23.44

D0521231

Handbook of
Real Estate
Terms

Dennis S. Tosh, Jr.
University of Mississippi

 Prentice Hall, Englewood Cliffs, New Jersey 07632

Library of Congress Cataloging-in-Publication Data

Tosh, Dennis S.
    Handbook of real estate terms.

       1. Real estate business—Dictionaries. 2. Real
property—Dictionaries. 3. Real estate business—
Abbreviations. 4. Real property—Abbreviations.
5. Real estate business—United States—Societies,
etc.—Directories. 6. Real estate business—
Canada—Societies, etc.—Directories.
       I. Title.
HD1365.T67 1990   333.33'03   89-3989
ISBN 0-13-372236-8

Editorial/production supervision: *Eleanor Ode Walter*
Cover design: *Lundgren Graphics, Ltd.*
Manufacturing buyer: *Laura Crossland*

 © 1990 by Prentice-Hall, Inc.
A Division of Simon & Schuster
Englewood Cliffs, New Jersey 07632

Printed in the United States of America

10 9 8 7 6 5 4 3 2

ISBN   0-13-372236-8

Prentice-Hall International (UK) Limited, *London*
Prentice-Hall of Australia Pty. Limited, *Sydney*
Prentice-Hall Canada Inc., *Toronto*
Prentice-Hall Hispanoamericana, S.A., *Mexico*
Prentice-Hall of India Private Limited, *New Delhi*
Prentice-Hall of Japan, Inc., *Tokyo*
Simon & Schuster Asia Pte. Ltd., *Singapore*
Editora Prentice-Hall do Brasil, Ltda., *Rio de Janeiro*

This Book Is Dedicated To

J. Ed Turner

Friend, Golfing Buddy, Real Estate Professional

CONTENTS

PREFACE

This book began as a result of being asked by people in real estate courses and seminars to define or explain a certain real estate term or abbreviation. What became ever more apparent was the simple fact that there are a great many real estate terms that need to be understood by anyone involved in real estate. Terms seem to be one way we explain real estate topics. Buzz words are everywhere. Abbreviations appear in the print media. Acronyms are used by lenders, appraisers, lawyers, real estate brokers, property managers, government officials, surveyors, and yes, even owners of real estate. Thus, the need exists for people involved in real estate, as well as those interested in becoming involved, to be able to identify and explain the more common real estate terms and concepts. In addition to knowing the meaning of a word, a person using any terminology should also be familiar with words similar in meaning and words that further explain a specific concept or principle. To assist the reader toward that objective, many of the words included in this handbook are cross-referenced. Thus, the reader can go to additional sources for further and more detailed explanations.

In addition to the more than 2,500 word entries included in this handbook, four appendices are also included. *Appendix A* lists a number of common abbreviations that appear in real estate text and that are used in conversation and gives the meaning of each. Contained in *Appendix B* are the major real estate organizations and agencies, their current mailing addresses and telephone numbers. The list includes all aspects of real estate activity. *Appendix C* includes the addresses and telephone numbers of all real estate commissions in the United States as well as the Canadian provinces. Anyone seeking information in regard to a real estate salesperson's or broker's license in a specific jurisdiction can contact the appropriate state for information regarding the licensing of people in that jurisdiction. Numerous uniform or standard forms exist in real estate transactions involving consumers. While the type of forms used may vary from jurisdiction to jurisdiction, certain documentation such as a settlement statement or a uniform appraisal report is standard and is used throughout the United States. Copies of these forms are included in *Appendix D*.

The author is indebted to many people who offered assistance in the development and preparation of this handbook. A sincere "thank you" to Vicki Coats, Warren Fisher, John Johnson, Robert Kern, Phil Malone, Eleanor Walter, and Carol Williamson. Thanks to all of you for your time and interest in this project. A special thanks to Gin-Chung (Jimmy) Lin who worked tirelessly in turning the manuscript into a finished handbook.

AAA TENANT

A tenant with a top credit rating. To a real estate developer, attracting such a tenant is important since the ability to arrange both construction and permanent financing for a major commercial project, such as a shopping center or office building, is often dependent upon preleasing a certain amount of the space to an AAA tenant(s).

A shopping center with one or two national chains or anchor tenants may result in other retailers wanting to lease the remaining space. This, in turn, will mean the developer/owner will be better able to meet the mortgage payments on the property. Thus, by having the AAA tenant(s) agree to lease space, the developer can show the lender that enough income will be generated to make the mortgage payments. In recent years, numerous national credit rating services have established criteria for deriving a rating such as AAA or AA for both retail and wholesale operations. (*See* **Anchor Tenant**)

AAE

Accredited Assessment Evaluator. A professional designation awarded by the International Association of Assessing Officers.

ABANDONMENT

The voluntary release of a claim or right one has in a piece of property with the clear intention of terminating possession or interest and without giving this

1

interest to anyone else. Abandonment includes both the intention to release any claim one has against the property as well as the actual act of "abandoning" the property. For example, a tenant (lessee) who walks away from a lease with the intent of not performing under the terms of the lease has abandoned the property. Such action gives the landlord (lessor) the legal right to take possession, but the tenant is still liable for all rent payments until the term of the lease expires.

A lessor does not show acceptance by entering on the realty in order to protect it after abandonment. The landlord may attempt to lease the property for the best terms that he or she can get in order to minimize damages, and to sue the breaching lessee for the actual injury suffered.

The owner of an easement can abandon the easement by taking steps that clearly indicate his or her intentions to give up any claim or right that he or she might have by rights of the easement. (*See* **Surrender, Uniform Residential Landlord and Tenant Act**)

ABATEMENT

A decrease or reduction in the amount of a charge such as rent. For example, a tenant receives an abatement of rent during the time the leased space cannot be inhabited due to fire or flood.

ABLE

A term referring to the financial capability of a purchaser. The word is often used in a phrase appearing in real estate listing agreements and sales contracts as "ready, willing and able."

ABNORMAL SALE

A sale that is not typical within the context of what is happening in the marketplace. An appraiser might discover that one of the comparables being used to appraise the subject property under the *market sales approach* was abnormal and thus is not a true indicator of normal market conditions. The abnormal sale could have been the result of a seller taking considerably less than the market value of the property because he or she had already purchased another home and was having to meet two mortgage payments. Likewise, in order to help a child purchase his or her first home, the parents might sell their home valued at $90,000 to the child for $60,000. Such a sale would be an abnormal sale. (*See* **Comparables, Market Value**)

ABODE

A home or place of residence. (*See* **Domicile, Residence**)

ABROGATE

To repeal or cancel. For example, a law could be repealed (abrogated) by legislative action.

ABSENTEE OWNER

The owner(s) of property who does not physically reside on the property. When this occurs both the rental as well as the upkeep of the property are normally done by someone other than the actual owner, such as a property manager. (*See* **Property Management**)

ABSORPTION RATE

The percentage of a particular type of real estate that can be sold or leased in a particular location during a certain period of time. For example, the developer of a 200-home subdivision needs to know how many houses can reasonably be expected to sell each month so as to project the time period necessary to sell all of the homes. Likewise, the owner of a new office building needs to know how long it will take to lease up the building in order to determine both income and expenses. (*See* **Feasibility Study**)

ABSTRACT OF TITLE

A condensed chronological history of all recorded instruments in the chain of title which affect the title. An abstract of title is prepared by an abstractor who may be an attorney, a public official or an employee of a title abstract company. The abstractor examines the records and condenses relevant information on each instrument affecting the title. No opinion as to the quality of the title is normally given.

A typical examination would begin by the abstractor examining the *grantor-grantee index* for each preceding year until the name of the current owner of the examined property is found. The same procedure is followed to find the source of title of the current owner's grantor. This is repeated as many times as is necessary until a satisfactory grantor is found, usually a government *patent*. The next step is to examine the grantor index and determine for each subsequent year whether the original grantor conveyed or in some manner encumbered title to the property prior to the conveyance to the grantee found in the first search. This procedure is repeated for each grantor in the chain of title. Occasionally, a break in the chain occurs, and this break must be satisfactorily explained. For example, the abstractor may find that George Harris granted Greensprings to Karen Harper in 1936. Later the examiner discovers that Greensprings was granted by Karen Adams to Fred French in 1942. The examiner has to determine if Karen Harper and Karen Adams are actually the same person. Other problems occur when there is a death or a mortgage foreclosure sale. The abstractor will need to examine other records to determine if the transfer was valid and confirmed by a court. Examination is normally made of proceedings of a probate court to determine if an executor's or administrator's deed was issued pursuant to proper authority. If a mortgage has been given, the examiner must determine whether it has been released or a satisfaction piece recorded. Judgment and lis pendens dockets must be examined to determine whether the property has any liens burdening it. Property tax liens, special assessments, mechanic's liens, federal tax liens and other such encumbrances should be checked for in the appropriate records by the title examiner. Normally, an abstractor will not examine records outside the jurisdiction nor physically inspect the property.

After the title examination, the abstractor prepares the abstract of title and issues a certificate. The abstract of title contains a caption which includes a legal description of the property. Following the caption is a condensation for each instrument examined. A typical condensation might look as follows:

	Special Warranty Deed Dated May 15, 1945
IRVING BERLIN **to** **JACK LONDON**	Acknowledged May 17, 1945 Recorded May 25, 1945 in Deed Book 503, Page 87 Consideration: $25,000.00 Revenue Stamps: $27.50 Attested by: Sam Tracy

Conveys caption property with easement to cross land to
reach fishing hole reserved to grantor.

This certificate issued by the abstractor states what records were examined and for what period of time the search was made. The certificate limits the liability of the abstractor to omissions in the search due to negligence. In some states the abstractor is liable for negligence only to those who paid for the search. No liability is accepted for unrecorded instruments such as mechanic's liens, or those instruments that were outside the chain of title or recorded outside the jurisdiction. (*See* **Attorney's Opinion of Title, Chain of Title, Title, Title Company, Title Insurance**)

ABUT

To border on or to share a common boundary. For example, a property owner could have land that "abuts" a highway, which means the two properties border each other.

ACCELERATED DEPRECIATION

The method(s) of depreciation for income tax purposes which increases the write-off at a rate higher than under the straight-line method of depreciation. (*See* **Straight-line Method of Depreciation**)

ACCELERATION CLAUSE

A clause in a promissory note, mortgage or deed of trust giving the creditor (mortgagee) the legal right to demand immediate payment of all future payments due to the occurrence of some event such as the default on an installment payment or the failure to keep the property adequately insured. To illustrate, assume John Jacobs borrows $80,000 from a savings and loan to purchase a house and agrees to make 360 monthly payments of $950 each. Assume that as of March of this year the outstanding balance had been reduced to $74,000. Next, assume John does not make payments for April, May, June and July, and consequently the savings and loan begins foreclosure proceedings. If the lender included an acceleration clause in the promissory note or mortgage, then the lender could claim the entire $74,000 as due and payable. Thus, all future principal reduction payments would be accelerated to the present. In this example, had the acceleration clause not been included, the lender could only demand payment for the four months in question and would have to take legal action each and every month to demand payment of the amount due that particular month. (*See* **Alienation Clause, Due-on-Sale Clause, Mortgage, Promissory Note**)

ACCEPTANCE

A voluntary expression by the person receiving the offer (the offeree, and quite often the seller of the property) to be bound by the exact terms of the offer in the manner requested or authorized by the person making the offer (the offeror, and quite often the potential buyer of the property). An acceptance must be *unequivocal* and *unconditional*. Any qualified acceptance which adds new conditions is an implied rejection of the offer. This implied rejection, called a *counteroffer*, has the legal effect of reversing the position of the original parties. The original offeror is now the new offeree and may accept or reject the counteroffer. This rule of implied rejection does not operate if the condition requested was already in the original offer by implication.

Example: Jay offers to sell his house to Barbara. Barbara replies: "I accept if you provide me with a good title." Unless Jay specifically limited the quality of the title in his original offer, his offer is considered to have implied good title. This means that Barbara's acceptance was unconditional and a binding contract would result. If, however, Barbara replies: "I accept if you provide me with financing," then this is a counteroffer and the original offer is rejected.

Once an offer is expressly or implicitly rejected, it is extinguished, and the offeree may no longer make a valid acceptance unless the offeror revives the original offer or in some way indicates that a counteroffer would not extinguish the original offer. The offer must be accepted in the manner requested or authorized by the offeror. In the case of a bilateral contract, the offer ordinarily requires that a return promise be communicated to the offeror. A *bilateral contract* is one in which a promise is given for the promise of another. A bilateral contract involves reciprocal obligations and becomes binding when mutual promises are communicated. An example would be a promise to pay $75,000 for a house at closing if the owner promises to sell the house and convey a warranty deed at the same time. A *unilateral contract* is one for which a promise is given for the act or performance of another. Acceptance occurs generally by the performance of the required act. A unilateral contract is not binding until the act has been performed. A common example of a unilateral contract is a listing contract where the seller agrees to pay a commission to a broker if the broker finds a suitable buyer. However, most modern listing contracts are written in a bilateral form in which the broker promises to use due diligence to find a buyer. As a general rule, in bilateral contract situations, an acceptance is effective immediately when properly dispatched by an authorized means of communication.

Example: Farmer Brown states: "You must accept by bringing an earnest money deposit of $1,000 in a brown paper bag and delivering it to me by sundown tomorrow while I am working in my cornfield." The only manner that the offeree may accept is by performing the requested act. (*See* **Communication, Contract, Counteroffer, Offer**)

ACCESS

The right to enter upon and leave property. The owner of land which abuts or adjoins a road or highway normally has a vested right to come and go from his or her land to the highway without obstruction, subject to limitations imposed by the governing body. For example, a state highway department constructs a limited access highway to aid in the flow of traffic and to decrease congestion along the road. Accordingly, adjoining landowners could only enter the highway at designated points of entry. (*See* **Easement by Implication**)

ACCESSIBILITY

The ease with which a person can either enter or exit a particular parcel of land. The accessibility of a particular parcel is a function of many things such as frontage to a road, traffic flow, and topography. Good accessibility will usually result in higher value; likewise, a parcel of land with poor accessibility will normally sell for less in the marketplace. (*See* **Amenity, Value**)

ACCESSION

The legal right that entitles the owner of land to all that the soil produces or all that is added to the land either intentionally or by mistake. For example, title may be given by nature through *accretion* to owners who have land adjoining rivers, lakes, or oceans. If a person builds a house or makes other improvements on the land of another by mistake, under common law that person loses the improvement to the owner of the land. However, some states have modified the harshness of this rule by statutes which permit the improvements to be moved after paying damages to the property owner. Any additions of fixtures other than trade fixtures by a tenant which are added without permission or agreement by the landlord belong to the landlord on the termination of the lease. (*See* **Accretion, Alluvion, Avulsion**)

ACCORD AND SATISFACTION

An agreed-to substitution of a different performance for the original obligation, the accord being the agreement and the satisfaction the execution or performance. For example, a new contract substituted for an old contract, which is now discharged, or an obligation which is, as a result of the accord and satisfaction, now settled.

Example: Mike claims Pat owes him $500 for services rendered while Pat says the amount is $300. If Pat offers Mike a check for $300 as "payment in full", the act of cashing the check by Mike would be an accord and satisfaction.

ACCREDITED RESIDENTIAL MANAGER (ARM)

A professional designation awarded by the Institute of Real Estate Management (IREM), an affiliate of the National Association of Realtors. The designation is intended for those persons specializing in the management of residential property.

ACCRETION

The accumulation of land (soil) as a result of the gradual washing or motion of water (*alluvion*). Title may be given by nature through accretion to owners who have land adjoining rivers, lakes or oceans. A similar process of acquiring new land is *reliction* or *dereliction*. This is a process by which water gradually recedes, leaving dry land where water was previously. Both concepts must be contrasted with *avulsion*, a sudden change in the bed of a river which had been used as a boundary by property owners. Such a sudden change conveys no new land; the dry bed remains as the boundary. (*See* **Accession**)

ACCRUED

An accumulation over a certain period of time, such as accrued depreciation or accrued interest. For example, if a person borrowed $1,000 for 10 years at 14% interest and agreed to pay the interest every two years, the accrued interest due at the end of the first two years would be $280.

ACCRUED DEPRECIATION

Any diminishment or loss of utility or value of a building from the time of initial construction to the present. Accrued depreciation is calculated as the difference between what it would cost to replace the building new and the current appraised value of the building. An accurate calculation of a building's accrued depreciation is used in the cost approach to value to derive an estimate of building value. (*See* **Cost Approach, Depreciation, Replacement Cost, Reproduction Cost**)

ACCRUED INTEREST

Unpaid interest that has already been earned.

ACCUMULATION OF ONE PER PERIOD

(*See* **Compound Amount of One Per Period**)

ACKNOWLEDGMENT

A formal declaration to a public official by a person who has signed (executed) an instrument which states that the signing was voluntary. Acknowledgment is required to ensure the authenticity of certain documents filed and is thus often necessary prior to recording important documents such as deeds in the public records. The public official, quite often a notary public or a justice of the peace, has the legal obligation to become assured of the true identity of the signor in order to prevent forgeries. Failure by the public official to properly identify the signor can result in the official being liable for damages caused by his or her negligence. (*See* **Attestation, Notary Public, Recordation**)

A typical acknowledgment would be as follows:

STATE OF

COUNTY OF

TO WIT:

I hereby certify, that on this _____ day of_____, 19_____, before me, the subscriber, a Notary Public of the State aforesaid, personally appeared _____ _____, known to me (or satisfactorily proven) to be the person(s) whose name(s) are subscribed to the within instrument, who signed the same in my presence, and acknowledged that _____ executed the same for the purposes therein contained.

AS WITNESS my hand and Notarial Seal.

_____

Notary Public

(NOTARY SEAL)   My Commission Expires_____

ACQUISITION

The act or process by which property ownership is achieved. The ways in which title to real property is transferred may be classified as (1) voluntary conveyance (*deed*), (2) transfer by *devise* (dying with a will) or *descent* (dying without a will), (3) transfer by *adverse possession*, (4) transfer by *accession* and (5) transfer by *public action* or by *operation of law*. (*See* **Deed, Transfer of Title**)

ACQUISITION COST

The total cost of purchasing or acquiring title to real property. In addition to the sales price, additional costs could also include loan origination fees, appraisal fee, credit report fee, title charges, attorney fees and other normal closing costs.

ACRE

A measure of land in whatever shape equal to 43,560 square feet, 4,840 square yards or 160 square rods. A square parcel of land measuring 208.71 feet on each side contains one acre. There are 640 acres in a section of land. (*See* **Government Survey Method**)

ACREAGE PROPERTY

A large tract of land that has had few, if any, improvements made either "to" the land, such as roads or the platting of individual lots, or "on" the land, such as buildings. (*See* **Unimproved Land**)

ACTION TO QUIET TITLE

A lawsuit filed by a person to remove a cloud on title or clear the claims of others filed against a parcel of property. The objective of such action is to have a court rule that the claims filed against the property are invalid. (*See* **Cloud on Title, Title**)

ACT OF GOD

Any act of nature such as rain, lightning, floods or earthquakes. Many casualty insurance policies do not cover losses resulting from an "Act of God."

ACTUAL AGE

The historical (*chronological*) age of a building, as for example a building constructed ten years ago is ten years old in actual age. Actual age should not be confused with *effective age* which is the age of a building that is indicated by the condition and utility of the improvement. It should be clear that the amount of maintenance and care given to a building helps determine its effective age. For example, a ten-year-old building might have an effective age of twenty-five years because of poor or deferred maintenance. (*See* **Appraisal, Cost Approach, Economic Life, Effective Age, Value**)

ACTUAL AUTHORITY

The power that a principal has expressly conferred upon an agent or any power that is incidental or necessary to carry out the express power of the agency. This power may be broad, general power or it may be limited, special power. The actual authority of a real estate broker is very limited since ordinarily, the broker is a *special agent*. When he or she is authorized to sell a house, for example, absent more specific authority, the broker is authorized only to find the purchaser and negotiate the transaction. The broker has no authority to make binding commitments on the principal to convey the property, to permit the third person to take possession or to enter the property to make repairs or modifications prior to closing. If the third person wishes to have permission to do these things, the broker should direct this person to the principal. If the broker is asked to buy a property for a principal, absent more specific authority, the broker is authorized to find the property and procure an offer for sale from the owner but the broker cannot actually disburse funds. (*See* **Agency, Agent, Authority**)

ACTUAL CASH VALUE

The monetary worth of a structure for insurance purposes. Actual cash value is calculated by taking the replacement cost of the property and then subtracting the value of the physical wear and tear of the property.

ACTUAL DAMAGES

The compensation received by an injured party for the actual injuries or loss suffered by the party. (*See* **Punitave Damages**)

ACTUAL EVICTION

The violation of any material breach of covenants by the landlord or any other act which wrongfully deprives the tenant of the possession of the premises. Eviction may be actual, partial or constructive. Since actual eviction refers to a physical ouster or dispossession from the premises, the tenant may bring a suit either to recover possession or for damages. (*See* **Constructive Eviction, Dispossess, Eviction**)

ACTUAL NOTICE

The actual knowledge that a person has about the existence of a particular fact. For example, Sally tells Ken that she sold her house to David. Ken has actual notice of the sale to David. A distinction should be made between actual notice and *constructive notice*. Constructive notice is the knowledge that the law presumes a person has about a particular fact, irrespective of whether the person knows about the fact or not. Any information which is recorded properly in the public records or announced in a official legal newspaper is constructive notice on every person in the world. In the example above, had Sally sold her house to David and David properly recorded the deed in the public records, Ken, as well as everyone else, would have constructive notice of the sale to David. (*See* **Constructive Notice, Recordation**)

ACTUAL POSSESSION

The physical occupancy and control by someone of a parcel of real estate. For example, if John has clear title to his house and is living in the house then he is in actual possession of the house. A distinction should be made between actual possession and *constructive possession* which occurs when a person has the legal right to assume occupancy but does not actually occupy the space. (*See* **Constructive Possession, Possession**)

ADC LOAN

A type of loan intended to cover the three phases of a project: (1) *acquisition*, (2) *development*, and (3) *construction*. Such loans, while considered more risky than some other types of real estate loans, are normally made with a variable interest rate and are expected to be repaid over a reasonably short period of time.

ADDENDUM

Something that is added and thus made part of a document. Quite often a real estate listing agreement or sales contract is a pre-printed form and thus may not have the space within the document to include specific and detailed information that the parties to the contract wish to include. In such instances, a separate instrument containing such information is drawn, being duly referenced in the primary instrument and referred to as an addendum.

ADD-ON INTEREST

A method of calculating the amount of interest due by taking the simple interest that would be charged if the loan principal amount was not amortized over the term of the loan. Periodic installments are thus calculated by dividing the sum of the add-on interest and original principal by the number of periods in the term. For example, a loan of $5,000 to be paid back over 36 months using add-on interest with an interest rate of 12% would require a monthly payment of $188.89 ($5,000 x .12 x 3 = $1,800; $5,000 + $1,800 = $6,800/36 = $188.89). Add-on interest is often used in consumer loans, such as mobile home loans, and with some second mortgages.

ADEQUATE PUBLIC FACILITIES ORDINANCE

A local government ordinance that requires that certain public facilities such as road and utilities be completed or soon to be completed before any new real estate development can be permitted. This technique is used by municipalities to control growth and direct new development toward areas where adequate public facilities exist. (*See* **Growth Management, Planning**)

ADJACENT LAND

Land lying close to or near another parcel, though the two parcels may not actually touch. The term should not be confused with adjoining land which exists when two parcels are actually jointed to each other. (*See* **Contiguous**)

ADJUNCTION

The process of adding or annexing a parcel of land to a larger parcel.

ADJUSTED COST BASIS

The value of property for accounting purposes used to determine the amount of gain or loss realized by the owner upon the sale of the property. Adjusted cost basis, also referred to as adjusted basis, is equal to the original tax basis at which the property was acquired (ordinarily the purchase price), plus any capital additions (cost of major improvements), minus any depreciation taken. (*See* **Basis, Capital Gain, Depreciation**)

ADJUSTED SALES PRICE

The estimated sales price of a comparable property after additions and/or subtractions have been made to the actual sales price for improvements and deficiencies when compared to the subject property being appraised. In theory, the adjusted sales price is what a comparable property would sell for if it were exactly equal in terms of all of its features to the subject property. (*See* **Comparables, Market Data Approach**)

ADJUSTMENTS

The additions and subtractions made in the market data or comparable sales approach to value to account for differences in location, design, age, etc. between the properties being used as comparables and the subject property being appraised. The comparable properties selected should be substantially similar to the subject property and should be "arms-length" transactions. However, since each comparable will be different from the subject property in terms of location, conditions of sale, amenities, time of sale, etc., adjustments must be made in the comparison process in order to derive a value for the subject property. The principal factors for which adjustments will normally be made can be divided into four general categories: (1) *date of sale*, (2) *location*, (3) *physical condition* and *features*, and (4) *terms* or *conditions of sale*. This adjustment process involves the adding and subtracting of dollars for those items where the comparable properties differ from the subject property. The dollar value of a feature present in the subject property but not present in the comparables is *added* while the dollar value of a feature present in the comparables but not present in the subject property is *subtracted*. The total adjustment for each factor when either added or subtracted will provide for an adjusted sales price for each comparable. The adjusted sales price of each comparable represents a value range of the subject property. (*See* **Appraisal, Comparable Sales Approach, Market Data Approach**)

ADMINISTRATOR

A person appointed by a court to administer or settle the estate of a deceased person who has died *intestate* (dying without a will). The person appointed may be a male (administrator) or a female (administratrix). The administrator will collect the assets of the estate, pay debts and distribute the remainder. The administrator is usually required to put up a bond and may sell that real property which is necessary to pay off the estate's debts if the sale of personal property produces insufficient proceeds. (*See* **Descent, Devise, Executor, Intestate, Testate**)

ADMINISTRATRIX

Feminine form of administrator. (*See* **Administrator**)

ADMINISTRATOR'S DEED

A conveyance of property which is issued to a grantee (purchaser) who purchases property from an estate. When a person dies *intestate* (without a will) the court appoints an administrator to pay the debts of the estate and to dispose of the property in a manner consistent with each state's statutes of descent and distribution. (*See* **Administrator, Deed, Intestate**)

AD VALOREM

A Latin prefix meaning "according to value." Local and state governments levy taxes on real property based on the *assessed value* of the property. Two different pieces of property with the same assessed value have the same ad valorem tax. Likewise, similar properties with different assessed values do not have the same property tax. Since property taxes are ad valorem taxes, the tax is in the form of a percentage of the property's value. In contrast, a specific tax, such as a tobacco tax or a gasoline tax, is imposed as a fixed sum on each unit sold, such as a 15-cents per gallon gasoline tax. (*See* **Appraisal, Assessed Value**)

ADVANCE

The word has two common meanings in real estate finance: (1) to pay or advance money before it is due, and (2) to disburse working capital to a builder/developer through a construction loan.

Under the first meaning, an owner might have both a first mortgage and a second mortgage on a parcel of real estate. Assume that he or she is behind in payments on the first mortgage. The holder of the second mortgage pays the amount of the first mortgage that is in arrears, so as to prevent foreclosure, and adds the "advance" to the amount owed on the second mortgage.

The more common use of the word "advance" deals with a construction loan and refers to the dollars that are transferred to the builder, or directly to the subcontractors, at various stages of construction. The idea of the "advance" is that as the building is being constructed, the builder receives advances to pay labor and material costs. While the exact schedule of disbursements will be specified in the loan agreement, a disbursement schedule for subdivision could be as illustrated below. (*See* **Construction Loan**)

SCHEDULE OF DISBURSEMENTS

No. of Advance	Work Required	Amount
1.	LOT Advance and settlement costs.	
2.	FOUNDATION Location survey, Builders Risk Insurance, Building Permit submitted. Excavation, footing and	

foundation complete. Individual
well, where applicable, complete
and county approved.

3. <u>ERECTION</u>
Floor joists and all framing com-
plete.
Subflooring installed.
Roof sheathing in place.

4. <u>DOORS, WINDOWS AND ROOF</u>
Exterior doors and windows in place.
Stairways in place.
Roof shingles in place.
Interior concrete complete.

5. <u>ROUGH-IN</u>
Plumbing, electric and heating
rough-in complete and county approved.

6. <u>INSULATION</u>
Insulation hung and installed.

7. <u>BRICK</u>
Brickwork complete, including fireplace,
if applicable.

8. <u>EXTERIOR SIDING</u>
Exterior siding in place.

9. <u>SHEETROCK</u>
All sheetrock hung, taped and spackled.
Heating plant in place.

10. <u>TRIM-OUT AND FINISH</u>
Interior trim complete, including hard-
wood floors.
Kitchen cabinets hung and set.
Prime painting complete.

11. <u>UTILITIES</u>
Individual sewer system complete and
connected; or, public water and sewer
connections complete.
Electric and gas connections complete.

12. FINAL
     Plumbing and electrical fixtures in
     place. Carpeting installed.
     Appliances installed. Interior and
     exterior paint complete. Exterior
     grading and driveways complete
     including landscaping. Use and Occu-
     pancy Permit issued, if applicable.

                    TOTAL LOAN $_____

ADVERSE POSSESSION

A method of acquiring title to real property by possession for a statutory period of time. In order to acquire title by adverse possession, which is also referred to as *title by prescription* in some jurisdictions, certain conditions must be fulfilled:

1. There must be *actual* possession which is *open* and *visible*. This means that the property must be openly used in a manner which could be readily observed. Such possession might be evidenced by the construction of improvements, the enclosure by fences and walls, the cultivation of fields or physical occupancy. Something like a hidden underground drainage pipe would not be considered sufficient.

2. The possession must be *hostile* to the true owner's title. Hostile means denial or opposition to the true owner's title. Such hostility might be evidenced by *color of title*. Color of title is any claim to title which for some reason is defective. For example, a deed which has been granted, but is void because it contains a vaguely worded legal description, may be used to support color of title. In cases where the claimant has color of title, many states shorten the required time period for possession. This claim to title must be *notorious*, which means that the claim must be made public.

3. Possession must be *exclusive*. This means that the claimant must claim right to the possession against the whole world; the claimant cannot share ownership in joint tenancy or tenancy in common with the true owner. Likewise, allowing the public to use the property would remove the exclusivity of possession.

4. The possession must be *continuous* and *uninterrupted* for a sufficient statutory period. If the claimant gives up occupancy the time period must begin again. If the true owner is out of the country, in the military, or is a minor, the period will not begin until the disability is removed. It should be noted that a person cannot claim

adversely against the state or federal government. Is the period interrupted if the claimant sells his or her interest to a purchaser? The law permits the original claimant's possession to be *tacked* to a person in privity with the claimant. Privity relates to succession of title by purchase, devise or other bond between the parties.
5. Some states require that property taxes be paid by the claimant during the time of possession.

(*See* **Color of Title, Easement, Prescriptive Easement, Tacking**)

AEDC

(*See* **American Economic Development Council**)

AFFIANT

The person who makes an affidavit. (*See* **Affidavit**)

AFFIDAVIT

Latin meaning "has pledged his faith." A written statement of facts made voluntarily and sworn to under oath before a public official or other persons authorized to administer such an oath.

An affidavit could be written as follows:

_____

STATE OF _____, _____COUNTY, To Wit:

_____ being duly sworn, deposes and states that

_____ is the person named in the attached

application and that each statement made in the application is true and

accurate to the best of _____ knowledge.

_____
(Signature)

Subscribed and sworn to before me this _____ day of _____, 19__

_____
(Notary Public)

My Commission Expires _____   (NOTARY SEAL)

AFFIDAVIT OF TITLE

A sworn statement by the seller of real estate that no defects of title other than those stated in the sales contract or deed exist in the title being conveyed. *(See* **Clear Title, Warranty Deed**)

AFFIRM

Ratification of a voidable contract by the party who is to be bound under the contract. *(See* **Ratification, Voidable Contract**)

AFFIRMATION

A solemn and formal declaration attesting to the truth of some matter. In certain instances, an affirmation is substituted for an oath, as for example, when a person for religious or personal reasons does not wish to take an oath.

AFFIRMATIVE FAIR HOUSING MARKETING PLAN

Action taken with the intent of encouraging minority integration in housing. The *Department of Housing and Urban Development (HUD)* has required an affirmative fair housing marketing plan from all subdivisions, multi-family projects and mobile home parks of five or more units before these projects are eligible for participation in various federal programs, including home mortgage programs. Authority for the marketing plan stems from *Title VIII (Fair Housing Law)* of the *Civil Rights Act of 1968.*

Affirmative marketing programs involve two aspects. (1) An initial sales or rental phase which involves "efforts to reach those persons who traditionally would not have been expected to apply for housing." HUD regulations specify the need for attracting minorities to predominantly white areas and whites to predominantly minority areas. (2) HUD regulations require continuing marketing activity to accomplish affirmative action goals whenever vacancies occur. Further, HUD requires non-discriminatory hiring of sales and rental personnel and the prominent displaying of HUD's fair housing logo or statements on equal opportunity. *(See* **Federal Fair Housing Act of 1968**)

AFTER ACQUIRED TITLE

Legal ownership in real property acquired by someone who had previously transferred his or her legal interest in the property.

AFTER-TAX CASH FLOW

The spendable cash from an income-producing asset, such as an office building or apartment complex, calculated by taking gross income and subtracting fixed and variable costs, replacement for reserves, debt service plus tax savings or minus tax liability.

Example: Each unit in a 75-unit apartment complex rents for $280 per month. A vacancy allowance of 8% is considered adequate, and operating expenses are calculated to be 45% of effective gross income. Debt service is $6,400 per month and the annual tax liability is $8,000. The calculation of cash flow for this particular project would be as follows:

Potential gross income	$252,000
Vacancy allowance	- 20,160
Effective gross income	231,840
Operating expenses	-104,328
Net operating income	127,512
Debt service	- 76,800
Pretax cash flow	50,712
Tax liability	- 8,000
After-tax cash flow	$ 42,712

(*See* **Cash Flow**)

AFTER-TAX EQUITY YIELD RATE
The internal rate of return on the equity investment after considering federal income taxes. (*See* **Internal Rate of Return**)

AFTER-TAX INCOME
(*See* **After-Tax Cash Flow**)

AFTER-TAX PROCEEDS FROM RESALE
The amount of money a property seller would receive from a property sale after subtracting transaction costs, capital gains taxes and other expenses. Generally, this figure is calculated by taking the selling price less the sum of the existing debt, the income or capital gains taxes, and the expenses of sale.

AGE-LIFE METHOD
A method of estimating accrued depreciation by applying to the reproduction cost new of the property the ratio of the property's effective age to its economic useful life. (*See* **Accrued Depreciation**)

AGENCY
A relationship in which one party (known as the *principal*) authorizes another party (the *agent*) to act as the principal's representative in dealing with *third parties*. Agency law generally involves rights and liabilities among these three parties. No agency relationship is ever created without some action or conduct, whether intentional or negligent, on the part of the principal. The exception to this rule is the special situation of an agency being established by operation of law. A purported agent cannot establish an agency by conduct or statements alone. Generally, a third person is under a duty to inquire as to the scope of an agent's authority. To rely on the agent's statements of the authority given by the principal is to act at one's own risk. A principal is not bound by acts of non-agents or

agents who act beyond the scope of their actual or ostensible authority. Any persons who are legally able to effect their legal relations with others are deemed to have the capacity to delegate to agents the authority to act on their behalf. A principal, however, may not empower an agent to do what the principal does not have the power to do. Thus, a legal nonentity such as an unincorporated club may not create powers in agents to enter into contracts on its behalf.

In order for an agency relationship to be valid, it must be for a legal purpose. The law will not provide remedies for breach of agency contract or breach of agency duties if the agency is for an unlawful purpose. As in other illegal contracts, this kind of contract is void, and the law will generally leave the parties as it found them. A real estate broker is considered to be a professional agent. Because the broker is usually employed to conduct a single transaction, he or she is also considered to be a *special agent*. Ordinarily, the primary function of a broker is to act as an intermediary between two parties, seller-buyer or lessor-lessee. Generally, the broker is limited in authority to bringing the parties together and assisting in the negotiation but generally not to binding the principal contractually. Because the broker is dealing with subject matter affecting the public interest, many of his or her duties and liabilities are defined to some extent by state licensing statutes. The broker is held to a strict code of ethics, not just to the principal but also to the public at large. He or she offers the skills and services of a professional and is expected to be knowledgeable of local market conditions and real estate values. The broker owes a duty to the principal to properly advise on all matters related to the real estate transaction where such matters are ordinarily within the scope of services provided by other brokers in the community.

A salesperson is considered to be an agent of the broker, not of the broker's principal. This means that the salesperson owes fiduciary duties to the broker and is obligated to follow all lawful instructions. As a result, a salesperson may not bring a suit against the broker's principal for a commission owed. Many people inappropriately refer to salespeople as subagents. Strictly speaking, a subagent has a contractual and fiduciary relationship with the original agent's principal. The subagent may sue the original agent's principal in the subagent's own right, and the original agent is not liable for the acts of the subagent unless the original agent was negligent in the appointment. Cooperating brokers may often be construed to be subagents. Since a broker is always liable for the civil acts of his or her salespeople, salespersons are not considered to be subagents when they act within the scope of employment.

An agency relationship or an agent's authority may be terminated by acts of the parties or by operation of law. Acts of parties include performance, mutual agreement, discharge, resignation, abandonment or breach of agency duties. Termination by operation of law includes expiration of term, death of parties, insanity, bankruptcy, change in law, destruction of subject matter or material change in circumstances. (*See* **Agent, Authority, Principal**)

AGENCY BY ESTOPPEL (Ostensible Agency)

A type of agency relationship that occurs when the principal in a principal-agent relationship leads a third person to believe that someone is an agent. The principal may create the impression of agency either intentionally or negligently. If the third person relies on the principal's manifestations and enters into a contract with the ostensible agent, the principal will be "estopped" from denying the agency. The agency may not be created solely by the purported agent's conduct or assertions, but where the principal has a duty to talk and remains silent the agency may nevertheless be created.

Example: Patty's brother-in-law, Abel, tells Terry that Patty has authorized him to sell her house for $50,000. Terry calls Patty on the telephone to inquire about Abel's authority to act. Patty tells Terry that she is planning to get rid of her house but fails to deny Abel's authority as an agent. Terry pays Abel $50,000 on the basis of the conversation. Patty refuses to deliver the deed saying that Abel was not appointed her agent. Some courts will hold that Patty is bound because she led Terry to believe that Abel was her agent. She is estopped from denying the agency. It should be observed that the statute of frauds may prevent any recovery because the contract was not in writing.

AGENCY BY NECESSITY

An agency relation in which authority to act is created by operation of law in an emergency. During such an emergency, it is generally unnecessary to gain consent from a principal in order for a person to act to protect property or person.

Example: While a broker is showing a prospect her principal's property, a large tree limb falls, breaking a plate glass picture window. If the broker is unable to contact the principal for instruction, she may by implication act to repair the window in order to prevent vandals or vermin from entering the house, or to prevent the elements from causing damage to the interior of the dwelling.

AGENCY BY RATIFICATION

A type of agency relationship that occurs when a principal agrees to be bound by the acts of a person purporting to act as an agent, even though the person was not in fact an agent. The principal may also be bound if there are acts of an agent who acted beyond the scope of authority. This agreement, called ratification, may be done by express affirmation or by implication.

Ratification may also be implied if the principal attempts to accept the benefits or attempts to affirm only part of the transaction. However, if part of the transaction is accepted, then all of it is accepted. Once a transaction is ratified, the principal is bound by the duties and the liabilities as well as being entitled to the rights.

AGENT

One who acts for and in the place of a principal for the purpose of affecting the principal's legal relationship with third persons. The power of an agent to affect the principal's legal relations for lawful purposes is called *authority*. The principal is bound by acts of the agent when the latter is operating within the scope of the agent's authority.

Agents may be classified on either the basis of the manner in which the agency was created on or the basis of the agent's authority. If the agency occurred on the basis of consentual agreement of the principal and agent, the relationship is called *actual agency*. If the agency occurred because of reasonable reliance on the part of a third party, the relationship is called *ostensible agency*. An ostensible agency may result from the principal's express, implied or negligent representation that an agency exists.

Agents classified on the basis of authority include universal, general and special agents. *Universal agents* have the authority to do all acts that can be lawfully delegated to a representative. Ordinarily, a universal agent is created by a *power of attorney*. Anyone of legal capacity may be an *attorney in fact*, a position created by the power of attorney. Care should be taken not to confuse this status with an *attorney at law*, a person who must be admitted to an appropriate bar. Power of attorney is useful when a principal wishes to empower a broker to sell a house while the principal must be out of the country and thus is unable to personally sign appropriate documents to convey title. It should be noted that power of attorney may be limited in authority so that a universal agency is not necessarily created.

A *general agent* is authorized to transact all of the principal's affairs within the context of a broad commercial or other kind of endeavor. A general agent is deemed to have broad discretionary powers. When a person is held out to be a general agent, the duty of a third person to inquire as to the scope of the agent's actual authority may be mitigated. An example of a general agent is a general manager of a store who has been delegated broad discretion to operate the business. A *special agent* is generally limited in authority to transacting a single business affair or a specific series of business affairs or to perform restricted acts for the principal. Ordinarily, a real estate broker is construed to be a special agent. A person dealing with a special agent must inquire as to the scope of the agent's actual authority.

A principal is bound by the acts of an agent performed within the scope of the agent's actual and implied authority. A principal is also bound by the reasonable reliance of a third person on the apparent or ostensible authority of the agent. A third person has a duty to inquire as to the scope of the agent's authority to bind the principal since generally the principal cannot be bound by unauthorized acts. When acting without authority or beyond the scope of authority, the agent may be liable to a third person for a breach of an *implied warranty of authority*. This is the warranty that the law will hold to be implied by the agent's actions in representing himself or herself as having authority which the agent in fact does not have.

Agents are considered by law to be *fiduciaries*. A fiduciary is a person who essentially holds the character of trustee. Thus, an agent has a duty to act primarily for the principal's benefit and not his or her own. The agent must act with the highest degree of care and good faith in relationship with the principal and on the principal's business. The penalties for failing in fiduciary duties may be quite severe. For example, a broker generally loses the right to a commission if the following duties are breached: loyalty, fidelity, obedience of legitimate instructions, due care, accounting, and the giving of notice of material facts affecting the subject matter of the agency. The extent of the penalty depends on the seriousness of the breach and the damages sustained by the principal. There are cases where the penalty was a loss of the brokerage license and even criminal sanctions.

When an agent is acting for a disclosed principal in negotiating with a third person, the general rule is that the agent is not party to the contract. He or she is not liable under the contract, nor is the agent entitled to enforce it against the third person. The principal alone is bound by the agent's act and is entitled to enforce the contractual obligations. The rule is different when the agent is acting for an undisclosed or partially disclosed principal in dealing with a third person. In this case, the agent is liable as a party to the contract. If the third person learns the identity of the principal, he or she may elect to hold either liable under the contract. An agent is always liable to third persons for his or her own torts. A *tort* is any civil injury which the law recognizes and gives remedy. The principal is also bound for the agent's torts if the agent is a servant under the principal's right to control. The principal is generally not bound if the agent is an independent contractor. (*See* **Agency, Independent Contractor, Listing, Principal**)

AG LAND

Land zoned for agricultural use such as farmland or land used to raise livestock.

AGREEMENT

An expression of mutual assent, or a meeting of the minds, by two or more parties on a given proposition.

AGREEMENT OF SALE

(*See* **Contract for Deed**)

AGRICULTURAL PROPERTY

Land zoned for agricultural or farming activities. (*See* **Zoning**)

AIR RIGHTS

The right to use, control and occupy the space above a particular parcel of real estate. Each unit of real estate is comprised of three-dimensional space. This space consists of the land's surface, the space beneath, which theoretically extends to the center of the earth, and the space above, which extends to the skies. If the surface unit were square, the space would form an inverted pyramid from the center of the earth stretching into space.

Possession of space gives access to numerous resources. For example, control of the surface gives the possessor use of the topsoil, crops, trees and other vegetation, manmade improvements, water passing on or next to the land and the natural features such as hills or scenic views. Control of the subsurface gives the possessor access to various mineral rights: oil, gas, coal, geothermal energy, subsurface water, and caves that are directly below the surface unit. Possession of air space permits the building of high-rise structures, gives access to solar and wind power sources, prevents others from using the space and gives the possessor various other rights enforceable by law. With the advent of air travel, the right to total control of air space has been limited to the space that the possessor could reasonably be expected to use. Space above that is shared with the public. Ownership of the surface gives the possessor control over several natural elements. Each element may be sold separately without selling the others, thereby increasing the economic worth of the real estate asset. Air rights are valuable property rights particularly in areas where the cost of land is high and the amount of available space is limited. These air rights can be transferred through selling them, leasing them and in some instances creating an easement. For example, in New York City buildings have been constructed over land owned by the New York Central Railroad by way of an easement. *(See* **Easement**)

ALIENATION

The voluntary transfer of property and possession of the land or tenements from one party to another. Alienation would include all means by which real property can be voluntarily transferred, such as by deed or will, as contrasted with passing the property by operation of law such as a mortgage foreclosure or a tax sale. Any restraints on alienation are strictly construed by the courts. *(See* **Deed, Fee Tail**)

ALIENATION CLAUSE

A provision often included in a mortgage or deed of trust that legally permits the lender (mortgagee) to demand payment of all the outstanding principal if the property is sold or transferred by the borrower (mortgagor). Such a provision is also commonly known as a *due-on-sale clause.*

In a fire insurance policy, a provision, also referred to as an alienation clause, is included which gives the insurance company the right to cancel the policy if ownership of the property is transferred. The reason such a clause is included is to provide the insurer a means by which an unsatisfactory risk would not have to be insured. *(See* **Acceleration Clause, Due-on-Sale Clause**)

ALLODIAL SYSTEM

The free and complete ownership of land by individuals. The allodial system is the system of property ownership in America today. The term allodial means free from the tenurial or vested rights in the king or feudal overlord. In other words, in the United States, a person may own full and complete property rights in land subject only to the various public and private restrictions, such as zoning, taxation and deed restrictions. Thus, full ownership, such as fee simple title, or something less than full ownership, such as the leasing of a building, may be transferred. Property owners may do such things since the law under an allodial system treats the rights and interests in land separately from the land itself. (*See* **Bundle of Rights, Feudal System**)

ALLUVION

The increase of soil, gravel or sand upon the bank of a stream or river or the shore of a sea due to the flow or current of the water. The actual act of the soil being added is known as *accretion*. (*See* **Accretion, Avulsion**)

ALONSO, WILLIAM

An urban economist who believed that urban sites are composed of both land and location. In his book, *Location and Land Use*, Alonso explained the trade-off that exists between land rent and the transportation cost incurred by individuals in determining where to locate within an urban area.

A. L. T. A.

(*See* **American Land Title Association**)

ALTERATION

An unauthorized modification of a contract by one of the parties to the contract. The alteration is considered *material* when it affects the rights of the parties to the contract. If the alteration is intentional and material, it will be treated as fraud and the innocent party may void the contract at his or her option. (*See* **Fraud, Material Fact**)

AMENITY

A feature or benefit received from a particular parcel of property which increases the satisfaction received by the owner or user of that property. Amenities may be both natural, for example, location or scenic view, and manmade, such as a swimming pool or tennis courts. Both material and manmade amenities increase the desirability of a certain location or parcel of land and thus that particular land will normally have a higher value than a parcel of land without the amenities. Likewise, the owner of an apartment complex who goes to the expense of adding swimming pools, tennis courts, game rooms and the like can more than likely command a higher rent than similar property without the amenities.

In regard to an easement, the word amenity has an entirely different meaning, namely preventing a landowner from using his or her property in some manner. Also called a *negative easement*, an example would be an easement for light and air which prevents a landowner from erecting a structure so high that it would cast shadows or restrict light and air from the property of the easement owner. A negative easement should be distinguished from an affirmative or positive easement, which permits a person to use another's property. (*See* **Easement, Negative Easement, Value**)

AMERICAN BANKERS ASSOCIATION (ABA)

Membership in the American Bankers Association is comprised of persons employed in the commercial banking business. The organization serves as a spokesman for the banking community. The Association is headquartered at 1120 Connecticut Avenue, N.W., Washington, D.C. 20036; (202) 663-5000.

AMERICAN ECONOMIC DEVELOPMENT COUNCIL (AEDC)

The American Economic Development Council is an international organization whose mission is to advance the art and science of economic development. AEDC publishes a journal, *Economic Development Review*, and awards two professional designations: (1) *Certified Industrial Developer (CID)*, and (2) *Certified Economic Developer (CED)*. The council's address is Suite 22, 4849 North Scott Street, Schiller Park, Illinois 60176; (312) 671-5646.

AMERICAN INSTITUTE FOR PROPERTY AND LIABILITY UNDERWRITER

The American Institute for Property and Liability Underwriters is the main professional organization of property insurance agents. In addition to numerous educational programs and seminars, a professional designation, *CPCU (Chartered Property Casualty Underwriter)*, is sponsored by the institute. The mailing address is Providence and Sugartown Roads, Malvern, Pennsylvania 19355; (215) 644-2100.

AMERICAN INSTITUTE OF ARCHITECTS

This institute awards the designation *AIA* and is the primary group for promoting architecture as a profession. Among the group's activities is its national committee on housing which provides numerous services in an effort to improve the quality of the living environment. The institute is located at 1735 New York Avenue, N.W., Washington, D.C. 20006; (202) 626-7300.

AMERICAN INSTITUTE OF HOUSING CONSULTANTS

This organizatin works with nonprofit sponsors in developing low-income housing. The institute also serves as a spokesman for low-income housing.

AMERICAN INSTITUTE OF PLANNERS

A professional trade association comprised of both publicly and privately employed planners. The designation, *AIP*, is sponsored by this institute which also publishes a journal. In addition, the institute attempts to keep its members informed as to various policy change in Washington. The institute is located at 1776 Massachusetts Avenue, N.W., Washington, D.C. 20036; (202) 872-0611.

AMERICAN INSTITUTE OF REAL ESTATE APPRAISERS (AIREA)

AIREA is affiliated with the National Association of Realtors. The institute publishes a great deal of professional appraisal literature, including *The Appraisal Journal*, and conducts appraisal, investment, and market analysis seminars throughout the United States. Two professional designations are awarded by AIREA: (1) *Member of Appraisal Institute (MAI)*, and (2) *Residential Member (RM)*. AIREA's address is 430 North Michigan Avenue, Chicago, Illinois 60611; (312) 440-8141.

AMERICAN LAND DEVELOPMENT ASSOCIATION (ALDA)

The American Land Development Association is a trade organization comprised primarily of land developers. The association's primary function is to represent the interstate land development industry in matters related to land development. The mailing address is 1200 L Street, N.W., Washington, D.C. 20005; (202) 371-6700.

AMERICAN LAND TITLE ASSOCIATION (ALTA)

An association, founded in 1907, representing more than 2,100 title abstractors, title insurance companies, title insurance agents, and associate members. Since the role and responsibility of the title industry, and of its ALTA members, is to guarantee the safe, efficient transfer of real property, the ALTA membership functions cooperatively and effectively to provide protection for consumers and lenders alike. Members of the association use standardized title insurance forms developed by ALTA to provide uniformity within the industry. The ALTA staff represents specialists in the fields of government relations, public affairs, research and state governmental affairs. ALTA's national headquarters is located at 1828 L Street, N.W., Suite 303, Washington, D.C. 20036; (202) 296-3671. (*See* **Abstract of Title, Title Insurance**)

AMERICAN REAL ESTATE AND URBAN ECONOMICS ASSOCIATION (AREUEA)

The principal professional organization of real estate education, AREUEA consist of both educators and professional practitioners. The association publishes a journal of articles dealing with land use, urban economics and related topics.

AMERICAN RIGHT OF WAY ASSOCIATION

The American Right of Way Association is comprised primarily of people involved in the appraisal and use of land for the public sector. This association sponsors the professional designation *SR/WA (Senior Right of Way Agent)*.

AMERICAN SOCIETY OF APPRAISERS

An appraisal organization consisting of persons involved in the appraisal of both real and personal property. The society sponsors the designation *ASA*. The society's mailing address is Dulles International Airport, P.O. Box 17265, Washington, D.C. 20041; (703) 478-2228.

AMERICAN SOCIETY OF CONSULTING PLANNERS

A professional society whose membership is limited to private planning firms. The society offers various services to its members and serves as a spokesman for consulting planners. The address is Suite 647, 210 7th Street, S.E., Washington, D.C. 20003; (202) 544-0035.

AMERICAN SOCIETY OF HOME INSPECTORS, INC. (ASHI)

A professional trade organization whose membership specializes in the physical inspection of homes. ASHI publishes numerous pamphlets and proceedings, conducts seminars and provides a Standards of Practice. The society's address is 7th Floor, 3299 K Street, N.W., Washington, D.C. 20007; (202) 842-3096.

AMERICAN SOCIETY OF PLANNING OFFICIALS (ASPO)

ASPO serves those people employed as planners with research material and various professional services. Membership consist of both private and public sector planners. The society is located at 1313 East 60th Street, Chicago, Illinois 60637; (312) 947-2560.

AMERICAN SOCIETY OF REAL ESTATE COUNSELORS (ASREC)

As an affiliate with the National Association of Realtors, this society consists of real estate brokers, appraisers, and consultants involved in assisting people in the buying and selling of real estate. The professional designation *CRE (Counselor, Real Estate)* is awarded by the society. The mailing address is 430 North Michigan Avenue, Chicago, Illinois 60611; (312) 440-8091.

AMORTIZATION

The repayment of a financial obligation over a period of time in a series of periodic installments. Specifically, this is the payback of the principal owed to the lender. The effect of amortization is to build up the paper value of the investor's (owner's) equity and to reduce the debt obligation. It should be noted that a portion of each payment consists of a blend of interest and amortization of principal. The interest portion is tax deductible, whereas the amortization is not.

A less common use of the word amortization refers to the allocation of the cost of an asset over the expected useful life of the asset. Examples include intangibles such as patents, trademarks or leaseholds. Real estate application would include a situation in which an investor purchased a 25-year leasehold interest for $100,000. In determining the profit realized during the 25 years, the investor would have to recoup the $100,000 investment over the term of the leasehold since at the end of the 25 years, the investor has no further interest in the property. (*See* **Amortized Loan, Leasehold**)

AMORTIZATION RATE

The percentage of a periodic payment that is applied to the reduction of the principal; in a level-payment mortgage this corresponds to the *sinking fund factor*.

AMORTIZATION TERM

The time period over which the principal amount would be retired on the basis of the periodic installments paid.

AMORTIZED LOAN

A financial obligation that is repaid over a period of time by a series of periodic payments. There are two types of amortized loans, *fully amortized* and *partially amortized.*

A fully amortized loan requires periodic (typically monthly) payment of both interest and principal. The first part of the payment covers interest on the outstanding debt as of the payment due date and the remainder of the payment reduces the outstanding debt. At the maturity date, the balance has been reduced to zero. The initial payments will consist of more interest than principal reduction; however, the percentage of the periodic payment reducing the outstanding balance will continue to increase as each subsequent payment is made. Fully-amortized mortgages are currently the normal means of securing permanent financing. The maturity date is usually much longer than with a *term loan.* For residential property, this type of mortgage usually covers twenty to thirty years and for commercial property the time period is ten to fifteen years.

The partially amortized loan also requires periodic repayment of principal. However, unlike the fully amortized loan, the balance at maturity under a partially amortized loan is not zero; rather the principal has been only partially reduced. The remaining balance is referred to as a *balloon payment.* This type of mortgage is often used with commercial property and in recent years has become more common with residential property. (*See* **Balloon Payment, Term Mortgage**)

AMOUNT OF ONE

(*See* **Compound Amount of One**)

AMOUNT OF ONE PER PERIOD

(*See* **Compound Amount of One Per Period**)

ANACONDA MORTGAGE

A type of mortgage in which a clause is included which states that the mortgage secures all debts of the mortgagor (borrower) that may be due and payable to the mortgagee (lender). Such a provision is also referred to as a *Mother Hubbard clause.*

ANALYST

An individual who performs various studies and calculations to help make decisions or solve problems concerning real estate investments. (*See* **Feasibility Study**)

ANCHOR TENANT

A well-known commercial retail business such as a national chain store or regional department store strategically placed in a shopping center so as to generate the most amount of customers for all of the stores located in the shopping center. In a strip shopping center the anchor tenants, such as a supermarket and a variety store, are often located one at each end with the smaller stores located in the middle. A regional shopping mall could have perhaps three anchors, one at each end and the third one in the middle with the smaller stores located between them. Such an arrangement helps to increase sales for all of the stores, and thus the landlord/owner is able to charge higher minimum rents for businesses desiring to locate in the shopping center. In addition, since shopping center lease rents are normally based on a percentage of gross sales, the higher volume of sales will mean higher rents for the landlord. (*See* **Percentage Lease**)

ANNEXATION

The act of adding, joining and attaching one thing to another. With respect to the annexing of land, from time to time municipalities legally incorporate into the existing town or city limits a certain amount of land or territory outside their legal boundary. This may be done to consolidate two governments into one or perhaps to increase property tax revenue for the municipality.

In regard to fixtures, annexing refers to the permanent attaching of personal property, both natural and manmade, to the land. The permanent attachment results in the personal property now becoming a fixture which means that in a transfer of the real property from one party to another, the fixtures go to the purchaser. For example, a bathtub becomes a fixture, and thus part of the real property, when it is annexed to the wall and plumbing system. (*See* **Fixture, Personal Property, Real Property**)

ANNUAL

Occurring once a year.

ANNUAL DEBT SERVICE

Total payments required in one year in regard to a loan. As can be seen in the table below, the amount of payment is affected by either a change in the interest rate or a change in the payback period.

TOTAL ANNUAL PAYMENT PER $1,000 DEBT

PAYBACK PERIOD	INTEREST RATE				
	5%	10%	12%	15%	20%
1	$1,050	$1,100	$1,120	$1,150	$1,200
5	231	264	277	298	334
10	130	163	177	199	239
15	96	131	147	171	214
20	80	117	134	160	205
25	71	110	128	155	202
30	65	106	124	152	201

ANNUAL PERCENTAGE RATE (APR)

The actual yearly cost of credit stated to the nearest one-fourth of one percent. Any lender subject to the federal *Truth-in-Lending Act* must fully disclose the APR to the borrower. The calculation of the APR is complex and involves the use of actuarial tables which are available from the Federal Reserve System and its member banks. The APR is usually different from the contract or nominal interest rate of interest and includes the impact on the effective rate from discount points and other finance changes.

Example: Tom borrows $1,000 from Christine which is repayable in one payment at the end of the year. The loan is to finance a real estate purchase. They agree to a contract rate of 10% plus four discount points. What is the APR?

Actual amount borrowed: $1,000 - $40 (discount points) = $960

Amount to be paid back: $1,000 + $100 (contract interest) = $1,100

Actual interest: $1,100 - $960 = $140

APR: $140/$960 = 14.58%

This calculation would differ depending on the term of the loan and the amortization period. If the interest is collected in the beginning, the APR could be twice the contract rate. (*See* **Add-on Interest, Discount Points, Nominal Interest Rate, Truth-in-Lending Act**)

ANNUITY

A series of payments made or received at even intervals either for life or for a fixed number of years.

ANNUITY IN ADVANCE

An annuity in which payments are made at the beginning of each period as contrasted with an ordinary annuity in which payments are made at the end of each period.

ANNUITY METHOD

A means of capitalizing future income streams from an investment.   The procedure uses compound interest formulas that treat the income stream as an annuity providing for both a return "on" the investment and a return "of" the investment.

ANTICIPATION, PRINCIPAL OF

A basic value principle which states that value changes in expectation of some future benefit or detriment affecting the property. For example, the value of a vacant parcel of land may increase if an office building is constructed next to it; likewise, use of land as an open dump may result in decreased values of surrounding residential properties. (*See* **Value**)

APPARENT AUTHORITY

In agency law such authority which a third person can reasonably assume that an agent has on the basis of actions or inactions of the principal. This is so despite the fact that the agent may not have actual authority. Such authority is also known as *ostensible authority*. A third person may justifiably rely on appearances and is not bound by secret instructions of the principal to the agent. Consider the case where John delivers a car to Honest Joe, a used car dealer. Honest Joe is instructed to sell the car for no less than $1,000. Honest Joe sells the car for $750 to Pam. Joe had apparent authority to sell the car at any price from the viewpoint of an innocent third party purchaser. John therefore cannot refuse to deliver title to Pam despite the fact that Honest Joe failed to obey his instructions. (*See* **Actual Authority**)

APPARENT TITLE

(*See* **Color of Title**)

APPEALS BOARD

A means by which a property owner can formally protest a tax bill and seek a change in the assessed value of his or her property. Jurisdictions that have such a board normally require the property owner to have first met with the tax assessor prior to appealing the property tax. (*See* **Assessed Value, Property Tax**)

APPORTIONMENT

A division or allocation of responsibility among two or more persons. In regard to the sale of real estate, the allocation is typically of a cost or expense such as property taxes between the purchaser and the seller, or, in the case of income-producing property, the allocation of rental income between the purchaser and seller. Normally the seller is responsible for expenses up to and including the day of settlement or closing.

Example: Annual property taxes of $600 have not been paid on a house which has sold with settlement scheduled for March 31. Thus, the seller is responsible for three months and the purchaser is responsible for nine months. Of the total $600 due, $150 would be payable by the seller and $450 payable by the purchaser. (*See* **Proration, Settlement**)

APPORTIONMENT CLAUSE

A clause normally included in standard insurance policies to prevent financial gain by the insured as a result of insuring the same property with two or more companies and hoping to collect more than the loss. Such a provision is also known as a *pro rata clause*.

Example: A building valued at $200,000 is insured with Company A for $160,000 and with Company B for $200,000. An $80,000 loss is incurred. Company A is liable for only $35,200 of the loss and Company B is liable for the remaining $44,800.

Solution:

$160,000 + $200,000   = $360,000

Company A's liability   = $160,000
                             $360,000   =   44% of loss

Company B's liability   = $200,000
                             $360,000   =   56% of loss

$80,000 x .44 = $35,200 for Company A

$80,000 x .56 = $44,800 for Company B

APPRAISAL

An estimate or opinion of value supported by factual information as of a certain date. Appraisals of real estate are made for a number of reasons; for example, when a potential purchaser is seeking a mortgage loan, or when property is condemned, taxed or insured. Normally, the purpose of an appraisal is to determine *market value* and the means of doing so is through the application of one or more of the three valuation approaches: (1) *comparable sales (market) approach*, (2) *cost approach* or (3) *income approach*. While all three approaches may be appropriate for a particular piece of real estate, often only two of the three will be relevant. Thus, it is up to the appraiser to pick the appropriate approach(es). (*See* **Appraisal Process, Cost Approach, Income Approach, Market Data Approach, Market Value, Value**)

APPRAISAL DATE

(*See* **Date of Appraisal**)

APPRAISAL FOUNDATION

An educational self-regulatory organization which functions for the purpose of developing appraisal standards and appraiser qualifications. The Appraisal Foundation is comprised of member organizations representing various appraisal groups, users of appraisal services and the public at large. The address is 1029 Vermont Avenue, N.W., Suite 900, Washington, D.C., 20005; (202) 347-7722.

APPRAISAL INSTITUTE OF CANADA

An appraisal organization comprised of persons doing appraisal work in

Canada. The institute offers membership to those appraisers in the United States who do appraisal work in Canada. The address is 177 Lombard Avenue, Winnipeg, Manitoba, Canada; (204) 942-0751.

APPRAISAL PROCESS

A systematic step-by-step analysis used by the appraiser to accurately reach an opinion of value. While each appraisal assignment varies according to the purpose of the appraisal and the approach(es) used, a well-done estimate of value will follow some standardized procedure. (*See* **Appraisal, Market Value, Value**)

APPRAISAL REPORT

A written report submitted by the appraiser to support and document the opinion of value rendered by the appraiser. The form of the appraisal report can be a letter of valuation, a single page standard form or a more elaborate report. In appraising single-family dwellings a standard form is normally used which provides space for recording neighborhood, site, and building data. Income-producing property normally requires a more detailed narrative report which not only gives the appraiser's opinion of value but also provides supportive evidence to substantiate the opinion. The documentation necessary with the narrative report is much greater than with the standard form. Professional standards of what is expected in a narrative appraisal report are available from the American Institute of Real Estate Appraisers, the Society of Real Estate Appraisers, the American Society of Appraisers, and other appraisal organizations. (*See* **Appraisal, Value**)

APPRAISED VALUE

An estimate of value based on the appraiser's analysis of data within the context of the appraisal problem that the appraiser was employed to solve.

APPRAISER

An individual who has the experience, training, and legal qualifications to appraise real or personal property.

APPRECIATION

An increase in an asset's market value over its value at some previous point in time. The increase can be a result of inflation, increased demand or some other related cause. The term denotes the opposite of *depreciation*.

APPURTENANCE

That which belongs to something else and thus passes with the property. Examples would include riparian rights, easements, barns and other outbuildings, gardens and orchards. Normally, a deed conveys the real property and then states, "Together will all tenements, hereditaments and appurtenances thereto belonging or in any wise appertaining." (*See* **Deed, Hereditament, Tenement**)

ARA

An appraisal designation for *Accredited Rural Appraiser* awarded by the American Society of Farm Managers and Rural Appraisers.

ARBITRATION

A procedure for resolving disputes out of court by an impartial third party chosen by the disputing parties who agree to abide by the decision of the arbitrator. While disagreements and disputes involving real estate often result in court action, disputing parties sometimes agree to settlement through arbitration. For example, a reappraisal lease which says that rent will be based on fair market value may result in a dispute between the landlord and tenant as to what is fair market value. To prevent such a dispute, the lease could contain a clause which states that a third party will settle the dispute if and when disagreement exists.

"ARM'S LENGTH" TRANSACTION

A transaction such as a sale of property or the lending of money in which all parties involved are acting in their own self-interest and are under no undue influence or pressure from the other parties. Such a situation is the basis for deriving fair market value, and if the transaction is not at arm's length then the actual selling price will likely be less than or greater than the market value. For example, a couple with a house valued at $50,000 might sell it to their child for $40,000; such a transaction would not be at arm's length.

ARPEN (ARPENT)

A French measurement term used to denote an area equal to seven-eights of one acre. (*See* **Acre**)

ARREARS

Money which is not paid on time, as for example, if a borrower has not made the last two mortgage payments, he or she is said to be in arrears. In many political jurisdictions, property taxes are paid at the end of the year rather than at the beginning and are thus referred to as due in arrears rather than in advance.

ARTERIAL STREET

A major road designed to be a through street and to handle a large volume of traffic.

ARTIFICIAL PERSON

A person created and recognized by law as having legal rights, an example being a corporation. Within a legal context, such a person should be distinguished from a *natural person*.

ASA

Senior Member, American Society of Appraisers. A professional designation awarded to individuals involved in the appraisal of both real and personal property. *(See* **American Society of Appraisers)**

AS IS

A phrase included in a contract of sale disclaiming any warranty or guarantee on the part of the seller. A person purchasing real estate "as is" takes it in exactly the condition in which it is found and must trust his or her own inspection of the property. However, with the trend towards consumerism in recent years, courts today will prevent the seller of a house from using an "as is" clause to shield him or her from not disclosing material facts that could affect the habitability of the house.

ASKING PRICE

The listed price of the property. Often such a price denotes a willingness on the part of the owner to sell the property for a lower price.

ASSEMBLAGE

The combining of two or more adjoining lots into a single large lot. Often the purpose of bringing a number of lots together under one ownership is to allow a developer/investor to construct a large building or buildings on a single lot. By assembling the lots, the single value of the one large lot is often greater than the total single values of each of the smaller lots. *(See* **Plottage)**

ASSESSED VALUE

The worth or value of a piece of property as determined by the taxing authority for the purpose of levying an ad valorem (property) tax. The assessed value of property is normally based on some percentage of market value. Property may be assessed at full market value or, as is more commonly the case, assessed at something less; for example, fifty percent. Generally, accepted appraisal techniques are used to derive an assessed value for the land and for the building. The assessed value is then multiplied by the tax rate or millage rate to determine the amount of taxes due.

Example: Capital city assesses property at 40% of market value.
If the market value of a parcel is $80,000, then the assessed value is:
$80,000 x .40 = $32,000
The $32,000 would be multiplied by the tax rate or millage rate to determine the taxes due on the property. *(See* **Ad Valorem, Assessment, Assessor, Millage Rate, Property Tax, Tax Rate)**

ASSESSMENT

(1) A determination of the value of a parcel for the purpose of levying a property tax on that parcel.

(2) The term also is used to denote the means by which local governments raise the money to pay for certain improvements which directly benefit property

owners adjoining or adjacent to the improvements. For example, the cost of paving a previously unpaved road could be assessed to the land on each side of the road. The actual cost to a particular landowner would be based on his or her front footage as a percentage of the total footage being improved.

(3) Joint forms of ownership such as condominiums and cooperatives allocate the expenses incurred for the maintenance and upkeep of the common areas and limited common areas and assess each unit owner for his or her proportionate share. (*See* **Homeowner's Association, Special Assessment**)

ASSESSMENT RATIO

The ratio of assessed value to full market value as set by a taxing authority. For example, a ratio of 40% would mean that a property with a full market value of $100,000 would be assessed at 40% or $40,000 for taxing purposes. In some jurisdictions all property is assessed at the same ratio, while in others various classifications of property have different ratios. (*See* **Property Tax**)

ASSESSMENT ROLL

A list of all taxable property showing the assessed value of each parcel. Such information is public and is normally available in the tax assessor's office or in the local land records.

ASSESSOR

A public official either appointed or elected to appraise property and place an assessed value on that property for the purpose of levying a property (ad valorem) tax. (*See* **Assessed Value, Property Tax, Value**)

ASSETS

An accounting term used to denote the real and personal property one possesses, as distinguished from debts and obligations which are known as liabilities. Assets minus liabilities equals net worth.

ASSIGN

To transfer to another. (*See* **Assignment**)

ASSIGNEE

The person to whom a claim, benefit, or right in property is made. (*See* **Assignment**)

ASSIGNMENT

The transfer of a claim, benefit or right in property belonging to one person (the *assignor*) to another person (the *assignee*). Real estate instruments in which assignments occur include sales contracts, mortgages, options, and leases. Rights under contracts are valuable property rights which can ordinarily be assigned to third persons. The legal effect of an assignment is to substitute the assignee for the assignor in the contractual relationship with the other original contracting party. All rights are considered terminated in the assignor after he or she makes the transfer. The assignee takes the contract subject to all defenses which existed prior to the assign-ment. Contract rights which may not be assigned include those rights which would materially change duties. Personal service contracts, therefore, are ordinarily not assignable. Rights which would materially vary the risk of a return performance are also not assignable. This means that contracts involving the personal credit of a party or a contract for insurance coverage may not be assigned. The parties may stipulate that a contract is not assignable, or they may agree that some rights which are ordinarily not assignable may in fact be assigned.

ASSIGNMENT OF LEASE

A transfer by the tenant (lessee) of his or her interest in the lease to a third person. Both the lessor and lessee may transfer their respective interests in a lease to a third person, unless prohibited by the terms of the lease. The lessor may sell, assign or mortgage the *leased fee* interest. Conveyance is taken subject to the rights of the lessee unless the lessee has agreed to subordinate the rights. The lessee may transfer the *leasehold* interest either by assignment or by sublease. If the lessee parts with the entire estate, retaining no interest, the transfer is called an *assignment*. If the lessee retains a reversion, the transfer is called a *sublease*. A provision may be included in the lease which prohibits the assignment or sublease of the leasehold without the written permission of the landlord. Restrictions against the transfer of property interests are called restraints on the *right of alienation*. These restrictions are not favored by the courts and will be strictly construed. Thus, a restriction against an assignment does not prevent a sublease, and likewise a restriction against subleasing does not prevent assigning. If a lessee makes an assignment, a *privity of estate* is created between the lessor and the assignee or new lessee. A privity of estate means that the lessor and lessee share a property interest in the land and owe reciprocal obligations as a result of this shared property interest. Therefore, both parties are bound by those covenants which run with the land, including the obligation to pay rent. However, since no privity of contract exists between the landlord and the new tenant, because the assignee did not sign the lease contract, the assignee may terminate all future liability to the landlord by making a new assignment. This is not true if the new tenant *assumes* the obligations of the lease. By creating privity of contract between the landlord and assignee, this assumption binds the assignee to all contractual obligations of the lease. In any case, the original tenant or assignor remains secondarily liable for the contractual obligations. (*See* **Sublease**)

ASSIGNOR

The person transferring a claim, benefit or right in property to another. (*See* **Assignment**)

ASSOCIATE BROKER

A person who has met the qualification necessary for a real estate broker's license but who works jointly with and is employed by another broker. (*See* **Broker**)

ASSOCIATED GENERAL CONTRACTORS OF AMERICA (AGCA)

AGCA serves as a leading spokesman for the construction industry. Four classifications of construction contractors are represented: buildings, heavy industrial, municipal utility construction, and highway. The association's address is 1957 E Street, N.W., Washington, D.C. 20006; (202) 393-2040.

ASSUMPTION FEE

A charge levied by a lender to a purchaser who takes title to property by assuming an existing mortgage. The charge can be a fixed amount; for example, $100, or perhaps a percentage of the outstanding balance, for example, one percent. The assumption fee is paid to the lender at the time of settlement or closing.

ASSUMPTION OF MORTGAGE

Taking title to property which has an existing mortgage and agreeing to be personally liable for the payment of the existing mortgage debt. A distinction exists between "assuming" a mortgage and taking title "subject to" a mortgage. If the purchaser agrees to *assume* the mortgage, he or she becomes personally liable on any deficiencies, such as not making payments, occurring in a foreclosure sale. When a purchaser takes title *subject to* the mortgage, no personal liability is undertaken to the lender; thus, the purchaser could walk away from the mortgage and lose nothing but the equity already invested. In both situations the original borrower is liable to the lender unless specifically released in a *novation*. A mortgage may obtain a *nonassumption clause* or *due on sale clause* which prohibits an assumption without consent of the lender. Such consent is normally given for a fee and a possible jump in the interest rate if the contract rate is below the prevailing market rate. (*See* **Due-on-Sale Clause, Mortgage, Nonassumption Clause, Novation, Subject to Mortgage**)

AT-RISK RULE

A part of the *Tax Reform Act of 1986* which limits the amount that an investor can claim as a loss suffered from a real estate investment.

ATTACHED HOUSING

Two or more units that are physically attached but intended and designed for occupancy as individual housing units. Such units may be in the form of a duplex, triplex or fourplex as well as row houses which may extend for a complete city block. In contrast, most residential units are in the form of *detached* units.

ATTACHMENT

The act of taking a person's property into the legal custody of a court for the purpose of serving as security for satisfaction of a judgment which has been filed.

The action itself is often called a *writ of attachment* and serves to create a lien against the property. As a result the property may not be sold free of the attachment unless the attachment has either been satisfied or released. (*See* **Lien, Lis Pendens**)

ATTESTATION

The act of witnessing a person's signing of a written instrument. Some states require that a deed be witnessed by at least two witnesses one of whom may need to be an official witness such as a notary. Without the attestation the deed is void in those states that have this requirement. Some deeds may require a witnessing in cases involving grantors who have not learned to write or are paralyzed. Such a grantor would be required to make a mark or at least a thumbprint which manifests intent to sign. Both the marking and the statement or declaration of intent by the grantor would need to be witnessed.

ATTORNEY AT LAW

A person authorized to practice law in his or her respective state and thus permitted to give legal advice, draft legal instruments, and represent clients in courts of law. (*See* **Attorney in Fact**)

ATTORNEY IN FACT

A person authorized to act on behalf of another by virtue of a *power of attorney*. Anyone of legal capacity may be an attorney in fact, and depending on the desire of the person creating the relationship, the attorney in fact's authority could be that of a universal, general, or specific agent. Care should be taken not to confuse this status with an *attorney at law*, a person who must be admitted to an appropriate bar. (*See* **Agent, Power of Attorney, Principal**)

ATTORNEY'S OPINION OF TITLE

A statement issued by an attorney as to the quality of title after examining an abstract of title. Commonly referred to as "opinion of title." (*See* **Abstract of Title, Title**)

ATTRACTIVE NUISANCE

A potentially hazardous object, such as a swimming pool, or a condition, such as an open pit on a parcel of land, that is inviting and potentially dangerous to young children. The owner is expected to take the same measures that a reasonable and prudent person would take to prevent injury to children who would be attracted to the "nuisance." Even though children would be technically trespassing if they entered the property, the owner may still liable for any injuries incurred.

AUCTION

The selling of real or personal property to the highest bidder by a person licensed and authorized to sell the property. The auctioneer is employed by the owner or seller of the property as an agent and normally receives a percentage of the sales price as his or her commission. With auctions being used frequently in the selling of hard-to-sell property, special rules exist in regard to offers and acceptances in auction sales. When an auctioneer places a property for sale, he or she is not making an offer but is merely soliciting offers. The auctioneer accepts bid offers when he or she slams down a gavel or says "Sold!" Auctions may be *with reserve* or *without reserve*. Unless it is stated to the contrary, an auction is considered to be with reserve. This means that the seller reserves the right to accept or reject bids and to withdraw the property from sale. Until actual acceptance, the bidder may withdraw a bid at any time.

The term auction is also used to denote the means by which the *Federal National Mortgage Association (Fannie Mae)* purchases mortgages in the secondary mortgage market. Periodically, the association accepts bids from approved lenders as to the amount, price and terms of existing mortgages that these lenders wish to sell in the secondary mortgage market. By purchasing these mortgages, Fannie Mae provides more money for the housing market.

AUCTIONEER

A person licensed or authorized to sell real or personal property belonging to someone else at public auction. In some states an auctioneer selling real property must be licensed as a real estate broker, whereas in others he or she is licensed as an auctioneer. (*See* **Auction, Broker**)

AUTHORITY

The power of an agent to affect the principal in legal relations with third persons for lawful purposes. Authority may be classified into: (1) *actual* authority, (2) *implied* authority, (3) *apparent* or *ostensible* authority, (4) *inherent* authority, and (5) *other* authority which may be implied from particular circumstances. Generally, the authority of an agent is strictly construed by the courts. An agent ordinarily only has that authority which is expressly given by the principal or that authority which is necessary to carry out the authority expressly delegated. Therefore, unless the principal has negligently or intentionally misled a third person as to the agent's actual authority, the third person has the duty to inquire as to its scope. A principal is bound by the acts of an agent performed within the scope of the agent's actual and implied authority. A principal is also bound by the reasonable reliance of a third person on the apparent or ostensible authority of the agent. A third person has a duty to inquire as to the scope of the agent's authority to bind the principal since generally the principal cannot be bound by unauthorized acts.

When a broker receives a listing from one who is not the owner of a property or if a co-owner such as a spouse is involved, the broker should be assured that the listing was authorized. It should be noted that familial relationship does not necessarily make one member of a household an agent for the others. If a broker negligently fails to inquire as to the authority of such a member to list the property, the broker may find it difficult to recover the commission. When a husband and wife are joint owners of a property, both should sign the listing contract. Likewise, when a broker receives a listing from a corporate officer, a duty arises on the part of the broker to inquire if the officer was in fact authorized to sell the corporation's assets. Often the sale of corporate land or personal property in the nature of a *bulk transfer* requires a resolution by the corporation's directors. (*See* **Agent, Principal**)

AUTHORIZATION TO SELL

A listing agreement entered into by the owner of property and a broker determining the rights and responsibilities of both in the selling of the property. (*See* **Listing**)

AVERAGE RATE OF RETURN

A technique used to estimate a rate of return. To compute this rate, investment outflows are subtracted from total investment inflows. The result is divided by the number of years the investment was held, and that result is divided by the total investment to arrive at the average annual rate of return.

AVULSION

A sudden loss or gain of land as the result of action of water or a shift in a bed of a river which has been used as a boundary by property owners. If land is lost as a result of avulsion the riparian owner does not lose title to the land that has been lost; the boundary lines remain the same. This is not true when land is lost by erosion. (*See* **Accretion, Erosion**)

AXIAL THEORY OF GROWTH

A pattern of land growth and development which takes the form of a star and occurs along the main transportation routes outward from a city. The city or central business district remains the center of the "star."

BABCOCK, FREDERICK

A real estate appraiser who studied urban growth and changes in the 1930s. Babcock characterized urban areas as "sliding, jumping, and bursting" in their growth. He is the author of *The Valuation of Real Estate*, one of the earliest texts concerned with valuation.

BACK-END FEES

Fees or commissions earned by a *syndicator* when a property owned by the *syndication* is sold. These fees are often subordinate to the investors getting their original investment back plus a guaranteed or preferred return.

BACKFILL

The dirt used to fill in around the foundation walls of a building after the walls have been constructed.

BACK-TITLE CERTIFICATE

A certificate issued by a title insurance company where it agrees to honor a valid search that continues a chain of title from the time the company last certified the title. (*See* **Title Search**)

BACK-TO-BACK ESCROW

A technique used by an individual who needs the cash proceeds from one sale to make a purchase in a second transaction. Back-to-back escrows can be structured so that one escrow is contingent on another escrow closing or concurrent with another escrow closing. (*See* **Escrow**)

BACKUP COMMITMENT

A loan commitment from a second lender to be used if the first lender's commitment is not honored. For example, the first lender may require a certain percentage of a project to be leased before the borrower qualifies for the loan. If the requirement cannot be met, the borrower may turn to the backup commitment for financing. The provider of the backup commitment may or may not charge a fee for the commitment.

BACKUP OFFER

A second contract on a parcel of real estate that is contingent on the first contract not going through closing. Sometimes a backup offer is made after the original offer has been accepted.

BAD DEBT ALLOWANCE

In income property appraisal, an adjustment to the potential gross income to account for expected rent collection losses. (*See* **Net Operating Income**)

BAD TITLE

(*See* **Defect of Record, Title**)

BAIL BOND LIEN

A lien placed on real property to allow someone who has been arrested to be released from jail without having to post a cash bond. (*See* **Lien**)

BAILEE

The person receiving delivery and possession of property under a contract of bailment. (*See* **Bailment**)

BAILMENT

Occurs when one person (the *bailor*) gives possession and control of personal property to another person (the *bailee*) for the purpose of carrying out or completing some specific assignment. During the period of this temporary possession, the property still belongs to the bailor. An example of a bailment is when a owner gives a real estate broker the key to a listed house. The owner is the bailor, the broker is the bailee, and the key is the subject of the bailment. Title to the key remains with the owner even though possession has been given to the broker. The broker must take care of the key until the owner asks for its return or in some way directs its disposition.

BAILOR

The person who delivers possession and control of property under a contract of bailment. (*See* **Bailment**)

BALANCE, MORTGAGE

The amount of money still owed to the lender on a mortgage loan. (*See* **Mortgage**)

BALANCE, PRINCIPLE OF

A valuation principle which states that there is an ideal equilibrium in assembling and combining the four factors of production (*land, labor, capital* and *management*). If too few are used, the result is *underimproved* land; if too many are used, the land may be *overimproved*. (*See* **Factors of Production, Highest and Best Use, Overimprovement, Underimproved Land**)

BALANCE SHEET

A statement that measures, from an accounting viewpoint, the financial position of a business enterprise as of a given date.

BALLOON DOWN PAYMENT

A creative financing technique used by a buyer to spread the down payment over two or more periods rather than making the entire down payment at closing. For example, for a down payment of $5,000, the buyer might agree to pay $1,000 at closing, a balloon payment of $2,000 in six months, and a second balloon payment of $2,000 at the end of one year.

BALLOON MORTGAGE

A mortgage in which the periodic payments do not result in the principal being fully amortized (paid back) at the end of the term, thus the last principal payment is substantially higher than those made during the life of the mortgage. Such a mortgage is commonly referred to as a *partially amortized mortgage,* as distinguished from a *fully amortized mortgage*, in which at maturity the outstanding balance has been reduced to zero. Balloon mortgages are often used in the financing of commercial property where the lender does not want to extend credit over a substantially long period of time. By using a balloon mortgage, the lender can receive a certain amount of the principal repayment with each payment of interest, the amount being less than would be received if the mortgage were fully amortized. At the end of the term the borrower either pays off the loan or seeks refinancing at current interest rates. (*See* **Balloon Payment, Fully Amortized Mortgage, Partially Amortized Mortgage**)

BALLOON PAYMENT

The final payment of principal under a balloon mortgage, possibly representing a substantial portion of the original amount borrowed.

Example: Mr. Garrett needs $1,000,000 to finance the purchase of an apartment building.   If he borrows the $1,000,000 for 25 years at 14% interest under a fully amortized mortgage, a monthly payment of $12,038 would be required. However, the lender will not make him a 25-year loan, but does agree to lend him the $1,000,000 for 10 years with the monthly debt service calculated on a 25-year maturity.   Thus, his monthly payment will still be $12,038; however, at the end of the 10 years, the outstanding principal of $856,843 is due as the balloon payment. (*See* **Amortization, Balloon Mortgage**)

BAND OF INVESTMENT METHOD

One of the common techniques used by appraisers and investors to derive an appropriate capitalization rate for a particular income-producing property.   The band of investment method is related to the typical capital structure of a particular project and to how much income would be necessary to compensate each provider of funds.   A weighted average is developed to determine the composite capitalization rate.

Example: An investor would like to purchase an office building.   The investor can finance 60 percent of the purchase with a first mortgage carrying an interest rate of 13 percent.   Fifteen percent of the purchase price can be financed with a second mortgage at a rate of 16 percent.   The remaining 25 percent must be contributed by the investor who desires a 20 percent return on equity.

The overall capitalization rate using the band of investment method would be:

SOURCE	AMOUNT		INTEREST REQUIRED		WEIGHTED VALUE
1st Mortgage	60%	x	.13	=	7.8%
2nd Mortgage	15%	x	.16	=	2.4%
3rd Mortgage	25%	x	.20	=	5.0%
			Overall Rate	=	15.2%

(*See* **Capitalization Rate**)

BANKER'S ACCEPTANCE

A short-term negotiable instrument representing a bank's obligation to pay on behalf of a depositor.

BANKER'S RATE SELECTION METHOD

A method used by appraisers to estimate a *capitalization rate* based on a bank's typical loan requirements for different classes of property.   (*See* **Capitalization Rate**)

BARGAIN AND SALE DEED

A deed conveying all of the grantor's interest in real property to the grantee by reciting a valuable consideration. Such deeds may be with or without covenants. A deed with covenants is like a special warranty deed in which the grantor covenants that the property has not been encumbered during the time that the grantor possessed the estate. A deed without covenants is similar to a quitclaim deed. There is an implication in both types of bargain and sales deeds that the grantor has possession and has some ownership interest, usually substantial, in the property. This type of deed is often used by trustees, executors, or officers of the court to convey property under their control. (*See* **Covenant, Quitclaim Deed, Special Warranty Deed**)

BASE (BASE INTEREST RATE)

In compound interest, one plus the interest rate per period. Mathematically, this is expressed as:

$$S = (1 + i)$$

where "S" represents the base, and "i" is the interest rate for the compounding period.

BASE LINES

Imaginary lines running east-west (latitude) which intersect with lines running north-south (longitude and referred to as *meridians*) to form the starting points in the rectangular survey or U. S. government survey system of land descriptions. (*See* **Government Survey Method**)

BASE PERIOD

A period that serves as a reference point for establishing an index for price changes. The index for the base period is normally set at 100. If, for example, a price change of 8% occurred, the new index would be 108. Base periods often appear in leases with index clauses and are used in conjunction with increasing rents due to changes in the level of prices. (*See* **Index Lease**)

BASE RENT

The minimum rent due the landlord in a percentage lease as stipulated in the lease agreement. For example, the rent clause in a commercial lease for a shopping center could say "$400 per month plus 2% of gross sales," in which case the base rent would be $400. (*See* **Percentage Lease**)

BASIC INDUSTRY

A term used in *economic base analysis* to refer to an industry which attracts income from outside the community or economic base. For example, an automobile assembly plant sells the vast majority of its finished product to customers outside the geographic area where it is located and thus dollars from outside are brought into the area. The growth and economic expansion of an area is dependent upon attracting basic industry. (*See* **Economic Base Analysis, Nonbasic Industry**)

BASIC MULTIPLIER

A ratio used in *economic base analysis* which compares an area's total economic activity (usually total employment) to basic activities (or basic employment). Basic activities are those which bring income from outside of the area. For example, automobile manufacturing in Detroit is basic, while a barber shop is a nonbasic or service activity. (*See* **Economic Base Analysis**)

BASIC RENT

In government subsidized housing, the amount of rent charged assuming the tenant qualifies for the maximum rent subsidy.

BASING INDEX

A measure of interest rates used to determine the interest rate charged on *adjustable rate mortgages*. Six-month U.S. Treasury Bill rates are one example of an index used to determine the rate on such mortgages. Normally the basing index is beyond the direct control of the lender.

BASIS

The cost of acquisition of property. Exceptions would be special situations such as property acquired by gift or inheritance. The adjusted basis is the original basis plus all *capital improvements*, minus *depreciation*.

BASIS POINT

An amount equal to one one-hundredth of one percent. The term is used to explain the absolute change in the marketplace of debt instruments, such as mortgages and bonds. A change in conventional mortgage rates from 14 percent to 13 1/2 percent would be 50 basis points.

BASKET LOAN

A type of loan that is not routinely made by a lender. Government regulatory provisions allow certain lenders such as insurance companies leeway to place a small percentage of their loan portfolio into otherwise unlawful investments. The regulation that permits this flexibility is referred to as a *basket provision* or *leeway provision*.

BASKET PROVISION

(*See* **Basket Loan**)

BASSETT, EDWARD M.

A leader in enacting the first comprehensive zoning ordinance in the United States. This took place in 1916 in New York City. Later, Bassett was influential in the zoning movement which spread throughout the United States in the 1920's and later.

BAY DEPTH

The distance from the tenant's side of a corridor wall to the building's exterior wall. Bay depth is one of the considerations in judging a building's efficiency.

BEAM RIGHT AGREEMENT

An agreement between two neighbors where one is allowed to use another's wall to attach beams for structural support.

BEDROOM COMMUNITY

An area consisting primarily of commuters located outside the *central business district (CBD)* of a city and for the most part void of any industry or high-employment centers. As urban sprawl took place beginning in the 1950's, bedroom communities began to appear around most of the metropolitan areas in the United States.

BEFORE-AND-AFTER RULE

A means of measuring compensation in an *eminent domain* taking. Also known as the *federal rule*, it involves finding: (1) the value of the whole property prior to taking and (2) the value of the property after taking and after considering any enhancement or damages to the property remaining. The difference is the measurement of damages that would be awarded. (*See* **Eminent Domain**)

BEFORE-TAX CASH FLOW

A term used by some investors referring to pretax cash flow as distinguished from after-tax cash flow. It is the sum of money generated from income-producing property after all operating expenses and mortgage payments, including principal and interest, have been made.

BEFORE-TAX CASH FLOW TO EQUITY

(*See* **Cash Throw-off**)

BEFORE-TAX EQUITY REVERSION

The amount received in cash by a seller after paying transaction costs and the remaining mortgage balance.

BELOW-MARKET INTEREST RATE MORTGAGE (BMIR)

A mortgage characterized by an interest rate that is less than the current market interest rate. Such mortgages are available if and when a third party, such as a builder, has "bought down" the interest rate with a cash payment to the lender at the time settlement occurs. The purpose of the *buydown* is to make the real estate being financed more attractive to the purchaser and/or to lower the monthly payment so as to qualify the purchaser. (*See* **Buydown**)

BELTWAY

A circumferential highway around a major city. As urban areas expanded outwardly in the late fifties and sixties, cities built roads some distance from the central business district that completely circled the city, thus providing a means by which automobile traffic could move in and out of the city.

BENCH MARK

A known point of elevation, usually in the form of an embedded brass disk set in a concrete monument, established throughout the United States by the *U. S. Coast and Geodetic Survey*. The elevation and complete description of all bench marks are published in booklet form for a given region by the U.S. Coast and Geodetic Survey (USC and GS). Numerous bench marks, other than those set by USC and GS, have been established. For example, bench marks are often established during the preliminary surveying on a construction site. These established elevations can then be used in preliminary design work and later during the actual construction of the project. Wooden stakes firmly driven into the ground and precisely identified are commonly used as bench marks on construction sites. (*See* **Datum, Mean Sea Level, Monument**)

BENCH MARK APPRAISAL

A detailed study of a specific property that an appraiser or bank wishes to use for the purpose of monitoring price changes in the market on an on-going basis. (*See* **Appraisal**)

BENEFICIAL INTEREST

A right recognized by law that gives an individual benefits from property, but legal title and control belongs to someone else such as a trustee. This concept is found in trusts and sales contracts. (*See* **Equitable Title**)

BENEFICIARY

One who benefits from the act or acts of another, such as the recipient of the proceeds of an insurance policy, the lender under a deed of trust, or an investor in a real estate investment trust. (*See* **Deed of Trust**)

BEQUEATH

To leave or give personal property by will. The term is distinguishable from *devise* which is the giving of real property by will. However, courts have ruled that if the clear intentions of the *testator* (the party giving the property) is to use the word bequeath as synonymous with devise then such wording can pass both personal and real property. (*See* **Devise, Testator**)

BETTERMENTS

Improvements to a structure that are more substantial than mere repairs.

BIANNUAL

Twice a year or semi-annually.

BID BOND

A bond required in some competitive bidding situations where the owner is compensated for the difference between the low bid and the next lowest bid if the low bidder refuses to honor the bid.

BIENNIAL

Once every two years. Some states require the renewal of a real estate broker's or salesperson's license on a biennial basis.

BIGGER FOOL THEORY

A theory used to explain why real estate speculators sometimes buy property which is overpriced. They hope that they can find a "bigger fool" who will pay them an even higher price.

BIKEWAYS

Paths designed for bicycles and other nonmotorized vehicles.

BILATERAL CONTRACT

A contract in which each party to the contract promises to perform some act or duty in exchange for the promise of the other party(ies). Most real estate contracts are bilateral contracts involving reciprocal obligations and become binding when the mutual promises are communicated. For example, modern listing agreements are normally bilateral contracts in that the seller "promises to pay to the broker a cash fee of _____ percent of the sales price upon consummation by any purchaser of a valid contract" and the broker "promises to make reasonable efforts to obtain a purchaser." Once such a contract is signed by the seller and the broker the contract is binding on both parties and failure to perform by one of the parties could result in legal action by the other. (*See* **Contract, Specific Performance, Unilateral Contract**)

BILL OF SALE

A written instrument used to transfer ownership of personal property in contrast to real property which is transferred by a deed. A bill of sale is used when personal property is being transferred in conjunction with real property. For example, the owner (seller) of a store might want to sell the current inventory along with the building and fixtures. In such an instance the deed, which would convey the building and fixtures to the new owner, might reference the bill of sale used to transfer the inventory. (*See* **Deed, Fixture**)

BINDER

A receipt for the earnest money deposit paid by the purchaser to secure his or her right to buy the property at the specific price and terms agreed to by both buyer and seller. Evidence of the actual receipt of the earnest money deposit is usually mentioned in the sales contract.

The term also denotes a written instrument issued by an insurance company which gives temporary protection or coverage to the insured until a formal policy is issued.

BIRD DOG

A real estate licensee, generally an inexperienced salesperson, who finds new prospects and then turns their names over to his or her broker or perhaps to another salesperson. The more experienced broker or salesperson, in turn, follows up on the names provided. For his or her services, the "bird dog" usually receives a finder's fee or part of the sales commission if a sale takes place.

BIWEEKLY MORTGAGE

A mortgage with a repayment schedule of every two weeks rather than the traditional monthly amortization. The recent popularity of such mortgages stems from the fact that since repayment is made every two weeks (twenty-six times per year), the total interest charge is less and, thus, more of the mortgage payment goes toward reduction of the principal. Thus, all things being equal, biweekly mortgages have shorter lengths of term than the traditional monthly amortized loan.

BLANK CHECK TRUST

A type of *Real Estate Investment Trust (REIT)* which is organized to raise funds from investors before a decision is made to buy any specific property. This trust gives flexibility to the trustees but investors earn little return of their investment until properties are actually purchased. The concept is similar to a *blind pool*.

BLANKET INSURANCE POLICY

(*See* **Master Policy**)

BLANKET MORTGAGE

A mortgage in which two or more pieces of property are used to cover a single debt. A blanket mortgage is often used by a developer to cover more than one parcel of land under the same mortgage. For example, a developer buys a large tract of land and plans to subdivide the land into one hundred lots and then build homes on the lots. Rather than going to the expense and time of obtaining one hundred separate mortgages, one blanket mortgage covering all the lots is obtained. Since the developer will probably be developing a few lots at a time, the mortgage will include a *partial release clause* which means that as the debt is repaid, individual lots will be released from the mortgage. Thus the developer can pay off part of the mortgage, have a certain number of lots released, build on the lots, and then sell them free and clear from the lien that still exists on the unreleased lots. (*See* **Partial Release Clause**)

BLEEDING A PROJECT

The withdrawal of income from a real estate project by an owner for personal use rather than making necessary repairs and maintenance expenditures on the property. Deferred maintenance is an example of bleeding a project. Potential investors should carefully examine property to ascertain whether or not the property has been bled.

BLENDED LOAN (MORTGAGE)

In refinancing, the name given to a loan if the new interest rate is a compromise figure between the old interest rate and the current market rate of interest.

BLIGHT

Decay in a neighborhood which normally leads to a lowering of property values. (*See* **Economic Obsolescence**)

BLIGHTED AREA

A geographic area in which property values are adversely affected by such things as physically deteriorating buildings, high vacancy rates, absentee ownership, high crime rates and lack of public services. In recent years many blighted areas have become the center of various public and private city renewal projects which have attempted to pump new life into them.

BLIND AD

An advertisement in which the name of the person placing the ad is not included. For example, a newspaper ad might say "House For Sale, $40,000, Call 234-7539." Real estate licensing laws often prohibit brokers and salespersons from using such ads. Normally, the name of the broker must be included in all advertising done by either the broker or salespersons licensed on behalf of the broker.

BLIND POOL

A blind pool, also known as a *nonspecified fund* occurs when a syndicator raises money and places it into a fund before making a purchase of any specific property. A blind pool allows the syndicator flexibility to take advantage of investment opportunities as they arise.

BLOCK

An area or portion of a city or town bound on all sides by streets or roads. The term is also used to denote a means of subdividing a large tract of land into smaller units, each of which is clearly identified, as for example, "Country Club Subdivision, Block A, Lot 2." (*See* **Lot and Block**)

BLOCKBUSTING

Any activity in which one party, hoping to benefit financially, induces another party to enter into a real estate transaction by implying or showing that a change in the neighborhood with respect to race, color, sex, religion or national origin may cause lowered property values, a change in the character of the neighborhood, an increase in criminal or antisocial behavior, or a decline in school quality. It should be noted that blockbusting does not occur from selling a house to a member of a minority group, but rather from attempting to drive out existing owners. Thus courts have construed even broad statements such as "This is a changing neighborhood" as falling under the heading of blockbusting. Blockbusting violates federal fair housing laws and in some states such practice violates state fair housing laws as well as real estate licensing law. (*See* **Civil Rights Act of 1866, Discrimination, Federal Fair Housing Act of 1968**)

BLUE LAWS

Statutes limiting activities, such as the selling of certain items or the opening of certain stores, which may take place on Sundays and other religious holidays.

BLUEPRINT

Reproduced plans of a building which are used by workers during construction.

BLUE SKY LAWS

State statutes providing for both regulation and supervision in the selling of securities. The purpose of such laws is to protect the citizens of the state from fraud in dealing with companies who promise one thing and deliver another. In some instances the laws prohibit certain practices while in others pertinent facts must be made available to all prospects. For example, a potential investor in a real estate limited partnership would have to be told what fees were being charged by the developer/general partner to put the project together. (*See* **Syndication**)

BOARD OF ADJUSTMENT

An appointed board authorized to grant variances from a zoning ordinance when a regulation imposes a unique hardship on a property. It may also serve as an appellate board for any complaints from property owners pertaining to the administration of the zoning ordinance. Also known as a *board of zoning appeals*.

BOARD OF EQUALIZATION

A local or state board authorized to hear formal property tax assessment complaints and to adjust the inequities which may exist. (*See* **Assessed Value, Property Tax**)

BOARD OF REALTORS

A local organization of Realtors and Realtor-Associates who are members of the State and National Association of Realtors. Currently, there are more than 1800 local boards throughout the United States.

BOARD OF ZONING APPEALS

(*See* **Board of Adjustment**)

BOARDING HOUSE

A residential dwelling containing numerous living units. The living units, while often quite small, normally contain sleeping and bath space, but no kitchen. Meals are often served in a main dining facility and are available to all residents.

BOECKH BUILDING VALUATION MANUAL

A national cost estimation manual published by the American Appraisal Company at 525 East Michigan St., Milwaukee, Wisconsin. The manual consists of several volumes covering various types of properties including residential, commercial, and industrial.

BOECKH INDEX

A national index of residential construction costs. (*See* **Boeckh Building Valuation Manual**)

BOILER AND MACHINERY INSURANCE

Special insurance that provides coverage for explosions and damages to building equipment.

BOILERPLATE

The standardized wording normally contained in a contract. Such wording, if it is commonly used, is often printed in a standard contract form with space provided for additions or specifics. Much of the language in a standard real estate listing agreement or sales contract is said to be "boilerplate."

BOILER ROOM OPERATION

A sales center using high pressure tactics over the telephone to sell securities, recreational lots, time share interests and other investment products. Products sold are often of questionable investment quality.

BOMA STANDARD

A method of measuring floor space in an office building. Such an approach is important in calculating the rentable space is to be included in the lease agreement.

BONA FIDE

Sincere, honest, in good faith.

BONA FIDE PURCHASER

One who purchases property in good faith without any knowledge or notice, by the seller, either constructive or actual, of any title defects. State statutes often protect such a purchaser against the rights of third parties who have not recorded their claims against the subject property. (*See* **Actual Notice, Constructive Notice, Lien, Title**)

BOND

A written promise by the borrower to pay back a specific sum of money at specified terms and at a specified time. The bond, or *promissory note* as it is also called, is the primary evidence of the debt obligation which is normally secured by a mortgage on the property. While there is no significant difference between a bond and a promissory note, a bond is more formal and is under seal.

The term bond has another meaning in real estate licensing law in that it refers to the amount of money required to be set aside to secure the performance of some obligation. Some states require, as part of the application for a real estate license, the filing of a bond. As a result, any person injured by any action arising out of a real estate transaction by a licensee may recover compensation from the bond. The normal procedure would be for the complaint to be filed with the real estate commission followed by an investigation, hearing, and possibly the awarding of compensation in the amount of the actual loss. (*See* **Mortgage, Promissory Note**)

BOND-TYPE SECURITY

A *Government National Mortgage Association (GNMA)* security in which a specified interest rate is paid to an investor on a semi-annual basis with the principal being returned at the end of the term.

BOOK DEPRECIATION

An accounting concept which refers to an allowance taken to provide for recovery of capital invested in *wasting assets*.

BOOK VALUE

The dollar amount of an asset as carried on the financial books of the owner. Book value is calculated as the initial cost of the asset plus capital improvements minus total accrued depreciation. It is the adjusted basis of the asset and can be significantly different than the market value of the asset. Book value is important in determining either capital gain or loss resulting from the sale of an asset. (*See* **Basis, Depreciation**)

BOOKIE SCREEN

A computer-based information system on federally backed mortgage securities made available only to a limited number of large securities brokerage firms.

BOOT

In taxation, money or something else of value, such as a land contract or a mortgage, given in the exchange of like-kind properties when the value of one of the properties is less than the value of the other. If there is boot, the gain of the party receiving the boot will be taxed to the extent of the boot received. (*See* **Tax-Free Exchange**)

BORROWER

The individual or company obtaining funds from the lender. (*See* **Mortgagor**)

BOTEL

An addition to a marina which offers sleeping accommodations for people traveling by boat.

BOUNDARY

The line of division between two contiguous properties. Boundaries can be both natural, such as a river, and artificial, such as an iron pipe driven into the ground. (*See* **Legal Description, Survey**)

BOUNDS

The external boundary lines of a parcel. The term is used in the oldest method of land description in the United States, *metes and bounds*, which involves identifying distances and directions in determining legal boundaries. (*See* **Metes and Bounds**)

BOY

Abbreviation for *beginning of year*. The term is used in regard to real estate financing and investment analysis.

BRACKETING

A process used by appraisers to select sales comparables that are better and worse, or bigger and smaller than the subject property being appraised. By including some comparables that are better and some comparables that are worse, the appraiser is better able to position the value estimate of the subject property within some value range.

BREACH OF CONTRACT

A failure to perform as promised on part or all of the terms and conditions of a contract. Each party to a contract has a duty to perform as promised. A failure to do so is called a breach of contract. If the breach is only incidental, it is called *minor*, and the remedy is the actual damage sustained by the innocent party; if the breach is serious it is called *major*. In the latter case, the innocent party has a number of remedies from which to choose. First, a material breach gives grounds for *rescission*. The innocent party is excused from performance and is entitled to a return of any consideration he or she may have rendered to the other party. Second, an injured party is entitled to collect any *actual damages* suffered. The rule that courts apply is that the injured party is entitled to be placed as nearly as possible in the same monetary position as if the contract had been performed. Punitive damages are normally not awarded in contract cases. Indirect damages called *consequential damages*, such as lost profits or lost business opportunities, are also ordinarily not awarded unless the breaching party could have reasonably foreseen them. An injured party has a general duty to *mitigate* (lessen) damages whenever reasonable. If the tenant breaks a lease, the landlord may not refuse to rent the premise to credit-worthy prospects in order to run up the damages against the breaching tenant. Third, if the contract is for the sale of unique goods or property, an alternative remedy, called *specific performance*, is available. Since by definition all real estate is considered unique, this remedy is available to both the purchaser and seller. Specific performance is an equitable remedy in which the court orders the contract to be performed as agreed to by the parties. In many cases, the contracting parties may have agreed in advance that, if the contract were breached, the injured party would be entitled to *liquidated damages*. Liquidated damages are an agreed upon sum which will be paid if the contract is breached. The courts will enforce the liquidated damages stipulation only if the agreed upon sum is reasonable. If the sum is unreasonably high, the courts will consider the sum to be a penalty, and will refuse enforcement. Liquidated damages are common in real estate sales agreements. Typically, a provision exists that, if a purchaser defaults on the contract, the earnest money that he or she may have paid will be kept by the seller or seller and broker as liquidated damages. Where a liquidated damages provision exists, other remedies are precluded, and the innocent party may not seek actual damages or specific performance.

BREAK-EVEN POINT

In finance, the point at which total income is equal to total expenses. For example, the break-even point in the ownership of an apartment complex would be reached when rental income was equal to all operating and fixed expenses plus debt service.

BRIDGE FINANCING

(*See* **Gap Financing**)

BROKER

A middleman acting as an intermediary for someone else and who, for a fee or commission, offers to perform certain functions such as those normally undertaken by a real estate broker or a mortgage broker. The legal relationship established between the broker and the customer is a *principal-agent relationship*. However, in the case of a real estate broker as an agent, custom, case law, and licensing legislation have altered traditional agency law principles by the creation of the real estate brokerage agency relationship. Ordinarily, a broker represents a property owner who desires to sell, lease, or exchange real estate, or the broker represents a prospective purchaser who wishes to find a property to purchase. When the broker provides the professional services contracted for, the commission is earned. (*See* **Agent, Brokerage, Brokerage Commission**)

BROKERAGE

The occupation or business of a broker. Specifically, real estate brokerage involves listing, selling, purchasing, exchanging, leasing, renting, or collecting rent for the use of real estate or attempting or offering to perform any of these functions. Thus, unless you are specifically exempt under the real estate licensing law in your jurisdiction, performing or attempting to perform any of these functions either for yourself or for others may result in your being defined as a real estate broker.

BROKERAGE COMMISSION

The compensation received by a broker for rendering the services he or she agreed to perform under the employment (listing) agreement. Commissions are set by custom, not by law, and any attempt by a group of brokers to fix brokerage rates is a violation of anti-trust laws. Unless there is an agreement to the contrary, a broker is usually entitled to a commission when a buyer is found *ready, willing, and able* to purchase the listed property on the terms specified by the seller. The right to the commission is not defeated by some subsequent events such as the inability of the seller to convey good title or an agreement between the seller and the buyer to cancel the sale. A prerequisite to compensation, however, is a proper license recognized by the state in which the transaction or property is situated. In the ordinary situation where the broker represents an owner seeking to sell a property, the broker is entitled to a commission if it can be proven that the broker is licensed, employed, and the efficient and procuring cause of the sale.

Generally, the license must be valid at the time the broker provides that particular service which entitled him or her to compensation. A lack of a license is fatal to the ability to recover the commission. In many states if the broker was not licensed at the time the listing was obtained, no recovery for commission would be permitted. A broker, therefore, would not be entitled to a commission if his license or the license of the broker's sales employee, who was the broker's instrument in a transaction, has lapsed. Even if a license is obtained before closing, this would generally not be enough to cure the defect. Further, most state license laws make it illegal for a broker to share a commission with a nonlicensed person or to pay a finder's fee to a nonlicensed person. Some states even make it illegal to pay a fee or split a commission with a nonresident broker licensed in another state.

BROKER'S BOND

A bond issued to guarantee the repayment of money improperly acquired by a broker.

BRUNDAGE CLAUSE

A clause that requires the mortgagor (borrower) to pay all taxes on a property. (*See* **Mortgage**)

BUBBLE CONCEPT

A process used by the *Environmental Protection Agency (EPA)* in which it examines all air pollutants, and will allow a new polluting industry to build only if it does not have a negative net effect on the air quality after offsets from other industries.

BUDGET MORTGAGE

A type of loan in which the payments cover more than principal and interest. Besides paying interest and principal each period, a borrower can also be required to pay a certain percentage of annual property taxes and property insurance. For a residential mortgage this means one-twelfth of the property tax and property insurance each month. The advantage to the borrower is that a budget mortgage allows the spreading out of these annual expenses into twelve equal payments. For the lender, who normally places these funds into an escrow or reserve account, the advantage is the assurance that these expenses will be paid when due.

BUFFER ZONE

A strip of land used to separate two adjoining parcels of land which have incompatible uses, such as a residential subdivision and an industrial park. The purpose of the buffer zone is to provide for the "blending" of the two incompatible uses with each other. The buffer can be created by both distance and barriers, such as fences or planting of bushes, and is intended to protect an adjoining property from noise, light and unsightliness of a particular land use or activity. When the buffer zone consists of undeveloped land, the area is referred to as *greenbelts*. (*See* **Zoning**)

BUILD TO SUIT

An agreement between a contractor and a tenant under which the contractor agrees to build the structure to meet the specific needs of the tenant. In return, the tenant agrees to lease the space for a certain period of time and for a certain rent.

BUILDER'S METHOD

A method of cost estimation in which the appraiser groups the cost of a building into major functional parts such as the foundation, walls, heating, etc. (*See* **Cost Approach**)

BUILDER'S RISK INSURANCE

Insurance which can be carried by the builder of a real estate project while the project is under construction. As the project undergoes increased stages of completion, the amount of insurance coverage increases, thus protecting the increased value of the project.

BUILDER/SPONSOR PROFIT AND RISK ALLOWANCE (BSPRA)

A fee that may be collected by developers of government-assisted low-income housing.

BUILDING AND LOAN ASSOCIATION

An organization incorporated for the purpose of accumulating a fund through the savings of its members and then lending those funds to its members for the purpose of building or purchasing a home. These associations are state chartered and are neither commercial banks nor, strictly speaking, savings and loan associations, although in some states they are viewed as a special type of savings and loan association. (*See* **Savings and Loan Association**)

BUILDING CAPITALIZATION RATE

A rate used in the residual appraisal technique to capitalize the income attributable to the improvements. The rate includes both a return "on" and a return "of" capital invested in the improvements. (*See* **Capitalization Rate**)

BUILDING CODES

Ordinances and regulations enacted by local governments which specify minimum standards for construction, maintenance, occupancy, and use of both new and used buildings. The legal right of local governments to enact building codes is granted under police power regulations for the purpose of promoting and maintaining the health, safety, welfare, and morality of the public. Violation of building codes by an owner can result in legal action to force the owner to meet the minimum building codes if he or she wishes to continue using the property. Most jurisdictions have more than one type of building code; for example, fire codes, electrical codes, plumbing codes, and others. It is important to be aware of the particular codes which exist in each locality since there is little uniformity throughout the United States. In addition to meeting local and state building codes, FHA financed properties must meet minimum standards established by the *Federal Housing Administration*. (*See* **Police Power, Zoning**)

BUILDING COST CALCULATOR AND VALUATION GUIDE

A national cost estimation service published by McGraw-Hill Information Systems Company at 1221 Avenue of the Americas, New York, New York 20011.

BUILDING EFFICIENCY RATIO

The ratio of the amount of the net rentable space to the gross building area. A higher ratio implies a more efficient use of the area.

BUILDING LIEN

A builder's claim or charge on a property for unpaid work performed. *(See* **Mechanic's Lien**)

BUILDING LINE

A line established by municipal authority on city streets beyond which the construction of buildings is prohibited. The line may also be used in placement of the fronts of all buildings on that street so as to provide a certain amount of uniformity. Building line is also referred to as the *setback requirement*.

BUILDING OFFICIALS AND CODE ADMINISTRATION INTERNATIONAL, INC. (BOCA)

BOCA is an organization that provides assistance to building code administrators in administering various building regulations. Membership consist primarily of persons involved in the administration and enforcement of building codes. The address is 1313 East 60th Street, Chicago, Illinois 60637; (312) 799-2300.

BUILDING ORIENTATION

The actual direction faced by a building.

BUILDING OWNERS AND MANAGERS ASSOCIATION INTERNATIONAL (BOMA)

An organization of owners and managers of commercial buildings. The group publishes periodically the *Office Building Experience Exchange Report*. The association serves as a spokesman for these owners and managers, and the address is 234 South Michigan Avenue, Chicago, Illinois 60604; (312) 236-5237.

BUILDING PERMIT

Written authorization required by local governments before a new building can be constructed, remodeled, or expanded. There is a charge for the issuing of the permit and normally the permit must be displayed on the construction site. A permit will not be issued if the proposed building or renovations violate local zoning ordinances or building codes. *(See* **Certificate of Occupancy, Zoning**)

BUILDING RESIDUAL TECHNIQUE

A method used in appraising income-producing property to estimate the total value of the property when the value of the land is known. To apply this technique the value of the land must be known or estimated prior to estimating the value of the building. In addition, the total income of the property must also be known. By subtracting the income attributable to the land from the total income generated by the property, the remainder or balance represents the income attributable to the building. This amount is then capitalized to arrive at an estimate of the building's value, which when added to the value of the land gives a total estimate of the value of the property.

Consider the following:

Net Operating Income (N.O.I.)	$100,000
Rate of Return on Investment	10%
Land Value	$250,000
Economic Life of Building	20 year
N.O.I.	$100,000
Income Attributable to Land	
($250,000 x .10)	-25,000
Income Attributable to Building	$ 75,000

Return "on" Investment	10%
Return "of" Investment (1/20)	5%
Overall Capitalization Rate	15%

Value = Income/Rate

V = $75,000/.15

V = $500,000

Land Value	$250,000
Building Value	$500,000
Property Value	$750,000

(*See* **Capitalization, Income Approach, Rate of Return**)

BUILDING RESTRICTIONS

Limitations and regulations as to the type and size of structures that can be constructed on one's property. Building restrictions can either be publicly imposed through zoning ordinances or privately imposed through deed restrictions. (*See* **Deed Restriction**)

BUILT-INS

Fixtures that are permanently attached to a building, such as kitchen cabinets or shelves.

BUILT-UP METHOD

A technique used by appraisers and investors for deriving a capitalization rate. The built-up method, or *summation method* as it is also called, is a process by which the appraiser or investor begins with a risk-free safe rate of interest as a foundation, such as the current yield on Treasury Bills, and upon this rate builds or adds the returns necessary to compensate the investor for risk due to the project itself, a premium for the loss of liquidity, and for the burden of managing the project. Since these returns are different for any two properties, using this method of capitalization will mean different capitalization rates for different projects.

The built-up method for deriving a capitalization rate for a particular property would be as follows:

Pure interest for risk-free investment	8.0%
Allowance for risk	4.0%
Allowance for nonliquidity	2.5%
Cost of management	1.0%
Rate derived by build-up method	15.5%

(*See* **Capitalization Rate**)

BULK TRANSFER

A major transfer of a company's inventory, land holdings, or other assets. Bulk transfers are regulated under the *Uniform Commercial Code (UCC)* to help eliminate fraud. In real estate brokerage activities, when a broker receives a listing on property from a corporate officer, a duty arises on the part of the broker to inquire if the officer was in fact authorized to sell the corporation's assets. Often the sale of corporate land or personal property is given in the nature of a bulk transfer which usually requires a resolution by the corporation's board of directors.

BULK ZONING

Regulations established by zoning ordinances intended to limit the intensity of development to prevent the overloading of public services and facilities. Area and bulk restrictions include setback and side-yard requirements, minimum lot sizes, and minimum and maximum floor area ratios (FAR). (*See* **Floor Area Ratio, Setback Requirement**)

BULLET LOAN

A loan of intermediate length with a balloon payment due at the end of the loan period. Such loans often carry substantial *prepayment penalties*, thus, the lender is more likely to receive payment over the entire life of the loan as opposed to early repayment. The term bullet refers to the balloon payment. If at the end of the term it is impossible to refinance the balloon payment due, the borrower's equity will be killed by the "bullet."

BUNDLE OF RIGHTS

A legal concept of real estate which gives the owner of real estate an aggregate of rights, powers, and privileges which are guaranteed and protected by the government. Property rights and interests are analogous to a *bundle of sticks*. Each stick represents a different right or interest. Ordinarily, the bundle includes rights of possession, use, enjoyment, and disposition, and the right to exclude others. Ownership, however, is not unlimited. Some of the sticks in the bundle of rights may have been sold or taken away. Society and the law may have shortened some of the sticks. Today, ownership of land entails both rights and duties. The *law of nuisance* states that a property owner may not use his or her property in such a manner as to interfere with reasonable and ordinary use of an adjoining property owner. Further, a property owner may have voluntarily accepted limitations on the property by agreeing to deed restrictions, accepting restrictions in a mortgage, signing contractual covenants with other property owners, selling easements, or leasing the property. Likewise, a property owner may have had involuntary restrictions or limitations imposed on the property. For example, prescriptive easements could exist on the property, a court could have issued an injunction prohibiting certain uses, a lien may have been placed on the property, or someone could be maintaining an encroachment. Finally, property ownership is subject to various restrictions by the public. These restrictions are: (1) *police power* regulations such as zoning ordinances or building codes, (2) the *power of taxation*, (3) the *power of eminent domain*, and (4) the *power of escheat*.

BUREAU OF LAND MANAGEMENT

The branch of the federal government in charge of surveying and overseeing public lands.

BURGESS, ERNEST W.

An urban economist credited with the development of the *concentric circle theory* of urban growth. Developed in the 1920s, the theory states that if there are no physical or legal barriers cities tend to expand from their centers or central business districts in concentric circles. Each circle or zone has land uses and income levels quite different from those of the other zones.

BURN OFF

A financing term referring to the amortization of the prepaid items on a loan.

BUYDOWN

A means by which a builder pays cash at closing to a lender who, in turn, makes a loan to the purchaser of the builder's property at a below-market interest rate. Quite often the period of the buydown is only one to three years, at which time the interest rate being charged the borrower will increase to whatever current interest rates are at that time.

BUYER'S EXTRAS

Additional features requested by a buyer that were not originally included in the sales contract.

BUYER'S MARKET

An economic situation in which supply is greater than demand. The result is greater opportunities for buyers to find properties on more favorable terms and conditions. For example, if there are numerous houses for sale in a town and few potential buyers, sellers might be forced to lower their asking price and might agree to assist in financing the sale with some type of owner financing. (*See* **Purchase Money Mortgage**)

BUYING POWER INDEX (BPI)

A ratio used to measure potential demand for retail uses or for a specific product line or service. The BPI is an average of local income, retail sales, and population relative to the United States as a whole.

BUY-SELL AGREEMENT

In finance, an agreement that an interim lender will assign a mortgage to a permanent lender when a building has been completed. When the loan also involves the owner, it is often referred to as a *tripartite agreement*.

BYLAWS

Legal documentation providing for the administration and management of a condominium. Bylaws provide for the establishment of the homeowner's association, enumerate the powers and authority given to the board of directors, and indicate various rights and responsibilities of the unit owners. Provisions are ordinarily included which define the use and maintenance of the common areas, establish the operating budget, give notice to the lenders of unpaid assessments, provide for property management, fire and hazard insurance, and general liability insurance. The board of directors may also be empowered to pass rules and regulations which regulate the use of common areas by unit owners and guests. Detailed provisions for meetings by the homeowner's association, election of officers, and amendments to the declaration are also included. Ordinarily, the bylaws may be amended by a simple majority of all the owners, although provisions may be made more stringent for important matters. Provisions are also included for the enforcement of liens and other matters necessary to assure that maintenance fees and special assessments will be paid. (*See* **Condominium**)

CAE

A professional designation which denotes *Certified Assessment Evaluator*, awarded by the International Association of Assessing Officers.

CALLABLE LOAN

A loan containing a clause which allows the lender to accelerate the due date at some point prior to the end of the original term. While uncommon in the majority of real estate loans, such a provision is sometimes included if the lender is uncertain as to the expected value of the property at some point in the future.

CANADIAN ROLL-OVER MORTGAGE

A type of mortgage used in Canada in recent years in which the maturity of the loan is fixed (for example, thirty years), but the interest rate is renegotiated periodically (for example, every three or five years). Recently this type mortgage has been used in the United States and is normally referred to as a *renegotiable rate mortgage*. (*See* **Renegotiable Rate Mortgage**)

CANCELLATION CLAUSE

A provision often added to contracts, such as a lease, granting one or more of the parties to the contract the right to terminate or cancel their duties and obligations upon the occurrence of some event. Normally, a cancellation clause includes some type of payment as consideration to the party whose rights are being cancelled.

CANON OF ETHICS
(*See* **Code of Ethics**)

CAP

A maximum on how much an interest rate or periodic mortgage payment on an adjustable rate mortgage can legally be changed. The cap is stated in the mortgage instrument and thus assures the borrower that the maximum rate charged or the maximum amount due each period cannot rise above a certain specified level.

CAPABLE

Qualified or fit to undertake something. As used in real estate finance, the term is used by lenders in reference to the three "C's" of credit: *capacity, capable,* and *competent.*

CAPACITY

The recognition through law that a person has the ability to incur legal liability or acquire legal rights. Parties to a contract must have *legal capacity* in order for the contract to be binding on them.

Some of the following classes of people are in some fashion protected or limited by the law:

Infants (minors): Infants are those persons who are below a state's statutorily prescribed age. In many states this age is twenty-one, whereas in others it is as low as eighteen. Most contracts entered into by an infant (or minor) are *voidable* at the infant's option. An infant may elect to *disaffirm* a contract any time before achieving majority. If the infant elects to disaffirm a contract, it must be done completely, and no attempt may be made to retain part of the benefits. In many states transactions involving the sale of real estate may only be disaffirmed during a reasonable time after achieving majority. The right of the infant to disaffirm is not defeated in most states if the infant lies about his or her age, even though a separate tort suit for fraud and deceit might be brought by the injured party. An infant may choose to *ratify* a contract after achieving majority. In addition, an infant is bound to pay the reasonable value for necessities. Necessities include food, shelter, and clothing which are appropriate for a person in the infant's station of life.

Insane Persons: If a person is insane but has not been so adjudicated, any contract that person enters into is voidable just as if he or she were an infant. The person is still liable for the reasonable value of necessities provided. A person who has been judged insane and is under guardianship enters into *void* contracts; only the guardian can act.

Intoxicated Persons: Generally, most states do not give relief for contracts entered into by a person under intoxication unless it can be shown that the person was incapable of understanding the effects of actions in entering into a contract. The exception is the rare situation where the person is so intoxicated that he or she has no understanding of the situation he or she is in. This rule also applies to people under the influence of various drugs and narcotics. Exception to this rule takes place if it can be shown that the other contracting party induced the state of intoxication for the purpose of taking unfair advantage. Where this can be shown, the drunken or drugged person may treat the contract as voidable.

Persons Under the Protection of the Courts: Spendthrifts and people in a state of senility may be placed under the protection of the court. Contracts made by such people are *void*.

Corporations: The power of a corporation to enter into certain transactions is defined by the corporation's charter and by the laws of the state where the entity was incorporated. Contracts entered into by the corporation which exceed its authority will not be enforced. Care should be taken that the agent which is dealing for the corporation is properly authorized to act. In the sale and purchase of real estate, it is ordinarily advisable to require a corporate resolution by the board of directors. The rules applying to corporations also apply to trusts and other artificial legal entities.

Unincorporated Associations: Unincorporated associations have no legal existence and thus cannot enter into contracts. Certain exceptions apply to fraternal organizations and to a few other groups.

Married Women and Men Jointly Owning Property: Under common law married women were merged into the legal person of the husband and could not independently enter into contracts. This disability has been changed, to some extent, in every state. Society has, however, imposed certain restrictions on contracts involving the sale of real estate as a result of the status of marriage. In many states both the husband and wife must sign a sales contract or a deed conveying an interest in land, or the conveyance may be subject to a cloud from unextinguished marital rights such as dower, curtesy, and other interests.

Trustees and Other Fiduciaries: Each state has its own guidelines on the limitations of trustees and other fiduciaries in entering into contracts on behalf of a trust. When the trustor establishes the trust, he or she may place limitations on what the trustee may do, for example, a restriction on the type of investments in which a trust's money may be invested. It is important to inquire as to the authority of the trustee or administrator of an estate or other party in a fiduciary capacity.

The term capacity is also used by lenders in reference to the three "C's" of credit: *capacity, capable, competent*. In this regard capacity refers to the ability of the borrower to accomplish what he or she has set out to do. For example, the willingness of a bank to make a construction loan to a developer is partly dependent upon the developer's "track record." How successful was the developer's last project? Was it completed? Was it profitable?

CAPITAL

An economic term referring to money, machinery, equipment, and buildings which, as one of the economic factors of production, are used to produce goods and services. Capital goods, such as buildings and equipment, are used to produce other goods as contrasted to consumer goods which are used to satisfy the consumption needs of a society. All income-producing real estate, such as commercial or industrial buildings, are capital or capital goods.

The terms capital also has an accounting meaning which refers to the amount of equity the owner(s) has in a business.

CAPITAL ASSET

In taxation, property other than inventory, receivables, or depreciable property used in a trade or business, and certain other assets. In general, assets of a more or less permanent nature.

CAPITAL EXPENDITURE

In accounting, an amount paid to acquire something of lasting value in contrast to something that will be consumed in the current year. Capital expenditures to real estate are normally made for the purpose of extending the useful life of the property as well as for increasing the property's value. Examples would include additions and remodeling.

CAPITAL GAIN

A capital gain or loss is the difference between the net sales price and the adjusted basis of a capital asset. The *net sales price* is cash, plus market value of other property received, plus the value of any liabilities such as a mortgage which will be paid off by the purchaser, minus transaction costs such as the broker's commission and various closing costs paid by the seller. *Adjusted basis* is the original tax basis at which the property was acquired, ordinarily the purchase price, plus any capital additions, cost of major improvements, minus any depreciation taken. Capital gains and losses may be classified as long-term and short-term. A long-term gain or loss results from the disposition of any capital asset which has been held at least one year. Previously, the holding period was six months, but as of 1978 it is one year. Under the *Tax Reform Act of 1986*, short-term capital gains are taxed at ordinary income rates. Long-term gains are taxed at a maximum rate of 28% even if the taxpayer is in a higher tax bracket.

CAPITAL IMPROVEMENT

Any permanent improvement made to real estate for the purpose of increasing the useful life of the property or increasing the property's value. For example, the addition of a garage to a house is considered to be a capital improvement whereas repairing of a door is not.

CAPITALIZATION

A mathematical process used in estimating the value of income-producing property by applying a certain capitalization rate to the net operating income of the property.   (*See* **Appraisal, Capitalization Rate, Capitalized Value, Income Approach**)

CAPITALIZATION RATE (CAP RATE)

The rate at which future income is converted into present value. In estimating the value of income-producing property, such as an office building or an apartment complex, value is defined as the present worth of future rights to income. This income, known as *net operating income* or *N.O.I.*, is what an investor could reasonably expect to receive after allowance for vacancies and operating expenses. Once this income has been projected, the investor must next determine a rate of capitalization to be used to convert the future income into a present value.

The capitalization formula is expressed as: $V = I/R$

$$
\begin{aligned}
\text{where } V &= \text{Value} \\
I &= \text{Net Operating Income} \\
R &= \text{Capitalization Rate}
\end{aligned}
$$

This formula converts future income into a single present value sum. Consider an apartment complex with a N.O.I. estimated to be $240,000 per year for some years to come. If an appropriate capitalization rate is believed to be 12%, what is the value of the project?

$$V = I/R \qquad V = \$240,000/.12 \qquad V = \$200,000$$

CAPITALIZATION RECAPTURE

The recovery of dollars invested in a parcel of real estate that is expected to decrease in value over the life of the investment. Thus, a return "of" the investment has to take place through the income generated by the real estate. (*See* **Capital Recovery**)

CAPITALIZE

To convert a future income stream to a present lump-sum value.

CAPITALIZED-INCOME APPROACH

Another name for the income approach to value. (*See* **Capitalized Value, Income Approach**)

CAPITALIZED VALUE

The estimated value of income-producing property derived by dividing the annual net operating income by a capitalization rate. The basic capitalization formula, $V = I/R$, means that the capitalized value of a piece of property is a function of the estimated net operating income and the particular capitalization rate.

Consider an office building with a net operating income of $500,000 and a capitalization rate of 10%. The capitalized value would be $500,000/.10 or $5,000,000.

What happens to the value if the net income increases to $550,000?

$$V = I/R \qquad V = \$550,000/.10 \qquad V = \$5,500,000$$

The capitalized value would increase to $5,550,000.

What would happen if the net income remained the same but the capitalization rate was increased to 15%?

$$V = I/R \qquad V = \$500,000/.15 \qquad V = \$333,333.33$$

In this case the capitalized value decreased to $333,333.33. Thus, capitalized value can increase as a result of either an increase in net income or a decrease in the capitalization rate. Likewise, a decrease in net income or an increase in the capitalization rate will result in a lower capitalized value. (*See* **Capitalization, Capitalization Rate**)

CAPITAL LOSS
(*See* **Capital Gain**)

CAPITAL RECOVERY
The recapture of dollars invested in real estate that is expected to lose part or all of its value during the time the property is owned. A capitalization rate must account for a return "on" the investment and a return "of" the investment. Return "on" investment is the interest that must be paid to an investor for the use of his or her money. Return "of" investment is the recovery of the capital invested. When the original amount used to purchase a piece of real estate is returned at the end of the holding period, no capital recovery is needed in the capitalization rate. If, however, the property is expected to decline in value over time, a portion of each year's income must be used to compensate for the expected decline.

Consider an investment in a warehouse currently worth $500,000 (land $100,000 and building $400,000). Assume that at the end of forty years, the improvement will be worthless. If this is the case, the value of the improvement, $400,000, must be recovered (recaptured) out of the net operating income. This can be done by increasing the capitalization rate by an amount necessary to recover the appropriate percentage that the asset is expected to decline over each year. If the economic life of the improvement is forty years, then, on a straight line basis, 2 1/2% of the value would have to be recovered each year. To determine how this would affect the capitalization rate, it is necessary to split the rate between the land and the improvements. If the land represents 20% of the total value, and the basic capitalization rate is 12%, the rate adjusted for capital recovery would be derived as shown on the next page:

CAPITALIZATION RATE ADJUSTED FOR CAPITAL RECOVERY

Part of Asset	Basic Rate	Adjustment	Weight	Weighted Average
Land	.12	+ none (assume no change in value)	x .20 =	.024
Improvements	.12	+ .025 (100% divided by 40 years)	x .80 =	.116
				.140

The total capitalization rate to provide for capital recovery would therefore be 14%. *(See* **Capitalization Rate, Depreciation**)

CAPITAL RECOVERY PERIOD
The period over which a property is expected to produce income to the particular investor and over which any loss in the capital invested must be recaptured through the net operating income stream.

CAP RATE
An abbreviation for *capitalization rate. (See* **Capitalization Rate**)

CAPRICIOUS VALUE
The apparent value placed on an item by someone as a result of an emotional or whimsical decision. For example, a person may pay what appears to be an extraordinarily high price for a home based on the fact that the person "likes it." Such a price paid is not necessarily what would be estimated as *market value* or *most probable sales price*.

CARRYING CHARGES
As used in real estate finance, the cost of owning nonincome-producing land or land currently under development or construction.

CARRYOVER CLAUSE
A provision often found in an *exclusive right-to-sell* listing agreement which provides that the broker will be entitled to receive a commission for a specified period after the expiration date of the listing if the property is sold to any prospect whom the broker showed the property to during the listing period. A broker could spend considerable time and money in trying to sell a piece of property during the listing period. Unless the broker delivers a ready, willing and able buyer during this period of time, no commission has been earned and thus, the seller owes the

broker nothing. However, it is quite possible that someone to whom the broker showed the property may decide to make an offer, after the listing has expired. By including a carryover clause, the broker is legally protected against an offer being accepted from someone initially shown the property by the broker. Common wording of such a clause would be as follows: "If the property is sold or exchanged by Owner, or by Broker or by any other person to any Purchaser to whom the property was shown by Broker or any representative of Broker within sixty (60) days after the expiration of the period of time mentioned above (a period of time such as 90 days covering the listing period would have also been included in the listing contract), Owner agrees to pay to the Broker a cash fee which shall be the same percentage of the purchase price as the percentage mentioned above" (a commission rate or sum would also have been included in the listing contract).

Prior to the expiration of the listing period, the broker should provide the seller with the names of everyone who was shown the property during the listing period so that there would be no doubt as to whether or not a particular person was shown the property by the broker. This clause is also known as an *extender clause*.

CASH

Money in U. S. legal tender, or its equivalent, payable on demand. Cash is a purely liquid asset. The liquidity of other assets, such as real estate, depends on how easily these can be converted into cash.

CASH EQUIVALENT

The price of a property reduced to a present value cash sum that takes into account the value of financial terms and any noncash items or services included as part of the consideration.

CASH FLOW

The sum of money generated from income-producing property after all operating expenses and mortgage payments, including principal and interest, have been made. Cash flow can be calculated on either a before-tax (pretax) or after-tax basis and normally investors refer to either *before-tax cash flow* or *after-tax cash flow*. Some investors refer to before-tax cash flow as *cash throw-off*.

Consider the following: Each unit in a 90-unit apartment complex rents for $350 per month. A vacancy allowance of 8% is considered normal and operating expenses are calculated to be 45% of effective gross income. Annual debt service is $95,000, of which $70,000 this year is interest and $25,000 is principal. An investor in the 28% tax bracket who owns the property is depreciating the building, valued at $875,000, over 25 years using a straight-line method of depreciation.

Cash flow on both a pretax and after-tax basis would be calculated as illustrated on the following page:

PRETAX CASH FLOW

Potential Income	$378,000
(350 x 90 x 12)	
- Vacancy Allowance	- 30,240
Effective Gross Income	$347,760
- Operating Expenses	-156,492
Net Operating Income	191,268
- Debt Service	- 95,000
Pretax Cash Flow	$ 96,268

AFTER-TAX CASH FLOW

Net Operating Income	$191,268
- Interest	- 70,000
Subtotal	121,268
- Depreciation	
($875,000 x .04)	- 35,000
Taxable Income	86,268
x Tax (28%)	x .28
Tax Liability	24,155
Pretax Cash Flow	$ 96,268
- Tax Liability	- 24,155
After-Tax Cash Flow	$ 72,113

In this example the after-tax cash flow was significantly less than the pretax or before-tax cash flow. The difference was due to the tax liability, which in turn is a function of the amount of interest paid, the depreciation taken and the tax bracket of the investor(s). Changes in any or all of these will have significant effects on the after-tax cash flow of a particular investment. (*See* **Tax Shelter**)

CASH-ON-CASH

The before-tax cash flow divided by the equity invested.

CASH THROW-OFF

A term used by some investors referring to pretax cash flow as distinguished from after-tax cash flow. (*See* **Cash Flow**)

CAVEAT EMPTOR

A Latin phrase meaning "let the buyer beware." Under common law a purchaser is responsible for physically inspecting the property and judging whether or not the property is sound since the purchaser takes the property "as is." The doctrine does not apply in situations of concealment of hidden defects. It should also be noted that in recent years courts have moved away from the doctrine of "let the buyer beware" as more states adopt consumer-oriented policies.   More and more of the burden to disclose information in regard to the property has been placed on the seller, particularly in the sale of new homes and condominiums. Also, the *Interstate Land Sales Full Disclosure Act* includes provisions for the disclosure of pertinent information by the seller of land falling under the act. (*See* **Implied Warranties, Interstate Land Sales Full Disclosure Act**)

CBD

(*See* **Central Business District**)

CD

(*See* **Certificate of Deposit**)

CED

Certified Economic Developer. A professional designation awarded by the American Economic Development Council to persons who have met minimum education, experience, and demonstrated requirements in the area of economic development. (*See* **American Economic Development Council**)

CENTRAL BUSINESS DISTRICT (CBD)

The downtown area of a city which contains the business, governmental and service activities of the city. The actual size of the CBD can be quite large depending upon the density of the area.

CERTIFICATE OF DEPOSIT (CD)

A receipt for money deposited in a lending institution in either one of two classifications, time or demand. Common reference is made to a "CD." Time certificates are payable at some specified date or maturity, such as six months, while demand certificates are payable on demand. In recent years lending institutions have relied more and more on CDs as a means of attracting funds. Interest rates payable on certificates have been significantly higher than the interest rate payable on passbook accounts and thus, the lender is more able to pay the going rate of interest. In addition, CDs are now sold in denominations small enough to attract savers who otherwise would have few alternative investment opportunities.

CERTIFICATE OF ELIGIBILITY

A certificate issued by the *Veterans Administration (VA)* to a veteran stating that he or she has qualified for a VA loan. (*See* **Veterans Administration (VA) Mortgage**)

CERTIFICATE OF ESTOPPEL

A legal instrument signed by the mortgagor (borrower) stating the unpaid balance of a mortgage, the interest rate being charged and the exact time up to which interest has been paid. Once he or she has executed this certificate, the borrower cannot claim that he or she does not owe the money or that the outstanding balance is incorrect. An estoppel certificate clause, or *certificate of no defense* clause as it is known in some states, is included in a mortgage to facilitate the selling of the mortgage by the lender to another investor. If the lender wishes to sell the mortgage it is necessary to determine what amount still remains on the principal. By requiring the borrower to issue this certificate, the lender prevents the borrower from disputing the amount of the outstanding balance.

CERTIFICATE OF NO DEFENSE

(*See* **Certificate of Estoppel**)

CERTIFICATE OF OCCUPANCY (CO)

A certificate issued by a local government indicating that the property passes a final inspection and is thus ready for occupancy. Most local governments have building inspectors who periodically inspect buildings while they are being constructed to ensure that the minimum standards of the building code are being met. (*See* **Building Codes, Zoning**)

CERTIFICATE OF REASONABLE VALUE (CRV)

A certificate issued by the *Veterans Administration (VA)* which states an estimate of the value of the property. Prior to final approval of a VA loan, the subject property must be appraised by a VA-approved appraiser and a CRV must be issued. The CRV is then used to set the ceiling on the amount of the loan the VA will guarantee. (*See* **Veterans Administration (VA) Mortgage**)

CERTIFICATE OF TITLE

A written statement issued by a title attorney or title examiner stating his or her opinion of the quality of the title to a particular parcel of real estate. The certificate will point out any defects which are revealed by an examination of the public records and is not a guarantee that the title has no defects but only that an examination of the records reveals no defects as of a given date. There are a number of defects that may exist which cannot be discovered by an examination of the record. Examples include delivery of a deed after the death of a grantor or grantee; deeds issued by persons who are legally incapacitated by virtue of insanity, minority, or other reasons; and deeds issued without release of dower, curtesy, or other marital rights. In addition, the record may contain forged deeds, satisfaction pieces, and others. The purpose for acknowledgment is to screen out such defective instruments, but this is not always successful. There may be errors in the indexing of instruments or other mistakes in the recordation process. When a person dies, there may be an invalid will or missing heirs. Other technical problems might include a deed given under an invalid power of attorney or failure of a co-owner to join in the conveyance. These types of title defects may be covered by a title insurance policy, not a certificate of title.

The person preparing the certificate of title is liable only for negligence in preparing the certificate. Liability is normally limited to his or her personal assets or to the assets of the company who employs the title examiner. In some states the certificate of title is provided by the seller as of the day of closing. The seller pays for the cost of the certificate and if the purchaser wishes to have the added protection of title insurance, the difference in cost between the certificate of title and title insurance must be borne by the purchaser. (*See* **Abstract of Title, Title Insurance**)

CERTIFIED CHECK

A check certifying that the signature of the person signing the check is genuine and that there are sufficient funds on deposit to cover the amount of the check. When a bank "certifies" a check, the dollar amount certified is set aside by the bank to pay the check when it reaches the bank and payment cannot be refused due to insufficient funds. A certified check for the amount owed by the purchaser at time of closing is often required by the closing attorney or escrow agent. This is especially true when the purchaser has a checking account with an out-of-town bank. In some instances a seller may require a certified check for the earnest money deposit prior to accepting an offer.

CERTIFIED PROPERTY MANAGER (CPM)

A professional designation awarded to qualified property managers who have demonstrated their professional competence through special course work and demonstration reports. The designation is given by the Institute of Real Estate Management (IREM), affiliated with the National Association of Realtors (NAR).

CERTIFY

To attest or guarantee in writing as being true; for example, a certified check.

CESSION DEED

A type of deed used to transfer a portion of an individual's property to a local government such as for streets or sidewalks. (*See* **Dedication**)

CHAIN

A unit of measurement used by land surveyors consisting of a series of wire links 7.92 inches long. The total length of a chain is 66 feet and ten square chains equal one acre.

CHAIN OF TITLE

The recorded history of matters such as conveyances, liens and encumbrances affecting title to a parcel of real estate. In order to determine whether title contains any defects or encumbrances which would mar its marketability, it is necessary to trace the chain of title in the public records. The chain of title is merely a successive series of title transfers from grantors to grantees. Since as a general rule a person can acquire no better title than that held by the previous grantor, it is necessary to trace the chain back to the origins of title in some government patent. Because this is time consuming, many states have passed laws which establish a statutory presumption that if the chain is unbroken for some period of time, such as fifty years, the title is presumed to be valid. For an instrument to have the legal effect of constructive notice, it must be within the chain of title. For example, John Brown on March 1 grants Yellow Valley by deed to Larry Johnson who promptly records on the same day. On March 15 John Brown grants the same property to Mary Smith, who also records. Mary Smith's recordation would have no legal effect. The recordation is not in the chain of title since John Brown had earlier passed title to Larry Johnson. What happens when there is a mistake in the recording of an instrument by the clerk? In most states the document is binding just as if it had been properly recorded. This is an exception to the rule that an instrument not in the chain of title is not binding. However, in some states it is the obligation of the party seeking the recording to make sure that the instrument is properly recorded. (*See* **Grantor-Grantee Index, Recordation, Title Search**)

CHAIN STORE

Any one of several retail stores owned, managed, and controlled by the same parent company. Each of the stores sells the same type of merchandise, often has similar store layouts, and uses the same marketing logo in advertising the store's name. A chain store is often sought as an anchor tenant in a shopping center. (*See* **Anchor Tenant**)

CHANGE, PRINCIPLE OF

A basic value principle which holds that the world is constantly changing and these changes affect land use which in turn changes the value of land. Most real estate passes through certain life states: (1) a period of *growth*, (2) a period of *stability*, (3) a period of *decline* and, in many cases, (4) a period of *renewal* or *restoration*. If a parcel of land goes through the fourth stage, the cycle can repeat itself.

CHATTEL

An item of movable personal property as distinguished from an immovable or real property. (*See* **Chattel Real, Fixture, Personal Property, Real Property**)

CHATTEL MORTGAGE

A type of mortgage in which personal property is pledged as security for a debt. Under *Article 9* of the *Uniform Commercial Code* chattel mortgages have been replaced by other types of security agreements. (*See* **Mortgage**)

CHATTEL REAL

A movable object which has become permanently attached or annexed to real property. Such an object, once attached, is normally referred to as a *fixture*. Chattel real also refers to any interest in land which is less than a freehold estate, for example, a lease. When a lessor (landlord) conveys property by a lease, he or she is said to do so by *demise*. The leasehold estate conveyed is ordinarily considered to be personal property even though it involves a real property interest. Some states distinguish between leaseholds which are chattel real and those which are real property on the basis of the length of the lease term. A lease which exceeds a statutory minimum period of time creates a real property interest. (*See* **Chattel, Demise, Fixture, Leasehold, Personal Property, Real Property**)

CHECK

The name given in the *government survey method* of land description to the 24 by 24 mile areas formed by the intersection of guide meridians and correction lines. Each check is divided into 6 by 6 mile areas known as *townships* which are further divided into *sections*. Checks are only approximately 24 miles square (576 square miles) since, due to the curvature of the earth's surface, meridian lines move closer together as they approach the North and South Poles. (*See* **Government Survey Method, Section, Township**)

CHRONOLOGICAL AGE

The actual age of an item as measured by a standard calendar. Also known as *actual age*.

CID

Certified Industrial Developer. A professional designation awarded by the American Economic Development Council to individuals who have met minimum education, experience, and demonstrated requirements in the area of industrial development. (*See* **American Economic Development Council**)

CIRCUIT BREAKER

Property tax legislation intended to relieve part of the financial burden of increases in property taxes on certain classes of people. Under a circuit-breaker approach a property owner is limited in the amount he or she must pay in property tax. The owner's income normally determines the exact amount of property tax and the difference between what is owed and what would be due without the circuit breaker is normally credited to the individual's state income tax. In addition to an individual's income level, some states also allow a tax credit on the basis of age or disability to homeowners who meet certain qualifying conditions. In a few states credit for property taxes under a circuit breaker also includes renters of dwelling units as well as owners. (*See* **Property Tax**)

CITY

A political entity established for the purpose of carrying out local government functions. A city government is normally headed by a mayor and governed by a city council. The term also refers to the geographic territory within the corporate limits.

CITY PLANNING

Effort on the part of a city to coordinate, direct and control the type of development taking place so as to ensure maximum benefits to the citizens of the city.

CIVIL RIGHTS ACT

Federal statutes enacted after the Civil War and more recently in the 1950s and 1960s to give further assurance to basic rights guaranteed by the Constitution of the United States. (*See* **Civil Rights Act of 1866, Civil Rights Act of 1968, Federal Fair Housing Act of 1968**)

CIVIL RIGHTS ACT OF 1866

A federal law which prohibits all racial discrimination in the sale or rental of real estate, whether public or private. This law, passed after the Civil War, provides that "all citizens of the United States shall have the same right, in every State and Territory, as is enjoyed by white citizens thereof to inherit, purchase, lease, sell, hold, and convey real or personal property."

In 1968, this law was revived and given substance by the U. S. Supreme Court in the case of *Jones v. Alfred H. Mayer Co.,* 392 U. S. 409 (1968). In this case the court prohibited any racially motivated refusal to sell or rent property. The case involved a refusal of a builder to sell a house to a black person in 1965. Three years later the builder was ordered to sell a house to the injured party at 1965 prices and to absorb the price difference. The 1866 Civil Rights Act may be enforced by bringing a civil suit in the federal district court. Proceedings of the Act give certain advantages to the plaintiff over the *Federal Fair Housing Act of 1968*. The courts are not restricted to $1,000 punitive damages, nor must the suit be brought within 180 days of injury. The time period for bringing a suit would be the appropriate state statute of limitations for tort actions. Under this act all real estate is covered, unlike the Federal Fair Housing Act of 1968 which just covers dwellings. Further, unlike the 1968 act, the 1866 act allows no exceptions. (*See* **Civil Rights Act of 1968, Federal Fair Housing Act of 1968**)

CIVIL RIGHTS ACT OF 1968

A federal law enacted to assure basic constitutional rights to certain protected classes of people. Of particular importance to the real estate industry is *Title VIII* of this act, which is commonly known as the *Federal Fair Housing Act of 1968*. As originally passed, the act prohibited discrimination in the sale or rental of residential dwelling units or vacant land intended to be used as such on the basis of race, color, religion, or national origin. Discrimination on the basis of sex was prohibited by an amendment in the *Housing and Community Development Act of 1974*. The *Fair Housing Amendments Act of 1988* bars discrimination on the basis of a handicap or because there are children in a family. (*See* **Civil Rights Act of 1866, Federal Fair Housing Act of 1968**)

CLEARING TITLE

The process of taking whatever steps or acts are necessary to clear up any title defects in order to establish a marketable title. (*See* **Marketable Title**)

CLEAR TITLE

A good and marketable title. Clear title is one that is free from burdens or limitations, such as an assumable mortgage or an easement, except those which the purchaser is aware of and has agreed to accept. (*See* **Marketable Title**)

CLERK OF COUNTY COURT

The public official, in most jurisdictions, with whom legal instruments such as deeds and mortgages are presented for proper recordation in the public records.

CLOSED-END MORTGAGE

A mortgage which prohibits the mortgagor (borrower) from pledging the mortgaged property as security for additional loans. (*See* **Open-End Mortgage**)

CLOSED MORTGAGE

A mortgage which cannot be prepaid during a specified time or until maturity. The lender uses such a mortgage so that he or she knows there will be a periodic payment of interest and principal for a specified period of time. By using a closed mortgage the lender is better able to accurately predict the repayment of his or her outstanding loans. Also, the use of such a mortgage prevents a borrower from prepaying the mortgage because another lender offers a lower interest rate. (*See* **Open Mortgage, Prepayment Penalty**)

CLOSING

The final meeting between buyer and seller in a real estate transaction at which time certain documents are delivered by each party, papers are signed, the closing statement is reviewed, the parties obtain certain documents, and funds are disbursed. This meeting, also referred to as *settlement*, will normally be attended by seller and buyer, or their representatives; attorneys representing various parties; representatives of the lending institution; and some representative of the real estate broker of record. Normally the sales contract specifies where closing is to occur. Depending on where the buyer and seller reside in the United States, settlement can take place at the lender's office, the closing attorney's office or at the title company. Also stated in the sales contract is the time and date of the settlement. Enough time should be allowed for the necessary requirements of closing such as inspection of the property, title search, drawing of the legal instruments, and appraisal and survey of the property. If the time of closing is not stated in the sales contract, a court will allow a reasonable period of time to complete the necessary requirements. Provision is often made in a sales contract to permit the seller a reasonable period of time to correct any defects reported by the title examiner. If the phrase *time is of the essence* is included in the sales contract, then the closing date must take place as specified in the sales agreement.

In some parts of the country the actual settlement does not involve a buyer, seller, attorneys, and brokers assembling at a meeting; rather, the transaction is closed by an *escrow agent*. This procedure is referred to as closing in escrow, and the person acting for all the parties is a neutral third party. The deed is delivered by the seller to the escrow agent and the money necessary to purchase the property is delivered from the buyer to the escrow agent. The escrow agent will hold all papers until the occurrence or nonoccurrence of some event or act. Normally, once an examination of title is completed and the escrow agent is satisfied that the seller has clear title, the money collected passes to the seller and the deed is delivered to the buyer.

CLOSING COSTS

Expenses in addition to the purchase price of the property which must be paid by the purchaser or deducted from the proceeds of the sale to the seller at time of closing. Since no two closings involve the same exact costs, the expenses incurred by both the seller and the purchaser will vary from sale to sale. In addition, in most jurisdictions certain closing costs are determined either by law, for example, transfer tax, or by custom, for example, the preparation of the deed.

Some of the more common closing costs are discussed below:

Broker's Commission: This is the sales commission due the broker for finding a qualified buyer who was ready, willing, and able to purchase the property. Usually paid by the seller, this fee will normally have been stated in the listing contract and is usually a percentage of the selling price.

Loan Fees: Certain fees will be charged by the lender in connection with the loan.

Loan Origination: This charge covers the administrative costs incurred by the lender and is typically stated as a percentage of the loan. For example, the lender might charge a 1% fee. On a $50,000 loan this charge would be $500. Generally, the buyer (borrower) pays this fee.

Loan Discount or Points: A discount point is one percent of a loan amount and is sometimes paid by someone other than the borrower. The reason discount points are paid is that lenders require minimum interest rates in order to make loans. This interest rate is normally the prevailing market rate. Often state usury laws will set an interest rate ceiling lower than the market rate of interest. A similar ceiling may also exist on VA mortgages. In these situations, the law is designed to prevent a lender from charging more than the ceiling to the borrower. However, without discount points a lender could not make loans because not enough interest could be charged. Thus, to increase the yield, someone will pay the bank discount points to make a loan.

Appraisal Fee: Since the property being purchased is used by the borrower to secure the loan, the lender wants some idea as to the worth or value of the subject property. Thus, either someone on the lender's staff or an independent fee appraiser will be employed to appraise the subject property. The appraisal report supplied to the lender will include supportive information used by the appraiser in reaching an estimate of value. This charge is normally paid by the borrower.

Credit Report Fee: Since the borrower signs a personal note for the loan, the lender is interested in the credit history of the borrower and wants to know how the borrower has handled other credit transactions. This fee is also normally paid by the borrower.

Assumption Fee: If the buyer is assuming an existing mortgage on the property, the lender might charge a certain fee for the processing of the necessary papers.

Items Paid in Advance: At the time of settlement the lender will require certain items to be paid in advance by the borrower.

Interest: Mortgages are normally written so that payment is due on the first day of the month. Since settlement can occur on any date, the lender will require the borrower to prepay interest on the amount borrowed from the date of settlement until the beginning of the mortgage period covered by the first full loan payment. For example, if closing takes place September 22, the first monthly payment will be due November 1, which will cover the interest due for the month of October. In this case the borrower would prepay on the amount borrowed from September 22 until October 1 at the interest rate established at settlement.

Mortgage Insurance Premium: If the loan is conventional and is insured the borrower is normally be required to pay the first premium in advance.

Hazard Insurance Premium: Insurance to cover loss due to fire, flood, wind, and natural hazards, plus additional risks such as personal liability and theft, will be required of the borrower. Normally the lender will require the borrower to show proof at settlement that a prescribed minimum amount of insurance coverage has been purchased. The coverage required is ordinarily for a minimum of one year.

Escrow Accounts: Escrow or reserve accounts are held by the lender to meet future payments incurred in connection with the property. To assure that these payments will indeed be made, the lender establishes escrow accounts at closing by requiring an initial payment and then adding a certain amount of each month's total payment to these accounts.

Property Tax: Local governments levy property taxes, which if unpaid can result in the property being sold at public auction. The lender may require a monthly payment into this account, and when the borrower receives the annual tax bill, payment is made out of this reserve account.

Hazard Insurance: At some point the hazard insurance policy required at closing will expire. In order to have adequate funds to renew the policy, the lender determines how much must be escrowed each month for insurance.

Mortgage Insurance: If the mortgage is insured and future premiums are due, the lender can require funds to be escrowed to cover this charge.

Annual Assessments: Annual assessments are levied by some municipalities for improvements such as sidewalks, roads, and parks. Also, homeowner's association fees are levied against property. The lender could require these charges to be escrowed.

Title Charges: Certain charges are incurred in connection with the examination of title. These expenses cover a wide range of services and vary greatly from jurisdiction to jurisdiction. In some instances all of the fees associated with the title search are included in one charge; in other cases they are itemized.

Title Examination: This charge covers the costs of searching the land records and determining whether the owner has clear title to the property. The abstract of title gives the history of the ownership and any liens or encumbrances that currently exist.

Title Insurance: In many jurisdictions it is customary for the lender to require the borrower to purchase title insurance. This one-time charge covers the mortgagee's interest against loss due to defects in title. For an additional fee, the borrower can also insure his or her own interest against title defects.

Attorney's Fees: A charge is sometimes made for legal services provided in the settlement procedures. This fee would be in connection with services provided the lender but charged to the borrower. Any charges made by an attorney representing the buyer or seller would be an additional expense.

Notary Fee: Various documents must be notarized to authenticate the execution by the parties involved.

Preparation of Documents: A fee may be charged for the preparation of certain documents presented at closing. These documents include deeds, mortgages, liens, and leases.

Government Recording and Transfer Charges: These fees are collected when the property changes hands and are paid when the deed is recorded in the land records. They can be paid by either buyer, seller, or both, depending upon the terms of the sales contract. The recording fees are normally a certain amount per page whereas transfer taxes and document stamps are based on a certain percentage of the sales price.

Survey: The lender or title insurance company may require a survey, conducted by a registered surveyor, to show the boundaries of the property and any encroachments.

Termite Inspection: A common condition of the sales contract is for the seller to pay for an inspection of the house for termites and other pest infestation. A termite certificate is normally required at closing.

Structural Inspection: An inspection of the property for structural soundness may also be a condition of the contract. With older property the lender might require all mechanical equipment to be inspected prior to consummating the loan.

Deed: A deed is prepared prior to closing by the party conducting settlement and is ready for delivery to the buyer. The cost of drawing this instrument can either be a specific charge or part of the attorney's fee. Who is to pay this fee should be stated in the sales contract.

CLOSING DATE

The actual date on which closing or settlement will occur. The time and place of settlement is normally stated in the sales contract, and is usually between 45 and 90 days after the signing of the sales contract. If the phrase *time is of the essence* is included in the sales contract, then the closing date must take place as specified in the sale agreement. (*See* **Closing**)

CLOSING STATEMENT

A written statement setting forth the credits and debits of both purchaser and seller and showing the total amount either due or to be received at closing. Normally the purchaser will "owe" a sum of money at closing while the seller normally "receives" a certain amount at closing. In certain parts of the country this statement is referred to as a *settlement statement*. (*See* **Real Estate Settlement Procedures Act, Uniform Settlement Statement**)

CLOUD ON TITLE

Any claim or encumbrance which, if valid, affects the title or interest that the present owner claims to have in the property. Examples of clouds on title found in title searches would include: (1) a recorded mortgage paid in full but with no satisfaction of mortgage recorded, (2) an heir to a previous owner claiming an interest in the property, (3) property being sold without the wife signing away her dower interest, and (4) an installment sales contract in which the buyer has defaulted but which is still recorded in the land records. A cloud on title is normally removed through an action to quiet title. (*See* **Quiet Title Action**)

CLUSTER DEVELOPMENT

A planning technique in which buildings are erected closer to one another than would normally be done with the remaining land used as open space or as common area for all of the occupants of the buildings. This technique allows the builder/developer to make more efficient use of terrain, trees and other physical components of the land. By allowing the higher density, a more efficient use of the land is realized. (*See* **Planned Unit Development**)

CLUSTER HOUSING

A type of residential construction in which individual housing units are attached in groups surrounded by common open space. (*See* **Planned Unit Development, Zero Lot Line**)

CLUSTER ZONING

A provision in a zoning ordinance which permits a developer to take the density level for an entire area and then disperse that density throughout the area in such a way as to make the most efficient use of the land. For example, rather than building thirty units on a thirty-acre tract, a developer could place all thirty units on eighteen of the acres and use the remaining twelve acres for open space and recreational facilities. (*See* **Planned Unit Development**)

CMB

The designation *Certified Mortgage Banker* awarded by the Mortgage Banker's Association. (*See* **Conventional Mortgage-Backed Securities**)

CMO

(*See* **Collateralized Mortgage Obligation**)

COASTAL ZONE MANAGEMENT ACT

A federal law enacted in 1972 which recognized the public interest in the planning, management, and use of the coastal zones. States are responsible for planning and developing management programs for the land and water in their coastal zones.

CO-BROKER

(*See* **Cooperating Broker**)

CODE OF ETHICS

A written statement of public and professional responsibility as adopted by a professional group. Many real estate professional groups, such as the National Association of Realtors, have adopted a code of ethics which must be adhered to by all of its members. In addition, many real estate commissions have included a code of ethics into their rules and regulations and violation of the code of ethics may result in disciplinary action against a licensee.

Following is the *Code of Ethics* of the *National Association of Realtors* which was approved by the delegate body of the association at its annual convention.

PREAMBLE. . .

Under all is the land. Upon its wise utilization and widely allocated ownership depend the survival and growth of free institutions and of our civilization. The Realtor should recognize that the interests of the nation and its citizens require the highest and best use of the land and the widest distribution of land ownership. They require the creation of adequate housing, the building of functioning cities, the development of productive industries and farms, and the preservation of a healthful environment.

Such interest imposes obligations beyond those of ordinary commerce. They impose grave social responsibility and a patriotic duty to which the Realtor should dedicate himself, and for which he should be diligent in preparing himself. The Realtor therefore, is zealous to maintain and improve the standards of his calling and shares with his fellow-Realtors a common responsibility for its integrity and honor. The term, Realtor, has come to connote competency, fairness, and high integrity resulting from adherence to a lofty ideal of moral conduct in business relations. No inducement of profit and no instruction from clients ever can justify departure from this ideal.

In the interpretation of his obligation, a Realtor can take no safer guide than that which has been handed down through the centuries, embodied in the Golden Rule, "Whatsoever ye would that men should do you, do ye even so to them."

Accepting this standard as his own, every Realtor pledges himself to observe its spirit in all of his activities and to conduct his business in accordance with the tenants set forth below.

Article 1

The Realtor should keep himself informed on matters affecting real estate in his community, the state, and nation so that he may be able to contribute responsibly to public thinking on such matters.

Article 2

In justice to those who place their interests in his care, the Realtor should endeavor always to be informed regarding the laws, proposed legislation, governmental regulations, public policies, and current market conditions in order to be in a position to advise his clients properly.

Article 3

The Realtor should endeavor to eliminate in his community any practices which could be damaging to the public or bring discredit to the real estate profession. The Realtor should assist the governmental agency charged with regulating the practices of brokers and salesmen in his state.

Article 4

To prevent dissension and misunderstanding and to assure better service to the owner, the Realtor should urge the exclusive listing of property unless contrary to the best interest of the owner.

Article 5

In the best interests of society, of his associates, and his own business, the Realtor should willingly share with other Realtors the lessons of his experience and study for the benefit of the public, and should be loyal to the Board of Realtors of his community and active in its work.

Article 6

The Realtor shall seek no unfair advantage over other Realtors and shall conduct his business so as to avoid controversies with other Realtors.

Article 7

In accepting employment as an agent, the Realtor pledges himself to protect and promote the interests of the client. This obligation of absolute fidelity to the client's interest is primary, but it does not relieve the Realtor of the obligation to treat fairly all parties to the transaction.

Article 8

The Realtor shall not accept compensation from more than one party, even if permitted by law, without the full knowledge of all parties to the transaction.

Article 9

The Realtor shall avoid exaggeration, misrepresentation, or concealment of pertinent facts relating to the property or the transaction. The Realtor shall not, however, be obligated to discover latent defects in the property or to advise on matters ouside the scope of his real estate license.

Article 10

The Realtor shall not deny equal professional services to any person for reasons of race, creed, sex, or country of national origin. The Realtor shall not be a party to any plan or agreement to discriminate against a person or persons on the basis of race, creed, sex, or country of national origin.

Article 11

A Realtor is expected to provide a level of competent service in keeping with the Standards of Practice in those fields in which the Realtor customarily engages.

The Realtor shall not undertake to provide specialized professional services concerning a type of property or service that is outside his field of competence unless he engages the assistance of one who is competent on such types of property or service, or unless the facts are fully disclosed to the client. Any person engaged to provide such assistance shall be so identified to the client and his contribution to the assignment should be set forth.

The Realtor shall refer to the Standards of Practice of the National Association as to the degree of competence that a client has a right to expect the Realtor to possess, taking into consideration the complexity of the problem, the availability of expert assistance, and the opportunities for experience available to the Realtor.

Article 12

The Realtor shall not undertake to provide professional services concerning a property or its value where he has a present or contemplated interest unless such interest is specifically disclosed to all affected parties.

Article 13

The Realtor shall not acquire an interest in or buy for himself, any member of his immediate family, his firm or any member thereof, or any entity in which he has a substantial ownership interest, property listed with him, without making the true position known to the listing owner. In selling the property owned by himself, or in which he has any interest, the Realtor shall reveal the facts of his ownership or interest to the purchaser.

Article 14

In the event of a controversy between Realtors associated with different firms, arising out of their relationship as Realtors, the Realtors shall submit the dispute to arbitration in accordance with the regulations of their board or boards rather than litigate the matter.

Article 15

If a Realtor is charged with unethical practice or is asked to present evidence in any disciplinary proceeding or investigation, he shall place all pertinent facts before the proper tribunal of the member board or affiliated institute, society, or council of which he is a member.

Article 16

When acting as agent, the Realtor shall not accept any commission, rebate, or profit on expenditures made for his principal-owner, without the principal's knowledge and consent.

Article 17

The Realtor shall not engage in activities that constitute the unauthorized practice of law and shall recommend that legal counsel be obtained when the interest of any party to the transaction requires it.

Article 18

The Realtor shall keep in a special account in an appropriate financial institution, separated from his own funds, monies coming into his possession in trust for other persons, such as escrows, trust funds, clients' monies, and other like items.

Article 19

The Realtor shall be careful at all times to present a true picture in his advertising and representations to the public. The Realtor shall also ensure that his status as a broker or a Realtor is clearly identifiable in any such advertising.

Article 20

The Realtor, for the protection of all parties, shall see that financial obligations and commitments regarding real estate transactions are in writing, expressing the exact agreement of the parties. A copy of each agreement shall be furnished to each party upon his signing such agreement.

Article 21

The Realtor shall not engage in any practice or take any action inconsistent with the agency of another Realtor.

Article 22

In the sale of property which is exclusively listed with a Realtor, the Realtor shall utilize the services of other brokers upon mutually agreed upon terms when it is in the best interests of the client.

Negotiations concerning property which is listed exclusively shall be carried on with the listing broker, not with the owner, except with the consent of the listing broker.

Article 23
The Realtor shall not publicly disparage the business practice of a competitor nor volunteer an opinion of a competitor's transaction. If his opinion is sought and if the Realtor deems it appropriate to respond, such opinion shall be rendered with strict professional integrity and courtesy.

NOTE: Where the word, Realtor, is used in this Code and Preamble, it shall be deemed to include Realtor-Associate. Pronouns shall be considered to include Realtors and Realtor-Associates of both genders. The Code of Ethics was adopted in 1913 and amended at the Annual Convention in 1924, 1928, 1950, 1951, 1952, 1955, 1956, 1961, 1962, 1974, 1982, 1986 and 1987.

CODICIL
A formal addition or amendment to a will. The addition, which normally does not revoke the original will, must be executed with the same formalities as the original will. (*See* **Will**)

COGNOVIT JUDGMENT
(*See* **Confession of Judgment**)

COGNOVIT NOTE
A note authorizing an attorney to confess judgment against anyone signing the note. It is written authority by a debtor for a judgment to be sought against him or her if the obligation in the note is not paid when due.

COINSURANCE
A provision normally included in insurance policies in which the insured party agrees to maintain a specified percentage, usually 80 percent of the replacement cost of the property. If a policy has a *coinsurance clause*, and the property is insured for less than the minimum required, any loss will be shared by the insured on a *pro rata basis*. Most losses due to fire or some other peril do not result in 100 percent loss. Since the cost of a policy is based on a certain amount per $100 or $1000 of coverage, the owner of a building might decide to insure for only a small amount of the building's total value and gamble that in case of damage there will only be a partial loss. If there is a loss and the policy has a coinsurance clause then the amount recovered from the insurance company is as follows:

$$\frac{\text{Amount of insurance carried}}{\text{Amount of insurance required}} \quad X \quad \text{Amount of loss} = \text{Recovery}$$

Example: The value of a building is $1,000,000 and the insurance policy has an 80% coinsurance clause. The owner has the property insured for $400,000.

There is a loss due to fire of $150,000. How much will the insured collect?

$$\frac{\$400,000}{\$800,000} \qquad X \quad \$150,000 \quad = \quad \$75,000$$

The insured will receive only $75,000 even though the actual loss, $150,000, was less than the $400,000 of insurance carried. (*See* **Insurance**)

COLD CANVASS

A technique used by real estate brokers and salespersons to obtain new listings by contacting potential sellers through telephone or door-to-door solicitation.

COLLATERAL

Property pledged as security for the satisfaction of a loan or debt. The collateral for a real estate loan is usually the mortgaged property itself and if the loan is not repaid as due then the creditor may take legal action to sell the property and use the proceeds of sale to satisfy the debt. (*See* **Default, Deficiency Judgment, Foreclosure, Mortgage**)

COLLATERIZED MORTGAGE OBLIGATION (CMO)

A multiple-class, pay-through bond, first issued by the *Federal Home Loan Mortgage Corporation (Freddie Mac)* in 1983, that is secured by a pool of mortgages or a portfolio of mortgage pass-through securities. The selling of CMOs provides liquidity to lenders who have sold their mortgages and, thus, those lenders can make additional loans. (*See* **Secondary Mortgage Market**)

COLOR OF TITLE

In the conveyance of property, an instrument that appears to convey title to the property, but in fact conveys no title at all. Any instrument of conveyance which has a grantor, a grantee, a legal description of the property and proper words of conveyance gives color of title. However, if for some reason, such as a forged deed, the instrument does not actually convey title, then it only passes color of title, or as it is also called, *apparent title*. In some states a claim to property through adverse possession is not permitted unless the possessor had color of title which he or she believed to be valid. If the defect(s) was obvious to a third party, then the person in possession could not claim title through adverse possession. (*See* **Adverse Possession**)

COMMERCIAL BANK

A financial intermediary authorized to accept deposits and lend funds for a number of loan activities. In terms of total assets, the more than 13,000 commercial banks are the largest financial intermediary directly involved in the financing of real estate. Commercial banks act as lenders for a multitude of loans. While they provide financing for permanent residential purchases, commercial banks' primary real estate activity involves short-term loans, particularly construction loans (typically six months to three years) and to a lesser extent home-improvement loans. Most large commercial banks have a real estate loan department and their involvement in real estate is through this department. Some of the largest commercial banks are also directly involved in real estate financing through their trust departments, mortgage banking operations and real estate investment trusts. All commercial banks are either federally (nationally) chartered or state chartered. National banks are chartered and supervised by the U. S. Comptroller of the Currency. The word "national" appears in their title, and they are members of the *Federal Reserve System (FRS)*. However, only one-third of all commercial banks are members of the FRS, even though the member banks control the majority of total bank assets. Nationally chartered banks are also required to maintain membership in the *Federal Deposit Insurance Corporation (FDIC)*. Federally chartered banks can make real estate residential loans up to 90% of the appraised value with a maturity of not more than 30 years. However, any government insured or guaranteed loans are exempt from these limitations. State chartered banks are regulated by various agencies in their particular state, and membership in both the FDIC and the FRS is optional. Banks not members of the FDIC are normally required to maintain membership in a state insurance corporation.

COMMERCIAL FRUSTRATION

Excuse of a party from performing on a contract if the performance is contingent upon the existence of a particular thing and such thing is not present. In regard to a lease, commercial frustration occurs if the purpose of the leasehold cannot be effectuated. For example, if the purpose of the leasehold were to sell liquor, and the tenant is unable to procure a liquor license, some courts may allow this lease to be terminated for hardship. This approach, however, is in the minority.

COMMERCIAL LEASE

A lease involving retail stores or office space as compared to an industrial lease or a residential lease. (*See* Lease)

COMMERCIAL PROPERTY

A zoning classification referring to income-producing property which would allow such uses as office buildings, retail stores, restaurants and service facilities. While zoning classifications vary from jurisdiction to jurisdiction, commercial property is normally classified as C-1, C-2, etc. which refers to the commercial uses legally permitted on the land. (*See* Zoning)

COMMERCIAL ZONE

A common zoning classification normally denoting commercial uses such as retail outlets and shops. (*See* Zoning)

COMMINGLING OF FUNDS

Mixing deposits or monies belonging to a client with one's personal account. A real estate broker is personally responsible for any money entrusted to him or her and is in violation of state licensing law if that money is placed in a personal account rather than a business account clearly designated as an escrow account. If found guilty of commingling funds, a broker is subject to either suspension or revocation of his or her license.

COMMISSION

The amount owed a broker as payment for services rendered in connection with the listing contract. Usually the commission is paid by the seller, since in most instances the broker is employed by the seller. The commission, normally stated in the listing contract as a percentage of the sales price, is generally earned when the broker has executed a valid sales contract by a ready, willing, and able buyer. In addition, real estate licensing laws require that in order to collect a commission one must have been properly licensed at the time one rendered the service. Courts will not award a commission to a person who brokers real estate if that person is not properly licensed.

Real estate brokers enter into agreements with the salesperson licensed to work on behalf of the broker in regard to how commissions will be split if the salesperson either lists the property or sells the property. A certain percentage, quite often as much as 50 percent of the commission, is kept by the broker to pay for overhead, selling expenses and profit. In many instances the amount of the total commission that goes to the salesperson increases as the salesperson's volume of sales increases. A common practice is for brokers in a particular city to charge the same rate. However, the amount of commission charged in a particular location is set by custom or practice, not by law, as to do such would be in violation of antitrust laws.

COMMISSIONER

A member of a state real estate commission or other public body, such as a county commission, who acts as the governing or policy-making body of the commission. (*See* **Real Estate Commission**)

COMMISSIONER'S DEED

A type of deed used for carrying out judicial purposes which is given to foreclose a deed of trust in lieu of a trustee's sale.

COMMITMENT

A pledge or promise to do something such as lend money at a certain interest rate within a certain period of time. (*See* **Commitment Letter, Loan Commitment**)

COMMITMENT FEE

A charge made by a lender at the time a loan commitment is made to compensate the lender for agreeing to keep the funds available for a stated period of time. The fee is normally a certain percentage, for example, one percent of the total amount the lender has agreed to loan. If the loan is actually made the lender may agree to return the commitment fee to the borrower. (*See* **Loan Commitment**)

COMMITMENT LETTER

A written agreement by a lender to loan a certain amount of money at a specified interest rate within a certain period of time. (*See* **Loan Commitment**)

COMMITMENT TO INSURE

A report issued by a title insurance company which shows the condition of the title and legally committing the title insurance company to issue a form policy of title insurance upon compliance with the requirements set forth in the commitment. (*See* **Title Insurance**)

COMMITTEE DEED

A deed issued by a group of people who have been appointed by a court to administer the property of someone who has been adjudged legally incompetent.

COMMON ELEMENTS

In a condominium, that part of the land and building which is jointly owned and used with other unit owners. Typically this may include the land, exterior walls, the roof, club houses, swimming pools, parking lots, and other amenities on the property. Each unit owner has an undivided interest on a pro rata basis in the common elements which are the responsibility of a *homeowner's association*, of which each unit owner is a member. The unit owner is obligated to pay a *maintenance fee*, ordinarily collected monthly, to the association which in turn pays for the maintenance and upkeep of the common elements. The percentage of each owner's interest in the common elements is usually based on the ratio of the square footage in an individual unit to the total square footage of the building. For example, a unit containing 1,500 square feet in a 60,000 square foot building would be assessed 2 1/2 percent (1,500/60,000) of the expenses for the upkeep of the common elements. In some condominium projects the pro rata share is based on the ratio of a unit's purchase price to the total purchase price of all the units. (*See* **Condominium, Homeowner's Association, Limited Common Elements**)

COMMON LAW

A body of legal principles and rules of action derived from accepted practices and procedures in England. Today, English common law serves as the foundation for most laws in every state except Louisiana.

COMMON WALL

A wall separating two living units in a condominium development. Such walls are normally treated as *limited common elements*. (*See* **Party Wall**)

COMMUNICATION

A sharing or passing of knowledge or information between two or more persons. In order to form a contract there must be an offer and an acceptance and in order to be effective an offer must be *communicated* by the *offeror* to the *offeree*. Ordinarily, an offer can only be effective when the offeror voluntarily communicates the offer. This voluntary communication is judged on the objective reasonable man standard. (*See* **Contract**)

COMMUNITY ASSOCIATION

An association of property owners in either a condominium or residential development which oversees the maintenance and upkeep of common areas and attempts to maintain property values in the area. Such associations are normally governed by a board of directors elected by the property owners. The board is responsible for seeing that deed restrictions and subdivision regulations are not violated as well as overseeing the upkeep of common spaces such as sidewalks and open space.

COMMUNITY ASSOCIATIONS INSTITUTE (CAI)

CAI provides assistance to builders, managers, and homeowners with the operation and management of condominiums and homeowner's associations. The mailing address is 1423 Powhatan Street, Alexandria, Virginia 22314; (202) 548-8600.

COMMUNITY PROPERTY

A form of property ownership in which husband and wife each have an undivided one-half interest in the property acquired by either spouse during the time of their marriage. Property acquired by a husband and wife during marriage in those states which recognize community property is owned in equal, undivided interests no matter how much either spouse contributed to the acquisition. In these states dower and curtesy do not exist. Any property which is acquired by purchase or as compensation by either spouse is considered to be owned in an undivided half-interest by each, and how much either contributed in acquiring the property is not relevant. This rule does not apply to property which each spouse owned prior to marriage or to property received as gifts or inheritance; this type of property is owned individually. To sell or otherwise convey community property, both wife and husband must join in the conveyance. Husband and wife share the *unity of possession* but no *right of survivorship* exists in community property, so if one spouse dies that spouse's interest will go to his or her heirs. If the property interest passes by will to a third person, the surviving spouse and the third person are considered to be tenants in common. Community property should not be confused with separate property, which is that property acquired before marriage or received by gift or inheritance after marriage. (*See* **Curtesy, Dower**)

COMMUNITY REINVESTMENT ACT

A provision of the *Housing and Community Development Act of 1977* intended to prevent the practice of *redlining* and disinvestment by lenders in central city areas. To comply with the act, lenders must prepare *Community Reinvestment Statements*. These statements contain up to four basic elements:

1.   The lender delineates a "community" in which its lending activities take place. The lender may use political boundaries, designate an "effective lending territory" in which a "substantial portion" of its loans are made, or any other "reasonably delineated local area." Care must be taken that such designations do not unreasonably exclude territory occupied by persons of low or moderate income.

2.   The lender must make available a listing of the types of credit it offers in each community

3.   Appropriate notice and information regarding lending activity by territory must be given or made available for public inspection. The specific language of the notice is dictated by the government.

4.   The lender has the option to disclose affirmative programs designed to meet the credit needs of the community.

COMPARABLES
Recently-sold properties which are similar to a particular property being appraised and are used to indicate the fair market value of the subject property. While comparables will not be identical to the subject property, they should be similar in terms of location, age, size, and physical design. (*See* **Market Data Approach**)

COMPARABLE SALES APPROACH
(*See* **Market Data Approach**)

COMPARATIVE UNIT METHOD
A technique used to estimate reproduction or replacement cost which measures the total square footage or cubic footage of a building and multiplies this total by a current cost per square foot or cubic foot factor. For example, if a house with 2,200 square feet of gross livable area (GLA) is located in an area where construction costs is $38 per square foot, the comparative unit method of calculating the replacement cost would be: 2,200 x $38 = $83,600. (*See* **Cost Approach**)

COMPARISON METHOD
One of the techniques used for deriving a capitalization rate based on determining how much more an investor has to be compensated for a particular real estate investment in comparison to an "ideal" real estate investment. Among the features which are considered in comparing an ideal investment are the reliability of the gross income, the likelihood of competitive construction in the market area, the income-expense ratio, the burden of management, the marketability of the property and the stability of each figure. If an ideal property would require a 7.5% return, and the subject property was considered to be 65% of the

ideal in quality, then the capitalization rate would be derived as follows:

$$\frac{7.5\%}{65\%} \quad = \quad 11.54\%$$

(*See* **Capitalization Rate**)

COMPASS POINTS

The marked points on a compass used to indicate a specific direction as, for example, when surveying land using the *metes and bounds* method of land surveying. (*See* **Metes and Bounds**)

COMPETENT

Legally capable or fit. (*See* **CONTRACT**)

COMPETITION, PRINCIPLE OF

A value principle which states that competition is a function of supply and demand and ordinarily results from excess profits which attract an increase in supply. For example, if only one fully leased apartment complex exists in a growing area of a city, normally competitors will construct additional apartments to take advantage of the anticipated demand. The fully leased project will be able to temporarily charge higher than normal rents, giving the owner excess profits.

COMPETITIVE MARKET ANALYSIS

An evaluation of recent sales of property in a specific neighborhood so as to better understand the current economics of the area. Sellers as well as real estate brokers and appraisers undertake such analysis in an effort to estimate the likely selling price of an owner's property. Normally, such analysis is done prior to listing the property for sale.

COMPLAINANT

One who files a complaint in court against another. The complainant is commonly known as the *plaintiff*.

COMPLETION BOND

A surety bond posted by a developer guaranteeing that a particular development will be completed as planned, free and clear of any liens. A completion bond is different from a *performance bond*, which is given by a contractor or as a party to a contract with an owner to assure the owner that so long as the contractor is paid, he or she will perform as agreed to in the contract. Local governments often require a developer to post a completion bond prior to approval of the developer's subdivision plans. Thus, if the development is not completed, the local government can use the proceeds of the bond to complete the project. (*See* **Performance Bond**)

COMPLIANCE INSPECTION

An inspection of a building to determine whether or not building codes have been met.

COMPONENT DEPRECIATION

A method of depreciation by which the individual components of the building are depreciated separately over their useful lives as contrasted to *composite depreciation*, in which the whole building is depreciated over its useful life. Components which may be separately depreciated include mechanical equipment, plumbing, air conditioning, roofing, carpeting, and paving. By breaking an improvement into different components and depreciating each separate component according to its useful life, a taxpayer may be able to increase the magnitude of the depreciation deduction. For example, assume an apartment building is valued at $1,000,000 and has a useful life of 40 years. Depreciation for each year would be: $1,000,000 x 1/40 = $25,000.

Now assume a component method of depreciation is used and observe what happens:

Component	Useful Life (Years)	Cost	Annual Depreciation
Building	40	$600,000	$15,000
Mechanical Equipment	15	180,000	12,000
Air Conditioning	10	75,000	7,500
Heating	10	75,000	7,500
Plumbing	15	50,000	3,333
Paving	10	10,000	1,000
Carpeting	5	10,000	2,000
			$48,333

In this example, the depreciation for the first year using a component method was almost double the amount under the composite method. (*See* **Depreciation, Useful Life**)

COMPOSITE DEPRECIATION

A method of depreciation by which the entire building is depreciated over its useful life. (*See* **Component Depreciation**)

COMPOSITE RATE

A blended rate of return that is a weighted average of different rates applicable to the property.

COMPOUND AMOUNT OF ONE

A factor used to calculate how much a present sum will be worth in the future if it is held for a certain period of time and earns an interest rate that is compounded periodically. The factor is calculated using the formula:

$$S^n = (1 + i)^n$$

AMOUNT OF $1 AT COMPOUND INTEREST

Year	Interest Rate			
	5%	10%	15%	20%
1	$1.05	$1.10	$1.15	$1.20
5	1.28	1.61	2.01	2.49
10	1.63	2.59	4.05	6.19
15	2.08	4.18	8.14	15.41
20	2.65	6.73	16.37	38.34

COMPOUND AMOUNT OF ONE PER PERIOD

A factor used to calculate how much a series of equal sums deposited at the end of the periodic compounding time intervals will be worth at the end of the total term. The factor is calculated using the formula:

$$S_n = \frac{(1 + i)^n - 1}{i}$$

The following factors show the future value of $1 accumulated per period at various interest rates and periods of time.

ACCUMULATION OF $1 PER PERIOD AT COMPOUND INTEREST

Year	Interest Rate			
	5%	10%	15%	20%
1	$1.00	$1.00	$1.00	$1.00
5	5.53	6.11	6.74	7.44
10	12.58	15.94	20.30	25.96
15	21.58	31.77	47.58	72.04
20	33.06	57.28	102.44	186.69

COMPOUND INTEREST

Interest upon interest; that is, interest that is paid on interest in addition to being paid on the original principal. If interest is compounded, then at the beginning of each new period, interest is added to the current principal, which creates a new principal amount. At the beginning of the next period, the interest paid will be based on the new principal. Interest may be compounded over any time period: daily, weekly, monthly, quarterly, semiannually, or annually.

Compound interest rate tables such as the one shown below are normally used to determine the total amount of principal and interest, given a certain interest rate and a specific compounding period.

COMPOUND SUM OF $1.00

Year	6%	8%	10%	12%	14%
1	1.060	1.080	1.100	1.120	1.140
2	1.124	1.166	1.210	1.254	1.300
3	1.191	1.260	1.331	1.405	1.482
4	1.262	1.360	1.464	1.574	1.482
5	1.338	1.469	1.611	1.762	1.925
6	1.419	1.587	1.772	1.974	2.195
7	1.504	1.714	1.949	2.211	2.502
8	1.594	1.851	2.144	2.476	2.853
9	1.689	1.999	2.358	2.773	3.252
10	1.791	2.159	2.594	3.106	3.707

Thus, a single dollar compounded at a 10 percent annual rate would increase to $1.61 at the end of 5 years ($1 x 1.611). Five hundred dollars compounded at a 14 percent annual rate would increase to $962.50 at the end of five years ($500 x 1.925). Compound interest tables are also useful to real estate investors in projecting the future value of real estate. Assume you own a parcel of land worth $10,000. You expect land values to increase 8 percent a year. How much will the land be worth in 10 years?

$10,000 x 2.159 (8% factor for 10 years) = $21,590

(*See* **Simple Interest**)

COMPS
(*See* **Comparables**)

CONCENTRIC CIRCLE THEORY
An economic theory used to explain the formation and growth of cities. The theory states that, if there are no physical or legal barriers, cities tend to expand from their centers or central business districts in concentric circles. Each circle or zone has land uses and income levels quite different from those of the other zones.

CONCESSION
A service or discount offered by the landlord to a tenant to induce the tenant to sign a lease. Reasons for offering concessions to tenants might include the desire to attract anchor tenants such as a national chain store or the desire to "rent

up" a certain amount of available space prior to the actual completion of the building.

Example: An office 100 x 75 rents for $6.00 per square foot. If a tenant will sign a five-year lease, rent will only be charged for the first four years.

Rent Calculation (without concession) = 100 x 75 x $6.00
    = $45,000 per year or $3,750 per month

Rent Calculation (with concession)   = $45,000 x 4 = $180,000/5
    = $36,000 per year or $3,000 per month

Even though less common than with commercial buildings, apartment complexes sometimes offer concessions. Examples would include such things as free membership in a private club or a twelve-month lease for eleven month's rent. An investor purchasing property that is currently being leased must carefully review all existing leases to determine if any concessions have been made that would result in the actual rent collected being less than the rent specified in the lease. If so, the value of the concessions should be estimated to determine their effect on the value of the property.

CONCILIATION AGREEMENT

A settlement or resolution to a dispute or complaint. Under the *1968 Federal Fair Housing Act*, the *Department of Housing and Urban Development (HUD)* has the responsibility to promptly investigate complaints brought before it. As a result of the investigation, HUD often seeks a conciliation agreement with the person or person accused with the discriminatory practice. The agreement may call upon the person to refrain from future discriminatory acts or to begin affirmative marketing plans.

CONCURRENT OWNERSHIP

Ownership of real estate by more than one person. The concurrent forms of ownership which were recognized under common law and which have relevance today include: (1) *tenancy in common*, (2) *joint tenancy*, and (3) *tenancy by the entirety*. Not every concurrent form of ownership is recognized in every state. In addition, each state may have peculiar rules which affect the creation, termination and rights associated with the concurrent form of ownership. A few states have enacted community property laws which are a form of concurrent ownership not recognized under common law. (*See* **Community Property, Joint Tenancy, Tenancy by the Entirety, Tenancy in Common**)

CONDEMNATION

The process of taking private property for public use or purpose through the power of eminent domain. Unlike police power, such as the denial of a zoning change, exercising the power of eminent domain requires *just compensation* be paid by the *condemnor* (the government agency taking the property) to the *condemnee* (the property owner). The amount of the just compensation is generally considered to be the appraised market value of the property as of the date of the condemnation. Examples of land being taken for public use would include highway expansions, urban renewal, and public parks. (*See* **Eminent Domain, Just Compensation, Police Power**)

CONDEMNATION APPRAISAL

An estimate of the market value of property which is being condemned through the power of eminent domain. (*See* **Appraisal, Condemnation**)

CONDEMNATION CLAUSE

A clause in a mortgage or lease specifying what is to occur in case any or all of the mortgaged or leased property is condemned under the power of eminent domain. The condemnation clause in a mortgage may require that the borrower apply any condemnation award received in a whole or partial taking to pay off the mortgage principal. (*See* **Condemnation, Eminent Domain**)

CONDITION

Any fact or event which, if it occurs or fails to occur, automatically creates or extinguishes a legal obligation. Conditions may be written so that they will void the entire obligation or merely part of it. It is common to include various conditions and contingency clauses in real estate contracts. These give the parties an opportunity to limit their liability if certain events occur or fail to occur and provide sufficient flexibility to truly express their contractual intent. Care should be taken to specify with definiteness and certainty the conditions and contingencies so that a reasonable person could know precisely what was intended. Poor drafting may cause the obligations to become illusory or too vague for enforcement. There is a difference between a condition and a *covenant*. A condition, upon the occurrence of the specified event, will automatically create or extinguish a legal obligation. A covenant is a promise. If a person fails to adhere to a covenant, this will result in a cause of action for damages, but it will not automatically create or extinguish legal obligations. (*See* **Condition Concurrent, Condition Precedent, Condition Subsequent, Covenant**)

CONDITIONAL COMMITMENT

An agreement by a lender to make a loan upon the fulfillment of specified conditions. (*See* **Loan Commitment**)

CONDITIONAL FEE ESTATE

A fee interest in land which is subject to a power in the original grantor or the grantor's heirs to terminate the estate upon the happening of an event. Such interest is also known as a *fee simple subject to a condition subsequent*. This type of estate is essentially the same as the *fee simple determinable*; however, the termination is not automatic, since the party with the future interest called the *right of re-entry* or *power of termination* must take steps to either enter upon the property or to bring a court action to recover the land.

Examples of a conditional fee estate include:
1. "to Mary Jones on the condition that the property be used as a camp for orphans"
2. "to James Smith on the condition that he remain single until he is thirty years of age"

In the second example, once James Smith has passed the age of thirty years and has remained single, the estate becomes a *fee simple absolute* since the condition can never be violated after that time. (*See* **Fee Simple Absolute, Fee Simple Determinable, Qualified Fee Estate**)

CONDITIONAL SALE CONTRACT

A contract for the sale of an item in which possession is given to the purchaser but title is retained by the seller until all of the conditions of the contract have been met, such as full payment of the purchase price. When all of the conditions of the contract have been met, title is transferred to the purchaser. Such contracts are used in real estate in the purchasing of personal property such as a refrigerator, stove, or equipment. When real property is involved, the contract used is an *installment sale contract*. (*See* **Installment Sale**)

CONDITION CONCURRENT

A condition which requires mutual performance of the parties. For example, at settlement one party is required to deliver a deed and the other party is required to pay the agreed-upon purchase price. If either party fails to perform, the other party is excused from performance as well. (*See* **Condition**)

CONDITION PRECEDENT

A condition which requires something to occur before a duty becomes absolute and enforceable. A common example is a condition included in a sales contract which states the contract is contingent upon the buyer acquiring financing at a specific loan-to-value ratio and at specific terms. If the financing is not available, the purchaser is not obligated to perform on the contract.

Example: Jack agrees to buy a house from Pam subject to receiving a loan of $50,000 at 11 1/2% for thirty years from First National Bank. If First National Bank refuses a loan or offers a loan which is less attractive, such as a loan for $50,000 at 11 3/4% for twenty-five years, then Jack is excused from performance. If the bank gives a more attractive loan, such as a loan for $50,000 at 11% for thirty years, then Jack is bound to perform. (*See* **Condition**)

CONDITION SUBSEQUENT

A condition which, if it occurs at some point in the future, extinguishes a duty to perform. An example is a contingency clause in a sales contract which states that the purchaser is excused from purchasing the house if the house is damaged by fire to the extent of ten percent of its market value. (*See* **Condition**)

CONDO

Common reference to a condominium. (*See* **Condominium**)

CONDOMINIUM

A form of property ownership which involves a separation of property into individual ownership elements and common ownership elements. Condominium refers to a legal form of ownership and not to a specific land use. Many people associate the term solely with residential housing. While much residential housing is in the condominium form of ownership, commercial, industrial, and mixed land uses are also being structured as condominiums. The popularity of the condominium form of ownership is a recent phenomenon in the United States. Before 1960 no state had enacted condominium legislation, while today every state has some form of condominium legislation. The titles of these acts differ; for example, some states call their enabling legislation *Horizontal Property Acts*.

Ownership elements in a condominium may be separated into: (1) *individual unit elements*, (2) *common elements*, and (3) *limited common elements*. Individual units are owned as separate fees by each individual owner. The *unit* refers to that portion of the condominium which is intended for the exclusive use and possession of the unit owner. The owner arranges for separate financing for the unit and is responsible for property taxes on the unit, plus taxes on a pro rata share of the common and limited common elements. Common elements relate to property which is jointly owned on a pro rata basis with other unit owners. Typically this may include the land, exterior walls, the roof, club houses, swimming pools, parking lots, and other amenities on the property. Ownership of the common elements is analogous to ownership by tenants-in-common. Each unit owner has an undivided interest on a pro rata basis in the common elements; however, unlike a tenancy-in-common, no right of partition exists while the condominium regime is in existence. Limited common elements are those portions of a condominium which are jointly owned by all unit owners but under the exclusive control or possession of only some of the owners. Limited common elements may include enclosed courtyards, balconies, shutters, and other features which may lie outside the description of an individual unit but are under the exclusive control of a percentage of the owners. An individual is responsible for the cost of operating and maintaining the individual unit. The common areas are the responsibility of a *homeowner's association* of which each unit owner is a member. The unit owner is obligated to pay a *maintenance fee*, ordinarily collected monthly, to the association. On occasion, the unit owner may also be charged a *special assessment* to pay for unusual costs which have not been adequately provided for in a reserve fund. Failure to pay maintenance fees or special assessments can lead to liens being placed on the individual unit, attachment, and foreclosure. These risks do not exist for individual property owners owning a fee in land and improvements. The establishment of a condominium regime requires the drafting and recording of several legal documents. These documents include: (1) *public offering statements*, (2) *condominium declaration*, (3) *condominium plan*, (4) *bylaws*, (5) *operating budget*, (6) *management agreement*, (7) *subscription and purchase agreement*, and (8) *unit deed.* The condominium form of ownership provides several advantages and disadvantages over other forms of ownership. Each of these should be carefully reviewed by anyone considering the purchase of a condominium. To consider residential condominiums as an example, unit owners are generally able to acquire more living space for the dollars spent on housing than they would get from acquiring a detached house. Likewise, these owners get a better amenity package than they might be able to afford as individuals. By cluster design, unit owners have access and ownership in more open space. There are fewer worries about maintenance and lawn care, since these tasks are handled by professional property managers. Unlike tenants leasing their housing, the unit owners are able to deduct interest on mortgage and property taxes. If the units appreciate, the benefits accrue to the unit owners; likewise, unit owners are protected against rent increases caused by under-supply of rental housing or inflation. Condominium ownership, however, also entails certain disadvantages. For example, in residential condominiums the unit owners do not have the same degree of personal freedom to control the environment as an individual property owner does. Many condominiums have architectural controls on the exterior of buildings, and any modifications such as patios or gardens might have to be approved by the association. Pets may be prohibited. Unit owners need to participate in frequent meetings of the homeowner's association to protect their property rights. In poorly constructed projects, unit owners may be annoyed by noise coming through thin walls from the adjoining unit. If repairs are needed, responsibility has to be determined, and if the interior of a unit needs repair, the individual unit owner is solely responsible unless the declaration specified otherwise. It may be difficult to approve major expenditures; thus, the project may be allowed to deteriorate.

CONDOMINIUM CONVERSION

The process of converting rental property to a condominium form of ownership. While most conversions involve residential properties, some conversions have included office buildings and other commercial properties. In many states, condominium conversions have proven to be very profitable to the original property owner. This has been especially true in residential rental properties and is partly a result of rentals not increasing as quickly as other real estate prices. With some communities imposing rent controls or rent rollbacks, the economic pressures for conversion have intensified. In addition, due to the nature of federal income tax rules, many projects need to be sold after being fully depreciated in order to avoid adverse tax consequences. Several communities have restricted or considered restricting residential condominium conversions. Typical restrictions include approval of a certain percentage of existing tenants or the payment of moving expenses to tenants who are displaced due to a conversion. Whether all of these types of restrictions are constitutionally justified is still open to debate and will need to be resolved by the courts. The social argument raised is that condominium conversion reduces the amount of rental housing in a community. This forces persons to purchase housing, pay higher rentals because of a shrinking supply, or move out.

CONDOMINIUM DECLARATION

The document which legally establishes the condominium regime. Such a document is also referred to as a *master deed*. The condominium declaration is prepared by a *grantor* or *declarant* who previously had the property under individual ownership. The declaration describes the individual units and authorizes the formation of the homeowner's association; also, the common areas are allocated in an undivided interest percentage to each unit. This determines the amount each unit owner will be assessed for maintenance, real estate taxes, and in some cases how much voting power the owner has. State law may define how the common areas will be allocated. Typically, allocation is made (1) by value of unit in proportion to the whole project as of a given date, (2) by living area of each unit in comparison to all other units, (3) by equal shares, or (4) by market value. The declaration also states the restrictions, covenants, conditions, right of access, and other rights and interests. Once a declaration is recorded, it extends the state condominium laws to the real estate. Ordinarily, future amendments to or changes in the declaration require consent of 100 percent of the unit owners. Care should therefore be taken that all relevant provisions are included in the original recording.

CONDOMINIUM MANAGEMENT

Control of a condominium regime which generally covers three phases: (1) control of management by the developer, (2) a period of transition, and (3) control by the homeowner's association.

Developer Control: At the inception of a condominium, the project is under the control of the grantor or developer. While the developer controls the condominium, the unit owners have little power to influence factors affecting the value of the units. Even though the developer wishes to sell out as soon as possible, marketing conditions may be such that he or she may decide to rent units until the likelihood of sales improves. Unless there are covenants in the declaration prohibiting this, the developer has the legal right to do so.

Transition: The declaration provides for the time when the control of the project will shift to the homeowner's association. Ordinarily, the declaration specifies a certain time or an event such as the sale of a certain percentage of units in the project. Problems may occur in cases of *expandable* or *incremental* condominiums. These are projects in which the developer reserves the right to add additional units to the project and to change the pro rata interest of each unit owner in the common elements. Problems occur from the viewpoint of the consumer when new units are added without the amenity package being expanded as well. One swimming pool for 100 units may be adequate, but if 400 additional units are added, this amenity may become overcrowded for the project.

Control by the Homeowner's Association: The homeowner's association has the authority and responsibility to manage the common elements of the project after the original grantor gives control. This, however, does not imply ownership. Each individual unit owner has an undivided interest in the common elements which leads to certain legal consequences. The individual homeowner is responsible for property taxes in the pro rata share; the association is not. A loan must be co-signed by all of the owners since they, not the homeowner's association, own the property. Condominium ownership also involves certain risks for liability which should be insured. Each unit owner is jointly and severally liable for negligence in the condition and management of common areas. If a third party were injured, any unit owner could be sued if the injury was due to negligence of the association in maintaining the property. Ordinarily, a package insurance policy is carried to cover the liability of each unit owner as a co-owner in the common areas, while a separate policy is carried by the unit owner for liability coverage within the unit itself. The package policy also provides coverage for the board of directors. In addition to liability coverage a blanket policy is usually carried for fire and hazard insurance. If the improvements are destroyed, many state condominium statutes provide for a termination of the condominium regime if the improvements are not replaced within a specified time. The insurance proceeds are therefore paid to the directors as agents or trustees for the purpose of replacing the destroyed improvements. Because a condominium involves the creation of a community with each member of the community having responsibilities to the other members, provisions in the declaration often provide for a *first right of refusal* by the association. This provision requires a unit owner seeking to sell his or her unit to notify the association and allow them to purchase the unit at a fair market price. This device may not be used to discriminate on the basis of race, color, creed, national origin, or sex.

CONDOMINIUM MANAGEMENT AGREEMENT

An agreement established with a professional property management company to maintain the common areas for a fee. Ordinarily, this agreement is authorized by the bylaws of the homeowner's association. In many cases the management agreement contains provisions for enforcement of rules by the management company. Care should be taken by unit purchasers that the management agreement is not for a long term with either the developer of the project or his associates. A problem can occur when the common areas are subject to a long-term recreational lease given by the grantor to some third party investor or retained by the declarant for his or her own investment. A long-term lease allows the lessee to charge user fees to the unit owners without adequate service in return. The user charges are usually mandatory and enforced by placing a lien on units which fail to pay the fees required. Many states have restricted this kind of practice to protect the public. (*See* **Condominium, Homeowner's Association**)

CONDOMINIUM PLAN

A graphic three-dimensional description of the various units and common areas in the condominium regime. The condominium plan, also called the *plat of the condominium subdivision* or the *record plat*, is normally included as part of the *declaration*. (*See* **Condominium Declaration**)

CONFESSION OF JUDGMENT

Written authority of a debtor permitting a judgment to be entered against him or her by a creditor in the event the debtor is in default in payment. Some mortgages include a provision called a *cognovit* or *confess judgment clause*, which empowers the mortgagee's (lender's) attorney to appear in court and confess default by the mortgagor (borrower) to the court. In many states such clauses are either prohibited or greatly restricted. (*See* **Foreclosure**)

CONFIRMATION OF SALE

The court's approval of the price, terms, and conditions of a sale ordered by the court. Examples would include the sale of property by executors, guardians, and administrators.

CONFISCATION

The taking or seizing of private property by the government without compensation to the owner, perhaps as a result of the owner being convicted of a crime or because the use of the property was in violation of the law. Unless taken in the valid execution of police power, due process prohibits confiscation without compensation. (*See* **Eminent Domain, Police Power**)

CONFORMITY, PRINCIPLE OF

An economic principle which states that a parcel of land must be used in such a way as to conform to surrounding land uses if maximum value is to be achieved. Zoning regulations, subdivision regulations, and deed restrictions are intended to maintain conformity. (*See* **Highest and Best Use, Value**)

CONNECTION LINE

A line used by surveyors in the metes and bounds method of surveying land to connect a monument to a permanent reference point such as a *bench mark*. (*See* **Metes and Bounds**)

CONSENT

Voluntary agreement or approval.

CONSEQUENTIAL DAMAGES

A monetary compensation made by a court to a person who has suffered loss or injury as a result of a breach of contract which could not reasonably have been prevented. Consequential damages, also known as *indirect damages*, such as lost profits or lost business opportunities, are ordinarily not awarded unless the breaching party could have reasonably foreseen them. (*See* **Breach of Contract, Damages**)

CONSERVATION

Action taken by private citizens and governmental agencies to protect and preserve natural resources so as to ensure their future well-being and existence.

CONSERVATOR

A guardian or protector appointed by a court to manage the affairs of a protected person, such as someone who has been adjudged incompetent. (*See* **Capacity**)

CONSIDERATION

The reason, motive or influence which induces a party to enter into a contract. In order to have a valid informal contract, there must be *legally sufficient* consideration which was *presently bargained for* by each promisor in exchange for his promise to the other. A legally sufficient consideration may consist of a promise, an act, or a forbearance to act. Legal sufficiency is not the same as adequacy. Ordinarily, the law will not inquire into the fairness of the consideration in the absence of fraud, undue influence, or other factors preventing reality of consent.

Example: A person sells her house for $50,000. Later she learns that the market value of the house was $60,000. She claims that she was ignorant of the fair market price and that because the consideration was inadequate she may rescind the contract. She has no valid case and will lose if this issue were litigated. While the price she bargained for was economically inadequate, it was legally sufficient; the courts will not assist persons who make bad business judgments.

A legally sufficient consideration may be a *legal detriment* suffered by the promisor or a *legal benefit* gained by the promisee. A legal detriment occurs when one does something that one is not obligated to do or gives up a legal right. It may be noted that promises to refrain from criminal, tortious, or immoral conduct are not detriments because everyone already has a general duty to society to avoid this kind of activity. Performance of a pre-existing legal duty is also not generally considered to be legally sufficient consideration. Examples of pre-existing duties include acts by officials which are duties prescribed by law, duties arising from the relationship of parties, and duties which arise from contract.

Example: A contractor agrees to build a house for $75,000. He finds out later that he miscalculated the difficulty of the design and that he will lose money on the contract. The contractor refuses to complete the job unless the landowner agrees to pay an extra $10,000. Because the contractor owed a pre-existing duty to build the house for $75,000, the promise for the extra $10,000 is not supported by a legally sufficient consideration.

A legal benefit occurs when one receives a promise, act, or forbearance to act to which he or she was not legally entitled. The benefit may or may not have any real monetary value. Because consideration is something which must have been previously bargained for, a number of acts or promises may be deemed legally insufficient. For example, a promise for a gift is not ordinarily enforceable against the promisor because the donee suffers no detriment if the gift is not made and the donor bargains for nothing in exchange. Moral consideration or love and affection are ordinarily held to be legally insufficient. Past consideration is likewise held to be legally insufficient because it is something which was given before the promise was made by the other party, and thus could not have been bargained for in exchange for the promise.

Example: Ms. Jones sells a warehouse to Ms. Smith. After the closing Ms. Smith asks Ms. Jones to paint the warehouse blue. Ms. Jones agrees to this request even though she will receive no extra money. Later Ms. Jones decides to back out of this commitment. She may do so with no penalty because Ms. Smith gave no present consideration in exchange for the promise. (*See* **Contract**)

CONSTANT
(*See* **Constant Annual Percent**)

CONSTANT ANNUAL PERCENT

The percentage of the original amount borrowed required to be repaid each year in order to pay the annual interest on the outstanding balance plus fully amortize (pay off) the loan over its maturity. The percent, or *mortgage constant* as it is also known, will vary with either a change in the interest rate or a change in the maturity of the loan, as can be seen below:

ANNUAL MORTGAGE CONSTANT (%)

Interest Rate	10 Years	20 Years	30 Years
8%	14.90	10.19	8.88
10%	16.27	11.75	10.61
12%	17.70	13.39	12.41
14%	19.17	15.10	14.28
16%	20.70	16.87	16.19

For example, $10,000 borrowed at 8% interest and repaid annually over 10 years would require a yearly payment of $1,490 ($10,000 x .1490), whereas, repaying the $10,000 over 30 years would require an annual payment of $888 ($10,000 x .0888).

While an increase in the maturity date decreases the annual payment, an increase in the interest rate has just the opposite effect. The same $10,000 repaid over 30 years but at an interest rate of 14% would require an annual payment of $1,428 ($10,000 x .1428). (*See* **Amortization**)

CONSTANT MONTHLY PERCENT

The percentage of the original amount borrowed required to be repaid each month in order to pay the monthly interest on the outstanding balance plus fully amortize (pay off) the loan over its maturity. Most real estate loans, commercial as well as residential, are amortized using a constant monthly percent. As is true with the constant annual percent, the monthly constant will vary with either a change in the interest rate or a change in the maturity of the loan, as can be seen on the following page.

MONTHLY MORTGAGE CONSTANT (%)

Interest Rate	10 Years	20 Years	30 Years
8%	1.2133	.8365	.7338
10%	1.3215	.9650	.8775
12%	1.4347	1.1010	1.0286
14%	1.5975	1.2583	1.1900
16%	1.7250	1.4058	1.3492

For example, a person borrowing $80,000 at 8% interest to purchase a house would need to make a monthly payment of $587 ($80,000 x .007338) in order to fully repay the loan over 30 years. However, with an interest rate of 14%, the monthly payment is $952 ($80,000 x .011900), an increase of $365. (*See* **Amortization**)

CONSTANT-PAYMENT MORTGAGE

A mortgage which requires equal periodic payments over its maturity. Residential loans are normally of this type. (*See* **Fully Amortized Mortgage**)

CONSTANT PERCENT

The installment payment, stated as a percentage of the original loan, required to pay the periodic interest on the outstanding balance plus fully amortize (pay off) the loan over its maturity. Precalculated tables are normally used by lenders to show the constant percent for various interest rates and various payment intervals, be it monthly, quarterly, semiannually, or annually.

CONSTRUCTION ADVANCE

Money transferred from a lender to a builder/developer at various stages of construction to pay labor and material costs. (*See* **Construction Loan**)

CONSTRUCTION LOAN

A short-term loan, sometimes referred to as *interim financing*, which provides the funds necessary for the building or development of a real estate project. The project can be a residential subdivision, a shopping center, an industrial park, or any other type of property requiring financing during the time required to complete construction. Normally, the full amount to be loaned is committed by the lender, but the actual disbursement is dependent upon the progress of the construction. Funds are sometimes distributed to the borrower in a series of *draws*, depending upon work required by the lender. Another method used is for the developer to submit all bills to the lender who in turn pays the bills. In either case interest is paid on what has been distributed and not on the total amount to be borrowed. Typically, the interest rate charged is tied to the lender's *prime rate* which is the interest rate charged to the lender's AAA customers. In addition to interest, the borrower is normally charged a one or two percent origination fee. Since construction mortgages are considered high risk loans, a lender often requires a *standby* or *take-out commitment* from a permanent lender. A standby or take-out commitment means that another lender will provide permanent financing when a certain event, generally the completion of the project, occurs. Sometimes permanent lenders require a certain percentage of a project to be rented before the financing is provided. This assures the construction lender that permanent financing will be available to repay the construction loan if the project is completed and other conditions are met. (*See* **Advance, Interim Financing, Takeout Commitment**)

CONSTRUCTION PERMIT
(*See* **Building Permit**)

CONSTRUCTIVE EVICTION
Action or inaction on the part of the landlord which results in the tenant's use of the premises becoming substantially disturbed or interfered with, thus forcing the tenant to vacate the premises without further obligation to pay rent. In order to have constructive eviction, the tenant must give up possession. Examples would include the landlord's failure to maintain heat in the winter, or to repair elevator service in a high-rise building. (*See* **Actual Eviction, Eviction, Partial Eviction**)

CONSTRUCTIVE NOTICE
Knowledge the law presumes a person has about a particular fact irrespective of whether the person knows about the fact or not. Examples of constructive notice would include the proper recording of a deed in the public records or the physical possession of property by an owner or tenant. Such notice, also known as *legal notice*, should be distinguished from *actual notice* which is knowledge actually given directly to a person. (*See* **Actual Notice, Notice**)

CONSTRUCTIVE POSSESSION
The power and intent to control property.

CONSUMER CREDIT PROTECTION ACT
(*See* **Truth-in-Lending Act**)

CONSUMER CREDIT REPORTING ACT
(*See* **Fair Credit Reporting Act**)

CONSUMER PRICE INDEX (CPI)
A statistical measure of changes in price levels of a predetermined mix of consumer goods and services. The index is prepared by the *Bureau of Labor Statistics* and is often used as a means of adjusting rental payments in a lease. (*See* **Index Lease**)

CONTIGUOUS

Adjoining or touching at a point or along a boundary. Two parcels of land are contiguous if they share a portion of their boundaries.

CONTINGENCY

A provision or condition included as part of a contract which requires the completion of a certain act or the occurrence of a certain event before the contract becomes binding. Contingency clauses, or *conditions* as they are also known, give the parties to a contract an opportunity to limit their liability if certain events occur or fail to occur and provide sufficient flexibility to truly express their contractual intent. A common contingency clause in a sales contract is a provision making the contract subject to the purchaser obtaining financing at a certain rate of interest within a certain period of time. Failure to find the prescribed financing results in the contract being voidable on the part of the purchaser. (*See* **Purchaser**)

CONTRACT

An agreement based on a promise or set of promises which results in some legally enforceable obligations between two or more parties. Contract law is the hub of most real estate transactions. Ordinarily, a broker and salesperson are involved with contracts on two levels of business activity. The first level involves the broker's employment through a listing contract. This contract defines the broker's right to a commission upon fulfilling the obligations agreed to in the listing. The second level involves the negotiation of some kind of contract between two or more parties. This contract may be a sales agreement, a lease, or some other agreement involving the disposition of real estate rights and interests.

For a contract to be valid and enforceable, the following essential elements must be present:

1. There must be an *offer* and an *acceptance*.

An offer is a promise conditioned upon some requested or asked-for act or promise. An acceptance is a voluntary expression by the offeree to be bound by the exact terms of the offer in the manner requested or authorized by the offeror. Together, offer and acceptance are referred to as *mutual assent*. (*See* **Acceptance, Counteroffer, Offer**)

2. There must be *consideration*.

In order to have a valid informal contract, there must be *legally sufficient* consideration which was presently bargained for by each promisor in exchange for his or her promise to the other. (*See* **Consideration, Legal Benefit, Legal Detriment**)

3. Contracting parties must have *legal capacity*.

Both parties to a contract must have legal capacity in order for the contract to be binding on both parties. Some classes of people, such as minors and insane persons, are in some fashion protected or limited by the law in regard to their contractual capacity. (*See* **Capacity**)

4. There must be *reality of consent* on the part of the contracting parties.

Contract law deals with the fulfillment of reasonable expectations of the contracting parties. A person who is forced or tricked into a contract cannot normally achieve reasonable expectations, and contracts induced without reality of consent are normally voidable at the option of the innocent party. (*See* **Duress, Fraud, Menace, Misrepresentation, Mistake, Reality of Consent, Undue Influence**)

  5. The object or the subject matter of the contract must be *legal*.

  The law will not enforce a contract in which either consideration or object is illegal or against public policy.

  6. The agreement must be in proper *legal form*.

  Certain classes of contracts must be in writing and contain certain essential elements in order to be enforceable. This requirement is called the *statute of frauds*. (*See* **Statute of Frauds**)

  Rights under contracts are valuable property rights which may be sold or otherwise transferred to third persons. The law has developed a number of principles which guide persons who wish to transfer contractual rights and obligations to third persons and which specify the legal relationship between the new set of obligors and obligees. (*See* **Assignment, Obligee, Obligor**)

CONTRACT FOR DEED

  A legal agreement between two parties in which the seller (owner) passes possession of the property but retains title until the total or a substantial portion of the purchase price is paid. It is essentially an agreement to deliver a deed at a certain time provided that the purchaser meets all of the conditions of the contract. A contract for deed is also referred to as a *land sales contract*, an *installment land contract*, an *agreement for purchase and sale*, and a *land contract*. If the purchaser defaults, the seller can normally cancel the contract and keep all payments as rent. This type of agreement is not favored by courts in many states because the failure to meet an installment payment date could cause a purchaser to lose all invested equity without the benefit of a foreclosure hearing and other protection, such as the equity of redemption or statutory redemption. A contract for deed is often used for the sale of unimproved lots and for recreation property. People who cannot qualify for long-term financing because of a poor credit rating may be able to purchase property through the use of this device. It is not uncommon for a land contract to require a low down payment and a term of seven or more years to pay off the obligation.

CONTRACT INTEREST RATE

  The nominal rate of interest, as stated in the note, being charged by the lender. This rate might differ from the *annual percentage rate of interest (APR)*, since the latter includes the impact on the effective rate from discount points and other finance charges. (*See* **Annual Percentage Rate, Discount Points, Truth-in-Lending Act**)

CONTRACTOR

  One who, for a sum of money, undertakes to perform a certain type of work or provide a certain service, such as a building contractor. Contractors are normally classified as either general contractors, in which case they are ultimately responsible for completion of the finished product, or subcontractors, such as an electrician or plumber, who are responsible for only a portion of the job.

CONTRACT RENT

The amount of rental income due from the tenant(s) as agreed to in the lease agreement. In contrast, the *economic rent* is what the leased property would be expected to rent under current market conditions if the property were vacant and available for rent. During inflationary times it is common for the contract rent to be less than the economic rent, which usually results in a raising of the rent when the lease is renewed. In contrast, if the contract rent is greater than the economic rent, a landlord may find the tenants vacating the property at the end of the lease period. (*See* **Economic Rent, Lease**)

CONTRACTUAL LIEN

A lien created by agreement of the parties, for example, a mortgage given to secure the debt represented by a promissory note. (*See* **Lien**)

CONTRIBUTION, PRINCIPLE OF

An economic principle which states that the value of a component part of a piece of property is equal to what that component part adds to the total value, less any costs incurred. For example, an old apartment building would not be remodeled unless the rent schedule could be increased enough to pay for the expense of remodeling. This idea of contribution is very important in the adjustment process described in the *sales comparison approach* to value. If a bedroom costs $5,000, a house with six bedrooms would not necessarily be worth $5,000 more than a house with five bedrooms because the value contribution of one additional bedroom might not equal the cost. (*See* **Comparables, Value**)

CONVENTIONAL LIFE ESTATE

An interest in land created by various acts of parties, such as by deed or will, in contrast with a legal life estate which is created by operation of law, such as dower, curtesy, and homestead. Conventional life estates are generally of two types. The first type is an *ordinary life estate* which lasts for the life of the grantee. An example of this is: "X," the owner of Blackacre, grants the property to "B" for life; when "B" dies the interest is automatically terminated. The second type of conventional life estate is one in which the term is measured by the life or lives of one or more third persons. This type of estate is called a *life estate pur autre vie*. An example of this is: "X" grants Blackacre to "B" for the life of "C"; when "C" dies, "B's" life estate is terminated. It might be noted that "B's" death would not terminate the estate so long as "C" were alive. The estate in that case would belong to "B's" heirs.

The life tenant may do nothing which will impair the value of the property to the owner of the future interest unless permitted to do so explicitly or implicitly in the grant. Impairment of the property is called *waste*. Examples of waste include the cutting of trees, mining, the failure to pay property taxes, and the failure to make reasonable repairs. However, if the property were originally a tree farm or a mine, the life tenant could continue in these operations without being considered to have committed waste. The life tenant is not obligated to make major repairs, restore destroyed buildings, or keep the premises insured. If the life tenant should happen to get ownership of the reversion or the remainder, the doctrine of *merger* would change the life estate into a fee simple absolute. (*See* **Fee Simple Absolute**)

CONVENTIONAL LOAN

A loan made in which real estate serves as the security without any government agency either insuring (FHA) or guaranteeing (VA) the loan. The majority of permanent residential financing provided in the United States is through the fully-amortized conventional mortgage. Since there is no third party to insure or guarantee the mortgage, the lender assumes full risk of a default by the borrower. A lender's decision to make a conventional loan is usually dependent upon: (1) the credit and income position of the borrower, and (2) the value of the property being used to secure the debt. As more and more conventional loans have been made, the *loan-to-value ratio* (relationship between amount borrowed and the appraised value of the property) has continued to increase even though most lenders still limit the amount they will lend to no more than 80% of value unless *private mortgage insurance* is carried. This down payment requirement is higher than with either FHA or VA loans. As the market price of residential real estate has continued to increase, more cash down payment has been required of the borrower, and thus many people have been eliminated from financing with a conventional mortgage. With both insured and guaranteed mortgages people have been able to purchase real estate with a smaller cash down payment. (*See* **Federal Housing Administration, Fully Amortized Mortgage, Private Mortgage Insurance, Veterans Administration (VA), Mortgage**)

CONVENTIONAL MORTGAGE-BACKED SECURITIE

Mortgage-backed securities that are not guaranteed by Freddie Mac, Fannie Mae, or Ginnie Mae.

CONVERSION

The process of changing the use of a building, such as from an apartment complex to a condominium. A conversion occurs when a building originally under one form of ownership is changed into a different form of ownership. During periods when the condominium form of ownership was first popularized in the United States many residential apartment projects were converted to condominium projects. (*See* **Condominium Conversion**)

CONVEYANCE

The transfer of title to land from one person to another by use of a written instrument such as a deed, assignment of lease, or mortgage. (*See* **Deed, Title**)

CONVEYANCE TAX

(See **Transfer Tax***)*

CO-OBLIGOR

One jointly bound with another under an obligation, such as a co-signor of a promissory note. *(See* **Obligor***)*

COOPERATING BROKER

A real estate broker, quite often the selling broker, who works with another broker (usually the listing broker), in bringing together a buyer and seller. When a seller lists his or her property with a real estate broker, an exclusive listing is often given, which means the property is listed with just one broker. Someone in the market for that type of property could be working with another broker. In order to bring about a sale the listing broker may agree to let the second broker show the property to his or her client with the understanding that if an offer is made and accepted, the commission paid to the listing broker will be divided, possibly 50/50, with the other broker. Many *multiple listing services* require that brokers who join the service must agree in writing to cooperate with all other brokers who belong to the service.

COOPERATIVE (OWNERSHIP)

An indirect form of property ownership in which individuals own shares of a corporation which in turn owns the real estate. Cooperatives have been established primarily for housing purposes; however, because of the complexity of this form of ownership it is not as common as the condominium form of ownership. A corporation is set up by filing articles of incorporation as specified in each state. The corporation bylaws define how the corporation will function. Persons wishing to occupy units which are owned by the corporation sign a *subscription agreement* for stock and enter into an *occupancy agreement* or *proprietary lease*. In the subscription agreement in the lease the member agrees to pay a proportional share of expenses incurred by the corporation for maintenance, property taxes, and debt service. Federal income tax law allows the tenant to deduct that portion of each payment which represents property taxes and interest just as in ownership in severalty. The tenant's right or interest in the cooperative is considered to be personal property. Much like a tenant in a lease, the occupant is restricted in the use to which he or she may put the property. If the tenant fails to pay monthly assessments the lease agreement may provide for the termination of the tenant's rights. Certain difficulties arise when the tenant wishes to sell an ownership interest in the cooperative. The corporation may retain the right to first refusal and may require that the occupant sell the shares for the original price paid. *(See* **Condominium***)*

COOPERATIVE SALE

A sale of real estate in which two brokers work together in bringing together the buyer and seller and thus agree to share the commission. (*See* **Cooperating Broker**)

CO-OWNERSHIP

(*See* **Concurrent Ownership**)

CORNER INFLUENCE

In appraising property, the additional value attributable to the fact that a parcel of land has a corner location. (*See* **Value**)

CORNER LOT

A parcel of land located at the intersection of two streets. (*See* **Corner Influence**)

CORPORATE VEIL

The legal buffer which protects a shareholder of a corporation from personal liability stemming from any transactions undertaken by the corporation. (*See* **Corporation**)

CORPORATION

A legal entity created under state law to have perpetual legal existence and to have legal power to carry on certain activities such as owning real estate. A corporation is organized by receiving a charter from the state where the entity is created. The corporation is authorized to carry out those acts which are specified in the corporate charter or by the state enabling legislation. In dealing with a corporation it is ordinarily advisable to assure that the officer with whom a real estate transaction is being negotiated is in fact authorized to act for the corporation. Ordinarily this is done by requesting that the board of directors pass a resolution. A corporation has certain advantages and disadvantages. The advantages include continuity of life, limitation on personal liability of the shareholders, freedom from state usury laws if the entity needs to borrow money, well-organized markets to transfer ownership interests in the corporation, and access to financial markets in issuing bonds, warrants, and various types of debentures. The disadvantages include an inability to pass through operation losses and other deductions, and double taxation of income, once on the corporate level and then again when dividends are distributed to the shareholders. There is also the possibility that a corporation which is owned by a single taxpayer might be declared a personal holding company, leading to disastrous tax consequences. Further, a corporation which in fact is merely a nominee might lose the shielding effect of personal liability on the individual owner. Courts are apt to "pierce the corporate veil" and impose personal liability on an individual who has failed to segregate personal activities from corporate activities.

Under tax law, a corporation which is organized under *Subchapter S* of the Internal Revenue Code provides for a pass through of expenses and revenues without being taxed on the corporate level. The availability of Subchapter S treatment is limited to 35 or fewer shareholders and not more than 20% of the gross income being derived from passive sources such as rentals or royalties. Further, while capital gains may be passed through, capital losses may not. Ordinarily a Subchapter S corporation is not very useful for the holding of real estate except during the construction phase of a project. A final disadvantage of a corporation is that its stock is classified as a security. Thus unless the entity meets certain exemptions, the stock must be registered with the Securities and Exchange Commission, certain disclosures must be made, and limitations on marketing are placed on the sale of the stock issue.

CORPOREAL PROPERTY

Possessory interests in land such as fee simple ownership and life estates. In contrast, *noncorporeal property*, such as easements, rents, and liens, does not entitle the owner to possession although it may include a right to use.

CORRECTION DEED

A deed used to correct errors or defects in a previous deed, as for example, when property has been resurveyed and the legal description in the original deed was found to be incorrect. This deed is also known as a *deed of confirmation*.

CORRECTION LINES

Adjustments in the *government survey method* or *U. S. government survey system* to compensate for the curvature of the earth's surface. Also known as *parallels*, these lines are located every 24 miles, or fourth township, north and south of a base line. (*See* Government Survey Method)

CORRELATION

A step in the appraisal process in which the appraiser weighs the appraisal approaches used to reach a rational conclusion regarding the value of the subject property. Also known as *reconciliation*. (*See* Appraisal Process)

CO-SIGNOR

A person who signs on a promissory note with another person and, thus, becomes legally liable for repayment of the debt.

COST APPROACH

One of the traditional ways to appraise property based on the reproduction or replacement cost of the building less total depreciation plus the value of the land. The cost approach to value is based on the economic *principle of substitution*, that is, the value of a building cannot be greater than the cost of purchasing a similar site and constructing a building of equal utility. Reproduction cost when added to the value of the land sets the upper limit for the cost approach. The chart on the following page outlines the basic steps for using the cost approach to value a subject property.

Cost Approach to Value

Value of Building: Reproduction Cost

1600 sq. ft. @ $50 per sq. ft. $80,000

    Less Depreciation:
      Physical Deterioration
        curable (deferred maintenance,
          painting, etc.) $3,500
        incurable (structural
          damages)   2,000
      Functional obsolescence   3,000
      Economic obsolescence   -0-
        Total Depreciation   - 8,500

    Building Value Estimate $71,500

Value of Land: Size 60 x 180 @ $170 per
                front foot   +10,200

      Total Property Value $81,700

The starting point, an estimate of *reproduction cost new*, is the total of what it would cost in today's dollars to build a similar structure. Reproduction cost new is the cost of actually replicating an improvement as of the date of the appraisal. Because this estimate is often difficult or impractical, many appraisers seek to find the *replacement cost new*, the cost of producing a structure of similar utility using modern materials and building techniques. While there are numerous techniques available to estimate reproduction or replacement cost, the more common ones are: (1) *quantity survey method* which requires calculating the quantity and cost of each material item plus the total cost of installation, (2) *unit-in-place method* in which the cost is grouped by stages of construction, (3) *builder's (trade breakdown) method* in which the cost is grouped by major functional parts of the structure such as foundation, walls, heating system, (4) *comparative unit method* which measures the total square footage or cubic footage and multiplies this total by the current cost per square or cubic foot, or (5) *index method* which takes the original cost of construction and multiplies that figure by a price index for the geographic area to allow for price changes.

Next, *accrued depreciation* must be subtracted from this replacement cost to derive an estimate of building value. Accrued depreciation is considered to be any diminishment of utility or value from the reproduction cost new. Depreciation is divided into three types: (1) *physical deterioration*, (2) *functional obsolescence*, and (3) *economic obsolescence*. Physical deterioration allows for actual wear and tear or the action of natural elements and can be either *curable* or *incurable*. Depreciation is considered curable if the cost of the repair would not exceed the contribution to value. For example, if a house valued at $60,000 had a leaky roof which would cost $5,000 to repair, and if the house would be valued at $68,000 after the repair, this defect would be considered curable. Curable physical deterioration estimates deferred maintenance, such as repairing the roof, while incurable physical deterioration estimates elements of the structure which are not economically feasible to correct. Functional obsolescence allows for conditions within the structure which make the building outdated compared with a new building. For example, inadequate loading facilities in a warehouse or a single bathroom in a five-bedroom house each subtract from the value of the structures. Functional obsolescence also includes features which are not fully valued by the market. For example, if a house had a marble sink with 24-karat gold faucets, the market might not add the cost of the sink to the value of the home. This sink would be called a *superadequacy*. Finally, economic obsolescence, also known as *location obsolescence*, considers factors outside the subject property such as changes in competition, desirability of the neighborhood, or surrounding land use. While all three types of accrued depreciation are difficult to measure, each must be estimated and subtracted to estimate the present value of the building. It should be noted that cost of improvements includes the cost in the marketplace, not the cost to an individual builder. This means that costs include materials, labor, indirect costs, and a reasonable builder's profit.

Finally, the value of the land is appraised as if the land were vacant and available for construction at its *highest and best use*. This is done by using the same basic techniques discussed in the sales comparison approach, namely, analyzing the current market conditions. By adding the land value estimate to the building value estimate, the total property value as indicated by the cost approach can be stated. While this approach can be used with all types of property, it is most applicable in appraising new buildings or nonincome-producing property, such as schools and churches. (*See* **Value**)

COST BASIS

The value of property for accounting purposes equal to the original price plus all acquisition expenses.

COST ESTIMATING

The process of calculating the approximate construction cost of an improvement through one of several alternative methods.

COST OF LIVING CLAUSE (COL)

A clause found in some leases providing for increases or decreases in the rent in accordance with changes in a price index, commonly the *Consumer Price Index (CPI)*.

COST-PLUS CONTRACT

A type of contract used by contractors in which the owner pays for all labor and material plus a certain percentage of these costs to the contractor as a fee for overhead and profit.

CO-TENANTS

Concurrent ownership by two or more persons of a single estate.   (*See* **Concurrent Ownership**)

COUNCIL OF HOUSING PRODUCERS

An organization comprised of some of the larger housing producers in the United States. The council represents these members in matters related to the production of housing.

COUNCIL OF STATE GOVERNMENTS

This agency is comprised of all 50 state governments. The council conducts research on a number of topics and maintains an information service for its members. The mailing address is P.O. Box 11910, Lexington, Kentucky 40511.

COUNCIL OF STATE HOUSING AGENCIES (CSHA)

Membership in CSHA is limited to state housing finance and development agencies. Associate membership is open to investment bankers, developers, investors, and others involved in state housing programs. The mailing address is 444 North Capital Street, Washington, D.C. 20002; (202) 624-7710.

COUNCIL ON ENVIRONMENTAL QUALITY (CEQ)

A council created under the *National Environmental Policy Act of 1969* to advise the President on environmental policy matters. Also created under the same act was the *Environmental Protection Agency (EPA)*, which has as its purpose the enforcement of environmental laws.

COUNTEROFFER

A reply to an offer to enter into a contract which introduces new terms or conditions and is thus an implied rejection of the original offer. A counteroffer has the legal effect of reversing the position of the original parties. The original offeror is now the new offeree and may accept or reject the counteroffer. (*See* **Offer**)

COUNTY

The largest governmental division for local administration in a state.

COVENANT

A promise contained in a deed by which one of the parties agrees or pledges to the other that something will be done or shall not be done, such as an agreement by the purchaser, (grantee) to restrict the use of the property to single-family residential use. Failure to adhere to a covenant can result in a cause of action for damages as a result of the breach.

COVENANT AGAINST ENCUMBRANCES

A covenant which provides the assurance that no encumbrances other than those specified in the deed exist. For example, if it is later discovered that an unrecorded prescriptive easement exists or that dower rights still cloud the title, the grantee may bring a suit for damages to the extent that the value of the estate has been diminished. Because of this covenant, care should be taken to specify all encumbrances in the drafting of the deed.

COVENANT NOT TO COMPETE
(*See* **Noncompetition Clause**)

COVENANT OF FURTHER ASSURANCE

A promise by a grantor that he or she will perform further acts reasonably necessary to correct any defects in the title or in the deed instrument. For example, if a cloud on title exists because the deed was improperly signed or contains other mistakes, the grantor has agreed by this covenant to give the grantee or the grantee's successor any legal documents necessary to perfect the title.

COVENANT OF QUIET ENJOYMENT

A promise that no one has superior or paramount title to that of the grantor and assurance to the grantee of peaceful possession without fear of being ousted by a person with a superior claim to the property. For example, if the grantee is evicted because an outstanding mortgage given by the grantor has been foreclosed, the grantee would be able to collect damages for breach of this covenant. Quiet enjoyment refers to right of peaceful possession free of hostile title and not to noise or loud neighbors.

COVENANT OF RIGHT TO CONVEY

The assurance that the grantor has the right, power, and authority to convey the title being granted. For example, in the case of a joint tenant or a tenancy by the entirety, this covenant would be violated if an attempt was made to convey the entire estate without the other co-owners joining in the conveyance. This covenant is very similar to the covenant of seizin and in some states both covenants are treated as one under the covenant of seizin.

COVENANT OF SEIZIN (OR SEISIN)

A covenant which gives the assurance that the grantor has the exact estate in the quantity and quality which in fact is being conveyed. For example, if the grantor is attempting to convey a fee simple absolute and in fact only has a fee simple determinable, this covenant would be violated. This is important because a grantor may legally convey only that title which is possessed and no better.

COVENANT OF TRUST

A covenant which makes the seller a trustee of the purchase price funds for the benefit of the buyer until the time for recording *mechanic's and materialman's lien* has expired. If the grantor has failed to pay off contractors and other workers who have performed work on the transferred property, the grantor would be obligated under state penal laws to satisfy any subsequently recorded liens. A covenant of trust has been established by statute in several states to protect the purchaser from unrecorded liens.

COVENANT OF WARRANTY OF TITLE

Sometimes called *warranty forever*, this covenant is the assurance that the grantor will underwrite the legal expenses if any person establishes a claim superior to the title given by the grantor. However, this does not mean that the grantor agrees to indemnify the costs for all court suits involving title, but only for those prior claims which actually put the grantee out of possession. This warranty applies to all claims which existed prior to the grantor's possession as well as those which occurred during it.

COVENANT RUNNING WITH THE LAND

A covenant which goes with the land and cannot be separated from the land nor can the land be transferred without the covenant. For such a covenant to exist, the covenant must be in writing, the intent of the grantor and grantee must have been that the covenant run with the land, subsequent grantees must have notice of the covenant, and the covenant must affect or concern the land with which it runs. An example would be a minimum square footage requirement for residences constructed on the land. (*See* **Restrictive Covenant**)

COVERAGE

In insurance, the extent of risk covered by the insurance policy.

COVERAGE RATIO

The relationship between the net operating income (N.O.I.) of income-producing property and the mortgage payment due the lender. The lender is interested in calculating this ratio in that it shows how much income is available for servicing the mortgage debt. The higher the ratio, the more likely the lender is to make the loan.

CPE

Certified Personalty Evaluator. A professional deisgnation awarded by the International Association of Assessing Officers.

CPM

A professional designation, *Certified Property Manager*, awarded by the Institute of Real Estate Management, an affiliate of the National Association of Realtors.

CRA

Certified Review Appraiser. A professional designation awarded by the National Association of Review Appraisers to persons involved in the appraisal review process.

CRB

A professional designation, *Certified Residential Broker,* awarded by the Realtors National Marketing Institute, an affiliate of the National Association of Realtors.

CRE

A professional designation, *Counselor of Real Estate,* which denotes membership in the American Society of Real Estate Counselors, an affiliate of the National Association of Realtors.

CREATIVE FINANCING

An all-encompassing term used to explain almost any type of financing arrangement undertaken in recent years. With periods of inflation and high interest rates, real estate sellers as well as buyers look for ways to "make the numbers work."

CREDIT

The ability of a person to borrow money. Because of the increased market value of real estate (both residential and income-producing property) the ability to borrow part of the purchase price is very important for most purchasers.

The term credit also refers to something due or to be received as compared to a *debit* which is something owed or payable. A closing statement consists of credits, as well as debits, to the buyer and seller. For example, the sales price of the house is a credit to the seller as the escrow deposit is a credit to the purchaser.

CREDIT APPLICATION

A written form completed by the lender at the time a person makes application for a loan. The information given as well as the verification of that and other pertinent facts are used by the lender as part of the loan decision.

CREDITOR

The person to whom a debt is owed.

CREDIT RATING

A measure of a person's or company's credit worthiness based on past credit history and current financial condition. The ability to borrow money as well as the interest rate one has to pay is largely dependent upon that individual's credit rating. A builder with good credit and a sound history of repaying loans might be able to acquire a construction loan at "prime plus 1 1/2%," whereas someone with a poorer credit rating might have to pay "prime plus 3%."

CREDIT REPORT

A detailed financial history of a person or company used by a lender in determining whether to extend credit.

CREDIT UNION

An organization comprised of members who deposit funds in accounts which generally pay an interest rate somewhat higher than that paid by savings and loan associations or commercial banks. While the majority of loans made by credit unions are consumer loans, some of the more than 16,000 credit unions provide mortgage money for both residential and nonresidential financing. In addition to permanent loans, credit unions also make home improvement loans directly to depositors. Credit unions normally use mortgage brokers to locate real estate investments for their portfolios.

CROSS INDEX

A means of indexing title records by which each party in the conveyance instrument is listed. The index is commonly referred to as a *grantor-grantee index*. (*See* **Grantor-Grantee Index**)

CRS

A professional designation, *Certified Residential Specialist*, awarded by the Realtors National Marketing Institute, an affiliate of the National Association of Realtors.

CRV

(*See* **Certificate of Reasonable Value**)

CUL-DE-SAC

A dead end street with a turnaround at one end. This type of street pattern is becoming increasingly popular in residential developments for two reasons. First, such a pattern allows the developer to make use of land which, because of topography or layout, is not suitable for a connecting street pattern. And second, by using cul-de-sacs, the amount of automobile traffic into such streets is significantly less than with a standard two-way street.

CURABLE DEPRECIATION

A loss in value which when corrected adds more to total value than the cost of the repair. For example, a house being put on the market for sale might be in desperate need of a good cleaning and some touch-up painting. In addition, a water faucet leaks and a door lock is broken. If the total cost of making these corrections, assume $150, is less than the increase in value as a result of correcting them, assume $500, then these items would be considered as curable. In contrast, if the cost of repair is greater than the increase in value as a result of making the repair, the loss in value is considered to be *incurable depreciation*.

CURRENT YIELD

The amount of cash return on an investment, normally expressed as a percentage.

CURTESY

The legal rights that a husband acquires in his wife's property upon her death. Under common law after a wife's death the husband acquired a life estate in all of the wife's property. In order for this right to exist, however, a child had to have been born of the marriage. If a child had not been born, the husband's rights would terminate upon the wife's death. Today, very few states recognize this type of life estate. (*See* **Dower, Legal Life Estate**)

CURTILAGE

The enclosed space of land and buildings surrounding a dwelling unit.

CUSTOM (BUILT) HOME

A dwelling unit containing unique features and amenities in contrast to a tract house which has little, if any, uniqueness. Custom built homes are normally built under contract between the builder and the owner.

DAMAGES

The court-ordered payment a person receives when his or her personal rights or property rights have been violated or injured through an unlawful act or negligence on the part of another. (*See* **Actual Damages, Breach of Contract, Consequential Damages, Liquidated Damages**)

DATE

The mention in a written instrument, such as a sales contract or deed, of the time (day, month, and year) when it was made or when a future event is to occur. Real estate contracts may have more than one date mentioned. For example, the contract could be dated March 19, 1990, which is the date the contract was accepted. In addition, a condition in the contract could say "conditioned upon buyer securing a VA loan within five banking days." Finally, the contract might say "settlement to occur on or before November 6, 1990."

DATE OF APPRAISAL

The day, month, and year as of which the opinion of value, as expressed in the appraisal, is based. Since changes in the value of property can occur very quickly, the date of appraisal is an important part of the appraisal form or report. The inclusion of the date makes it clear to anyone examining the appraisal that the value estimate is as of a specific date.

DATE OF CLOSING
(See **Closing Date***)*

DATUM

A level surface to which the elevations of points used in legal descriptions are referred. Besides the *mean sea level datum* some arbitrarily chosen datum such as a bench mark is often used in surveying work. *(See* **Bench Mark***)*

DEALER

One who holds property for sale to customers. If a person is classified as a dealer for federal income tax purposes, any gain or loss on the exchange or sale of property is treated as ordinary gain or loss and not as capital gain or loss. Dealers also may not take advantage of tax-free exchange rules which can be used by nondealer investors. *(See* **Tax-Free Exchange***)*

DEAD END STREET

A street with only one entrance, the other end being closed.

DEBENTURE (BOND)

A long-term bond or note issued by corporations and governments and not secured by a mortgage or lien on any specific property. Since there is no specific property securing the debenture, the ability to repay the debt is based solely on the financial strength of the issuer.

DEBIT

An amount due or owing, as compared to a *credit* which is an amount due or to be received. Debit entries are made on closing statements to reflect charges made to both parties. For example, the sales price of the property is debited to the purchaser whereas unpaid property taxes would be debited to the seller. If total debits exceed total credits, the difference is owed. Likewise, total credits in excess of total debits would show the amount to be received by the party. *(See* **Closing Statement***)*

DEBT

An obligation of money, goods, or service either in the present or in the future from one person to another.

DEBT COVERAGE RATIO

The relationship between the annual net operating income (N.O.I.) of a property and the annual debt service of the mortgage loan on the property. Lenders and investors calculate the ratio to assist them in determining the likelihood of the property generating enough income to pay the mortgage payments. From the lender's viewpoint, the higher the ratio, the better. For example, an apartment complex with annual net income of $750,000 and annual mortgage payments of $500,000 would have a debt coverage ratio of 1.5:

$$\frac{\$750,000}{\$500,000} = 1.5$$

If, however, due to increases in the vacancy rate and higher operating expenses, the net operating income falls to $550,000, then the debt coverage ratio would only be 1.1:

$$\frac{\$550,000}{\$500,000} = 1.1$$

and a lender would feel less secure in making a loan that would require a $500,000 annual mortgage payment. *(See* **Debt Service, Net Operating Income)**

DEBT EQUITY RATIO

The relationship between the total loan amount owed to the lender(s) and the invested capital of the owner(s). In real estate investments this ratio, also known as the *leverage ratio*, can be very high due largely in part to the loan security of real estate, thus real estate investments are often highly leveraged. Owner-occupied residential real estate typically has a high debt-equity ratio, particularly homes recently purchased. A $100,000 home purchased with $20,000 cash and an $80,000 mortgage would have a debt-equity ratio of 4:1 ($80,000/$20,000). *(See* **Leverage, Loan-to-Value Ratio)**

DEBT FINANCING

The use of borrowed funds, or *other people's money*, to purchase real estate. Also known as *debt capital* as compared to *equity capital*, which is the amount of one's own money used to purchase real estate.

DEBTOR

One who owes debt.

DEBT SERVICE

The periodic payment (monthly, quarterly, annually) necessary to pay the interest and principal on a loan which is being amortized. *(See* **Amortization, Mortgage Constant)**

DEBT SERVICE CONSTANT

(See **Mortgage Constant)**

DEBT-TO-INCOME RATIO

The relationship between a person's periodic (normally monthly) debt and his or her income. While lenders use various rules of thumb in determining the maximum amount of money a person can borrow, the ratio often used is that the total principal, interest, taxes, and insurance *(PITI)* due each month should not exceed 25 to 28 percent of the borrower's monthly gross income.

DECEDENT

A deceased person. One who is deceased with a will is known as a *testator* while a deceased person without a will is said to have died *intestate*.

DECLARATION OF CONDOMINIUM

(*See* **Condominium Declaration**)

DECLARATION OF HOMESTEAD

(*See* **Homestead Exemption**)

DECLARATION OF TRUST

Acknowledgment by a person who holds legal title to property that he or she is holding the property as trustee for someone else or for a specified purpose.

DECLINING-BALANCE DEPRECIATION

An accelerated method of depreciation for tax purposes in which the remaining depreciable balance each year is the base for calculating the subsequent year's depreciation. The result is a faster write-off in the early years than would be possible using a straight-line method of depreciation.

DECREASING ANNUITY

A series of periodic payments or receipts that progressively decline over time.

DECREE

A court order or declaration announcing the legal consequences of the facts.

DECREE OF FORECLOSURE

A court order following the actions of a mortgagee who has a lien against a parcel of real property which states the amount of the outstanding debt and orders the sale of the property with the proceeds being used to satisfy the debt. (*See* **Foreclosure**)

DEDICATION

A donation of property by a property owner to a public authority such as a local government without payment and for a public use. Examples would include roads, schools, and open spaces. The dedication may consist of either the owner's entire fee simple interest or an easement such as a right-of-way to cross the land. (*See* **Subdivision Regulation**)

DEDUCTION

Any ordinary and necessary expense paid or incurred in a taxable year which is related to business or the production of income. Such deductions are in addition to any other deduction permitted by law and depend upon the accounting method used by the taxpayer. Except where specifically authorized by Congress, expenses for personal or family purposes are usually not deductible. A deduction has the effect of reducing the amount of taxable income and thereby reducing a taxpayer's tax liability. If a person owns a house which serves as his or her personal residence, Congress permits mortgage interest, property taxes, and casualty losses as allowable deductions. In addition to these deductions, owners of real estate held for other purposes may be entitled to deductions for maintenance expenses, minor repairs, insurance premiums, and depreciation.

DEED

A written instrument, usually under seal, conveying some property interest from a *grantor* to a *grantee*. A grantor is the person who conveys the property interest; the grantee is the person to whom the grant is made. In order for a deed to be effective in transferring title, it must be in proper legal form and executed as specified by the law in the state in which the property is located. The title is actually transferred the moment the deed is properly delivered to and accepted by the grantee. In order to protect the validity of the title from subsequent innocent third parties purchasing the same property from the original grantor, the deed must be recorded as required by the particular state's recording statute. This also gives assurance to third parties that no one else has good title unless the title has been recorded. This gives *constructive notice* to third parties. When a deed is delivered, all prior oral and written agreements are merged into the deed and are collateral. This means that when a deed is delivered and accepted all prior agreements which are inconsistent with the deed are superseded and have no legal effect. An exception to this rule occurs in cases of fraud and mutual mistake. Another exception exists when the contract specifically provides that the obligations will survive the closing.

Requirements: In order for a conveyance to have legal effect, the deed must be in *proper legal form* and meet other requirements specified by law in the state in which the land is located. The basic requirements for a valid deed in most states include the following:
1. The grantor and grantee must be named.
2. Both grantor and grantee must have legal capacity.
3. Consideration must be recited.
4. An appropriate granting or conveyance clause must be included.
5. The quantity and quality of the property interest must be stated.
6. There must be legally adequate description of the property.
7. The deed must be signed by the grantor and other formalities which are required, such as a seal or witnessing, must be met.
8. There must be delivery and acceptance.
9. In most states in order to be legally effective against innocent third parties the deed must be recorded.

Contents: For the purpose of analysis, a deed may be divided into three sections: (1) the *premises*, (2) the *habendum*, and (3) the *testimonium*.

The Premises

The premises is the introductory section of the deed. Ordinarily, the premises will contain the date that the deed was signed, identification of the parties, a recital of consideration, a granting clause, the legal description, any reservations or exceptions, the recital, any "subject to" clauses, and the conveyance of the appurtenances.

1. *Date*. The date on the deed is the *date of execution* and does not necessarily indicate when title passes. Title is transferred only when the deed is actually delivered and accepted. In some states, "Sunday" laws exist which prohibit transactions on the Sabbath. A deed which is dated on a Sunday will nevertheless be valid if it is delivered on a weekday.

2. *Grantor*. The grantor must be identified with the same name that was used when the title was received as grantee. For example, if the title was received as "George S. Hinds, grantee" it would not be proper to convey property from "G. Sims Hinds, grantor." This might cause a cloud on title since the title examiner could not be certain that "George S. Hinds" and "G. Sims Hinds" are the same person. If the name has been changed because of marriage or other reason, both the new name and the old name should be indicated.

Example: Fanny Hart Brice, formerly Fanny Hart

The grantor should be identified according to marital status. In states that recognize curtesy, dower, homestead, or community property both spouses should join in the grant.

Other state requirements may specify that the grantor's name be followed by the address of the grantor's residence. If the property is in some form of co-ownership, all co-tenants should be indicated and join in the conveyance. The grantor must be of legal capacity.

If the grantor is a guardian, or some other representative, the authority to act should be indicated in the deed. When the deed is recorded, the written authority to act, such as the power of attorney, should also be recorded.

3. *Grantee*. The grantee must be identified and be legally capable of receiving title. A conveyance to a fictitious person, a nonexistent person, or an entity which is not recognized by law is a void conveyance. For example, a conveyance to an unincorporated association or to a deceased person could not take place. The grantee may use a fictitious name so long as he or she exists. However, if the deed is ambiguous as to the identity of the grantee, the deed will be void on account of vagueness.

4. *Consideration*. Except in some states such as Nebraska and Maryland, the actual consideration does not need to be stated if the stated consideration is clearly nominal, e.g., "$10.00 and other valuable considerations." Deeds which are given by fiduciaries such as trustees or executors should state the actual amount of consideration involved.

5. *Granting Clause*. The granting clause contains the operative words of conveyance. Without these words there can be no effective transfer of title through the deed. Care should be taken to use the appropriate words which convey the quantity and quality of title intended. State law generally specifies the words of conveyance that create a certain type of deed such as a warranty deed or a quitclaim deed.

Examples of operative words:
>   A. *Warranty deed*: "Grant, bargain, sell, and convey"
>   B. *Bargain and sale deed*: "Grant, release, bargain and sell"
>   C. *Quitclaim deed*: "Release, remise, convey, and quitclaim"

6. *Legal Description*. A deed that does not sufficiently identify the property to be conveyed is void. The description should be a formal legal description and not just a street address.

7. *Reservation or Exception*. The grantor may wish to limit the estate to be conveyed. A *reservation* creates a right which is retained by the grantor. For example, the grantor might wish to keep a life estate or an easement in the property. This could be done by including a reservation at this point in the deed. An *exception* is an exclusion of a specified portion of the land previously described in the deed. For example, Tom grants a 500-acre farm to Christine except for a quarter-acre family graveyard. (Legal description of the graveyard is included.)

8. *Deed Restrictions*. A deed restriction is a clause which limits the future use of the property granted in some manner. The restriction may be in the nature of a *condition* or a *covenant*. A condition creates a conditional fee such as a fee simple determinable. The breach of a condition can lead to the forfeiture of the estate. In cases of ambiguity, the courts will attempt to interpret a deed restriction as a covenant. A covenant is a contractual promise on the part of the grantee to restrict the use of the granted property in some manner. If a *restrictive covenant* is breached, remedy is restricted to a suit for money damages or injunctive relief. Through restrictive covenants or restrictive conditions it is possible to limit the land-use activities that are permitted, to limit height and density of structure, to require minimum floor area ratios, and other such restrictions. Deed restrictions accomplish the same things for the individual that zoning and subdivision regulations accomplish for local government. If there is a conflict between the application of a zoning restriction and a deed restriction, the more restrictive of the two applies.

Example: Jane grants Hillyvalley, which is zoned R-3, to Anne, with the restrictive covenant that the land must be used for a single-family house. R-3 zoning permits duplexes. Anne may not construct a duplex permitted by the zoning ordinance.

Certain covenants which discriminate against persons on the basis of race or other reasons will not be enforced by the courts because they violate the U. S. Constitution. In order to be enforced, deed restrictions may be included directly in the deed or cited by reference to a previously recorded plat. In addition, the restriction must be reasonable and usually must be limited in time. Many states limit deed restrictions to twenty, thirty, or fifty years.

9. *Recital.* The recital is not mandatory, but is included to give information useful in title examinations. The recital may be used to explain the reason for the transaction or to indicate how the grantor acquired the title.

10. *"Subject-to" Clause.* In a warranty deed, title is assumed to be free and clear of all encumbrances except for those which are specifically stated in the deed. All existing encumbrances and clouds on title would be noted in this portion of the deed. This includes all unrecorded prescriptive easements, encroachments, unpaid tax assessments, and any other specific liens.

11. *Appurtenances.* The premises normally end with the words, "Together with all tenements, hereditaments, and appurtenances thereto belonging or in any wise appertaining." The purpose of this clause is to convey all of the property rights associated with the land. A *tenement* refers to houses, improvements, and other permanent things that go with the land. *Hereditaments* refers to real and personal property which would pass to heirs by inheritance. This is to distinguish chattel real from items which are clearly personal property. *Appurtenances* refers to all incidental rights such as riparian rights or easements which belong with the land.

The Habendum

The Habendum refers to the formal words which define the extent of ownership which is granted.

12. *Habendum.* This is a term which comes from the Latin phrase "habendum et tenendum" which means "to have and to hold." Today a habendum begins with these same words.

13. *Covenants of title.* The covenants of title, which follow the habendum, should be carefully examined to determine the quality of deed which is actually being delivered.

The Testimonium

The testimonium contains the execution, attestation, and acknowledgment of the deed. In addition some states may have additional requirements such as provision for release of a spouse's interest.

14. *Execution.* The execution refers to the signing of the deed by the grantor. Originally the signature of the grantor had to be under *seal*. A seal was an impression in hot wax which was affixed to the document in order to give it the necessary formality. Today the need for wax is no longer present. Seals are impressed on wafers of paper affixed to the deed. Many states recognize the initials L.S. which mean "in place of the seal," or the word, "seal," as a substitute. Other states have no requirement for a seal unless a corporation is the grantor. As a general rule the owner of the property personally signs a deed. However, certain circumstances may require a representative to sign on the owner's behalf. Such a representative is called an *attorney in fact* and derives authority from a *power of attorney*. A power of attorney is a formal statement of authority which is drafted with all of the formalities of a deed. The instrument should clearly specify the

extent of authority being given and contain a legal description of the property which the attorney in fact is authorized to convey. An example of how the agent would sign a deed follows:

John Doe

by Mary Smith
His attorney in fact

15. *Attestation.* Some states require that the deed be witnessed by at least two witnesses, one of whom may need to be an official witness such as a notary. The process of witnessing is called *attestation.* Without the attestation the deed is void in those states that have this requirement. Some deeds may require a witnessing in cases involving grantors who have not learned to write or are paralyzed. Such a handicapped grantor would be required to make a mark or at least a thumbprint which manifests intent to sign. Both the marking and the statement or declaration of intent by the grantor would need to be witnessed.

Example: John Doe   *Example*:   HIS

_____   John X Doe (SEAL)

X   (SEAL)   MARK

HIS MARK

16. *Acknowledgment.* An acknowledgment is necessary to permit recording of important documents such as deeds in the public records. Acknowledgment is required to ensure the authenticity of documents filed. An acknowledgment is a formal witnessing of the grantor's signature by a competent officer such as a notary public or a justice of the peace. The grantor must declare that the deed is a voluntary act; it is the legal obligation of the official to become assured of the true identity of the signer in order to prevent forgeries.

Delivery and Acceptance: In order to be legally effective, a deed must be delivered within the lifetime of the grantor. The deed may be delivered directly to the grantee or placed into escrow. There must be an objective intent to give up present control of the deed. A deed cannot pass title after the grantor's death unless it also meets the state's formalities of a will.

Example: George prepared a deed conveying title to his niece, Frances. He intended that the deed be given to Frances upon his death. After George died, the deed was found among his personal possessions. Because the delivery had not taken place within his lifetime the deed was void and Frances received nothing. It might be noted that George could have achieved a different result by conveying his land to Frances while he was still alive and reserving a life estate for himself.

In order to complete the delivery, the grantee must accept the deed. However, acceptance is ordinarily presumed if the grantee is silent.

Recording and Taxation: Recording is not necessary in order to make an effective conveyance of title. However, if the grantee wishes to have good title against a subsequent third party purchaser to whom the grantor fraudulently conveys the same property, recording is usually essential. Prior to January 1, 1968, there was a requirement for U. S. revenue stamps on deeds at the rate of $.55 per $500. Since the end of this requirement, some states have passed their own requirements for revenue stamps. In order to record a deed these stamps must be attached to the instrument.

DEED BOOKS
Part of the public records found in the county clerk's or recorder's office in which copies of deeds transferring real property in that jurisdiction are recorded. These books are also known as *libers*. (*See* **Liber**)

DEED IN LIEU OF FORECLOSURE
A special purpose deed used by a borrower (mortgagor) who is in default to convey the property to the lender (mortgagee) in order to eliminate the need for a foreclosure. (*See* **Foreclosure**)

DEED IN TRUST
A special purpose deed for carrying out fiduciary purposes in which the real property is conveyed to a trustee in a land trust. The power to sell, lease, mortgage, and so forth are given to the trustee under the provision of the trust agreement. (*See* **Land Trust**)

DEED OF CONFIRMATION
(*See* **Correction Deed**)

DEED OF GIFT
(*See* **Gift Deed**)

DEED OF RECONVEYANCE
A deed used to transfer title from the trustee back to the trustor (borrower) after the outstanding debt has been paid in full. (*See* **Deed of Trust**)

DEED OF RELEASE
A special purpose deed given by lien holders, remaindermen, or mortgagees to relinquish their claims on the property.

DEED OF SURRENDER

A special type of deed used to merge a life estate with a reversion or remainder. (*See* **Conventional Life Estate**)

DEED OF TRUST

A deed to real property which serves the same purpose as a mortgage but instead of two parties, three parties are involved. The third party holds title for the benefit of the lender. The borrower under a note secured by a deed of trust or trust deed is called the *trustor* or in some states the grantor. The lender is called the *beneficiary*. When a loan is made the borrower conveys *naked title* to a third party called the *trustee* who holds the title for the benefit of the lender although the instrument itself may remain in the lender's possession. A state's deed of trust act specifies who may act as a trustee. Some states have created the office of public trustee, while others allow individuals such as attorneys or brokers or entities such as title insurance companies or savings and loan associations to serve in that capacity. As with mortgages, states have title theory and lien theory deeds of trust.

If a note is in default, the trustee may hold a *trustee's sale* or use a court-ordered foreclosure. As procedures differ slightly from state to state, care should be taken to consult the local law. A foreclosure based on a trustee's sale normally takes the following steps:

1. Lender notifies the trustee of the borrower's default in a document called a *beneficiary's notice of default and election to sell*.
2. The trustee files a notice of default in the public records and notifies the borrower of this fact.
3. For a statutory period of time (90 to 180 days depending on the particular state law) the borrower may make good on the default and this will terminate the proceedings. This right is analogous to *equitable redemption* in the mortgage.
4. Once the statutory waiting period has passed, the trustee may begin advertising the sale for a statutory period. After the advertising is placed, but before the actual sale, the borrower may pay off the note plus any accrued interest and expenses incurred by the trustee.
5. After proper advertising the property is put up for bid at public auction in the jurisdiction where the property is located.
6. The successful bidder receives a *trustee's deed* with whatever title the original borrower has possessed. In many states the bidder must be able to produce cash at the sale.

As with mortgages, state rules on statutory redemption differ. One advantage of the deed of trust may be the cutting off or limitation on the statutory redemption period. Foreclosure of a deed of trust by a trustee's sale may be speedier than the process needed to foreclose a mortgage. Care should be taken, however, because some states do not permit deficiency judgments unless there is a judicial foreclosure. When a note or bond is paid off, the lender will deliver the note or bond and the deed of trust to the trustee for cancellation. The trustee then will issue a *trustee's deed of reconveyance* to the borrower. This has the same effect as a mortgage release or satisfaction piece. To clear any clouds on title created by the recording of the deed of trust, the deed of reconveyance may also be recorded.

DEED POLL

A deed made by only one party who binds only himself or herself to the deed.

DEED RESTRICTION

(*See* **Restrictive Covenant**)

DEFAULT

The failure to perform a contractual obligation or duty. Since each party to a contract has a duty to perform as promised, the nondefaulting party has a number of alternative remedies from which to choose. Quite often real estate contracts such as sales agreements, leases, and mortgages specify the act(s) that will result in default as well as the remedies available to the innocent party. (*See* **Breach of Contract, Specific Performance**)

DEFAULT JUDGMENT

A judgment entered by a court against a person who fails to answer a complaint or appear in court at an appointed time.

DEFAULT POINT

(*See* **Break-Even Point**)

DEFAULT RATIO

A ratio used in financial analysis that compares the effective gross income (the rent collected from a project) to the operating expenses plus the debt service. For example, an apartment building with rental income of $200,000, operating expenses of $90,000, and debt service of $70,000 would have a default ratio of $200,000/$160-,000 = 1.25:1. A ratio greater than one means that the debt payment can be made from the rental income generated by the property. However, a default ratio of less than one means the rental income is not enough to pay both the operating expenses and the debt service which could result in the owner/investor defaulting on the mortgage(s). Thus the higher the ratio the more likely a lender will provide the financing necessary to fund the project.

DEFEASANCE CLAUSE

A provision found in a mortgage which "defeats" the passing of title to the lender (mortgagee) had the borrower (mortgagor) not met the terms and conditions specified in the mortgage. When the debt is repaid this clause nullifies any interest the lender may have had in the property. Typical wording of a defeasance clause would be as follows:

"Provided, however, if the said mortgagor, his heirs, personal representatives, or assignees, shall make or cause to be made the payments, and perform and comply with the covenants and conditions herein mentioned on his part to be made and done, then this mortgage shall be void." (*See* **Mortgage, Title Theory States**)

DEFEASIBLE

Subject to be revoked or defeated upon the occurrence of a future event or the performance of a condition subsequent, generally used in regard to rights and interests in real estate. For example, a lender's (mortgagee's) interest in a certain parcel is defeated or defeasible by the borrower (mortgagor) exercising his or her equity of redemption.

DEFEASIBLE FEE TITLE

(*See* **Fee Simple Determinable**)

DEFECT OF RECORD

Any lien, claim or encumbrance on a particular piece of real estate that has been properly recorded in the public records. Recorded defects impair clear title and may result in the title being unmarketable. (*See* **Clear Title**)

DEFENDANT

The person against whom a lawsuit has been brought or against whom recovery is sought by the plaintiff.

DEFERRED ANNUITY

A series of periodic payments or receipts that begin at some point in the future.

DEFERRED CHARGES

In accounting, expenditures for intangible assets, such as mortgage placement fees or property leasing commissions, that are to be written off over the life of the service provided.

DEFERRED INCOME

Income to be received in the future. (*See* **Installment Sale**)

DEFERRED INTEREST MORTGAGE

A financing technique in which a lower interest rate and thus a lower monthly mortgage payment is charged. Upon the selling of the property the lender receives the deferred interest plus a specified fee for postponing the interest that would normally have been paid each month. This type of mortgage is particularly aimed at those people who only plan to keep the property for a short period of time.

DEFERRED LIABILITY

A debt that need not be paid currently. Accelerated depreciation frequently causes a deferred income tax liability for income-producing property.

DEFERRED MAINTENANCE

Inadequate repair and upkeep of a building which results in physical depreciation and loss in value. Examples would include failure to paint or inadequate servicing of the heating and cooling systems. (*See* **Physical Deterioration**)

DEFERRED-PAYMENT SALE

(*See* **Installment Sales**)

DEFICIENCY

The lack of an item or its inadequate capacity.

DEFICIENCY JUDGMENT

A personal claim based on a court order against a borrower (mortgagor) for the difference between what is owed the lender (mortgagee) and the amount realized following a foreclosure on the property. The deficiency occurs when the property fails to sell at foreclosure for a price which covers the outstanding mortgage amount. Some mortgages, particularly commercial loans, are written so that the lender has recourse only against the property (*nonrecourse mortgage*) and thus, if the property fails to sell at foreclosure for the amount owed, no personal judgment can be brought against the borrower.

DEFLATION

A decline in the general level of prices.

DEGREE

A land surveying measurement denoting 1/360th part of a circle. The term is used in metes and bounds method of surveying and is denoted by the symbol "°", as in 90°. (*See* **Metes and Bounds**)

DELINQUENCY DATE

A specific time after which a penalty is incurred for nonpayment of a debt. In real estate lending, promissory notes normally have a due date, typically the first day of each month, and a delinquency date, normally sometime between the tenth and the fifteenth.

DELINQUENCY RATIO

A ratio used by commercial banks and other lenders to denote the number of overdue loans relative to the total loans being serviced.

DELIVERY

The formal surrender of control or ownership of something to someone else. Legal documents such as deeds and mortgages do not become valid until they have been delivered and accepted. What constitutes delivery depends upon the intent of the parties. For a deed, there must be an objective intent on the part of the grantor to give up present control of the deed. (*See* **Acceptance, Deed**)

DELTA

A land survey term denoting the angle between two intersection lines. The angle is generally shown on a metes and bound description by the Greek "Δ", as for example, $\Delta = 90°$. (*See* **Metes and Bounds**)

DEMAND

An economic term commonly used to denote a qualified buyer(s) who is ready, willing, and able to make a purchase. For example, a builder might say "There is a great deal of demand in this city for condominiums priced between $70,000 and $85,000." What the builder is saying is that he or she believes people would buy condominiums selling in that price range.

DEMAND DEPOSIT

Funds on deposit with banks which are subject to immediate withdrawal by the depositor(s). Commonly known as *checking accounts*, demand deposits are different from time deposits, commonly referred to as savings accounts, which require the depositor to wait a specified period of time before withdrawing or else pay a penalty for early withdrawal.

DEMISE

A conveyance of an estate to someone for life, for a certain number of years, or at will by means of a lease. The word demise is synonymous with "lease" or "let" and use of the word in a lease implies a covenant for quiet enjoyment which means the landlord (lessor) guarantees that the tenant (lessee) will not be disturbed by someone having superior claims against the property. (*See* **Lease**)

DEMISED PREMISES

The part of a property which is leased to a tenant. (*See* **Lease**)

DEMOGRAPHY

The study of populations with respect to density and distribution. Demographic information is of particular importance to people involved in market analysis and highest and best use analysis in determining potential land uses of a particular site.

DEMOLITION LOSS

A tax deduction which may be taken under certain circumstances when an improvement is voluntarily demolished. No deduction may be taken if there was an intent to demolish the building at the time the property was acquired. If the building is used in trade or business or for production, and a decision is made to demolish the building after acquisition, then the taxpayer will ordinarily be entitled to the demolition loss deduction.

DENSITY

The number of buildings or persons occupying a certain area of land, generally an acre. For example, if a certain zoning district is zoned R-2, then the maximum density permitted in that district would be two units or houses per acre.

DEPARTMENT OF HOUSING AND URBAN DEVELOPMENT (HUD)

A federal agency actively engaged in housing programs and related activities including urban renewal, model cities, block grants, public housing and subsidy programs. The *Federal Housing Administration (FHA)*, the *Government National Mortgage Association (GNMA)*, and the *Office of Interstate Land Sales Registration* are all under HUD's jurisdiction.

DEPARTMENT STORE

A large store divided into sections or departments selling a wide range and variety of products. Local department stores are often used as anchor tenants in shopping centers. (*See* **Anchor Tenant**)

DEPENDENCY, PRINCIPLE OF

An economic principle which states that the use and thus the value of a particular parcel of land can change as a result of modifications of other parcels or other changes in the land-use pattern or environment. (*See* **Spillover Effect**)

DEPLETION

A tax deduction which may be taken by taxpayers who own property interests in extractive industries such as mines, oil, gas, or other natural deposits.

DEPOSIT

Money offered by a prospective purchaser to indicate his or her good faith in entering into a sales contract. If the sale is completed then the deposit is credited to the purchaser and applied towards the purchase price. However, if the purchaser defaults then the deposit is normally kept by the seller as liquidated damages. Depending upon the terms of the listing agreement, the seller may split the deposit with the listing broker. Default by the seller results in all of the deposit being returned to the purchaser, with the broker having no legal claim to any of the money. (*See* **Earnest Money, Escrow, Liquidated Damages**)

DEPOSIT INSURANCE ACT

A federal act enacted during the Great Depression creating the *Federal Deposit Insurance Corporation (FDIC)* to insure deposits of member commercial banks. (*See* **Federal Deposit Insurance Corporation**)

DEPOSIT INSURANCE CORPORATION

(*See* **Federal Deposit Insurance Corporation**)

DEPOSIT OF TITLE-DEEDS

The placing of title-deeds to land in the hands of a lender for the purpose of securing a loan.

DEPOSITION

The testimony of a witness taken outside of court for the purpose of using the testimony during a trial.

DEPRECIABLE BASIS

The amount on which depreciation deductions are based for income tax purposes. Allocation must be made between land and improvements, since ordinarily only the improvements to and on the land may be depreciated. For example, if a taxpayer purchases an apartment building for $550,000, a determination must be made as to how much of the purchase price is attributable to the land and how much to the building. The taxpayer must be able to justify the allocation made.

DEPRECIABLE LIFE

The estimated economic useful life of a depreciable asset such as a building. Depreciable life is not a measure of how long the building will remain standing, but rather how long the improvements are expected to provide an economic return. As an analogy, automobiles may last for decades, but the cost and annoyance of repairs and the modern equipment of newer cars gives most automobiles a short useful life. Improvements to real estate are long-lasting, but without renovation, they steadily march to the junkyard.

DEPRECIATED COST

In taxation, the cost new minus any depreciation taken.

DEPRECIATION (ACCOUNTING)

A method of allocating the cost of a wasting asset over its estimated useful life. For income tax purposes, depreciation is a provision for the estimated wear and tear of an asset. Depreciation deductions can be claimed as a tax deduction on real estate improvement (not land), regardless of whether the market indicates an increase or decrease in the value of the property. To claim depreciation on an income tax return, a bookkeeping entry is required, not a cash payment. In many real estate investment situations, depreciation deductions are of significant value. The deductions reduce income taxes without a cash payment. However, there will be a day of reckoning. Ultimately, the tax implications catch up with the real economic situation. Depreciation deductions serve to reduce the adjusted tax basis of property; so, upon a resale, there will be a greater capital gain on which a tax is due. Most investors prefer to enjoy substantial amounts of current depreciation deductions in the face of a future tax because of (1) the time value of money, and (2) the possibility of lower tax rates upon resale. Lower tax rates may be due to more favorable capital gains rates, or planning the sale to occur in a tax year when there are off-setting losses. The time value of money implies that taxpayers would rather pay taxes later than now. It is like getting an interest-free loan from the U. S. Government. (*See* **Accelerated Depreciation, Depreciable Life, Depreciation Methods**)

DEPRECIATION/AMORTIZATION RATIO

The relationship between depreciation deductions and mortgage principal payments for income-producing property. Depreciation claimed for income purposes allows a tax deduction without a cash payment. Mortgage payments that apply toward principal reduction require an actual cash payment but are not deductible for income tax purposes, so they have an opposite effect. Since all other operating expenses such as maintenance and property tax are tax-deductible, the difference between the depreciation claimed for tax purposes and the mortgage principal payments is clearly reflected in taxable income. Thus, any excess of depreciation over mortgage principle payments in a taxable year will cause some of the before-tax cash flow (cash throw-off) to be tax-free. When the principal amortization payment equals depreciation, all of the cash throw-off will be taxable. Should the principal amortization payments exceed depreciation, taxable income will exceed cash throw-off. Replacement reserves require cash payments but are not tax-deductible; thus, they must be added to the mortgage amortization payments when estimating the relationship of taxable income to cash throw-off.

DEPRECIATION (APPRAISAL)

A loss in utility, and hence value, from any cause. In the cost approach to value, the depreciation factor attempts to make adjustments between the attributes of the selected building, as if it were new, and the subject property's physical condition and economic setting. It is a way of adjusting the hypothetical new structure on which the cost estimate was based and distinguishing it from the subject property. An appraiser may estimate depreciation through observation and/or by applying a formula based on the effective age and remaining life of each component of the property. The indirect method of estimating depreciation is to subtract values for the property, estimated from the market or income approach (or both), from the reproduction cost of the subject property, plus the value of the land. The difference obtained is the total depreciation sustained. For example, if reproduction cost plus the land at market value is $750,000, and both market and income approaches yield a value of $500,000, then the $250,000 difference is

accrued depreciation. A direct method is to estimate each type of depreciation for each component of the property that is being appraised. The three types of depreciation to be recognized are:
1. *Physical deterioration* (wear and tear)
2. *Functional obsolescence* (becoming outmoded)
3. *Economic obsolescence* (due to changes outside the subject property)

(*See* **Economic Obsolescence, Functional Obsolescence, Physical Deterioration**)

DEPRECIATION METHODS

Those methods allowed for depreciating real estate improvements (not the land) as prescribed by the *Internal Revenue Code.*

DEPRECIATION RECAPTURE

A provision contained in the *Internal Revenue Code* that makes excess depreciation taken on real property subject to income tax upon the sale or disposition of the property.

DEPTH TABLE

A table showing the percentage relationship between the depth of a lot being appraised and the value as compared to values indicated by a standard lot in the market. Such tables are sometimes used by appraisers and tax assessors in estimating the value of a particular parcel of land. Several rules of thumb for depth adjustment have been developed. Among the more common are the *4-3-2-1 rule*, the *Hoffman rule*, the *Hoffman-Neill rule*, the *parabolic formula*, and the *Milwaukee rule*. Little reliance can be placed on these rules without first testing market behavior. In some markets very little price differentiation exists between different-sized lots within acceptable rates. In other markets prices may be affected by size. A much preferable approach is the use of linear or multiple regression. This is a statistical technique used to calculate the mathematical relationships between variables. It requires the use of large numbers of data points to provide reliability. Using one of many calculators currently available, the appraiser can use regression to determine the existence of a relationship between lot depth and sales price. (*See* **4-3-2-1 Rule, Hoffman Rule, Hoffman-Neill Rule, Parabolic Formula**)

DERELICTION

A process by which water gradually recedes, leaving dry land where water previously was. (*See* **Accretion**)

DERIVATIVE CONVEYANCE

A conveyance of property which presupposes that a conveyance of the property has previously occurred. Such a conveyance only serves to alter or confirm the interest originally conveyed. (*See* **Conveyance**)

DESCENT

The transfer of title to property upon the death of the owner who has died without a will (*intestate*) to those heirs related by blood or marriage, whom the law designates. If a person dies intestate the disposition of the person's property will pass as defined by state laws called *statutes of descent and distribution*. Real estate will pass directly to a person's heirs as defined by the state law in which the real estate is located subject to the debts of the decedent. A court in the state where the decedent lived will appoint a person called an *administrator* to dispose of the property of the estate. The administrator will collect the assets of the estate, pay debts and distribute the remainder. The administrator is usually required to put up a bond and may sell that real property which is necessary to pay off the estate's debts if the sale of personal property produces insufficient proceeds. The real estate remains charged with debts of the estate until the state's statute of limitations has run. States have different rules as to who receives property of the decedent. For example, depending on the state, a wife might receive half the property, the same share as the children, a dower's share, or the entire property. (*See* **Curtesy, Dower, Testate**)

DESCRIPTION

The part of a deed, mortgage, sales contract, or other such legal instruments which identifies the real estate involved in the transfer. When land is conveyed from one party to another the instrument of conveyance needs to contain a *legally sufficient description* of the parcel. Courts have interpreted this to mean that property is sufficiently described if a competent civil engineer or surveyor could locate the subject property given the land description. Since no two parcels of land could ever be exactly alike in location, each parcel requires a unique description. A legal instrument, such as a deed, which does not have a legally sufficient description is void and not enforceable. (*See* **Government Survey Method, Lot and Block, Metes and Bounds, Monument, Street Address**)

DESIGNATED REAL ESTATE BROKER

An officer of a corporation who has been designated by the corporation as its broker of record. The person so designated must meet the minimum qualifications for acquiring and maintaining a broker's license and is responsible for the corporation's real estate brokerage activities.

DETACHED SINGLE-FAMILY HOME

A free-standing structure designed for one family unit.

DETERIORATION

A loss in value due to wear and tear by action of either the natural elements or use of the property. (*See* **Physical Deterioration**)

DETERMINABLE FEE
(*See* **Fee Simple Determinable**)

DEVELOPER

One who does whatever is necessary to transform an undeveloped tract of land into parcels ready for construction. This could mean acquiring a 100-acre tract of land from a farmer, subdividing the large parcel into one-half acre tracts, putting in roads, curbs, gutters, sewers, and water mains and then selling the individual lots to either builders or private individuals who in turn construct houses on the lots. Land development can also involve commercial property such as the development of a large shopping district or industrial property such as an industrial park.

DEVELOPMENT LOAN

A loan to fund the cost of converting an undeveloped tract of land into parcels ready for construction. Such loans, intended to be short-term, are normally tied to the prime rate and are made by lenders expecting repayment when the improvements to the land are completed.

DEVELOPMENT RIGHTS

The rights to improve or develop land that are sold or given by one property owner to another. (*See* **Transfer of Development Rights**)

DEVISE

Transferring title to real property by means of a will. In order to make a valid formal will a person must be of statutory age, generally eighteen or twenty-one in most states, although some states set the age as low as fourteen. In addition, the person must be of "sound mind" at the time of the execution of the will. A formal will must be in writing, which may be typed, printed, or handwritten. Real estate must be described with sufficient certainty, but it is not required that a complete legal description be included. A formal will must be signed. In addition, states impose a strict requirement that the will be witnessed. Some states recognize nonwitnessed wills called *holographic wills*. A holographic will is one which is entirely handwritten. Such a will is valid only in some jurisdictions and there only if it is free from suspicion of fraud or other defects. In addition many states recognize *nuncupative wills*. A nuncupative will is an oral will which a terminally ill testator or testatrix declares before qualified witnesses. This will must be reduced to writing within a statutorily prescribed time period in order to be admitted into probate. Unlike a deed which cannot be changed or withdrawn by a grantor after it has been delivered and accepted, a will may be changed or revoked by the testator at any time during his or her lifetime. A will may be changed by making out a new will or by drafting a *codicil* to a will. A codicil is a supplement or addition to the original will and must be executed with the same formality. Any attempt to modify the original will by crossing out a provision will not ordinarily be effective. The courts may view such as alteration as a revocation of the will.

DEVISEE

The person to whom real property is given by will.

DEVISOR

A giver of real property by means of a will; also known as a *testator*.

DIMINISHED UTILITY

(*See* **Accrued Depreciation**)

DIMINISHING RETURNS, POINT OF

The point in time or production where returns fail to increase in proportion to additional investments of labor, capital, management, or land.

DIPLOMAT CLAUSE

A provision included in a lease allowing for immediate termination of the lease when the tenant, who is a diplomat of a foreign government, is transferred to another country.

DIRECT CAPITALIZATION

A method of capitalizing income based on dividing net operating income by a rate of return derived by analyzing similar properties and comparing their net income to their selling price. Also known as the *overall capitalization rate*, this approach takes into account the unique operating characteristics of each property. The table below illustrates how an appraiser could have derived an indicated overall rate from recent sales.

OVERALL CAPITALIZATION RATES DERIVED FROM MARKET

Sales Comparable	Date	Net Operating Income	Sales Price	Overall Rate
A	3/23/90	$ 324,000	$ 2,700,000	= .120
B	2/17/90	$ 960,500	$ 8,500,000	= .113
C	4/ 8/90	$1,180,000	$10,000,000	= .118
D	1/25/90	$ 827,640	$ 6,840,000	= .121
E	2/14/90	$1,470,600	$12,900,000	= .114

After examining the data, the appraiser determines that Sales Comparable D is most like the subject property. Even though an average of the five capitalization. rates indicate 11.7%, most weight is given to D, and a rate of 12% is selected.

DIRECT COSTS

Costs directly associated with the physical construction of a project, such as steel, brick, lumber, and labor.

DIRECTIONAL GROWTH

The direction towards which a city or area tends to be growing. Land values, and thus the uses to which land is put, are directly affected by the direction the growth takes.

DIRECT REDUCTION LOAN

(*See* **Amortized Loan**)

DIRECT SALES COMPARISON APPROACH

A means of estimating value by compiling recent sales of comparable properties to the subject property after making appropriate adjustment for any difference. Also known as the *market (sales) approach*, this method is effective in an active market in which sales comparables can be identified and information collected. The comparable properties selected should be substantially similar to the subject property and should be arms-length transactions. However, since each comparable will probably be different from the subject property in terms of location, condition of sale, amenities, time of sale, etc., adjustments must be made in the comparison process in order to derive a value for the subject property. The principal factors for which adjustments will normally be made can be divided into four categories: (1) *date of sale*, (2) *location*, (3) *physical condition* and *features*, and (4) *terms* or *conditions of sale*. This adjustment process involves the adding and subtracting of dollars for those items where the comparable properties differ from the subject property. The dollar value of a feature present in the subject property but not present in the comparables is *added* while the dollar value of a feature present in the comparables but not present in the subject property is *subtracted*. The total adjustment for each factor when either added or subtracted will provide for an adjusted sales price for each comparable. The adjusted sales price of each comparable represents a value range of the subject property. A weighted average or straight average is often used to derive the indicated value of the subject property. It should be noted that an appraiser must use his or her judgment and experience to determine how much weight to place on each adjusted comparable.

DISAFFIRM

To disclaim or refuse consent previously given. For example, most contracts entered into by a minor are voidable at the minor's option and thus the minor has the ability to disaffirm the contract any time before reaching the age of majority. (*See* **Contract**)

DISASTER LOAN

A loan either made or guaranteed by a governmental agency to owners of property which has been damaged or destroyed as a result of such natural disasters as floods, riots, or earthquakes.

DISBURSEMENT

A cash expenditure for the purpose of settling a debt.

DISCLAIMER

Rejection or refusal of a legal claim, power, or property. In real estate, a disclaimer would be the refusal by a party to accept an estate which had been conveyed to him or her.

DISCLOSED PRINCIPAL

A kind of principal in a principal-agent relationship whose identity is known to the third person before the third person enters into contractual relationships negotiated by the agent. Under such a principal-agent relationship the agent is not considered liable under the contract in the absence of personal wrongdoing. Most real estate transactions involve a disclosed principal. (*See* **Agency**)

DISCLOSURE STATEMENT

A written statement required under the *National Consumer Credit Protection Act*, referred to as the *Truth-in-Lending Act*, to be given by a lender to individual borrowers for certain types of consumer loans. All real estate lending transactions involving consumers are covered, as is all credit extended in five or more installments and not in excess of $25,000 for personal, family, household, or agricultural purposes. Two important disclosures included are the *finance charge* and the *annual percentage rate (APR)*. (*See* **Truth-in-Lending Law**)

DISCOUNT

The amount of money paid at the front end to acquire a loan. This amount is deducted from the principal at the time the loan is made and thus represents interest paid in advance. The discount is normally stated in terms of *points* or percent. For example, a 3 percent discount on a $50,000 loan would be $1,500, which would result in the borrower receiving $48,500 ($50,000 - $1,500) but having to repay the full $50,000. This type of activity is particularly common during periods of tight money when as a result of either artificial constraints, such as VA rates set by the federal government, or uncertainty of the future, lenders anticipate selling off the loans they are originating. If a difference exists between the face value of the loan and the loan's market value, the lender may require a certain amount of money be paid at the front end of the loan period. (*See* **Discount Points**)

DISCOUNT CENTER

A type of retail store offering a wide variety of general consumer merchandise such as clothing, household supplies, toys, and automobile supplies. Such stores often serve as anchor tenants for strip centers.

DISCOUNTED CASH FLOW (DCF)

A technique used by appraisers/investors to convert income anticipated in the future into a present worth or value. A particular discount rate or present value factor is applied to the cash flow expected each year over the life of the investment. The result is a series of reversions which when added together estimates the total present value of the cash flow stream.

DISCOUNTED CASH FLOW AT 15%

YEAR	CASH FLOW	PRESENT VALUE FACTOR AT 15%		AMOUNT AT PRESENT VALUE
1	$10,000	.8696	=	$ 8,696
2	12,000	.7561	=	9,073
3	13,000	.6575	=	8,548
4	15,000	.5718	=	8,577
5	15,000	.4972	=	7,458
6	16,000	.4323	=	6,917
7	18,000	.3759	=	6,766
8	20,000	.3269	=	6,538
9	23,000	.2843	=	6,539
10	25,000	.2472	=	6,180

TOTAL PRESENT VALUE $75,292

DISCOUNTED MORTGAGE

A mortgage sold below the amount of the remaining principal balance in order to provide a satisfactory yield to the purchasing mortgage investor.

DISCOUNTED RATE OF RETURN

(*See* **Discounted Cash Flow**)

DISCOUNTING

The process of converting investment inflows to a present value. Since money has a time value, one dollar to be received in the future is worth less than one dollar now. How much less (the amount of discount) depends on: (1) the time span between the cash outflow and inflow, and (2) the necessary rate of interest or discount. For example, at a 10% rate of interest (discount rate), $100.00 that is expected to be received one year from now has a present value of $90.91. As a check on the arithmetic, if an investor has $90.91 now and can earn 10% during the next year, the interest will amount to $9.09; so with the interest added, the principal in one year will be $100.00 ($90.91 + $9.09 = $100.00). An investor who expects to receive $100.00 in two years and pays $82.64 now will receive a 10% annual rate of interest. As a check, after one year, $82.64 will grow to $90.91 with 10% interest, then to $100.00 in two years. An application of this technique in real estate would be the problem of estimating the amount to pay today for land that is expected to be resold in the future at a gain. For example, an investor expecting to resell certain property in two years for $10,000 is faced with the problem of how much to offer for the land today. If the investor requires a 10% annual rate of return on capital invested, the maximum offer would be $8,264. A price lower than that will result in a higher rate of return on investment. Conversely, a higher price would prevent achievement of the 10% annual required rate of return.

DISCOUNT POINTS

A fee charged by a lender at closing or settlement that results in increasing the lender's effective yield (internal rate of return) on the money borrowed. Each discount point represents a one-time charge by the lender equal to 1% of the loan principal. Often sellers pay these point to comply with government regulations since by law the buyer cannot pay discount points on VA mortgages. Why would third persons want to pay discount points if the loan is actually being given to the borrower and not to themselves? The third person usually stands to benefit from the loan indirectly. For example, the third person might be a seller, and the borrower might be a purchaser of a house. Without the loan, the transaction might not take place. How do discount points increase the effective yield to the lender? First, consider what would happen without discount points. Assume a lender makes a loan of $1,000 at 11%. Over the term of the loan, the lender would receive interest at 11% effective yield plus repayment of the original principal of $1,000. With discount points the following would happen:

Example: Assume the third person must pay four (4) discount points in order for the lender to make the same $1,000 loan. The lender would given $1,000 to the borrower but would receive $40 back from the third person.

How much did the lender actually lend? $1,000 - $40 = $960

How much must the borrower pay back? $1,000

This means the bank receives 11% interest on $1,000 even though it only lent $960. Further, since it will receive back $1,000 instead of $960, it makes an additional $40 over the life of the loan. If the loan is paid off over a period of 30 years, this will increase the effective yield of the loan from the nominal rate of 11% to an effective rate of 11.5%. In other words, as a rule of thumb, each discount point paid will increase the effective yield by 1/8 of one percent over the full term of the loan. Or in order to increase the yield by 1/2 of one percent, four (4) discount points should be charged; or to increase the yield by one full percent, eight (8) discount points should be charged. What happens if the loan is paid off early? In that case, the lender's yield increases. The table below shows what happens to the lender's yield if a loan is paid off early. You will notice the rule of thumb does not work with short loan terms such as one or two years.

INTERNAL RATE OF RETURN

Thirty year loan payable in equal monthly installments
Interest rate on original loan = 11%
Rate of return is annual rate compounded monthly

	Payout Time from Origination				
Points	6 Months	12 Months	36 Months	60 Months	360 Months

RATE OF RETURN

Points	6 Months	12 Months	36 Months	60 Months	360 Months
1	13.08	12.07	11.40	11.27	11.13
2	15.18	13.15	11.80	11.53	11.26
3	17.31	14.24	12.21	11.81	11.39
4	19.47	15.35	12.62	12.08	11.52
5	21.65	16.47	13.04	12.36	11.66
6	23.86	17.60	13.46	12.64	11.80
7	26.10	18.75	13.88	12.93	11.94
8	28.36	19.91	14.32	13.22	12.08
9	30.67	21.08	14.75	13.51	12.23
10	32.99	22.27	15.20	13.81	12.38

DISCOUNT RATE

The rate of interest charged by the *Federal Reserve System* to banks who borrow money from the Federal Reserve. An increase in the rate not only discourages banks from borrowing, but it also serves as a signal to the money market that interest rates are probably going to increase. Accordingly, interest rates charged by banks to their customers usually increase as a result of an increase in the discount rate. (*See* **Federal Reserve System**)

DISCOUNT REAL ESTATE BROKER

A licensed real estate broker who charges a lower sales commission than normally charged in exchange for the seller performing some of the activities normally performed by the broker. A discount broker may charge as little as one or two percent commission if the seller agrees to, for example, be available to show the house to potential buyers and pay the advertising expenses normally incurred by the broker.

DISCRIMINATION

Failure to treat all people equally. It is the stated policy of the federal government to eradicate discrimination in real estate markets. Two major laws which have been enacted by Congress are of particular concern. The first law is the *Federal Fair Housing Act of 1968* which was passed as *Title VIII of the Civil Rights Act of 1968.* As originally passed, the act prohibited discrimination in the sale or rental of residential dwelling units or vacant land intended to be used as such on the basis of race, color, religion or national origin. Discrimination on the basis of sex was prohibited by an amendment to the *Housing and Community Development Act of 1974.* The *Fair Housing Amendments Act of 1988* bars discrimination on the basis of a handicap or because there are children in a family. The second law is the *Civil Rights Act of 1866.* This law, passed after the Civil War, provided that "all citizens of the United States shall have the same right, in every State and Territory, as is enjoyed by white citizens thereof to inherit, purchase, lease, sell, hold, and convey real and personal property." This law prohibits discrimination in all real estate transactions based on race. In 1968, this law was revived and given substance by the U. S. Supreme Court in the case of *Jones v. Alfred H. Mayer Co.,* 392 U. S. 409 (1968). In this case the court prohibited any racially motivated refusal to sell or rent property. The case involved a refusal of a builder to sell a house to a black person in 1965. Three years later the builder was ordered to sell a house to the injured party at 1965 prices and to absorb the price difference. In other cases the Supreme Court ruled that the two laws are to be given very broad construction in order to accomplish the national goal of fair housing for everyone. This interpretation is important because it makes it more difficult to disprove allegations that a broker has violated the provisions of the laws. Hence, the broker must use extreme care not to give even the appearance of violating the intent of the laws. A broker may not defend on the basis that his or her principal instructed the discriminatory action or that it was the principal who was practicing the discrimination. Further, a principal cannot defend for discriminatory acts performed by a broker on the basis that the broker was an independent contractor. (*See* **Civil Rights Act of 1866, Federal Fair Housing Act of 1968**)

DISINTERMEDIATION

The withdrawing of funds from financial institutions by depositors who in turn invest directly into short-term financial instruments, such as treasury bills and commercial paper. Such activity occurs when the interest rate paid on these short-term instruments is higher than the rate(s) offered by savings and loan associations, mutual banks, and commercial banks. The result is less mortgage money available for loans, since the short-term instruments being purchased are normally not made available for real estate loans.

DISPOSSESS

The removal or eviction of someone from real estate through legal action.

DISPOSSESS PROCEEDINGS

Legal action undertaken by a landlord to remove a tenant and regain possession of the property for breaking a condition or term of the lease such as nonpayment of rent.

DISTRAINT

The taking by a landlord of personal property belonging to the tenant to satisfy past-due rents. Under common law a landlord had the right to seize the tenant's property on the premises and to sell or hold the property to satisfy a claim for rent. Today, a court action is required and the priority of the landlord's lien will depend upon local law.

DISTRESS

The common law right of a landlord to seize the personal property of a tenant to satisfy past-due rent. (*See* **Distraint**)

DISTRESSED PROPERTY

Real estate which must be sold due to a pending mortgage foreclosure.

DIVISION WALL

(*See* **Party Wall**)

DOCUMENT

An official paper establishing facts or giving instructions.

DOCUMENTARY STAMP

A tax levied by some local and state governments at the time legal instruments such as deeds and mortgages are entered into public record. Prior to January 1, 1968, there was a requirement for U. S. revenue stamps on deeds at the rate of $.55 per $500.

DOG

A parcel of real estate that is very difficult to sell due to location, condition, or design. Such property normally remains on the market for an extended period of time and may sell at substantially below the listing price.

DOMICILE

The legal residence of a person. A person has only one domicile, which is the place to which he or she intends to return, even though he or she may now reside someplace else.

DOMINANT ESTATE

The tract of land that benefits as a result of an easement on a servient estate. (*See* **Easement**)

DONEE

The recipient of a gift.

DONOR

The giver of a gift.

DOUBLE-DECLINING BALANCE DEPRECIATION

In accounting, an accelerated depreciation method restricted to certain qualified properties. The method calculates depreciation at twice the rate of the straight-line method on a balance that is reduced each year as the depreciation is taken. Also known as *200% declining balance depreciation* and *DDB depreciation*. (*See* **Depreciation**)

DOUBTFUL TITLE

A situation in which there exists some doubt as to the validity of title and thus a court will not force a purchaser to accept title. In contrast, a court will compel a purchaser to accept a *marketable title* when the purchaser has previously agreed to buy the property. (*See* **Title**)

DOWER

A legal life estate, recognized in some states, that a wife acquires in her husband's fee simple property. Conventionally, this right was a life estate in one-third of all the property that the husband owned at any time during the marriage. While the husband was alive this right was *inchoate* or an expectancy. This expectancy could not be defeated by the husband by sale or mortgage. In order to convey property which was freed from the dower interest, the wife had to sign a *release*. When the husband died, the wife's interest was called *consummate*, and she was entitled to one-third of the property to be held in life estate, despite any will provisions which sought to dispose of the property otherwise. Many states have abolished dower because of the uncertainty this right has placed on title assurance. Other states have created substitutes such as community property or a statutory share in lieu of dower. Some states give the widow a one-year's support which could conceivably tie up all of the husband's estate until the right was exercised. Other states give the widow 25 percent to 50 percent of the estate. However, if the husband sells his property before his death then there will be nothing for the wife to receive under the statutory share. In some states the husband as well as the wife is entitled to dower rights. (*See* **Curtesy, Legal Life Estate**)

DOWN PAYMENT

The amount of cash paid by a purchaser which when added to the mortgage amount equals the total sales price. At the time of closing this is referred to as the purchaser's *equity*.

DOWNSIDE RISK

The probability that an investor may lose the money he or she has invested in a particular venture.

DOWNZONING

Action by a local government to reduce the allowable density for a parcel of land, as for example, from apartment to single-family residential. *(See* **Zoning***)*

DRAGNET CLAUSE

A clause included in a mortgage instrument which extends the lien of the mortgage to any and all other debts, both past and future, of the borrower. *(See* **Mortgage***)*

DRAIN

A ditch or other means by which water flows off land. A landowner may not obstruct or divert the natural drain of water to the detriment of another landowner.

DRAW

An advance of money, as for example the periodic receipt of money by a builder from a lender under the stipulations of a construction loan to pay for labor and materials. The term also refers to a practice by some brokers to advance money to certain salespersons with the money being repaid from future commissions.

DREI

Designated Real Estate Instructor. A designated awarded by the Real Estate Educators Association to persons involved in real estate education. *(See* **Real Estate Educators Association***)*

DRY MORTGAGE

A mortgage in which the lender has a lien on the property but does not have any recourse against the borrower in case of default. Such a mortgage is commonly known as a *nonrecourse loan.*

DUAL AGENCY

Action by an agent in a principal-agent relationship resulting in the agent representing the third party and, thus, creating two principals. As such, the agent is in violation of agency law which requires that he or she represent the principal, not the third party. A principal-agent relationship establishes a fiduciary relationship which means that the agent owes his or her loyalty to the principal. In addition, in some states the real estate licensing law prohibits a licensee from representing both buyer and seller in the same transaction. *(See* **Agency***)*

DUE DATE

A date set on which a payment is to be paid. If the payment is not made on or before the due date, then it is past due. Most real estate loans carry with them a first of the month due date as well as a *grace period* up to fifteen days during which time the payment can be made without penalty. The last day of the grace period is known as the *delinquency date* and payment after that date normally must also include a past payment charge.

DUE-ON-SALE CLAUSE

A clause included in many mortgages permitting the lender to require the borrower to repay the outstanding balance when the property is sold. Also known as a *nonassumption clause*, the effect is that mortgages with such a clause are nonassumable unless the lender permits the assumption. The lender may allow the mortgage to be assumed only after adjusting the interest rate to reflect current market conditions. All FHA and VA mortgages are assumable. (*See* **Assumption of Mortgage**)

DUMMY

Someone who buys or holds legal title to property on behalf of someone else. In certain instances, the true buyer wishes to keep his or her true identity hidden and thus someone else is used to purchase the property.

DUPLEX

A house divided into two dwelling units with separate living facilities. The units may be side-by-side or one on top of the other.

DURESS

The use of force or improper actions against a person or property in order to induce a party to enter into a contract. Examples of duress include blackmail, extortion, unlawful retention of property, a threat to bring criminal action, or threats against family.

DWELLING

The building in which a person lives.

DWELLING UNIT

Used in zoning ordinances and building codes to denote the room or rooms joined for occupancy by a family and containing a kitchen.

EARNEST MONEY

Money paid by a buyer at the time he or she enters into a contract to indicate both the ability and intent of carrying out the contract. If the contract is fulfilled then the earnest money is applied towards the purchase price. Default by the buyer will generally result in the earnest money being paid to the seller as damages. Extreme caution should be exercised by any licensed real estate broker or salesperson who receives earnest money deposits. First, real estate licensing laws are very specific as to the handling of such funds. In most states such monies must be deposited in the broker's trust account within a reasonable period of time after the contract has been formed. In addition, a broker is not permitted to *commingle* his or her personal funds with earnest money deposits. Finally, the broker is responsible for the safekeeping of such funds. This means that the broker should not dispense of the money until he or she has been properly advised. (*See* **Commingling of Funds, Contract, Damages**)

EASEMENT

A right to the limited use or enjoyment by one or more persons in the land of another. An easement is a nonpossessory and intangible interest. The right to use land does not include with it the right to remove any part of the land. A right to remove part of the land such as trees, soil, and minerals is called a *profit a prendre*, normally called a *profit*. Examples of easements include such rights as the permission of passage across one's land to reach a fishing pond, right-of-way access roads, telephone lines, pipelines, drainage and flooding rights, support of adjoining buildings, and support for pillars used in air-space construction. Easements may be *affirmative* or *negative*. An affirmative easement permits one to use another's property. A negative easement is used to prevent a landowner from using his or her property in some manner. One example of a negative easement is an easement for light and air. This easement prevents a landowner from erecting a structure so high that it would cast shadows or restrict light and air from the property of the owner of the easement. Another common negative easement is one which prevents the impairment of a scenic view or prevents any construction. Such an easement is called a *scenic easement*. The extent of the rights or limitations created by the easement is a matter of contract or grant. An easement may be created by *express agreement* between parties. Since an easement is considered to be an interest in land, it falls under the statute of frauds and the agreement must be in writing. A deed is usually used to convey an easement. An easement may also be created by *reservation* or *exception* by the grantor when the land is conveyed to another by retaining in the conveyance the right to use the land in some particular fashion. An easement may also be created by *implication* (*necessity*), *prescription*, and by the government's power of *eminent domain*. Easements may be terminated by written release, by merger when the dominant and servient estates come under one ownership, by the cessation of the necessity, by prescription when the owner of the servient estate acts adversely to the owner of the dominant estate for a sufficient period of time, by abandonment or by destruction of the purpose for the existence for the servient or dominant estate. An example of the latter is the destruction of two buildings where there was a mutual easement for support. Easements may be recorded. If a person purchases a servient estate without actual or constructive notice of the easement, the unrecorded easement will be extinguished by operation of law.

EASEMENT APPURTENANT

An easement which belongs to and passes with a particular tract of land. In order to create an easement appurtenant there must be at least two tracts of land. One tract is called the *dominant estate*, the tract which benefits from the easement. The other tract is called the *servient estate*, the tract which is burdened by the easement. An easement appurtenant "runs with the land." This means that when the land is sold or otherwise conveyed, the easement is also one of the rights which is conveyed, even if the instrument conveying the land is silent about the easement. Unless there is a specified limitation on the time of the easement it is considered to exist indefinitely.

EASEMENT BY IMPLICATION (NECESSITY)

An easement created by operation of law such as in the conveyance of landlocked property. The grantor by implication must give the purchaser the right to pass over his or her property in order to access a public road. An easement by implication may also be created because the purchaser had reasonably believed that an easement would be conveyed with the grant.

Example: Ann owns two adjoining houses with a common driveway. Mary purchases one of the houses, but nothing is stated about the common driveway which is totally on the adjoining lot. At the time that Mary was examining the property, Ann had indicated that the drive had been used by both properties. In this situation Mary would have an implied easement to use the common driveway unless it was clear at the time of the transaction that this would not be the case.

EASEMENT BY PRESCRIPTION

A means of acquiring title to property by long-continued use. If a person uses another's land for a sufficient period of time, the owner of the land may not be able to prevent further continued use. (*See* **Adverse Possession**)

EASEMENT IN GROSS

A personal right to use the land of another. No dominant estate exists, only a servient estate. Ordinarily, this personal right may not be conveyed or assigned. Modern commercial necessity has caused the creation of commercial easements in gross which may be transferred. Such easements include pipelines, telephone lines, and billboards.

ECOA

(*See* **Equal Credit Opportunity Act**)

ECONOMIC BASE ANALYSIS

A technique used by market analysts and appraisers that attempts to measure the current economic activity and expected future economic growth in a specific geographic area.

ECONOMIC DEPRECIATION

(*See* **Economic Obsolescence**)

ECONOMIC DIVISION

An economic concept which occurs if real property rights can be subdivided into two or more property interests resulting in an overall increase in aggregate value. Division can take place in many different ways. For example:

Physical division: separating air rights, surface rights, and mineral rights; or subdividing a tract of land

Division of time of possession: leases, life estates, future interests

Division of right to use: easements, licenses, deed restrictions

Division by right of ownership: joint tenancies, partnerships, trusts, corporations, options, conditional sales contracts

Division by security interests: first mortgages, junior mortgages, tax liens, judgment liens, equity interests

ECONOMIC LIFE

The time period over which an improvement to land earns more income than the cost incurred in generating the income. Thus, economic life is a function of materials used, construction quality, methods of engineering and architectural design, and various environmental or climatic factors. Under the *principle of anticipation*, an investor is willing to pay a price equal to the value of all future benefits, minus the cost of all future expenses, discounted to a present value. The longer an improvement is usable, the more the investor is generally willing to pay. The remaining years that a real estate improvement is productive is referred to as the *remaining economic life*. The difference between the economic life and the remaining economic life is the *effective age*. (*See* **Effective Age**)

ECONOMIC OBSOLESCENCE

A loss in value due to factors outside the subject property, such as changes in competition or surrounding land uses; for example, busy streets or an industrial plant near a residential area. Economic obsolescence, also called *environmental* or *locational obsolescence*, is always considered *incurable* since the expense makes it impractical to buy surrounding properties and remove the offending elements just to increase the value of one property that is affected. (*See* **Curable Depreciation, Incurable Depreciation**)

ECONOMIC RENT

The amount of rental revenues a parcel of real estate would receive in an open, freely competitive market, as opposed to *contract rent*, which is the amount of rent specified in the lease.

EFFECTIVE AGE

The age of an item, such as a building, as indicated by its physical condition and utility compared to its useful life, in contrast to its chronological age. It should be clear that the amount of maintenance and care given to a building helps determine its effective age. A ten-year-old building might have an effective age of twenty-five years because of poor or deferred maintenance.

EFFECTIVE CAPITAL RECOVERY RATE

The difference between the overall rate of return and the discount rate. An annual capital recovery rate weighted by the fraction of property considered to be wasting. (*See* **Capitalization Rate**)

EFFECTIVE GROSS INCOME

Gross actual cash receipts (net of vacancy and collection losses) from income-producing property. Effective gross income includes rental receipts, parking income, and other miscellaneous income. This is the amount that is available for meeting the necessary expenses of operating the project. (*See* **Gross Income**)

EFFECTIVE GROSS RENT

(*See* **Effective Gross Income**)

EFFECTIVE INTEREST RATE

The percentage rate of interest actually being paid by a borrower.

EFFICIENCY RATIO

The ratio of leasable space to total space. For example, a high-rise office building that has 200,000 square feet might be only 80 percent efficient because 20 percent of the building area is used for elevators, hallways, etc.

EFFICIENCY UNIT

A type of dwelling unit consisting of a living area-bedroom combination, kitchen, and bathroom. Also known as a *studio apartment*.

EFFICIENT AND PROCURING CAUSE

The legal test to determine if in fact a real estate licensee is entitled to a sales commission when property sells other than through an exclusive right to sell agreement. The licensee must be able to show that he or she procured the buyer and, as a result of the licensee's action, a sale took place. The primary reason for the exclusive right to sell listing agreement among real estate brokers is that under such an agreement, the broker has earned the commission if and when the property sells regardless of whether the broker actually sold the property.

EGRESS

The means by which a person exits from a property, as contrasted to *ingress* which refers to the entrance taken onto property.

EIS

(*See* **Environmental Impact Statement**)

EJECTMENT

Legal action to regain possession of property by the person who is legally entitled to it.

ELECTIVE SHARE

A statute present in many states which permits a surviving spouse to choose either what he or she has been left under the will of the deceased spouse or what is provided for under state statute, for example, one-third of the estate. (*See* **Descent, Devise**)

ELLWOOD, L.W.

A real estate appraiser who originated the use of the "Ellwood" technique of mortgage-equity capitalization used in the appraising of income-producing property. Mr. Ellwood (1896-1974) was the author of *Ellwood Tables for Real Estate Appraising and Financing.*

ELLWOOD TECHNIQUE

A mortgage-equity technique used in investment analysis for estimating the value of income-producing property on the basis of the present value of cash flows and resale proceeds before income taxes. The technique is named after L. W. Ellwood, noted real estate appraiser.

EMBLEMENTS

Crops which require annual planting. Emblements are considered to be a form of personal property, unlike other vegetation, which is considered real property. In cases of indefinite leases and other indefinite estates, if notice is given to terminate the estate, the tenant is entitled to harvest the crops even after the end of the lease term. However, if a fee owner sells unencumbered real estate, the emblements pass with the realty unless an express reservation excepts the crops from the sale.

EMINENT DOMAIN

The right of government to acquire private property for a public use or purpose. The process used to acquire the property is known as *condemnation* and the person(s) whose property is taken must receive *just compensation. (See* **Police Power)**

EMPTY NESTER(S)

A married couple or widow(er) whose children are no longer in the home. Such persons often sell their large homes and move into condominiums or apartments.

ENABLING LEGISLATION

Statutes which confer powers to persons or corporations to do something which before they could not do. Local governments receive authority to engage in land-use planning from enabling legislation passed by the state. Some states provide this power as part of the home rule powers in the municipal charter or state constitution. Most states have passed enabling legislation based on the *Standard City Planning Enabling Act* which was developed by the *U. S. Department of Commerce* in 1927. The enabling act provides for the creation of a planning commission or board. This commission is usually a board of citizens, often including real estate brokers, architects, lawyers, business people and others, who advise local government officials and legislators on planning matters. In passing a zoning ordinance, the planning commission usually recommends whether or not an ordinance should be approved by examining the proposed change and weighing its impact on the community on the basis of planning criteria. The planning commission's powers are usually limited, with the actual planning being handled by professional planners in the planning department and with final authority resting with the legislative body of the local government.

ENCROACHMENT

The extension of some improvement or object across the boundary of an adjoining tract. Examples of encroachments include walls, fences, cornices or buildings. If an encroachment exists and appropriate and timely steps are not taken to secure the removal of the encroaching object, an easement may be formed by prescription or the boundary of the property may change in favor of the encroaching party. The innocent landowner may seek removal or damages for trespass. The court will weigh the cost of removal with the benefits to be derived. In some cases if the cost is excessive, the remedy will be restricted to damages. If the court finds gross negligence or wrongful intent, the remedy may be very harsh. Cases have been decided in which a person has constructed a house on someone else's property and has lost the house. The landowner, in effect, has received a gift. An encroachment may affect the marketability of title. A purchaser might be freed of the obligation to buy the property where an encroachment prevents the title from being marketable.

ENCUMBRANCE

Any interest in or claim on the land of another that in some manner burdens or diminishes the value of that property. (*See* **Title**)

ENFORCEABLE

Any agreement, such as a valid contract, in which the parties to it can be compelled to perform.

ENJOIN

To require, by court order, a person to perform or to abstain from some act. (*See* **Injunction**)

ENTREPRENEUR

A person who on his or her own initiative undertakes the organization and management of a new business.

ENVIRONMENTAL IMPACT STATEMENT (EIS)

A requirement under the *National Environmental Policy Act of 1969* designed to require that in every recommendation or report on proposals for legislation and other major federal actions significantly affecting the quality of the human environment, a detailed statement by the responsible official must be filed. The impact statement must include the following:
1. The environmental impact of the proposed action
2. Any adverse environmental effects which cannot be avoided should the

proposal be implemented
3. Alternatives to the proposed action
4. The relationship between local short-term uses of man's environment and the maintenance and enhancement of long-term productivity, and
5. Any irreversible and irretrievable commitments of resources which would be involved in the proposed action should it be implemented.

ENVIRONMENTAL OBSOLESCENCE
(*See* Economic Obsolescence)

ENVIRONMENTAL PROTECTION AGENCY (EPA)
A federal agency that oversees and enforces federally enacted minimum standards dealing with environmental protection, specifically pollution control programs. EPA was created under the *National Environmental Policy Act of 1969* which had as its purposes: (1) to declare a national policy which will encourage productive and enjoyable harmony between man and his environment; (2) to promote efforts which will prevent or eliminate damage to the environment and biosphere and stimulate the health and welfare of man; (3) to enrich the understanding of the ecological systems and natural resources important to the nation; and (4) to establish a *Council on Environmental Quality.*

EPA
(*See* Environmental Protection Agency)

EQUAL CREDIT OPPORTUNITY ACT (ECOA)
As originally passed in 1974, the act prohibits discrimination by lenders on the basis of sex or marital status in any aspect of a credit transaction. As of 1977, the act was extended to cover additional protected groups of borrowers. These include individuals who are discriminated against on the basis of race, color, religion, national origin, age, receipt of income from a public assistance program, and good faith exercise of rights under the *Consumer Protection Act.* Exceptions to the protection of the law are individuals who do not have contractual capacity (minors) and individuals who are noncitizens and whose status might affect a creditor's rights and remedies in the case of a default. The purpose of this law and *Regulation B,* which was issued by the Board of Governors of the Federal Reserve System, was to assure that lenders would not treat one group of applicants more favorably than other groups except for reasonable and justifiable business reasons. Strict rules have been established to require fair dealing in all aspects of a credit transaction. A creditor failing to comply with the law is subject to civil liability for damages in individual or class actions. These damages can be actual or punitive. Punitive damages are intended to punish a wrongdoer. These are limited to $10,000 in individual actions or the lesser of $500,000 or one percent of a creditor's net worth in class actions. A class action occurs when a specific group of individuals has been harmed from a violation of the law. In general, lawsuits must be filed within two years of a violation.

The law is very broadly worded and covers all phases of a credit transaction. The following is a lender's lists of "do's" and "don'ts":

1. Do not ask about a person's birth control practices or intentions to bear children; however, a neutral question such as whether the applicant expects his or her income to be interrupted in the future is considered proper.
2. Do tell the applicant that income from alimony or child support need not be disclosed unless the applicant wishes this source of income considered.
3. Do tell the applicant that the federal government needs certain information for monitoring purposes but that this information will not be used as a means of discrimination. Note that the applicant may decline to furnish this information.
4. Do not require a spouse to co-sign a credit instrument except where state laws such as California's community property law require a signature to create a proper lien on property serving as security for a loan.
5. Do not use age in evaluating an applicant's creditworthiness. One exception to this rule is if the applicant is considered "elderly" (age 62 or over), and the age is being considered to favor the applicant.
6. Do not require the applicant to reveal marital status. This extends to the use of courtesy titles (Ms., Mr., Mrs., Miss) unless requested by the applicant.
7. Do furnish credit information in the names of both spouses for the purpose of establishing a credit history in each name if both are participating in the loan.
8. Do notify the applicant within 30 days whether you are approving the loan or taking an adverse action.
9. Do give a specific reason for an adverse action. Specific reasons could include: no credit file, insufficient credit reference, lawsuits, liens, excessive obligations, delinquent credit obligations, unable to verify employment or income, denial by FHA or other government program, inadequate collateral.
10. Do retain records for at least 25 months after notifying applicant of action taken.

EQUAL DIGNITIES RULE

A rule of agency law which states that if the principal, for example the seller of a home, wishes to empower the agent, for example the listing real estate broker, to enter into a contract on the principal's behalf and the contract falls within the requirements of the statute of frauds, the appointment must also be in writing. A power of attorney, for example, authorizing a broker to sign a sales contract must be in writing to be enforceable. (*See* **Power of Attorney, Statute of Frauds**)

EQUALIZATION BOARD

A local governmental agency established to supervise the review and inequities in property tax assessments and to hear property owner's complaints. (*See* **Property Tax**)

EQUITABLE CONVERSION

A legal doctrine that conveys title to property to the buyer even though actual legal title to him or her has not been transferred. For example, when a real estate sales contract is signed which is not subject to any unfulfilled contingencies, under common law equitable conversion occurs and *equitable title* passes to the purchaser. The result of this is that the risk of loss also passes to the purchaser. If the subject matter is destroyed before closing, the purchaser suffers the loss. This is the rule in many states. However, a number of states have modified the common law rule by passing the *Uniform Vendor and Purchaser Risk Act*. This act provides for risk of loss to shift only if either legal title or possession has been transferred. Either under common law or statute, the purchaser and seller may specify in the contract who has the risk of loss. (*See* **Equitable Title**)

EQUITABLE LIEN

A type of lien created when justice and fairness would require a court of equity to declare that such a lien exists or when conduct of the parties would imply that a lien was intended. For example, if a tenant in common made necessary repairs to a house which was in danger of collapse and in violation of the housing code, an equitable lien would attach to the other co-tenant's undivided interest for a proportionate share of the expenses.

EQUITABLE MORTGAGE

An agreement that sets aside certain property for security of a debt before the security agreement is formalized.

EQUITABLE OWNERSHIP

(*See* **Equitable Title**)

EQUITABLE REDEMPTION

The process by which a borrower (mortgagor) redeems his or her property upon full payment of the outstanding debt. (*See* **Equity of Redemption**)

EQUITABLE SERVITUDE

A restriction of the use of land.

EQUITABLE TITLE

The ownership interest that one has in real property upon the consummation of a valid sales contract. Upon delivery and acceptance of a deed, the equitable title becomes legal title to the property. (*See* **Equitable Conversion**)

EQUITY

The excess of a property's fair market value over the outstanding indebtedness. The term is also used to denote the principle of fairness and legal jurisprudence as contrasted with the strict interpretation of common law.

EQUITY BUILD-UP

The increase of the owner's share of the property as a percentage of the total as the property appreciates and/or the mortgage principal is amortized over time.

Example: Joe Smith purchases a $80,000 home with a $60,000 mortgage and $20,000 cash. His equity is 25 percent ($20,000/$80,000). Three years later the value of the house has increased to $110,000 and the outstanding mortgage balance has been reduced to $58,000. His equity is now $52,000 ($110,000 - $58,000) and represents 47 percent ($52,000/$110,000) of the value of the property.

EQUITY DIVIDEND

(*See* **Before-Tax Cash Flow**)

EQUITY DIVIDEND RATE

(*See* **Cash-on-Cash**)

EQUITY KICKER

(*See* **Kicker**)

EQUITY OF REDEMPTION

The right of the mortgagor (borrower) to reclaim his or her property by paying the outstanding loan, interest, and court costs prior to a foreclosure sale. (*See* **Foreclosure, Statutory Period of Redemption**)

EQUITY PARTICIPATION

A lender's share in the equity of property in addition to the interest earned on the mortgage note. Equity participation, also called *mortgage participation*, entitles a lender to receive a share of income and/or appreciation from the property in addition to payments for interest and principal repayment. Each participation agreement is unique. Some agreements require the payment of a stated percentage of effective gross income, net operating income, or cash flow. Other agreements require a share of income in excess of a base amount, such as 5 percent of effective gross income above $500,000. Still other agreements allow the lender to share in the appreciation or resale proceeds of the property.

EQUITY PURCHASER

One who purchases another's equity in a project without necessarily assuming personal liability for the loan.

EQUITY RATIO

The percentage relationship between the down payment and the total purchase price or equity value at any point in time to total property value.

EQUITY YIELD RATE

The internal rate of return on an equity investment calculated without regard to the impact of federal income taxes.

EROSION

The gradual eating away of soil due to the actions of water, wind or other elements.

ERRORS AND OMISSIONS INSURANCE (E & O)

A type of liability insurance that protects real estate brokers and salespersons from errors and mistakes committed during the day-to-day activities of brokering real estate.

ESCALATOR CLAUSE

A clause inserted in certain types of contracts permitting an increase or decrease in the amount of payments due. For example, some leases contain such a clause which permits the lessor (landlord) to raise the rent upon the occurrence of certain stipulated conditions such as an increase in property taxes or property insurance. Thus the landlord is able to pass these higher costs on to the tenants and therefore protect his or her investment from inflation. An escalator clause may also appear in some mortgages, thus permitting the lender to raise the interest rate upon the occurrence of certain stipulated conditions such as a rise in the prime interest rate. (*See* **Renegotiable Rate Mortgage, Variable Rate Mortgage**)

ESCAPE CLAUSE

A provision in a contract or other legal document which under specified circumstances frees a party from performance or certain responsibilities.

ESCHEAT

The legal right or claim of government to ownership of property which is left by a deceased property owner who leaves no will and dies without descendents or heirs. The state is thought of as analogous to a feudal lord who was entitled to enter upon land which became vacant because no competent tenant was left.

ESCROW

The deposit of funds or documents with a neutral third party who is instructed to carry out the provisions of an agreement. The neutral third party is known as an *escrow agent* and his or her duties are specified in the agreement. In some locations in the country real estate closings are handled through escrow, referred to as *closing in escrow*, which means that the deed is delivered by the seller to the escrow agent and the money necessary to purchase the property is delivered from the buyer to the escrow agent. The escrow agent will hold all papers until the occurrence or nonoccurrence of some event or act. Normally, once an examination of title is completed and the escrow agent is satisfied that the seller has clear title, the money collected passes to the seller and the deed is delivered to the buyer.

ESCROW ACCOUNT

A bank account held in the name of the depositor, for example a mortgagor, by a lender, the mortgagee, for the purpose of paying periodic expenses such as property taxes and property insurance. The borrower, in addition to making principal and interest payments each month, is required to pay a pre-calculated portion of the taxes and insurance when they become due, typically monthly. In some states lenders are required to pay interest on the money placed in escrow accounts.

The term is also used to refer to the bank account maintained by a real estate broker holding funds, such as an earnest money deposit, belonging to others. State real estate licensing law generally requires that such an account be maintained and that the money held in the account cannot be *commingled* with the broker's personal bank account.

ESCROW AGENT

An independent third party legally bound to carry out the written provisions of an escrow agreement. *(See* Escrow)

ESCROW CLOSING

(See Escrow)

ESTATE

A legally recognized interest in the use, possession, control, and disposition that a person has in land. An estate defines the nature, degree, extent, and duration of a person's ownership in land. Estate relates to the degree of interest that a person has in land. The degree of interest may be classified by: (1) the *quantity and quality of the interest*, (2) the *time of enjoyment*, and (3) the *number of individuals connected with the ownership*.

One important characteristic of the estate concept is that ownership is divisible. The original owner may separate his or her full ownership into different interests which may be granted to several persons. These interests may change over time as different contingent events occur or fail to occur. Further, one estate may be divided into two or more estates, all of which can exist simultaneously.

ESTATE AT SUFFERANCE

(See Tenancy at Sufferance)

ESTATE AT WILL

(See Tenancy at Will)

ESTATE FOR YEARS

A conveyance of realty for a definite period of time. This is the most common type of leasehold and is one that has a specified beginning and ending to the term. Although the *leasehold* is called an estate for years, it may in fact be for a shorter time. The term may be one month, one week, or even one day. In most states if the term is less than one year, it may be created by oral agreement. Some states permit leaseholds for less than three years to be created orally. During the term of this lease, a tenant has a right to possess, control, enjoy, and dispose of the property rights. If the tenant were to die during the term of the leasehold, the property interest would pass to the tenant's estate. If the tenant retains possession of the property after the expiration of the term, this is referred to as *holding over*. The landlord has the option to treat the holdover tenant as a trespasser and proceed to dispossess him or her from the property, or he may elect to treat the term of the lease as renewed, thereby converting the leasehold into a periodic tenancy, or in some states into a tenancy at will.

ESTATE FROM YEAR TO YEAR

A leasehold interest in real estate also known as a *periodic tenancy* or an *estate from period to period*, which is automatically renewed for the same term as in the original lease; thus, the conveyance is for an indefinite period of time. If the lease term is for more than one year, the term upon renewal is considered by most states to be for one year.

Example: If Jan signs a lease for a five-year period with an automatic renewal provision, then at the end of the term, if Jan has failed to give proper notice to terminate the lease, the tenancy will automatically renew for an additional term of one year.

Where no term is specified, the manner and time that the rent is paid establishes the term by implication. For example, if the rent is paid quarterly, the implication is that the term is from quarter to quarter. What is proper notice to prevent renewal of the term? Ordinarily, this is specified by the lease itself, or where the lease is silent, by statute. Under common law, where a lease term was for less than one year, notice had to be given at least one period in advance. If the lease was for one year or more, six month's advance notice was considered sufficient. Despite notice, if the tenant held over by even one day past the expiration of the term, the courts under common law construed this as a renewal of the lease for another term. As with the estate for years, death of either the lessor or lessee does not terminate a periodic tenancy.

ESTATE IN FEE

(*See* **Fee Simple**)

ESTATES LESS THAN FREEHOLD

(*See* **Leasehold**)

ESTATE TAX

A tax imposed upon the value of the property transferred from the deceased to his or her heirs or beneficiaries. The tax is levied on the estate rather than on the person(s) receiving the property.

ESTOP

To stop or prevent. (*See* **Estoppel**)

ESTOPPEL

A legal doctrine which prevents a person from alleging something to be true or a fact which is contrary to a previous affirmation or allegation made by that same person.

ESTOPPEL BY DEED

A legal doctrine that prevents a grantor in a warranty deed who does not have title at the time of conveyance but who later acquires title to the property from denying that he or she had title at the time of the original transfer. The after-acquired interest of the grantor is thus automatically transferred to the grantee.

ESTOPPEL CERTIFICATE

(*See* **Certificate of Estoppel**)

ESTOVER

The right of a tenant to use the wood on property he or she is leasing to provide for necessary fuel and agricultural operations.

ET AL

Abbreviation for *et alius* which means "and another."

ETHICS

Professional rules of duties or conduct. (*See* **Code of Ethics**)

ET UX

Abbreviation for *et uxor* which means "and wife."

EVALUATION

A study of the usefulness or utility of a parcel of land without reference to a specific valuation estimate. Evaluation studies take the form of land utilization studies, highest and best use studies, marketability studies, and demand and supply analysis. (*See* **Appraisal**)

EVICTION

Any action by the landlord which interferes with the tenant's possession or use of the leased premises in whole or in part. (*See* **Actual Eviction, Constructive Eviction, Partial Eviction**)

EVIDENCE OF TITLE

A deed or other legal instrument establishing title to property. (*See* **Title**)

EXAMINATION, LICENSING

(See **Licensing Examination**)

EXAMINATION OF TITLE

A search of the land records to determine whether or not the title is marketable. *(See* **Abstract of Title**)

EXCESS ACCELERATED DEPRECIATION

The amount by which annual or accumulated depreciation, under a repaid method of depreciation, exceeds straight-line depreciation, considering the same asset useful life. *(See* **Depreciation, Depreciation Recapture**)

EXCESS RENT

The amount of rent being paid under a lease that exceeds the current market rent being paid on similar properties. *(See* **Contract Rent**)

EXCEPTION

A clause included in a deed excluding a specified portion of the land previously described in the deed. For example, the exception could be: "Tom grants a 500-acre farm to Janet except for a quarter-acre family graveyard (legal description of the graveyard is included)."

The term is also used to refer to all discovered defects and encumbrances against which a title company will not insure. *(See* **Perfecting Title, Reservation, Title Insurance**)

EXCHANGE

(See **Tax-Free Exchange**)

EXCLUSIONARY ZONING

Zoning action which excludes the poor and minority groups from a geographic area. In zoning ordinances certain area and bulk restrictions such as minimum lot sizes serve to regulate the intensity of development to prevent the overloading of public services. A minimum lot size requirement might be a two-acre lot for each house. Such a restriction has been criticized for raising the cost of housing so that lower socioeconomic groups are unable to afford houses in a particular neighborhood. *(See* **Zoning**)

EXCLUSIVE AGENCY

An agreement between an owner and a real estate broker in which the owner employs only one broker but retains the right to personally sell the property and thereby not pay a sales commission. If any other broker negotiates a sale, the listing broker is nevertheless entitled to the full commission unless the listing broker had agreed otherwise with the procuring broker. Thus, if a procuring broker has a prospect who is interested in a house that another broker has under an exclusive listing, the listing broker should first be contacted and arrangement for a cooperation agreement should be made.

EXCLUSIVE LISTING

(*See* **Exclusive Agency**)

EXCLUSIVE RIGHT TO SELL LISTING

A listing agreement whereby only one real estate broker is employed and that broker is entitled to a commission no matter who sells the property during the listing period. This is true whether another broker or the owner sells the property. It may be noted that general rules of law may be modified by specific agreement. One modification which occasionally appears in listing contracts is an exclusion by the owner from the contract of people the owner has been negotiating with prior to the listing. If the owner sells the property to one of these excluded people, he or she would not be liable to the broker for a commission, despite the general exclusive right to sell provision. Another problem often occurs when a house is sold after the expiration of the listing period to a purchaser procured by the broker during the stipulated period. Normally, unless the sale was imminent and effectively completed during the period or if the buyer and seller acted in bad faith to conspire to deprive the broker of the justly earned commission, no commission is owed. The broker can be protected with an *extender* or *carryover provision* in the original listing contract. This clause provides that the broker will be entitled for a specified period after the expiration date of the listing to receive a commission if the property is sold to any prospect to whom he or she had shown the property during the listing period.

EXCULPATORY CLAUSE

A clause inserted in a contract, such as a mortgage or a lease, which frees a party from liability. For example, such a clause in a mortgage could free the borrower from personal liability in case he or she defaults on the mortgage. A landlord could, by inserting an appropriate exculpatory clause in a lease, be free from any liability for personal or property damages to the tenants.

EXECUTE

To perform or complete as in the signing and delivery of a deed.

EXECUTED CONTRACT

A contract in which the obligations have been performed on both sides of the contract and nothing is left to be completed. (*See* **Contract**)

EXECUTION SALE

A judicial proceeding in which the property of a debtor is seized and sold to satisfy a judgment lien.

EXECUTOR

A person appointed in a will to carry out the instructions of the testator, pay the debts of the estate and dispose of the property as instructed.

EXECUTOR'S DEED

A deed issued by the executor of an estate in conveying the real property of the estate.

EXECUTORY CONTRACT

A contract in which obligation to perform exists on one or both sides of the contract. Real estate sales contracts are good examples of executory contracts. In a typical sales contract the seller agrees "to convey the property to the purchaser by deed with the usual covenants of title and free and clear from all encumbrances," while the purchaser agrees "to pay the sales price in full at time of closing." (*See* **Contract**)

EXEMPT

To relieve from liability.

EXISTING MORTGAGE

A mortgage which has not been fully repaid, and thus is an encumbrance against the property. The mortgage may or may not be assumed if the property is sold. (*See* **Assumption of Mortgage, Due-on-Sale Clause**)

EXISTING USE

In zoning, a particular use of land which, as a result of the enactment of a zoning ordinance, does not conform to the ordinance. However, since zoning is not retroactive such a use would have to be permitted to continue for a reasonable period of time.

EXPENSE RATIO

The fraction found by dividing stabilized operating expenses by the effective gross income of a particular real estate project. Such a ratio is used by property owners to see how their property compares to similar properties.

EXPRESS CONTRACT

An agreement formed through the oral or written words of the parties as compared to an *implied contract* which is one formed through the acts or conduct of the parties involved. (*See* **Contract**)

EXTENDED COVERAGE

An insurance term referring to the extension of a standard fire insurance policy to cover damages resulting from wind, rain, and other perils. The term is also used with a title insurance policy to refer to additional coverage under a policy. For example, a mortgagee may wish to have an endorsement which will extend coverage for any subsequent loss of priority of lien by any unrecorded mechanic's lien which is later properly filed.

EXTENDER CLAUSE

A clause included in some listing contracts which provides that the broker will be entitled for a specific period of time following the expiration date of the listing to receive a commission if the property is sold to any prospect to whom the broker showed the property during the listing period. This clause is also known as a *carryover clause*.

EXTENSION AGREEMENT

A formal agreement entered into between two parties lengthening the time of performance. For example, a mortgagor (borrower) and a mortgagee (lender) could formally agree to lengthen the amortization period of a loan.

EYE APPEAL

Positive features of a property which make it more appealing and thus easier to sell. Examples would include a landscaped yard, a beautiful view, and a clean interior.

FACADE

The exterior wall of a building.

FACE RATE OF INTEREST

The stated interest rate in a promissory note. Also known as the *contract rate* or *nominal rate*, the face rate of interest will be less than the *annual percentage rate (APR)* if additional charges such as origination fees and discount points are charged by the lender. (*See* **Annual Percentage Rate**)

FACE LIFT

Changes other than structural that result in an improved appearance of a building. Such things as repairs, paint, new windows, and general cleaning all serve to improve the appearance of a building and, thus, give it a face lift.

FACE VALUE

The value of a debt such as a mortgage as stated in the instrument itself. If current interest rates are greater than the contract rate of interest, the *market value* of the debt instrument will be less than the face value since the instrument would have to be *discounted* to generate the market rate of interest. Conversely, if the contract rate of interest is greater than current market rates, the instrument, if sold, will sell for a *premium* and, thus, its *market value* will be greater than its face value.

FACTOR

Any number or symbol that when multiplied by another forms a product; the reciprocal of a rate.

FACTORS OF PRODUCTION

An economic principle which refers to the inputs necessary to create goods or services. There are four factors of production: (1) *capital*, (2) *labor*, (3) *entrepreneurship* or *management*, and (4) *land*. Each factor must be compensated in order for the owner(s) to be induced to part with the factor. Since land is the only immobile factor of production, it must attract the other three factors of production. As a result, land receives its payment only after the other factors have been compensated. This means that real estate is *residual*. Thus, the value of real estate is dependent upon how much compensation is left after the other three factors have been rewarded. (*See* **Highest and Best Use**)

FAIR CREDIT REPORTING ACT

A federal act which became effective April 1, 1971, and attempts to regulate the actions of credit bureaus that give out erroneous information regarding consumers. First, banks and credit companies must make a customer's credit file available to the person in question. Further, the consumer, upon examining the file, has the right to correct any errors that may appear in the credit reports. Secondly, if a creditor denies a loan to an applicant, the applicant must be given the name and address of the credit bureau that supplied the credit information to the creditor. Upon request the credit bureau must supply the consumer with the pertinent information contained in the applicant's credit file. Finally, the act limits the access of the consumer's credit records to people who: (1) evaluate an applicant for insurance, credit or employment, (2) secure the consumer's permission, or (3) secure court permission.

FAIR HOUSING

(*See* **Federal Fair Housing Act of 1968**)

FAIR HOUSING AMENDMENT ACT OF 1988

A federal act which amended the *Federal Fair Housing Act of 1968* to include two new protected classes, the handicapped and the "familial" status, or those with children under eighteen. The amendment became effective March 12, 1989. (*See* **Federal Fair Housing Act of 1968**)

FAIR MARKET VALUE

An economic concept denoting the price, in terms of money, at which a willing seller and willing buyer will agree when both parties are acting prudently, knowledgeably, and under no compulsion. (*See* **Value**)

FANNIE MAE

Nickname commonly used in reference to the *Federal National Mortgage Association (FNMA)*. (*See* **Federal National Mortgage Association**)

FAR

(*See* **Floor Area Ratio**)

FARM AND LAND INSTITUTE (FLI)

(*See* **Realtors Land Institute**)

FARMER'S HOME ADMINISTRATION (FmHA)

An agency of the *U. S. Department of Agriculture* that provides credit to farmers, rural residences, and certain communities. Currently, FmHA administers two loan programs for rural housing: (1) a direct loan program, and (2) a guaranteed loan program. Properties securing such loans may not be located in urban areas and, like FHA and VA, FmHA requires that the property meet certain minimum requirements. Although there is no statutory loan limit for such loans, the property must appraise for the contract sales price. Information on both loan programs is available from any office of the Farmer's Home Administration.

FARMLAND

A classification of land which denotes land primarily used for the raising of crops and or livestock.

FARM MORTGAGE

A loan secured by agricultural real estate. Such loans are normally used by farmers to raise capital for the purchase and operation of their farms.

FASA

Fellow, American Society of Appraisers. A professional designation awarded by the American Society of Appraisers to individuals involved in the appraisal of both real and personal property. (*See* **American Society of Appraisers**)

FEASIBILITY

The reasonable likelihood of satisfying certain investment objectives within the context of the market, finances, and other resources or constraints.

FEASIBILITY STUDY

A detailed analysis of a real estate project to determine the most profitable use and the likelihood of the proposed use being a financial success. The study is often used by the promoter or developer to inure would-be investors to participate in the venture and to assist lenders in making their decision whether or not to loan the necessary funds. (*See* **Financial Feasibility**)

FEDERAL DEPOSIT INSURANCE CORPORATION (FDIC)

An independent agency functioning within the executive branch of the U. S. Government. FDIC was established following the run on banks that occurred prior to the Great Depression and its purpose is to insure the deposits of all banks who hold FDIC membership. All nationally chartered commercial banks must maintain FDIC membership and, in addition, state chartered banks may apply for and be granted membership. The corporation insures deposits up to a statutory limit.

FEDERAL FAIR HOUSING ACT OF 1968

A federal fair housing law which was passed as Title VIII of the *Civil Rights Act of 1968*. As originally passed, the act prohibited discrimination in the sale or rental of residential dwelling units or vacant land intended to be used as such on the basis of race, color, religion, or national origin. Discrimination on the basis of sex was prohibited by an amendment in the *Housing and Community Development Act of 1974*. The *Fair Housing Amendment Act of 1988*, which became effective March 13, 1989, adds two new protected classes, the handicapped and the "familial" status, or those with children under eighteen.

What Is Prohibited by the 1968 Fair Housing Act? This law prohibits the following discriminatory acts if the discrimination is based on race, color, religion, national origin, sex, handicap, or a family with children in all instances, except where otherwise specified:

1. It is unlawful to refuse to sell or rent, to refuse to negotiate to sell or rent, or otherwise make unavailable or deny a dwelling to any person in the protective classification.

Example: Joan is an apartment manager for Frosty Pines Apartments which are rented by many people who originally came from Pakistan. A prospective tenant who came from India seeks to rent an apartment. Because of trouble between the countries of Pakistan and India, Joan's tenants tell her that if she rents to an Indian, they will move out. Joan refuses to rent to an Indian. She has violated the law.

It should be noted that under this provision the practice of *steering* would be considered illegal. Steering is defined as a real estate broker or salesperson channeling prospective home purchasers or renters into homogeneous neighborhoods and actively discouraging them away from neighborhoods of different racial or ethnic composition. Thus, if a broker intentionally fails to make a house available to a prospect because of the prospect's race, sex, religion, color, national origin, handicap, or a family with children, the broker is in violation of the law. The prospect, not the broker, is entitled to choose which neighborhoods are suitable.

2. It is unlawful to modify terms, conditions, or privileges of sale or rental or change the provisions of services or facilities in connection with the sale or rental of a dwelling on the basis of race, color, sex, religion, national origin, handicap, or a family with children.

Example: John Developer is selling houses in a subdivision which he has completed. When a purchaser buys a house he or she is automatically given a free membership in a club which is part of the subdivision. Harry Gold, a member of the Jewish faith, buys a house but is told by John that the club is for Gentiles only. John offers to give Harry a rebate on the purchase price. John is in violation of the law.

3. It is unlawful to make any statement or advertise that sale or rental is limited to certain groups or that certain groups are preferred.

Example: Jan tells a white couple that the project is restricted to whites and that no blacks will ever be welcome so long as she is manager. This statement is illegal.

It might be noted that the U. S. Supreme Court in *Trafficante v. Metropolitan Life Insurance Company*, 409 U. S. 205 (1972) permitted a white plaintiff to recover against an owner of an apartment project because the plaintiff was denied the social benefits of associating with blacks due to the owner's discriminatory practices.

4. It is unlawful to represent to a person in a protected classification that any dwelling is not available for inspection, sale, or rental when such dwelling is in fact so available.

Example: Mike and Janet, an interracial married couple, answer an advertisement for an apartment. The manager of the apartment shows the couple the apartment. When the couple seeks to place a deposit on the apartment, the manager tells them that unfortunately he cannot accept the deposit because someone has previously made a deposit on the apartment. The manager's statement is false. The statement violates the law.

5. It is unlawful to make representations that a person or persons of any classification are entering into a neighborhood to induce sales for the purpose of profiting from the sale or rent of any dwelling.

Example: Mary and Joe are concerned that their neighborhood may be racially transitional. They ask their broker, Ann Smith, if there is any danger of minorities or foreigners moving into their neighborhood. Ann Smith urges them to list their house because Vietnamese refugees are moving into the neighborhood and will undoubtedly drive prices down. Ann Smith is acting illegally by blockbusting.

Any activity which attempts to drive prices down for the purpose of causing transition from one ethnic group to another is illegal. It should be noted that *blockbusting* does not occur from selling a house to a member of a minority group, but from attempting to drive out existing owners. Thus, courts have construed even broad statements such as "this is a changing neighborhood" as falling within this provision.

6. It is unlawful for any bank, building and loan association, insurance company, or other lender to modify the terms or conditions on a loan as the basis of discrimination where the purpose of this loan is to buy, build, or repair a dwelling.

Example: The Friendly Finance Company of Anystate tells Mary Jones, who is seeking to borrow money to paint her house, that because she is likely to become pregnant, they will require that she pay back the loan within nine months. This kind of restriction on the terms of the loan is illegal.

7. It is unlawful to deny or to impose on any person discriminatory conditions because of the person's race or other protected classes in order to participate in any multiple-listing service or any other real estate business organization.

Example: Anytown Listing Association refuses to list any house in a neighborhood which is racially transitional. This restriction would be illegal.

Who Is Exempt From the Provisions of the 1968 Fair Housing Act?   There are four exemptions noted in the law. The reader is advised that these exemptions do not apply to the provisions of the 1866 law where discrimination is on the basis of race.

1. The sale or rental of single-family homes rented by an owner is exempt provided that the following conditions are met:
   A. Only one sale within any twenty-four month period is permitted if the owner was not residing in the home at the time of the sale or was not the most recent resident of the home prior to the sale.
   B. The owner cannot own any more than three homes at one time.
   C. A broker or salesperson or the services of any person in the business of selling or renting dwellings cannot be used.
   D. Discriminatory advertising cannot be used.

The reader should note that if a person who is in the business of selling or renting dwellings assists in the sale, the exemption does not apply. Such a person is anyone who has participated as a principal in three or more rental or sales transactions within the preceding twelve months, or if the person has acted as an agent in two or more rental or sales transactions within the preceding twelve months, or if the person is the owner of any dwelling designed for five or more families.

2. Rentals of dwellings designed for four or fewer families are exempt if the owner occupies one of the units.

3. Religious organizations may give preference to members of their own religion in sales and rentals so long as the groups do not discriminate on the basis of color, race, sex, national origin, handicap or a family with children.

4. Private clubs may restrict rental or occupancy to their own members if the lodgings are not operated commercially.

Complaints and Enforcement.   Under the 1968 Fair Housing Act, a complaint may be handled in three ways:

1. A complaint may be filed with HUD. HUD must promptly investigate complaints before it, unless state or local law provides rights and remedies which are substantially equivalent. If the latter is the case, then the complaint must be referred to the appropriate state or local agency. While HUD has broad investigatory and subpoena powers, it is not empowered to issue cease and desist orders. HUD is restricted to informal conciliation to seek a resolution to complaints. While this process is time consuming, the advantage to the complainant is that HUD bears the cost of investigation and discovery. This information may be used as evidence in a private civil suit for damages and for injunctive relief. If HUD or the state agency is unable to cure the discriminatory

practice or correct the damage, the injured party may then bring a civil suit in the federal district court.

2. A civil suit may be filed in federal district court. As per the *Fair Housing Amendment Act of 1988* a civil suit must be filed in federal district court within two years of the discriminatory act. The two years rule does not apply where the complaint is first filed with HUD. The federal district court may give injunctive relief and award actual damages and up to $1,000 in punitive damages. It might also be noted that a complaint to HUD and a separate civil suit may take place simultaneously.

3. Action may be taken by the Attorney General. The Attorney General of the United States may file a civil suit where there exists a pattern or practice of discrimination or if a number of persons have been injured by such practices. This avenue of enforcement is ordinarily restricted to cases of general public importance.

Example: A large brokerage firm makes it a practice to have white agents show houses to white prospects, while black agents show houses to black prospects. The Attorney General could become involved in a case such as this to correct this type of pattern of discrimination.

A technique which is used by plaintiffs or government investigators to gather evidence of discrimination is that of "testing" or "checking." A typical example of this technique is described: Assume that a broker is suspected of not treating whites and blacks in the same manner. A complaint has been filed that the broker has discouraged blacks from purchasing homes. The following sequence of events might take place to investigate the complaint. First, a white couple of a certain socioeconomic status would approach a house that the suspected broker was showing. They would ask certain questions and give certain facts about themselves to the broker. After the first couple left, a black couple of the same socioeconomic status would come and ask the same essential questions and give the same essential facts about themselves. After the black couple left, another white couple would repeat the same procedure. A comparison would be made to determine if the attitude and representations made were different in the treatment of the black couple than with the two white couples. The findings of this checking would be admissible in court. (*See* **Civil Rights Act of 1866**)

FEDERAL HOME LOAN BANK BOARD (FHLBB)

A board established by the *Federal Home Loan Bank Act of 1932* which charters and regulates federal savings and loan associations. The purpose of the board in regard to savings and loans is much the same as that of the Federal Reserve System in regard to commercial banks. All federally chartered savings and loan associations must maintain membership in their regional home loan bank.

FEDERAL HOME LOAN MORTGAGE CORPORATION (FHLMC)

In 1970 under the *Emergency Home Finance Act*, the *Federal Home Loan Mortgage Corporation (FHLMC)* or "Freddie Mac" was created as a wholly-owned subsidiary of the *Federal Home Loan Bank System*. Freddie Mac was established as a secondary mortgage market for savings and loan associations who are members of the FHLBS. The creation of FHLMC was of added importance since S & L's make such a high percentage of the total conventional residential mortgages and many of these lenders would like to roll over their mortgages. While Fannie Mae deals heavily in FHA and VA mortgages, the majority of mortgages in Freddie Mac's portfolio are conventional. In recent years, this agency has referred to itself as *The Mortgage Corporation.*

FEDERAL HOUSING ADMINISTRATION (FHA)

A federal agency established as part of the *1934 National Housing Act* that insures mortgages made by FHA-approved lenders on real estate that meets FHA minimum standards. The establishment of the 1934 Housing Act immediately resulted in more construction jobs for the unemployed. This, in turn, helped to stimulate the depressed economy. In order to provide the means by which these new homes could be purchased, FHA established an insurance program to safeguard the lender against the risk of nonpayment of people purchasing these homes. The result was that the majority of homes financed were FHA insured. Even though the percentage of homes insured under FHA coverage has continued to decrease, the standards and requirements under FHA programs have been credited with influencing lending policies and techniques in financing residential real estate. Under an FHA-insured mortgage, both the property and the borrower must meet certain minimum standards. Prior to 1983, the borrower was charged an insurance fee of one-half percent on the unpaid balance and could, under certain conditions, receive up to 97% financing on the appraised value of the property. However, on December 1, 1983, FHA changed to a one-time *mortgage insurance premium (MIP)* of 3.8 percent of the loan amount, which is either paid in cash at closing or added to the amount of the loan and thus repaid as part of the monthly debt service.

If a purchaser using FHA financing is paying more than the appraised value, the difference between the appraised value and the sales price must come from the purchaser's assets. Borrowers are not permitted to obtain second mortgages to use as down payments. Also, FHA sets limits as to the maximum loan origination fee charged by the lender. The subject property must be appraised prior to the loan being made; this fee is normally absorbed by the mortgagor. FHA insures these loans for up to thirty years. Thus the low closing costs, the relatively low down payment and the long amortization period permitted under FHA have all aided in providing residential financing for millions of people who otherwise would not have been able to purchase a home. On a conventional mortgage, the interest rate is determined by the lender subject to state usury laws. A recent change in the law makes FHA interest rates also determined by the lender rather than by the Secretary of Housing and Urban Development. This rate is periodically raised or lowered to reflect changes in the cost of money, although historically interest rates on FHA mortgages have been slightly below conventional mortgage interest rates. In addition, borrowers financing with FHA coverage may be charged discount points since points can be paid by either the buyer or the seller. In recent years FHA has expanded its operation; currently the agency administers a number of programs dealing with housing. The basic home mortgage program is normally referred to as 203(b), and the program which provides insured mortgages for low or moderate income families is referred to as 221(d)(2).

FEDERAL LAND BANKS

Regional banks established as part of the *Farm Credit Administration* which are a source of long-term mortgages to farmers. The Federal Land Banks make first mortgages though local federal land bank associations to farmers, ranchers, rural residents, and farm-related businesses. A majority of the funds used to make these loans come from the selling of securities by the Federal Land Banks to investors.

Each of the banks is known as "the Federal Land Bank of _____," and is located in the following twelve cities: Baltimore, Maryland 21203; Berkeley, California 94701; Columbia, South Carolina 24202; Houston, Texas 77001; Louisville, Kentucky 40201; New Orleans, Louisiana 70150; Omaha, Nebraska 68101; Springfield, Massachusetts 01101; Spokane, Washington 99204; St. Louis, Missouri 63166; St. Paul, Minnesota 55101; and Wichita, Kansas 67202.

FEDERAL NATIONAL MORTGAGE ASSOCIATION (FNMA)

Commonly known as "Fannie Mae", the FNMA is the largest and best known buyer of existing mortgages. The Federal National Mortgage Association was originally organized by the federal government in 1938 to purchase FHA-insured mortgages. The association was reorganized in 1968 as a quasi-private corporation whose entire ownership is private. Fannie Mae raises capital by issuing corporate stock which is actively traded on the New York Stock Exchange and by selling mortgages out of its portfolio to various investors. Over the past twenty years Fannie Mae has purchased many times more than it has sold. At the end of 1989 current mortgage holdings exceeded $100 billion, the majority being conventional mortgages. The mortgage purchase procedure used by FNMA is conducted through an auction process referred to as the *Free Market System Auction.* Periodically, the association accepts bids from approved lenders as to the amount, price, and terms of existing mortgages that these lenders wish to sell to Fannie Mae. Upon deciding how much money it will spend during a given time period, FNMA notifies the successful bidders (determined by those mortgages offered for sale that will generate the highest yield to FNMA) and these bidders have a certain time period in which they can choose to deliver the mortgages. Once the mortgage has been delivered to Fannie Mae, the originator of the mortgage continues to service the loan (collect monthly payments, escrow property taxes, etc.) and for this service the originator receives a *servicing fee.* By selling to Fannie Mae a lender is allowed to roll over its money. That is, by selling $1,000,000 worth of mortgages to FNMA, a mortgage banker now has $1,000,000 that can be used to originate new mortgages. Thus funds are provided that would not have been available had Fannie Mae not purchased the mortgages. (*See* **Secondary Mortgage Market**)

FEDERAL RESERVE BANK

One of twelve banks located in the twelve federal reserve districts throughout the United States. *(See **Federal Reserve System**)*

FEDERAL RESERVE SYSTEM (FRS)

The central bank of the United States which functions to control the money supply, availability of credit and interest rates. The FRS is comprised of twelve *Federal Reserve Banks* to which all nationally chartered commercial banks must belong and to which state chartered banks may choose to join. The system was created by Congress in 1913 and is governed by a seven-member Board of Governors each of whom are appointed for fourteen year terms by the President of the United States.

FEDERAL REVENUE STAMP

A U. S. revenue stamp which until January 1, 1968, was required to be placed on deeds prior to recordation. The rate was $ .55 per $500 of consideration, and proof that the stamps had been purchased was evidenced by the actual placement of the stamps on the instrument being recorded. Since the end of this requirement in 1968, some states have passed their own requirements for revenue stamps.

FEDERAL SAVINGS AND LOAN INSURANCE CORPORATION (FSLIC)

A corporation established in 1934 as an agency of the federal government which insures the deposits of member savings and loan associations. Federally chartered S & Ls must maintain membership and state chartered associations may be members. Well over 90 percent of all deposits in S & Ls are insured by the FSLIC.

FEDERAL TAX LIEN

A federal lien which attaches to the real property of a person when that taxpayer has violated either federal estate tax laws or federal income tax laws. When a person dies his or her estate is subject to a federal estate tax. This tax causes a lien to attach on all real and personal property in the estate for a statutory period of ten years or until the tax is paid. If a person fails to pay federal income taxes, the government may issue a tax warrant which, when recorded in the federal tax docket in the county records, attaches a federal tax lien.

FEDERAL TRADE COMMISSION (FTC)

An agency of the federal government created in 1914 that has as its primary function the promotion of free and fair competition in interstate commerce through the prevention of unfair and deceptive trade practices. In addition, FTC enforces the *Fair Credit Reporting Act* and those parts of the *Truth-in-Lending Act* related to real estate brokers.

FEE APPRAISER

A person who charges a fee for rendering his or her opinion as to the value of a parcel of real estate. It is unethical for appraisers to charge a percentage of the derived value estimate as their compensation. (*See* **Appraisal, Value**)

FEE SIMPLE

The largest quantum of ownership recognized by law; also referred to as *fee simple absolute* or *fee*. The owner of the fee simple has unlimited power to dispose of the interests during his or her lifetime and upon death the property is automatically passed on to the owner's heirs and devisees either by will or by descent. Ownership in this country is ordinarily in the fee simple form. The only restrictions on use are those restrictions defined by the *law of nuisance* or those necessarily imposed by law in order to protect the interests of society. A fee simple owner may convey lesser estates, sell easements, mortgage the property or do whatever else he or she wishes with the property so long as others are not harmed by the improper use of the property. The fee simple absolute is created by using the words "to (name) and his heirs and assigns forever."

FEE SIMPLE ABSOLUTE

(*See* **Fee Simple**)

FEE SIMPLE DETERMINABLE

A qualified fee simple estate created to exist only until the occurrence or nonoccurrence of a particular event. The words, "so long as" are ordinarily used to create the estate. *Examples* of a fee simple determinable include:
1. "To John Smith and his heirs so long as the premises not be used to sell intoxicating liquor or illegal drugs."
2. "To XYZ Church so long as the land be used exclusively for church purposes." If the property is not used as designated or if the property is used for a prohibited use, the estate will automatically expire. The original grantor or the grantor's heirs have a future interest called a *possibility of reverter*.

FEE SIMPLE SUBJECT TO A CONDITION SUBSEQUENT

A qualified fee estate which is subject to a power in the original grantor or the grantor's heirs to terminate the estate upon the happening of an event. The termination is not automatic, since the party with the future interest called the *right of reentry* or *power of termination* must take steps to either enter upon the property or to bring a court action to recover the land. *Examples* of a fee simple subject to a condition subsequent include:
1. "To Mary Jones on the condition that the property be used as a camp for parentless children."
2. "To James Smith on the condition that he remain single until he is thirty years of age."

FEE SIMPLE SUBJECT TO AN EXECUTORY LIMITATION

A qualified fee simple estate which will *automatically* pass on to a third person upon the occurrence or nonoccurrence of a stated event. *Examples* of fee simple subject to an executory limitation include:

1. "To Mary Smith until Linda Jones has a child, then to Linda Jones"
2. "To ABC Church so long as the land be used for church purposes, then to the XYZ University"

FEE TAIL

An estate in land which was designed to restrict the conveyance of title to the descendants of the grantee. This estate is established by a grant in which the following words of conveyance are used, "to X and the heirs of his body." Effectively the fee tail created a long series of successive life estates. This estate was designed to promote the landlord aristocracy in England by keeping property in the family. Most states in this country have abolished this estate, and where it has not been abolished, the estate has been severely restricted. In those states that still recognize the fee tail, the first grantee is given a life estate, but the remainder-man receives a fee simple. It is also ordinarily easy to defeat the estate by court action. The reason for this is that any restraint on *alienation* is not favored in this country. Alienation is a term which means the transfer of title from one person to another. Any restraints on alienation are strictly construed by the courts.

FELONY

A crime more serious than a misdemeanor. (*See* **Misdemeanor**)

FEUDAL SYSTEM

A system of land ownership established in England after the Norman conquest of 1066, in which all property theoretically resided in the king. In return for military service or other duties the king would give a *feud* or *fief* to a lord. This lord would not have full ownership, but held the property under the paramount title of the king. The lord would be a tenant or vassal of the king. This lord would give a lesser fief to a sublord in return for services, and the process would repeat itself. At the very bottom of the land tenure chain would be the serf who would hold land in return for crops and other services. This system of land tenure caused society to be organized in the form of a pyramid with all ownership being derived from some superior lord who ultimately derived his ownership from the king. In other words, the feudal system never conveyed full ownership but rather various rights and interests. Some of these rights and interests evolved into inheritable estates or fees. The term "fee" is derived from the terms "fief" or "feud" and is related to inheritable estates. Other rights and interests conveyed possession, but not title. This included various tenancies which are defined by the law of landlord and tenant. (*See* **Allodial System**)

FHA

A common reference to the *Federal Housing Administration*. (*See* **Federal Housing Administration**)

FHA INSURANCE

An insurance fee charged the borrower on all FHA mortgages. The insurance payment is retained by FHA for use in buying any mortgage in default that is being held by a lender. (*See* **Federal Housing Administration**)

FIABCI

(*See* **International Real Estate Federation**)

FIDELITY BOND

(*See* **Surety Bond**)

FIDUCIARY

A person who essentially holds the character of a trustee. Real estate brokers and salespersons are considered by law to be fiduciaries, thus they have a duty to act primarily for the principal's (the person who employed them) benefit and not their own. A fiduciary must act with the highest degree of care and good faith in relations with the principal and on the principal's business. The penalties for failing in fiduciary duties may be quite severe. For example, a real estate broker generally loses the right to a commission if the following duties are breached: loyalty, fidelity, obedience of legitimate instruction, due care, accounting, and the giving of notice of material facts affecting the subject matter of the agency. The extent of the penalty depends on the seriousness of the breach and the damages sustained by the principal. There are cases where the penalty was a loss of the broker's license and even criminal sanctions. (*See* **Agency**)

FIEF

An interest in land given under a feudal system. The term "fee," as used to denote the extent of one's interest in land, is derived from the term fief. (*See* **Feudal System**)

FIFTEEN-YEAR MORTGAGE

A loan with a less than traditional payback period, specifically one of fifteen years. During the past thirty years, the vast majority of long-term residential loans have been made with twenty, twenty-five, and thirty year payouts. However, in recent years more and more homebuyers have opted for loans with shorter maturity periods, such as fifteen-year mortgages. The primary advantage of a early-payout mortgage is the fact that considerably less interest is paid over the life of the mortgage since the principal is borrowed for a shorter period of time. However, offsetting this advantage is the fact that since the principal is borrowed for a less than normal period of time, the principal repayment each period is greater than with twenty-five and thirty-year mortgages. Thus, higher monthly payments eliminate many people from qualifying for fifteen-year mortgages. For example, $80,000 borrowed at a 10 percent rate of interest requires a monthly payment of $702.06 to fully amortize the loan over thirty years. However, the monthly payment increases to $859.68 if the loan is amortized over a fifteen-year pay-back.

FILTERING DOWN PROCESS

The means by which housing once occupied by middle- and upper-income groups becomes available to lower-income families. Normally the property has physically deteriorated and thus is less expensive than when originally occupied.

FINAL VALUE ESTIMATE

The estimate of value reached after the appraiser has analyzed the data, reconciled the value indications provided by the application of the various approaches to value, and made a final judgment. (*See* **Appraisal Process**)

FINANCE CHARGES

The total of all costs paid to the lender by the borrower directly or indirectly as an incident to the extension of credit. The *Truth-in-Lending Act* requires that consumers be told of the following charges: interest, finder and origination fees, discount points, service charges, credit report fees, and other such charges.

FINANCE FEE

(*See* **Discount Points, Loan Origination Fee**)

FINANCIAL FEASIBILITY

The likelihood that a proposed project will attain a cash flow of sufficient quantity, quality, and duration to allow investors to recover the capital invested and achieve the necessary and expected rate of return. Factors to be considered are the timing of inflows and outflows of cash, revenues, costs, debt service, and the proceeds of a sale or refinancing.

FINANCIAL INSTITUTION

An organization that attracts funds through some type of deposit mechanism and lends those funds to individuals or corporations in order to make an acceptable return. The major financial institutions involved in financing real estate are savings and loan associations, commercial banks, mutual savings banks, life insurance companies, credit unions, finance companies, and pension funds.

FINANCIAL INTERMEDIARY

A financial institution that serves as a middleman between depositors and borrowers. Savings and loan associations, for example, attract many deposits from individuals. In turn, these deposits are made available to borrowers through a loan. The difference between what the financial intermediary pays to attract deposits and what it charges on its loan is its gross profit.

FINANCIAL LEVERAGE

The use of borrowed money to complete an investment transaction. If the asset purchased with borrowed money offers annual financial benefits at a rate in excess of the loan's interest rate, leverage is said to be *positive* or favorable. The investor makes money by borrowing. Conversely, if an asset purchased with borrowed money fails to increase in value or if it fails to provide benefits in excess of the interest rate paid on the borrowed money, then leverage is *negative*. Leverage is neutral when the property earns at the same rate as the interest rate on borrowed money. (*See* **Leverage**)

FINANCIAL MANAGEMENT RATE OF RETURN (FMRR)

A modified internal rate of return model designed to remedy some of the deficiencies of the *internal rate of return (IRR)* technique. Two rates are considered by the FMRR: (1) a safe, liquid after-tax rate, and (2) a run-of-the mill reinvestment rate. (*See* **Rate of Return**)

FINANCIAL RATIO ANALYSIS

A means by which an investor/lender detects facets of a business or investment that are within norms as well as those that become unhealthy. An astute investor uses financial ratio analysis to compare potential acquisitions and select the ones offering the greatest potential. By monitoring constantly changing ratios, it is possible to detect areas of weakness for both management and capital employment in order to take steps necessary to bring ratios back to the desired balance level of safety and risk.

FINANCIAL SOLVENCY

The expected normal condition of a business present when current assets exceed current liabilities.

FINANCIAL STATEMENT

A written statement of the financial position of a person or company, showing total assets and liabilities as of a certain date. Many lenders require a financial statement as part of a loan application.

FINANCIAL STRUCTURE

The mix of equity and debt used in the purchase price of an asset.

FINANCIER

A person or financial institution engaged in the lending and management of money.

FINANCING

The difference between the purchase price and the down payment, commonly referred to as *debt* or the *mortgage*. One of the features distinguishing real estate from some investments is the ability to finance all or a significant part of the purchase price with borrowed dollars. (*See* **Financial Leverage**)

FINANCING COSTS

(*See* **Finance Charges**)

FINANCING PACKAGE

The total of all loans used to develop and/or purchase a real estate project. For example, the financing package assembled by a builder might include the loan to purchase the land, a construction loan, gap financing, and permanent loans prearranged for the purchasers of the finished homes.

FINANCING STATEMENT

A written notice filed in the public records by a creditor who has extended credit for the purchase of personal property. The purpose of filing the statement is to establish the creditor's interest in the personal property which is the security for the debt but which may become a fixture when it is attached to real property. For example, if a homeowner purchases a dishwasher on time and has the dishwasher installed, then the dishwasher becomes a fixture and thus is subject to liens which may exist or be placed against the house. However, by filing the financing statement, the store who sold the dishwasher protects its lien position against the dishwasher and the store's claims are superior to the rights of lien-holders of the property.

FINDER'S FEE

A payment made by one party to another for locating a prospect. This payment is often used in the financing of real estate when a mortgage banker locates a lender willing to loan money to a borrower. In addition, in most states real estate brokers may legally split a real estate sales commission with another broker who was partly responsible for bringing about the sale. However, an unlicensed person may not legally accept a finder's fee from a real estate broker since by doing so the unlicensed person is brokering real estate without a license and is thus in violation of licensing law. The term is also known as a *referral fee*.

FIRE AND EXTENDED COVERAGE INSURANCE

A basic fire insurance policy protecting the insured against losses suffered from fire or lightning. In addition, the owner can receive extended coverage which insures against losses suffered due to windstorm, hail, explosion, riot or civil commotion, aircraft, vehicles, smoke, theft, and vandalism and malicious mischief. Coverage of these extra perils normally adds very little to the premium. (*See* **Homeowner's Insurance**)

FIRM COMMITMENT

An agreement by a financial institution to loan a specified sum of money for a specific time period and at a certain interest rate, provided all conditions set by the lender are met by the borrower.

FIRM OFFER

An offer made by a potential buyer that will not be further negotiated.

FIRM PRICE

A stated sales price that is fixed and, thus, non-negotiable. While uncommon in real estate transactions, occasionally an owner will put his or her property on the market at a firm price and will instruct the listing sales broker not to accept any offer below the listed price.

FIRST LIEN

A legal claim with the highest priority against a certain property; also known as a *senior lien*.

FIRST MORTGAGE

A lien on property in which the lender's claims are superior to the rights of subsequent lenders. Such a lien position means less risk to the lender and thus normally results in a lower interest rate charged to the borrower than that charged on second or junior mortgages. Certain lenders only make first mortgages due to regulatory requirements; others limit mortgages to these senior instruments due to company policy.

FIRST STEP OF REFUSAL

(*See* **Right of First Refusal**)

FISCAL YEAR

A business year used for accounting or tax purposes as compared to a calendar year. The fiscal year of many governmental units, including the federal government, runs from July 1 through June 30 of the following year. Whether or not a local government operates on a fiscal or calendar year is particularly important in prorating property taxes between buyer and seller. (*See* **Proration**)

FIXED EXPENSES

Expenditures such as property taxes, license fees, and property insurance that do not vary given changes in the occupancy rate. Fixed expenses are one of the items subtracted from effective gross income to determine the net operating income of property. (*See* **Net Operating Income, Operating Expenses**)

FIXED RATE MORTGAGE

A loan carrying a constant interest rate over the full life of the mortgage. Historically, fixed rate mortgages have been the norm in permanent financing, particularly residential real estate. Thus, when a borrower secures a fixed rate mortgage he or she knows that the lender cannot raise the interest rate regardless of what the market rate of interest is doing. However, in recent years lenders have in some instances been reluctant to loan money for a long period of time without including in the loan provision a clause allowing them to vary the rate of interest if and when market conditions change. (*See* **Variable Rate Mortgage**)

FIXER UPPER

(*See* **Handyman's Special**)

FIXING-UP EXPENSES

The money spent to repair and/or refurbish real estate so as to improve its marketability.

FIXITY OF LOCATION

A physical characteristic of land which makes it subject to the influence of surrounding land uses. Since real estate space is fixed in location it cannot be moved. While it is true that the various elements within the space may be moved, such as the topsoil or the minerals, the space itself remains in the same geographic location. This immobility leads to several legal and economic results. From a legal standpoint only the legal rights and not the asset itself can be physically transferred to a purchaser. Accordingly this transference requires a description of the space which is dependent on clearly defined reference points. Without a sufficient description, courts will not recognize legal instruments purporting to convey rights in the real estate. From an economic standpoint, in order to use the real estate as part of a productive good, other factors of production must be attracted to the land; the land cannot go to the other factors of production. Likewise, the real estate is highly dependent on the surrounding environment. If someone builds a store, a factory or a house on a site nearby, this change in land use will have some effect, either positive or negative, on the subject property. The dependency of each parcel of real estate on the surrounding environment leads to a reliance on public goods such as highways, utilities, nearby schools, and parks. The immobility also causes real estate markets to be very local in nature.

FIXTURE

Personal property which for some reason, such as the manner of attachment, has become realty. Such property is also referred to as *chattel real*. Examples of fixtures include built-in cabinets in a kitchen, bathtubs, permanent bookcases, and other such objects.

The tests that courts consider in determining if an item is indeed a fixture include the following:

1. *Reasonable intent of the party annexing the object.* Where custom ordinarily presumes an object to be a fixture, the secret subjective intent of a party annexing (attaching) an object will have little weight. However, where there is a doubt, the intent of the party will be controlling. Care should be taken with such objects as refrigerators, stoves, and washers to determine whether they are locally considered

to be fixtures or personal property. If a doubt arises, care should be taken to specify disposition of the property in a contract.

2. *Adaption of the object.* If an object has been custom-made to be used with and as part of the realty, this will lead the courts to believe that the intent was for the object to be a fixture. An example of this might be custom-made drapes or storm windows.

3. *Method of annexation.* If the removal of an article or object will cause permanent damage to the realty, it is ordinarily considered to be a fixture. For example, wall to wall carpeting is often considered to be a fixture while a large rug would be considered as personal.

4. *Relationship of parties.* In cases where property is leased to a commercial tenant, any fixtures that the tenant brings into the realty for the purpose of conducting business such as shelving and counters will not be considered as realty. These fixtures are called *trade fixtures* and retain their character as personalty unless otherwise specified in the lease contract. (*See* **Personal Property**)

FLAG LOT
A parcel of land that is shaped like a flagpole and flag with the land being the "flag" and the only access being the "pole."

FLAT
A floor or part of a floor in a building designed for occupancy by a single family for residential purposes.

FLAT LEASE
A type of lease requiring the tenant to pay equal rent payment each period, be the period monthly or annually. Rental payments under this type of lease do not change during the term of the lease and thus because of expected inflation are not generally used by a landlord when the lease is for a significant period of time. (*See* **Graduated Lease, Index Lease**)

FLEA BAG
An inexpensive, run-down rental property such as an apartment or hotel room.

FLEXIBLE LOAN INSURANCE PROGRAM (FLIP)
An innovative financing technique developed to overcome the negative amortization aspects of the *graduated payment mortgage*. The key to the FLIP mortgage is the use of the buyer's down payment. Instead of being used as a down payment, the cash is deposited in a pledged, interest-bearing savings account where it serves as both a cash collateral for the lender and as a source of supplemental payments for the borrower during the first few years of the loan. During the early years of the mortgage, each month the lender withdraws predetermined amounts from the savings account and adds them to the borrower's reduced payment to make a full normal mortgage payment. The supplemental payment decreases each

month and vanishes at the end of a predetermined period (usually five years). By using this type of program, a borrower is likely to qualify for a larger loan than with a conventional fully-amortized mortgage. (*See* **Graduated Payment Mortgage**)

FLIP

The near simultaneous buying and selling of a parcel of real estate at an inflated price for the purpose of leveraging the transaction. For example, a financial institution would pay $6 million for a project and immediately sell it to a prearranged buyer for $8 million, and agree to finance the $8 million purchase. In turn, the buyer, anticipating a significant increase in the value of the property, agrees to what might normally be considered a high interest rate.

FLOAT

The time period in which a person has free use of someone else's money. For example, building materials could be charged on the first day of the month and the bill for those materials would not be sent until the end of the month. In addition, a finance charge would not be charged as long as the bill is paid by the tenth day of the following month. The builder delivers a check for the material on the tenth. The check is not deposited until the next day and does not clear the bank until the fourteenth of the month. Thus, the buyer who charged the material a full forty-four days ago has the benefit of the float, or in essence an interest-free loan for forty-four days.

FLOATING RATE

A finance term used to explain the spread on a variable interest rate loan. Developers and builders often borrow money at an interest rate tied to the prime rate, for example, "prime plus two." This means that if the prime rate is 10% the builder pays 12% on the money borrowed. However, if the prime increases to 11%, then the interest rate charged by the lender floats upward to, in this case, 13%.

FLOOD INSURANCE

Insurance that protects a property owner from damages resulting from flooding. Due to the high cost of flood insurance when written through a private insurance company, Congress enacted the *National Flood Insurance Program* in 1968. The intent of this legislation was to provide insurance coverage for those people suffering both real and personal property losses as a result of floods. Due to the lack of public interest in the program, Congress enacted the *Flood Disaster Protection Act* in 1975. Under this law, no real estate located in a floodplain area can be financed through a federally regulated lender unless flood insurance is purchased.

FLOODPLAIN

The land bordering or surrounding a river or stream that can be under water when the river or stream are at their high-water mark.

FLOOR AREA

The total of all the horizontal areas of all the floors in a building. For example, a ten-story building with 5,000 square feet of floor space on each floor would have a total floor area of 50,000 square feet. Minimum floor areas are sometimes included in the restrictive covenants by a developer so as to maintain some degree of conformity throughout the subdivisions. For example, the covenant could require a minimum of 2,000 square feet livable space. Thus, a buyer of one of the lots could not build a house that contained fewer square feet than this minimum.

FLOOR AREA RATIO (FAR)

The relationship between the floor area of a building and the total area of the land under the building. Minimum and maximum floor area ratios are often established as part of a zoning ordinance. For example, a 2:1 FAR means that two square feet of floor space may be constructed on one square foot of land. In other words, a two-story building covering the entire lot could be built. If only one-half of the lot were covered, a four-story building could be constructed, while if only one-quarter of the lot were covered, an eight-story building could be developed.

FLOOR DUTY

A procedure used in many real estate brokerage offices in which one or more sales associates are responsible for answering all telephone inquiries and office visits during a specific period of time. The benefit to the company is the assurance that all inquiries will be handled, while the benefit to the person(s) on floor duty is the opportunity to acquire new clients that would otherwise not be known.

FLOOR LOAN

(*See* Floor-to-Ceiling Loan)

FLOOR PLAN

The layout of a building showing the exact specifications as to size and shape of each room.

FLOOR-TO-CEILING LOAN

A financing technique in which the total amount of the loan is a function of the projected net operating income of the project. The total amount of the loan is funded by the lender in two separate payments. The "floor loan" is made upon satisfactory completion of the project and may be as high as 50 to 75 percent of the total loan. The remainder of the loan, the "ceiling," is funded only if certain predetermined occupancy and or net income requirements are met. For example, 90 percent of the total loan may be funded when 50 percent of the building's available space has been leased, and 100 percent of the loan will be funded only after 70 percent of the total space is under lease. Lenders use floor-to-ceiling loans to minimize their exposure in case the building does not lease enough space to generate the income necessary to pay the mortgage. If, in fact, the building is short on tenants and thus the lender funds less than is needed, the builder must turn to other sources of funds or, as it is commonly called, seek *gap financing*. (*See* **Gap Financing**)

FLOW OF INCOME

The total amount of income projected from a real estate investment as stated in either annual figures or the total flow over the economic life of the investment. (*See* **Capitalization**)

FMHA

(*See* **Farmer's Home Administration**)

FNMA

(*See* **Federal National Mortgage Association**)

FORBEARANCE

Refraining from action by a creditor against the debt owed by a borrower after the debt has become due. For example, while a lender may be legally able to foreclose against property after the debt is in arrears, a lender does not have to foreclose and, in fact, may choose not to as long as the borrower is taking positive steps to pay what is in arrears.

FORECASTING

An estimate of future events based on present knowledge, facts, theory, and judgment. Numerous real estate associations and organizations are constantly forecasting what lies ahead for their particular membership. For example, homebuilders use forecasts made by both private associations and government agencies in determining how many housing units they will build during a particular period. Forecasts of both long- and short-term interest rates are important to would-be real estate investors as these investors choose where they will make their investments.

FORCED SALE

The selling of an asset under less than favorable conditions in order to liquidate the asset, such as the selling of mortgaged property through foreclosure by the lender.

FORECLOSURE

A legal procedure by which mortgaged property in which there has been default on the part of the mortgagor (borrower) is sold to satisfy the mortgage debt. The most common type of foreclosure in most states is *foreclosure by sale*. Foreclosure by sale takes two general forms: (1) *foreclosure by judicial sale*, and (2) *foreclosure by power of sale* (also known as *foreclosure by advertisement*). While procedures differ from state to state, under a foreclosure by judicial sale, a petition is usually filed with the court against the defaulting mortgagor and all persons having junior lien interests in the property. The petition states the nature of the default, the amount due, and the property involved. A person who has a junior lien position and is not included in the foreclosure suit is unaffected by the court decree. In order to prevent new liens from attaching while the property is being foreclosed, it is customary to file a *notice of pendency* which gives constructive notice to the world that the property is in litigation. A person who has a junior position is able to foreclose the rights of all persons in a junior position but not persons in a senior position. However, the junior lienholder may take the property subject to the senior position or redeem the senior interest. Once all parties have been notified according to state procedure, the court will make a determination whether there has been a default. If a default is declared and the mortgagor is unable to make good, the court will order the property sold at auction. Depending on local rules, a person such as a sheriff or referee will place the property for sale. After the sale is made, the court will be asked to confirm the price. In the process of confirmation the court will determine whether the foreclosure sale was fairly held. If the price achieved is unreasonably low, the court has the power to set the sale aside. If there is a surplus, the lienholders will be paid off in the order of their priority according to state rules. The mortgagor will receive any remaining amount. In situations where the proceeds from the foreclosure sale are insufficient to pay off the mortgage note, the note holder may seek a *deficiency judgment* from the court, a personal claim against the debtor.

Foreclosure under a power of sale is permitted in many states as a substitute for a foreclosure by judicial sale. A provision is included in the mortgage which gives the mortgagee the right to sell the property upon default by giving proper statutory notice. There are both advantages and disadvantages to such a foreclosure. The advantages include speed and efficiency in disposing of the property. As in the judicial sale, the foreclosure under power of sale is held at a public auction with the property going to the highest bidder. Some states severely limit the right to a deficiency judgment and there may also be some question as to the marketability of title acquired pursuant to such a sale. Rather than going through the process of a foreclosure the mortgagor may be willing to give a *deed in lieu of foreclosure.* When a mortgagee accepts a deed in satisfaction of the mortgage debt, the mortgagor's redemption rights are terminated in the absence of any fraud. One disadvantage to the mortgagee, however, is that the property is taken subject to all of the junior liens on the property. These liens would have been terminated if the property had undergone a foreclosure sale. A few states recognize *foreclosure by entry and possession.* This is a peaceful possession or possession by a court order called a *writ of entry* by the mortgagee upon the default by the mortgagor. Some states such as Pennsylvania recognize a special type of foreclosure procedure called a *foreclosure by scire facias.* This is essentially the same as a sale by judicial sale but cannot take place until one year after default. Other peculiarities exist, and the reader should become familiar with local and state requirements. (*See* **Deed of Trust, Equity of Redemption, Mortgage, Statutory Period of Redemption**)

FOREIGN CORPORATION

A corporation not incorporated or chartered in a particular state yet conducting business in that state. Even though it is not chartered in states where it is doing business, a foreign corporation must consent to certain requirements and conditions before it may legally operate in the state. (*See* **Corporation**)

FORESHORE

The part of a parcel of land lying between the high water mark and the low water mark.

FORFEITURE

Loss of property for some specified reason such as nonperformance of a condition or legal obligation. (*See* **Fee Simple Subject to a Condition Subsequent**)

FORGERY

Altering a written document with the intent to injure or defraud someone. For example, two people claiming to be husband and wife attempt by use of a deed to convey property which is actually owned by one of these two people and a third person. Such a deed would be void and an innocent third party who purchased this property would not have valid title to the property. (*See* **Title Insurance**)

FORMAL CONTRACT

A written contract under seal that is enforceable because of the way it is written and does not depend upon sufficiency of the consideration. (*See* **Contract**)

FORWARD COMMITMENT

An agreement by a lender or investor to either make or purchase a loan within a certain period of time into the future. For example, a builder might receive a commitment from a lender to borrow a certain sum of money at an agreed upon rate and the commitment might be good for a specified period of time, such as 90 days. By having this forward commitment the builder knows how much money can be borrowed plus what the money will cost. For such a commitment, the lender may charge the builder a fee such as so many points if and when the money is actually borrowed. Purchasers in the secondary mortgage market such as Fannie Mae and Freddie Mac make forward commitments to lenders for a specified time such as six months and at a certain interest rate. By having this commitment a lender knows what interest rate a borrower will have to be charged if the loan is going to be sold in the secondary mortgage market. (*See* **Secondary Mortgage Market**)

4-3-2-1 RULE

A rule of thumb used by appraisers in estimating the value of land. The rule states that in a standard sized lot, 40 percent of the total value is allocated to the front (street frontage) quarter of the lot, 30 percent to the second quarter, 20 percent to the third quarter and 10 percent to the back quarter. Such an approach is nothing more than an approximation and should not be used if a more definitive estimate is desired.

FRACTIONAL APPRAISAL

An appraisal of one component or legal interest of the whole property. For example, an appraisal of a leasehold interest would be an example of a fractional appraisal.

FRACTIONAL INTEREST

A partial interest in real estate, such as an easement.

FRACTIONAL OWNERSHIP

(*See* **Time Sharing**)

FRANCHISE

A business arrangement undertaken for the purpose of marketing a product or service. One party (the *franchiser*) provides marketing and selling expertise for a fee to another party (the *franchisee*) who in turn sells the product or service in the marketplace. In recent years franchised brokerage operations have become very popular ways to market real estate services. National franchises such as Century 21, Gallery of Homes, and Realty World are located in large and small towns alike. Independent real estate brokers enter into contractual agreement with the franchiser for the purpose of leasing the franchise name, referral services, sales training programs and other marketing services. Typically, the broker is charged a franchise fee plus a percentage of gross sales.

FRAUD

A misrepresentation of a material fact which is made with knowledge of its falsity and with intent to deceive a party who in fact relies on the misrepresentation to his or her detriment and injury. Fraud can result from words spoken or written, acts, or nondisclosure where there is a duty to inform. Fraud is a defense against the enforcement of a contract. In addition, it is grounds for damages in a separate tort action and in many circumstances a criminal violation. While ordinarily the doctrine of *caveat emptor* or "let the buyer beware" is used to justify that the purchaser is responsible for observing defects in a house, this doctrine does not apply in situation of concealment or hidden defects. If should also be noted that courts are moving away from the doctrine of caveat emptor as more states adopt consumer-oriented policies.

Example: Don is planning to sell a house which has a flooded basement whenever it rains. He paints the basement in such a manner that all water marks are removed. Shirley inspects the house and makes no inquiry as to whether there is a leaky basement. She buys the house. One week after closing, the basement floods after a thunderstorm, and she wishes to rescind the contract. Many courts will find fraud in Don concealing the water marks and then failing to advise Shirley of the flooding problem.

The National Association of Realtors' Code of Ethics states that it is the duty of the Realtor to protect the public against fraud, misrepresentation, and unethical practices in real estate transactions. In addition, real estate licensing laws in every state include provisions for either the suspension and/or revocation of a broker or salesperson's license for fraudulent acts. *(See* **Misrepresentation**)

FRAUDS, STATUTE OF
(See **Statute of Frauds**)

FREDDIE MAC
A common name used to refer to the *Federal Home Loan Mortgage Corporation.* *(See* **Federal Home Loan Mortgage Corporation**)

FREE AND CLEAR
Title to property which is unencumbered by any mortgages or other liens.

FREEHOLD
An estate in real property which continues for an indefinite period of time. Freehold estates may be *inheritable* or *noninheritable*. Inheritable estates include the fee simple absolute, the qualified fee, and the fee tail. Noninheritable estates include various life estates which are created by acts of parties, such as an ordinary life estate, or by operation of law, such as dower and curtesy.

Less than freehold estates are generally referred to as *leaseholds*. These estates are considered to exist for a definite period of time or successive periods of time until termination by notice. Conventionally, nonfreehold estates may be classified as follows: (1) *estate for years*, (2) *estate from period to period* or *periodic tenancy*, (3) *tenancy at will*, and (4) *tenancy at sufferance*. *(See* **Fee Simple, Conventional Life Estate**)

FREEHOLDER
One who owns a freehold interest in real property. *(See* **Freehold**)

FREE MARKET SYSTEM AUCTION
An auction process used by the *Federal National Mortgage Association* in which the association accepts bids from approved lenders as to the amount, price, and terms of existing mortgages that these lenders wish to sell to Fannie Mae. Upon deciding how much money it will spend during a given time period, Fannie Mae notifies the successful bidders (determined by those mortgages offered for sale that will generate the highest yield to FNMA), and these bidders have a certain time period in which they can choose to deliver the mortgages. Once the mortgages have been delivered to Fannie Mae, the originator of the mortgage continues to service the loan (collect monthly payments, escrow property taxes, etc.) and for this service the originator receives a servicing fee.

FRM

(See Fixed Rate Mortgage)

FRONTAGE

The distance of property facing a street or water which is available for the construction of a building.

FRONTAGE ASSESSMENT

An assessment made by local governments to pay for improvements such as roads. Improvements such as roads or sidewalks can be paid for by assessing the property facing or abutting the road based on the proportion of a particular property's frontage to the total distance being improved.

FRONT-END FEE

Charges made by a lender to a borrower for expenses incurred in determining whether or not a loan will be made. Such expenses would include credit report, appraisal, survey, structural inspection, and various legal fees. The fee may be stated as a set amount or as a percentage of the requested loan. Such fees are not payment for the use of money and thus are not considered to be interest.

FRONT FOOT

A property measurement for purposes of valuation that is measured by the front footage on the street line. When the dimensions of a lot are given, such as 200 by 600, the first measurement, 200, normally refers to the front footage.

FRONT MONEY

Money that must be raised by a builder/developer before obtaining financing in order to start a project. Front money is needed to pay for such expenditures as options on the land, legal fees, feasibility, and engineering studies, and architectural drawings. The money, also known as *seed money*, is normally provided by the equity investor(s) since at this stage in the development of a project financing has not been finalized.

FSBO

An acronym denoting property *for sale by owner*, which means the owner is attempting to sell without listing the property with a real estate broker.

FULL DISCLOSURE

The obligation to reveal all material facts. Under agency law a real estate broker or salesperson acting as an agent is required to fully disclose all material facts to a third party. Failing to do so may result in legal action against the agent. In addition, federal and state acts such as the *Truth-in-Lending Act* and the *Interstate Land Sales Full Disclosure Act* require that certain information be made available to the consumer.

FULL-PRICE OFFER
An offer to purchase real estate at the exact price and with the exact conditions stated by the owner. Most real estate offers are not full-price offers, although in some isolated markets offers are made above the listing price due to the high demand and short supply of available property.

FULLY AMORTIZED MORTGAGE
A loan that is fully repaid at maturity by periodic reduction of the principal. The first part of each payment covers interest on the outstanding debt as of the payment due date and the remainder of the payment reduces the outstanding debt. (*See* **Amortized Loan, Balloon Payment**)

FUNCTIONAL OBSOLESCENCE
A loss in value within a structure due to changes in tastes, preferences, technical innovations, or market standards. The item in question may be *curable*, such as lack of air conditioning in Florida, or *incurable*, such as exceptionally low ceilings in a warehouse, depending on the costs of correcting the item as compared to the benefits expected if the correction is made. (*See* **Cost Approach**)

FURTHER ASSISTANCE
(*See* **Covenant of Further Assurance**)

FUTURE ADVANCES
Money loaned by a mortgagee (lender) to a mortgagor (borrower) after the mortgage has been placed on the property and secured by the original security agreement. A *construction loan* often calls for future advances in which dollars are dispersed to the developer as various stages of construction are completed.

FUTURE ADVANCES CLAUSE
(*See* **Dragnet Clause**)

FUTURE INTEREST
A present ownership interest or possibility of ownership in land with the right of possession postponed into the future. Essentially a future interest is a present nonpossessory right which will or may become a possessory right at some future date. Future interest may be classified as follows: (1) *possibility of reverter*, (2) *right of reentry* or *power of termination*, (3) *reversions*, and (4) *remainders*.

FUTURE WORTH OF ONE
A factor used to calculate how much a present sum will be worth in the future if it is held for a certain period of time and earns an interest rate that is compounded periodically. The factor is calculated using the formula:

$$S^n = (1 + i)^n$$

The formula can be used in real estate to calculate the value of a parcel of real estate at some point in the future given the current value of the parcel and its estimated periodic increase in value.

Example: A parcel of land has a current value of $10,000. What will the land be worth in 5 years if it is expected to increase in value 10% per year?

$$S^n = (1 + i)^n$$
$$S^n = (1 + .10)^5 \quad = \quad 1.6105$$
$$\$10,000 \times 1.6105 \quad = \quad \$16,105$$

The future worth will be $16,105.

FUTURE WORTH OF ONE PER PERIOD

A factor used to calculate how much a series of equal sums deposited at the end of periodic compounding time intervals will be worth at the end of the total term. The factor is calculated using the formula:

$$S_n = \frac{(1 + i)^n - 1}{i}$$

Example: How much will be accumulated if $1,000 is deposited each year for 15 years and compounded at an interest rate of 10%?

$$S_n = \frac{(1 + i)^n - 1}{i}$$

$$S_n = \frac{(1 + .10)^{15} - 1}{.10}$$

$$S_n = 31.7725$$

$$\$1,000 \times 31.7725 = \$31,772.50$$

The future worth will be $31,772.50

GAP FINANCING

A loan covering the period between the expiration of the construction loan and the time when conditions set by a permanent lender have been met. Gap financing often covers a shorter period than permanent financing and because of risk, the "gap" lender usually charges a higher interest rate. When used to supplement permanent financing, gap financing becomes a *junior mortgage* For example, the developer of a shopping center might be able to borrow $2,000,000 if 80% of the available space is leased, but only $1,600,000 if 70% of the space is leased. In this case, the permanent lender will have first claim on the property, while the lender who fills the $400,000 financing "gap" will have a secondary claim. If gap financing is the sole method used during a period, it becomes a *senior mortgage.*

GARDEN APARTMENT

A type of apartment dwelling which includes a grass or lawn area.

GARNISHMENT

A legal process whereby a person's property or money which is in possession or control by a third party (*garnishee*) can be legally applied towards paying debt owed to a third party in order to satisfy the debt.

GENERAL AGENT

One authorized to transact all of the principal's affairs within the context of a broad commercial or other kind of endeavor. A general agent, for example the manager of a store, has broad discretionary powers in acting for his principal. As a result, the duty of a third person to inquire as to the scope of a general agent's authority may be mitigated. (*See* **Agent**)

GENERAL CONTRACTOR

A person who agrees to construct all of a real estate project, such as an office building or warehouse, rather than just a portion or part of the structure. The general contractor is responsible for hiring the subcontractors (plumbers, electricians, drywallers, etc.), coordinating all construction activities and making payments to all of the subcontractors. A general contractor is also known as a *prime contractor.*

GENERAL IMPROVEMENT

A public improvement, such as a power line, which benefits the public in general. The cost of making the improvement, therefore, cannot be assessed against specific property owners even though the improvement may incidentally benefit specific property owners.

GENERAL LIEN

A claim on all the property owned by an individual. The types of general liens include judgment liens established by courts, creditors' liens on the estate of a deceased person, and federal and state tax liens. Judgment liens may be *in personam*, applying to all personal property, or *in rem*, applying to a specific property. Only judgments in personam are general liens. (*See* **Special Lien**)

GENERAL PARTNER

One of two or more people who join together to carry on a business and who are personally liable for all debts incurred by the partnership. All partnerships, whether limited or general, must have a general partner. (*See* **General Partnership**)

GENERAL PARTNERSHIP

A form of multiple ownership in which two or more persons associate for the purpose of carrying on a common business for the purpose of making a profit. Under a general partnership each partner is jointly and severally liable for the expenses and claims against the partnership. Unless care is taken by providing appropriate provisions to the contrary in the partnership agreement, the death or bankruptcy of one of the general partners will terminate the partnership. (*See* **Limited Partner**)

GENERAL WARRANTY DEED

An instrument in which the grantor formally guarantees that good and marketable title is being conveyed. *Good title* implies that the property is free from encumbrances such as liens, pending litigation, and other such defects. *Marketable* or *merchantable title* means that the property is free from reasonable doubts or objections. The courts will compel a purchaser to accept such title under the terms of a sales contract. A general warranty deed contains three present and three future covenants. Present covenants include: (1) *seizin*, the assurance that the grantor has the exact estate in the quantity and quality he claims to be conveying; (2) *right to convey*, assurance that the grantor has the right, power, and authority to convey the title being granted; and (3) *against encumbrances*, the assurance that no encumbrances exist other than those specified in the deed. Future covenants include: (1) *further assurances*, the promise that the grantor will perform further acts reasonably necessary to correct future defects in the title; (2) *quiet enjoyment*, the promise that the grantee will peacefully possess the property without someone with superior title ousting him or her; and (3) *warranty of title*, in which the grantor promises to underwrite legal expenses for title disputes which put the grantee out of possession if the hostile claims existed before or during the grantor's possession of the property. Some states, such as New York, also include a *covenant of trust*. This covenant makes the seller a trustee of the purchase money for the buyer until the time for recording mechanic and materialman liens has expired. The grantor is responsible for paying off all such liens with the purchase money. (*See* **Deed**)

GENTLEMEN'S AGREEMENT

An oral agreement made between two or more people who because of good faith expect performance on the agreement.

GEORGE, HENRY

An American economist who advocated a "single-tax" remedy for raising revenues for state and local governments. Under this approach, increases in the value of land as a result of public action or public improvements should be returned to the people from which it came. His so-called unearned value increment theory was included in his book *Progress and Poverty*, published in 1879.

GHETTO

An urban area inhabited by low-income people living in substandard housing.

GIFT DEED

A deed used to convey property which is given without valuable consideration. The deed is supported by "good consideration," which is "love and affection" instead of something material such as money. General creditors may sometimes set a gift deed aside, because something of legal worth has not been substituted for the property being conveyed. To assure the grantee's right of possession, many gift deeds state valuable consideration in addition to "love and affection", for example, $10.

GI LOAN

(*See* **Veterans Administration (VA) Mortgage)**

GIM

(*See* **Gross Rent Multiplier)**

GINNIE MAE

(*See* **Government National Mortgage Association)**

GLUT

An oversupply of available real estate in a specific type market such as warehouse space, condominiums or office space. Quite often a market is referred to as a *glutted market* which denotes excess supply relative to recent and current demand.

GNMA

(*See* **Government National Mortgage Association)**

GNMA DEALERS ASSOCIATION

This trade organization is for investment banking firms acting as principals in GNMA mortgage-backed securities. The association is headquartered at 55 Water Street, New York, NY 10041.

GNMA FUTURES MARKET

A central trading market operated by the Chicago Board of Trade which specializes in the buying and selling of GNMA contracts.

GOING RATE

The current rate normally being charged in the marketplace. The particular rate can refer to current interest rates on new homes or current real estate brokerage commission rates or construction loan rates.

GOOD CONSIDERATION

"Love and affection," as opposed to *valuable consideration* such as money. (*See* **Deed)**

GOOD FAITH

Reasonable and fair dealing with other individuals. In contract law, the test of what a "reasonable man" would do or think is often used to test whether the parties to a contract have acted in good faith.

GOOD FAITH MONEY
(*See* **Earnest Money**)

GOOD FAITH PURCHASER
An innocent purchaser of real estate who is unaware of material circumstances which if known would cause the person to inquire as to the marketability of the seller's title. (*See* **Marketable Title**)

GOOD TITLE
Title which is free from encumbrances such as liens, pending litigation, or other such defects.

GOODWILL
The favorable and good reputation of a business as shown by its customers. In the selling of a business, goodwill denotes the difference between the purchase price and the value of all net assets.

GOVERNMENT NATIONAL MORTGAGE ASSOCIATION (GNMA)
Nicknamed "Ginnie Mae," this HUD agency operates as a participant in the secondary mortgage market. It is involved with special government financing programs for urban renewal projects, elderly housing, and other high-risk mortgages. GNMA also carries out the liquidation and special assistance functions performed by the *Federal National Mortgage Association* prior to its reorganization in 1968. The association is involved with the *mortgage securities pool* and the *tandem plan*.

GOVERNMENT PATENT
(*See* **Patent**)

GOVERNMENT SURVEY METHOD
Also referred to as the *rectangular survey system*, this method of land description was established in 1785 and is used is some 30 states. The system is based on imaginary lines of longitude (north-south and referred to as *meridians*) and latitude (east-west and referred to as *base lines*). There are 36 principal meridians, some designated by names, other by numbers. Each principal meridian has an intercepting base line. *Guide meridians* are located every 24 miles east and west of a principal meridian, and parallels or corrections lines are located every 24 miles north and south of a base line. These 24 by 24 mile areas formed by this checkerboard pattern are the basic quadrangles called *checks*. Checks are only approximately 24 miles square; since the earth is not perfectly flat, the meridian lines move closer together as they approach the North and South Poles. *Ranges* are located every 6 miles east and west of each principal meridian. These are imaginary lines numbered Range 1 East (R1E), Range 2 East (R2E), Range 1 West (R1W), etc. Imaginary township lines are drawn every 6 miles north and south of

a base line. Where they intersect with the range lines a 6 by 6 *township* is formed. Each tier or row of townships is numbered according to its proximity to a base line. For example, Township 1 South (T1S), Township 2 South (T2S), Township 7 South (T7S) lie south of the base line. T3S, R3E would identify the township lying in the third tier south of the base line and the third range east of the principal meridian. Each township is divided into 36 *sections* of 1 mile square. Sections are numbered 1 through 36 beginning in the northeast corner. Since a section is 1 square mile it contains 640 acres. The subdividing of each section is done by quartering the section. This is referred to as aliquot parts and the quartering continues with reference to the quadrants of a compass (NE, NW, SE, SW).

GPARM

An acronym for *graduated payment adjustable rate mortgage*, a type of financing in which the interest rate can legally be changed to reflect changes in market interest rates. (*See* **Graduated Payment Mortgage**)

GPM

(*See* **Graduated Payment Mortgage**)

GRAASKAMP, JAMES A.

A real estate appraiser noted for his writing in the area of site location and feasibility analysis. In his text, *A Guide to Feasibility Analysis*, Graaskamp explained the various ways in which a particular land use may come about, including "a site looking for a use," "a use looking for a site," and "capital looking for an investment opportunity."

GRACE PERIOD

A period between the time an obligation is due and the time default actually occurs. For example, a mortgage payment while due the first day of each month can normally be paid by the tenth without either financial penalty or the borrower being in default.

GRADUATED LEASE

Sometimes called a *stair-step lease*, this lease has provisions calling for periodic increases in the rental payments. Graduated leases are used by landlords who do not wish to be bound by a fixed-payment, long-term lease in times of inflation. For example, in a five-year graduated lease, the rental may be $500 per month for the first two years, $550 per month for the next two years and $625 per month for the last year. Such an agreement can be part of either a *gross lease* or a *net lease*.

GRADUATED PAYMENT MORTGAGE (GPM)

A financing technique for residential real estate in which monthly payments start at a lower level and increase periodically over the life of the mortgage. The rationale behind GPMs is that first-home buyers are likely to be young couples unable to make the high monthly payments required by present interest rates. With a GPM, the home buyer starts with a lower monthly payment, and the payments increase as (presumably) his or her salary increases and he or she can afford to allocate more money to the mortgage payment. *(See* **Innovative Financing Techniques)**

GRADUATE, REALTORS INSTITUTE

A professional real estate designation awarded to Realtors and Realtor-Associates who have successfully completed a prescribed set of educational courses as determined by their State Association of Realtors.

GRANDFATHER CLAUSE

A clause which creates an exemption from application of a new law due to previously existing circumstances. For example, states have enacted prelicensing educational requirements which must be met before someone may be licensed as either a real estate broker or salesperson. In some instances, all persons currently licensed may be "grandfathered" in or exempted from having to meet the new education requirements.

GRANT

To transfer real estate by means of a deed.

GRANT DEED

A deed much like a special warranty deed in that it limits the responsibility of the grantor to the time that he or she actually possessed the property. The grantor is not responsible for any liens, clouds on title, or other encumbrances that may have attached to the property before he or she owned it, but the grantor guarantees that he or she has not encumbered the property during his or her ownership, unless otherwise specified in the deed.

GRANTEE

One who receives title to property. The grantee must be legally capable of receiving title and thus a conveyance to a fictitious person, a nonexistent person, or an entity which is not recognized by law is a void conveyance. For example, a conveyance to an unincorporated association or to a deceased person could not take place. The grantee may use a fictitious name so long as he or she exists. However, if the deed is ambiguous as to the identity of the grantee, the deed will be void on account of vagueness. *(See* **Deed)**

GRANTOR

The person who is conveying interest or title in a piece of property. The grantor must be identified with the same name that was used when the title was received as grantee. For example, if the title was received as "George S. Hinds, grantee" it would not be proper to convey property from "G. Sims Hinds, grantor." This might cause a cloud on title since the title examiner could not be certain that "George S. Hinds" and "G. Sims Hinds" are the same person. If the name has been changed because of marriage or other reason, both the new name and old name should be indicated.

Example: Fanny Hart Brice, formerly Fannie Hart

The grantor should be identified according to marital status. In states that recognize curtesy, dower, homestead, or community property both spouses should join in the grant. Other state requirements may specify that the grantor's name be followed by the address of the grantor's residence. If the property is in some form of co-ownership, all co-tenants should be indicated and join in the conveyance. The grantor must be of legal capacity. If the grantor is a guardian, or some other representative, the authority to act should be indicated in the deed. When the deed is recorded, the written authority to act, such as the power of attorney, should also be recorded. (*See* **Deed**)

GRANTOR-GRANTEE INDEX

A means of indexing title records by which each party in the conveyance instrument is listed. Two sets of indexes are used, one for grantors and one for grantees, and each is kept alphabetically by year. If, for example, John Doe grants Hillydale to Mary Jones, the deed would be referenced in the grantor index under John Doe's name and in the grantee index under Mary Jones' name. Depending on the sophistication of the records, this index is computerized or is handwritten in a book by the clerk or recorder. Sometimes all of the names beginning with a particular letter are only indexed chronologically by when the instrument was filed, requiring a title examiner to check all of the names under that letter; sometimes the index is refined enough for all names to be in alphabetical order.

GREATER FOOL POLICY

A belief on the part of some that real estate can be purchased today and resold to another investor in a relatively short period of time at a price higher than originally paid. The theory is based on certain investments that occurred during inflationary times when some values increased and, thus, some investors concluded that any and all real estate investment would automatically increase in value.

GREENBELT

A geographic area of land set aside for local governments upon which nothing can be built. The purpose of such an undertaking being to establish a buffer between certain types of land uses. (*See* **Buffer Zone**)

GRI

(*See* **Graduate, Realtors Institute**)

GRIDIRON PATTERN

A type of subdivision layout comprised of straight streets and right angles, the result being the creation of lots with approximately the same size and shape.

GRIEVANCE PERIOD

A period of time during which the public may formally register complaints with the local government with regard to tax assessments.

GROSS INCOME

The actual income received from a property before deducting any expenses, including taxes, depreciation, and operating expenses. Also known as *effective gross income*, gross income is calculated by taking the potential gross income and subtracting the vacancy and bad debt loss and then adding any additional income of the property other than rent.

GROSS INCOME MULTIPLIER

(*See* **Gross Rent Multiplier**)

GROSS LEASE

A lease in which the landlord pays for most of the operating expenses, including property taxes, maintenance, and repairs. A gross lease is typically used in short-term leases such as apartment leases. Specific details vary according to the lease agreement provisions and local market customs. (*See* **Net Lease**)

GROSS LEASABLE AREA (GLA)

Total floor area designed for exclusive tenant use and occupancy, expressed in square feet. Generally the GLA is measured from the center line of joint partitions and from outside walls.

GROSS POSSIBLE RENT

(*See* **Gross Income**)

GROSS RENT MULTIPLIER (GRM)

A handy rule of thumb used in estimating the market value of residential rental property. The multiplier is derived by dividing the sales price of comparable properties by their gross annual or monthly rent. By taking the sales price of other properties and dividing each by its gross income, a GRM of the group can then be multiplied by the gross annual or monthly rent of the subject property to estimate a value. This popular method is a quick and easy means of comparing properties based on what the market is paying for similar properties.

Example: Assume three comparable properties are currently rented. The monthly rental of each house can be used to derive a GRM.

	Sales Price	Monthly Rental	GRM
Comparable A	$76,000	$600	127
Comparable B	$74,500	$575	130
Comparable C	$80,000	$600	133
Correlated Gross Rent Multiplier			130

Assuming that the subject property is renting for $575 per month, an estimate of its value based on the gross rent multiplier approach would derive a value of $74,750 ($575 x 130). In inflationary times it is not uncommon for the value derived by the GRM to be less than the value based on the other approaches to value. Consequently, this technique for deriving value is generally not given the same weight as the market and cost approaches.

GROUND COVER

Grass, ivy and other plants grown to keep dirt from washing and eroding.

GROUND LEASE

A long-term lease for a parcel of unimproved land. Under a ground lease, the tenant pays what is known as a *ground rental* and pays all taxes and other charges associated with ownership. The landlord receives a net amount which may have an escalation clause to periodically adjust the ground rental so that the rental payment reflects the changing values of the land. Normally, a ground lease contains a *subordination clause*. A subordination clause is an agreement that the first lienholder will agree to take a junior position to another lienholder. Without a subordination clause, it may be more difficult to construct improvements on the land. A lender, without a subordination agreement by the lessor of the land, will only consider the value of the leasehold in making a loan, while with a subordination clause, the lender will consider the full value of the property. In certain parts of the country, most notably Baltimore, Maryland, the land under residential real estate is leased through a long-term lease agreement whereby the owner of the land receives periodic rent for the use of the land. Such an agreement covers an extended period of time, possibly ninety-nine years, renewal at the lessee's option and results in a lower purchase price of the home, since the land is not owned in fee simple. Thus, less money has to be borrowed. The owner of the ground rent has a superior lien position to that of the lender, and therefore the lender normally requires the borrower to include the ground rent as part of the monthly debt service. State statutes regulate land leases. (*See* **Net Lease**)

GROUND RENT

A payment made by the tenant under a ground lease. Also known as *ground rental.* (*See* **Ground Lease**)

GROUND WATER
Water located in the subsoil of the earth.

GROWTH MANAGEMENT
The process of controlling the size, timing and direction of growth in a community. Growth management is accomplished through the use of zoning regulations and other types of police power, eminent domain, taxation, and capital budgeting by the community.

GUARANTEED LOAN
A loan which contains a clause guaranteeing payment to the lender by a third party in case the borrower defaults on the loan. For example, VA loans are guaranteed by the Veterans Administration.

GUARANTEED PURCHASE
A contractual agreement between a real estate brokerage firm and a property owner in which the broker promises to buy the property at a guaranteed price; thus, assuring the owner that if a better offer is not forthcoming, his or her property will still sell. This marketing technique is used by brokerage offices as a means of obtaining listings that might not otherwise be obtained and is particularly appealing to property owners during times of over-supplied markets.

GUARANTY
A pledge made by one person, known as the guarantor, that the obligation, or promises of another person will be performed as specified.

GUARDIAN
A person who has been given the legal power and responsibility of taking care of another person. The person under care might be a minor, an insane person, or a spendthrift.

GUARDIAN'S DEED
A type of deed issued by the guardian of a minor, insane person or spendthrift.

GUIDE MERIDIAN
A surveying measurement used in the *government survey method* denoting imaginary lines located every 24 miles east and west of a principal meridian. Parallel or correction lines are located every 24 miles north and south of a base line. These 24 by 24 mile areas formed by this checkerboard pattern are basic quadrangles called *checks*. (*See* **Government Survey Method**)

HABENDUM CLAUSE

The part of the deed defining the extent of the estate granted. Coming from the Latin phrase "habendum et tenendum", which means "to have and to hold", the habendum clause states the owner's exact interest in the property, whether it be fee simple or some lesser interest.

HABITABLE

Suitable for occupancy. Local building codes ensure that structures are habitable through requirements for *building permits* and *certificates of occupancy*. Anyone wishing to construct a new building or make a major addition to an old one must obtain a building permit which binds the builder to minimum standards of construction. Before a new structure can be occupied, the owner must obtain a certificate of occupancy to certify that the building has passed a final inspection by local officials. Though building codes differ from locality to locality, most areas have regulations regarding fireproofing structures, electrical wiring, and plumbing.

HAMLET

A small village.

HANDYMAN'S SPECIAL

A parcel of real estate, normally residential, that is in need of major work and repair in order to bring the property up to market standards. Normally, such property is on the market at a price significantly below current prices, reflecting the loss in value due to wear and tear. (*See* **Sweat Equity**)

HARBOR LINE

An arbitrary line set by the appropriate authorities on navigable rivers, beyond which permanent structures may not be build.

HARD SELL

Action by a salesperson that results in an aggressive sales presentation. Hard sell tactics are sometimes used with certain types of real estate such as time sharing and second home sites. In both instances, a substantial amount of time and money is often spent in attempting to bring about a sale.

HARRIS, CHAUNCEY D.

An urban economist who, along with Edward L. Ullman, is credited with developing the *multiple nuclei growth theory* of urban development. The theory is used to explain how development of different types of land use occurs.

HAVE AND TO HOLD

(*See* **Habendum Clause**)

HAZARD INSURANCE

An insurance policy on property to protect the insured against loss due to physical damage to the property.

HEAVY HITTER

A real estate developer or investor who has substantial financial resources and or financial backing.

HEDGING

The sale or purchase of mortgage future contracts by a mortgage banker or lender for the purpose of protecting cash transactions made at a future date.

HEIGHT ZONING

A zoning technique used to establish height restrictions so as to protect the sunlight and flow of air to adjoining properties. (*See* **Zoning**)

HEIR

A person who is entitled to the real property of a deceased person who died *intestate* (left no will).

HEREDITAMENT

Any property capable of being inherited, be it real, personal, corporeal, incorporeal, or mixed.

HETEROGENEOUS

Different or diverse. Heterogeneity is one of the physical characteristics of real estate. Because no two parcels of land are the same, investors should carefully evaluate the characteristics of a particular site for suitability for proposed uses since a use that works on one parcel of land may fail for another. In addition, heterogeneity makes *specific performance* a viable remedy for breaches of contract involving real estate. If a person contracts for a particular parcel of land, receiving its value in money or receiving another similar parcel does not substitute for the original land.

HFA

(*See* **Housing Finance Agency**)

HIDDEN AMENITIES

Features of a property which, even though they may not be easily recognizable, add to the value of the property. Examples would include extra wall insulation, high quality paint, and better grade materials.

HIGHEST AND BEST USE

The legal use of a parcel of land which, when capitalized, will generate the greatest net present value of income. Existing uses of land are not always the highest and best use. For example, a parcel of land may be used for a parking lot until building permits and capital are obtained to build an office building. The parking lot is an *interim use* of the land. Uses that violate the law (for example, building a resort hotel in an area zoned single-family residential or running a liquor store in a dry county) can, by definition, never be highest and best uses. The first step in deriving the highest and best use is to determine *land capacity*. This refers to the ability of land to absorb other factors of production profitably. Once the capacity of the land has been determined, the next step is to calculate *land efficiency*. While land capacity is a quantitative measure, land efficiency is qualitative. It refers to how factor inputs are used. If a parcel of land can profitably absorb more units than are currently being employed, then the land is said to be *underimproved*. This means that, given the current economic, social, and political environment, more income could be generated for the land than is currently being done. However, if the landowner has combined more factor inputs with the land than can be profitably absorbed the land is *overimproved*. (*See* **Value**)

HIGHEST AND BEST USE STUDY

A study of two or more possible uses of a particular parcel of land to determine which use will be the most profitable. (*See* **Feasibility Study**)

HIGH RISE

A commonly used expression referring to a building, usually an apartment or condominium complex, that is high enough to require an elevator.

HIGH WATER LINE OR MARK

The line or mark on a shore to which the water rises at high tide under normal weather conditions.

HIGHWAY

A free and public road or street which anyone has the right to use.

HIL

(See Home Improvement Loan)

HISTORICAL COST

Actual cost of a project when it was first constructed.

HISTORIC DISTRICT

A zoning classification referring to a geographic area of a city that has been singled out as having unique architectural styles and historic significance. Normally, alterations of buildings within such a district cannot be made without permission of appropriate authorities.

HOA

(See Housing Finance Agency)

HOFFMAN RULE

A rule of thumb used by appraisers in estimating the value of land. The rule states that the front half of a 100-foot-deep lot is worth two-thirds of that lot's value, with the back half is worth the remaining one-third.

HOFFMAN-NEILL RULE

A rule of thumb used by appraisers and developers many years ago based on a set of depth factors published by Henry H. Neill. These factors were an extension of similar factors developed by Judge Murray Hoffman which originally came to be known as the *Hoffman Rule*. Such set factors are not widely used today and reliance on this rule is highly questionable. *(See Depth Table)*

HOLDBACK

That portion of a contractor's draw under a construction loan that is withheld by the lender until all work is completed to the satisfaction of the lender. Quite often the amount withheld is equal to the contractor's profit, which means that enough of the loan is dispersed so that the subcontractors can be paid. *(See Construction Loan)*

HOLDER IN GOOD FAITH

One who takes property without any knowledge of defective title. (*See* **Good Title**)

HOLD HARMLESS CLAUSE

An exculpatory clause freeing one from personal liability.

HOLDING COMPANY

A company that is not actively involved in business operations but which owns enough stock in other companies so as to have control over their operation.

HOLDING PERIOD

The period of property ownership, from the date of purchase to the date of sale.

HOLDOVER TENANT

The retention by a tenant of possession after the lease on a property has expired. Holding over creates a *tenancy at sufferance*. (*See* **Tenancy at Sufferance**)

HOLOGRAPHIC WILL

An entirely handwritten will which is not properly witnessed. Such a will is valid only in some jurisdictions and then only if it is free from suspicion of fraud or other defects.

HOME

The place in which a person lives.

HOME EQUITY LOAN

A loan secured by a second mortgage on a person's home and characterized by an open line of credit based on the homeowner's equity. As a result of the *Tax Reform Act of 1986*, consumer interest on credit cards, automobile loans, and similar purchases is not fully deductible when itemizing deductions for federal income tax purposes. However, the interest paid on a home equity loan is fully deductible as long as certain guidelines are met, namely that the amount borrowed must be used for home improvements, medical expenses, or education. Thus, home equity loans have become very popular in recent years. Adding to the popularity is the ease within which such a loan can be made. Most lenders will establish a line of credit to the homeowner up to a total loan-to-value ratio of 75 or 80 percent. For example, a home valued at $100,000 with an existing first mortgage of $50,000 could qualify for a home equity loan of $30,000. In addition, once such a loan is set up, the homeowner can borrow up to the established line of credit at any time. Repayment is normally monthly based on a small percent of the amount borrowed or a set dollar amount, such as $50 or $100, whichever is greater. The interest rate is also substantially less than current rates being charged on revolving credit cards.

HOME IMPROVEMENT LOAN

A loan made to a homeowner in which the home is used as collateral for the loan. In recent years one result of increased housing costs and higher market prices has been the relatively fast equity build-up for owners of real estate. To an owner this equity can become a source of capital that can be drawn out of the home for home improvements or personal or business reasons. Numerous commercial banks and finance companies make short-term (three to five years) junior mortgages based on a percentage of the homeowner's equity. Since they are junior mortgages, such loans normally carry an interest rate three or four percentage points above that charged on senior instruments or first mortgages.

HOME INSPECTION SERVICE

A professional service available to homebuyers normally undertaken prior to the transfer of title to the property. Quite often, particularly in the case of older homes, a buyer will make an offer contingent upon an inspection of the property being done by a qualified person and if the property does not pass the minimum inspection requirements, the offer is voidable. Home inspection services charge from one hundred to several hundred dollars, with the fee normally paid by the buyer.

HOME INSPECTOR

A person who inspects real estate for the purpose of determining whether or not the property meets minimum structural and code standards. Such persons normally have engineering and or building backgrounds and are employed on a fee basis.

HOME LOAN BANK

(*See* **Federal Home Loan Bank Board**)

HOMEOWNER'S ASSOCIATION

The organization in a condominium made up of all the unit owners and which is responsible for maintaining the common areas of the condominium. The homeowner's association also decides on matters affecting the common areas, such as whether an individual unit owner may put up window boxes or plow a garden. Most homeowner's associations have a *right of first refusal*, or right to purchase a unit at market value before the owner seeks other purchasers; however, this right may not be used to discriminate against prospective buyers on the basis of race, color, creed, national origin, sex, handicap, or families with children.

HOMEOWNERSHIP

Owning the home in which one lives. One of the successes of the American economic system has been its ability to provide a decent home to a broad number of households. Approximately 60% to 65% of all occupied housing in the United States is owner occupied. Homeownership offers several advantages to an individual. It provides a sense of security and belonging to a community. There is a certain pride and satisfaction in controlling one's own territory without being restricted by rules established by a landlord or having one's privacy intruded upon by strangers. In a privately owned home, there is generally more living space, more rooms, more storage space, and more privately controlled outdoor space for the dollar spent. This is particularly important for large families with young children. Homeownership often gives a person more social status and a better credit rating. In addition, there are certain financial benefits; monthly payments for a mortgage include a build-up of equity and tax deductible interest. There are other tax advantages as well. Property taxes are deductible, and capital gains on the sale may be deferred if a person reinvests in another house of same or greater price. Except for certain types of variable rate mortgages, the mortgage debt service remains constant, providing protection against inflation while the asset generally appreciates in value. However, homeownership is not for everyone. It may lead to constraints on one's ability to relocate. For example, in housing markets which are overbuilt or in times of tight mortgage money, it may be very difficult to arrange a quick sale at a reasonable price. Homeownership also entails certain responsibilities that not everyone is willing to accept. The yard must be maintained, taxes and mortgage payments must be paid, risks must be insured against. This means there is generally less leisure time and during the early years of homeownership, a person often has less discretionary income. Owning a home ties up capital and in some situations causes a drain on savings. For example, a home may suffer damage from an uninsured peril or the local government may unexpectedly raise property taxes. In addition, if the homeowner fails to make mortgage payments, all invested equity could be wiped out in foreclosure.

HOMEOWNER'S INSURANCE

A package insurance policy available to anyone who owns a one-family house, condominium, cooperative, mobile home, or who resides in an apartment. It is quite common for a homeowner to purchase and maintain insurance coverage for his or her residence. For a relatively small and certain amount of money the homeowner buys protection against a potentially large and unpredictable loss. Numerous types of policies are available. The homeowner can buy a standard fire insurance policy which insures only against fire and lightning, whereas for an additional premium, the coverage is broadened to include damage from wind, hail, smoke, explosion, riot, vehicles, and falling aircraft. Or one can purchase protection against burglary, injuries suffered by parties while on the property, and damages the policyholder causes to the property of others. Besides being able to purchase any number of separate policies, one can also purchase a package policy called a *homeowner's policy* that includes all of the above mentioned risks. A homeowner's policy can be purchased by anyone who owns and occupies either a one- or two-family residence. The advantages to purchasing such a policy are numerous: (1) only one policy is purchased, (2) only one premium has to be paid, (3) the coverage is for a wide variety of perils, and (4) the cost is considerably less than if the same perils were covered through individual policies.

What properties are covered? First, the house or the dwelling is covered. In addition to the living quarters, this includes such structures as garages or other additions. Other structures referred to as appurtenant structures are covered such as a tool shed or a detached garage. However, buildings located on the property that are either rented to others or used for commercial purposes are not covered. Personal property including all household contents and personal belongings is covered. This would include losses both at home or away from home. Pets are not protected, nor are automobiles, which have their own special insurance. Another added feature of a homeowner's policy is the coverage of additional living expenses, which is intended to cover the increase in living expenses incurred while a house cannot be occupied because of damages caused by an insured peril.

What perils are insured against? The number of perils insured against under a homeowner's policy depends upon what form is purchased. Three forms are available: (1) the *Basic Form (HO-1)*, (2) the *Broad Form (HO-2)*, or (3) the *Comprehensive Form (HO-5)*. The Broad Form, which is the most common, insures against eighteen different perils. The Basic Form insures only against the first eleven, whereas the Comprehensive Form covers the eighteen perils, plus additional coverage. While the HO-5 is often referred to as an all-risk policy, it still has certain exceptions listed in the policy.

Is there a policy for renters? For those who rent, the Tenant's Form (HO-4) of the homeowner's policy is available. It insures contents and personal property against the same perils included in the Broad Form. However, since a renter does not own either the dwelling or other private structures on the property, the dwelling is not insured. Such a policy does, however, provide coverage for additional living expense.

HOMEOWNER'S ONCE-IN-A-LIFETIME TAX EXCLUSION

A forgiveness of $125,000 in capital gains taxes for taxpayers 55 years or older who sell their principal residence. To qualify, a taxpayer must be at least 55 years old on or before the date of the sale. The house must have been the principal residence in at least three of the five years preceding the sale. If married, only one spouse must be 55 years old, but both must join in making the election. If filing separately, each spouse is only allowed half the exclusion or $62,500. There are other more technical provisions which may require consultation with an attorney or tax accountant for an understanding of how the law applies in the situation of any particular individual.

HOMEOWNER'S (HOMESTEAD) TAX EXEMPTION

The amount of the assessed value of property not subject to property tax due to the fact that the taxpayer resides on the property and declares it as his or her homestead. Those states that provide for a homestead exemption normally require the homeowner to file for the exemption within a statutory period of time within the tax year. (*See* **Property Tax**)

HOMEOWNER'S WARRANTY (HOW) PROGRAM

A ten-year warranty program administered by a subsidiary of the National Association of Home Builders and available from some builders of new homes. The program has strict building standards, and it requires the builder to give a one-year warranty against defects in workmanship, a two-year warranty against defects in electrical and mechanical systems, and a full ten-year warranty against major structural and sanitary defects. The warranty is transferable to new owners and provides for arbitration in case of owner/builder disputes.

HOME RULE

The power of local self-government given either by the state constitution or legislation to a municipal corporation. Home rule powers allow local governments to pass zoning ordinances and other land-use regulations.

HOMESTEAD EXEMPTION

A statutory or constitutional right which gives a person who is defined as the head of a household protection from creditors for property known as the homestead. The homestead is ordinarily defined as the primary dwelling and surrounding land, and usually there must be a family which owns and occupies the dwelling. This exemption does not normally apply to rented premises. Many states define this exemption. Ordinarily, any recorded debts which existed before the declaration of the exemption are not affected. In some states homestead exists automatically by operation of law, while in other states the head of the household must file a declaration of homestead with the appropriate public official in the jurisdiction. Debts incurred to finance and to repair the homestead may or may not be affected by the exemption. The exemption may be waived and each state has its own requirements for what constitutes a waiver. Upon the death of the head of the household, the surviving spouse may be entitled to the exemption. In some states the homestead is also important in calculating property taxes. A certain statutory amount may be subtracted from the assessment of the homestead before the tax rate is applied.

HOMOGENEOUS

Similar in type. Real estate is the opposite of homogeneous, since no two parcels of land are exactly alike. (*See* **Heterogeneous**)

HORIZONTAL PROPERTY ACT

The name, in some states, for legislation authorizing the creation of the condominium form of ownership. Before 1960, no such legislation existed, while today every state has some form of condominium legislation. (*See* **Condominium**)

HOSKOLD FACTOR

A factor used to value an annuity that is based on reinvesting capital recapture at a safe rate of interest, named after H. E. Hoskold.

HOSKOLD, H. E.

An English mining engineer who originated the use of the "Hoskold" method of valuing coal mines, timberland, and other types of real estate with depleting assets.

HOTEL

A building offering its facilities as lodging to the public rather than to a limited private group.

HOT LISTING

A listing on property that, in the opinion of the real estate broker acquiring the listing, is located in a market with much more demand than supply. In theory, hot listings do not remain on the market for a very long period of time.

HOUSE-POOR HOMEOWNER

A homeowner who has bought more house than he or she can comfortably afford and, thus, spends a more than normal percentage of his or her income on the mortgage payment. First home buyers who have financed a high percent of the purchase price are sometimes referred to as being "house poor."

HOUSING AFFORDABILITY INDEX

A monthly index published by the *National Association of Realtors* showing the financial ability of the median income family to purchase the median-priced home with an 80 percent loan. An index greater than 100 means that the median income family could qualify for more than the median-priced home with an 80 percent loan. A less than 100 index means that the same median income cannot qualify to buy the median-priced home, which is normally the case during times of inflation and higher than normal interest rates.

HOUSING AND URBAN DEVELOPMENT (HUD)

An agency of the federal government which oversees many federal housing programs, including enforcement of fair housing laws. (*See* **Department of Housing and Urban Development**)

HOUSING ASSISTANCE COUNCIL (HAC)

The Housing Assistance Council is funded by the *Department of Housing and Urban Development (HUD)* and provides assistance, training, and loans for the development of low-income housing in rural areas. The mailing address is 1025 Vermont Avenue, N.W., Washington, D.C. 20005; (202) 842-8600.

HOUSING CODE

Local government codes which specify minimum standards that a dwelling unit must meet. (*See* **Building Permit, Certificate of Occupancy, Habitable**)

HOUSING FINANCE AGENCY

A state financing program that provides direct loans at a preferred interest rate to citizens of that state who, for various reasons, have been unable to obtain financing from private institutions. Applicants must be residents of the state for a specified period of time and under most programs may not own other real property. In recent years, cities and counties have also established mortgage funds in order to meet the needs of the housing market in their political jurisdictions.

HOUSING FOR THE ELDERLY

A real estate project specifically built for elderly persons and normally, in addition to living accommodations, provides recreational facilities and nursing services.

HOUSING STARTS

The number of housing units (including apartments) placed under construction during a specific period of time. Since the construction industry is such a vital component of the overall economy, the number of housing starts is an important barometer for how well the economy is doing.

HOW

(See **Homeowner's Warranty (HOW) Program**)

HOYT, HOMER

An urban economist who, in the 1930s developed the *sector theory* of urban growth. Hoyt's explanation of urban growth was based on wedge-shaped neighborhoods which he believed would surround the central business district of a city. New, higher-income neighborhoods would, in Hoyt's opinion, develop along highways and other transportation facilities.

HUD

(See **Department of Housing and Urban Development**)

HUNDRED PERCENT LOCATION

The location which generates the highest per square foot revenues for a particular type of use in a geographic area. This particular location generally commands the highest rentals or cost per square foot.

HURD, RICHARD

A mortgage banker who compiled statistics and information on the expansion and growth of American cities. Hurd concluded that cities grow along the lines of least resistance or greatest attraction.

HYPOTHECATE

The process of pledging something as security but retaining possession of it. The borrower who gives a mortgage to a lender but keeps possession of the mortgaged property has hypothecated the property.

I

IAAO

(See **International Association of Assessing Officers)**

IFA

Member, National Association of Independent Fee Appraisers. A professional appraisal designation awarded to individuals who have met minimum education, experience, and demonstrated requirements as outlined by the association. *(See* **National Association of Independent Fee Appraisers)**

IFAC

Appraiser/Counselor, National Association of Independent Fee Appraisers. An appraisal/counselor designation awarded to IFAS members who have had a minimum of five years experience in counseling. Applicants must submit an approved thesis of an actual counseling experience. *(See* **National Association of Independent Fee Appraisers)**

IFAS

Senior Member, National Association of Independent Fee Appraisers. An advanced appraisal designation awarded to those IFA members who have demonstrated knowledge, and experience in the appraisal of income producing property. *(See* **National Association of Independent Fee Appraisers)**

ILLIQUIDITY

When an asset cannot readily be converted into cash. Depending on the demand for particular types of land in a given area, real estate can be a relatively illiquid asset. Certainly one would normally have a harder time converting real estate to cash than selling bonds or other, more liquid assets.

ILLUSORY OFFER

An offer which does not bind the offeror to any real commitment. For example, the statement "I will buy your house if I can find acceptable financing" is illusory because "acceptable financing" can mean different things to different people. No firm commitment has been made. (*See* **Offer**)

IMMOBILITY

Incapable of being moved, fixed in location. One of the important physical characteristics of real estate is its immobility, which means that a parcel of real estate must be used where it is located. (*See* **Fixity of Location**)

IMPLIED AGENCY

An agency relationship that is created by the acts and conduct of the parties involved.

Example: Pam advertises her lot for sale with the words: "Seven percent commission paid to licensed brokers finding a buyer accepted by purchaser." If Bob, a licensed broker, brings a purchaser and this purchaser is accepted, Bob will be entitled to a commission in most states even though no actual listing contract was signed and no words were exchanged between Pam and Bob.

IMPLIED AUTHORITY

Authority which is created by the actions or conduct of the principal, giving to the agent the reasonable impression that the scope of authority is broadened from that actually expressed in words. Implied authority is also described as that authority which is customary in carrying out the duties of the agency. In relation to real estate brokers, implied authority is very narrowly construed. For example, a broker is not deemed to have implied authority to collect the purchase price in the sale of real estate. Because a broker is held to be a special agent with limited powers from the seller-principal, if a buyer pays cash to the broker, the broker is considered to be an agent for the buyer and not for the seller-principal. Thus if the money is destroyed or stolen, the risk of loss is on the buyer and not on the seller. This rule does not apply if the broker is authorized by the principal to accept cash, or to accept a promissory note as an earnest money deposit unless specifically authorized by the principal. If the third person were to default on the note, the broker would have to make it good as a surety to the principal. Generally, deposits must be in cash or, where customary, by check.

IMPLIED CONTRACT

A contract formed through the acts or conduct of the parties involved, rather than through words, either written or spoken. (*See* **Contract**)

IMPLIED EASEMENT

(*See* **Easement by Implication**)

IMPLIED WARRANTIES

Guarantees in a deed assumed by law to exist even though they are not specifically stated. The term is also used to denote unstated promises that courts will find in a transaction when circumstances and justice require it.

IMPLIED WARRANTIES OF FITNESS AND MERCHANTABILITY

Representation or promise by the contractor or seller of personal and real property with respect to the quality of the item(s) of the transaction. While the implied warranty may be neither written or spoken, facts and/or circumstances may lead the purchaser to assume warranty is being given. For example, a purchaser of a house reasonably assumes the normal components of the house, such as the electrical system or plumbing system, are in fact in working order. Even though the owner may not say specifically that such is the case, the fact that the property is for sale gives an implied warranty of fitness and merchantability that such is the case.

IMPLIED WARRANTY OF AUTHORITY

When an agent acts on behalf of a principal the agent implies to a third party that he has the authority to act. For example, a property manager who contracts with painters and carpenters for maintenance work at an apartment complex implies that he has received authority from the complex owner to hire and pay these workmen. Implying authority falsely is a breach of agency law and may result in a real estate salesperson or broker losing his or her license.

IMPOUND ACCOUNT

(*See* **Escrow Account**)

IMPROVED LAND

Any land to which improvements such as roads or buildings have been made. Improvements generally increase the value of a parcel of land.

IMPROVEMENT

An immovable object that has become annexed (attached) to or a part of real estate. Improvements can be either "to" the land or "on" the land. Examples of improvements to the land would include sewers, sidewalks, streets, and utility hook-ups, while improvements on the land would include buildings, walls, and other such structures.

IMPROVEMENT RATIO

A ratio or fraction that compares the value of the improvements to the value of all property. The improvement ratio normally indicates that part of the total cost that can be depreciated for tax purposes. For example, if the total value of land and improvements is $1,000,000 and the value of the improvements is $750,000, the improvement ratio is 75 percent ($750,000/$1,000,000). For improved income-producing property, this ratio normally has a range from 60 percent to 95 percent.

INCHOATE

Pending, possibly occurring in the future.

INCHOATE INTEREST

Someone's possible future right to property. For example, in those states that recognize dower rights, a wife's interest in her husband's property during his lifetime is an inchoate interest.

INCOME

Financial and other benefits. Income should be qualified as to the degree of "netness," that is, *gross* or *net*. (*See* **Cash Flow, Gross Income, Net Operating Income, Potential Gross Income**)

INCOME APPROACH

One of the traditional means of appraising property based on the assumption that value is equal to the *present worth of future rights to income*. To estimate the value of an income-producing property, an appraiser would take the following steps:

1. Estimate the stabilized *net operating income* of the property.
2. Select an appropriate *capitalization rate*.
3. Apply the *capitalization formula* to derive the estimated value.

$$\text{Value} = \frac{\text{Net Operating Income}}{\text{Capitalization Rate}}$$

(*See* **Capitalization, Net Operating Income**)

INCOME-EXPENSE RATIO

The relationship between the gross income of an income-producing property and its operating expenses. For example, an apartment building with gross income of $1,000,000 and operating expenses of $450,000 would have an income-expense ratio of 45% ($450,000/$1,000,000). The ratio is a good barometer for measuring how a particular property compares to similar properties.

INCOME MULTIPLIER

A factor that expresses the value of property as a multiple of the periodic income that the property generates. (*See* **Gross Rent Multiplier**)

INCOME PARTICIPATION

The right of a party to share in part of or all of the income generated by an investment. (*See* **Equity Participation, Kicker**)

INCOME PROPERTY

Property that generates income for its owner, for example, an office building or apartment complex.

INCOME PROPERTY LOAN

A loan secured by income property such as a loan on an office building or shopping center. The amount of the loan is generally a function of the amount of income the property is expected to generate. (*See* **Net Operating Income**)

INCOME TAX LIABILITY

The tax a property owner must pay, based on the taxpayer's taxable income multiplied by the tax rate in each marginal tax bracket.

INCOMPETENT

One who is legally unable to take care of himself or herself. Persons judged insane or mentally incompetent by the courts do not have contractual capacity; therefore, any contract such a person enters into is void. However, the guardian of an incompetent person may contract for that person.

INCORPORATE

The act of creating a corporation.

INCORPOREAL PROPERTY

Intangible property that is not visible but exists as a legal right. Examples include riparian rights, easements, patents, and mineral rights.

INCREASING AND DECREASING RETURNS, PRINCIPLE OF

Similar to the economic rule of diminishing marginal returns, this economic principle states that the addition of more factors of production will add higher and higher amounts to net income (additional revenue minus additional cost) up to a certain point, which is the point of the asset's maximum value (*highest and best use*). Any further addition of factors of production will do nothing to increase the property's value. Factors of production include land, labor, capital, and managerial (entrepreneurial) ability. (*See* **Highest and Best Use**)

INCREASING ANNUITY

An income stream that promises or requires systematic increases in the periodic payment.

INCREMENTAL CONDOMINIUMS

Condominium projects in which the developer reserves the right to add additional units to the project and to charge the pro rata interest of each unit owner in the common elements. (*See* **Condominium**)

INCUMBRANCE

(*See* **Encumbrance**)

INCURABLE DEPRECIATION

Physical elements of a structure which would cost more to correct than the value added by correction. (*See* **Cost Approach, Depreciation**)

INDEMNIFY

To reimburse or compensate someone for a loss already suffered by him or her.

INDEPENDENT APPRAISAL

An estimate of value performed by a qualified, disinterested party. (*See* **Appraisal**)

INDEPENDENT CONTRACTOR

One who is retained by another to complete a certain task and is subject to the control of the hiring person only as the final result of the work effort. How and where the work was done is determined entirely by the independent contractor. A real estate broker working for a principal (for example, a broker employed under a listing agreement) is considered to be acting as an independent contractor. A typist or clerk in a real estate broker's office is generally considered to be in a *master-servant relationship*. The test to be applied is whether the employer has the right to control the method and mode of service. Salespeople working for a broker can be either servants or independent contractors. Which status a salesperson has depends on the method of compensation and the agreement between the broker and salesperson as to the broker's right to control activities. Some state licensing laws specify that a salesperson is essentially a servant under the control of the broker. (*See* **Master and Servant Relationship**)

INDEPENDENT FEE APPRAISER

(*See* **Fee Appraiser**)

INDEX LEASE

A lease whereby the rental is tied to some commonly agreed to price index such as the *Consumer Price Index (CPI)* or the *Wholesale Price Index (WPI)*. The clause which connects the rent to this index is called an *escalator clause*, and the index lease is often referred to as an escalation lease. An escalation clause may also include factors other than inflation. For example, an escalation clause may provide increases in the tenant's gross rents if the landlord's property taxes go up or if the cost of heating oil increases. Through escalation clauses, a lessor may build in some of the same financial safety features of a net lease. Ordinarily, the index is used to adjust the rent on an annual basis. The application of the index is, however, as mutually agreed to by the lessor and the lessee.

Example: If the rent for office space is $8.00/square foot and the rent is tied to a commonly agreed to index which is 1.87, what will the rent per square foot be if the index goes to 2.03 at the time the rental terms are reassessed? First, the percentage rate that the index has increased must be determined. This calculation is as follows: 2.03/1.87 = 1.8056

This factor will then be multiplied by the per square foot rate to get the new rate. This calculation is as follows: $8.00 x 1.0856 = $8.68/square foot.

INDEX METHOD

An appraisal technique used to estimate reproduction or replacement cost which takes the original cost of construction and multiplies that figure by a price index for the geographic area to allow for price changes. (*See* **Cost Approach**)

INDIRECT COSTS

Costs associated with construction that cannot be actually identified in the structure, including insurance, interest and taxes during construction, architect's fees, management costs, and the like.

INDIRECT DAMAGES

(*See* **Consequential Damages**)

INDUSTRIAL BROKER

A real estate broker who specializes in brokering industrial real estate. (*See* **Society of Industrial and Office Realtors**)

INDUSTRIAL PARK

A large parcel of real estate specifically zoned to be used as a manufacturing facility or other light industrial uses. Normally facilities needed by industrial plants such as roads, water, rail service, and automobile parking are made available by the developer of the park.

INDUSTRIAL PROPERTY

Real estate that is used as a manufacturing facility; also a zoning classification that restricts land to certain uses.

INDUSTRIAL REVENUE BOND (IRB)

A type of bond issued by a municipality to raise funds for building a plant for a company which in turn enters into a long-term lease with the municipality to lease the building. The rental payment is used by the municipality to pay interest on the bonds and to retire the bonds at maturity. Local governments use this as a means of attracting industry that might otherwise not locate in their town.

INFILTRATION

The absorption of water into the earth.

INFLATED APPRAISAL

An estimate of value that appears to be greater than the market value of the property being appraised. While it is unethical to do so, some appraisers find themselves under pressure from developers and borrowers to "make the numbers look good" in an attempt to justify a higher than normal loan.

INFLATION

A decrease in the purchasing power of currency, typically measured by the *Consumer Price Index (CPI)* published by the *Bureau of Labor Statistics*.

INFRASTRUCTURE

A municipality's services and facilities such as public transportation, parks, water and sewer.

INGRESS

Access or entrance to land. (*See* **Egress**)

INHABIT

To occupy.

INHERITANCE TAX

A tax imposed by the state on the heirs of an estate upon their right or privilege of receiving the property. Such a tax is not levied against the property itself, but rather on the right to acquire the property. (*See* **Estate Tax**)

INITIAL EQUITY

The amount of cash and/or valuable consideration used as a down payment by a real estate owner. (*See* **Equity**)

INITIAL INVESTMENT

The down payment on the purchase price of property. The initial investment within real estate is often a much lower percentage of the purchase price than with other types of investments.

INJUNCTION

A court order prohibiting or compelling a person to perform or refrain from performing a certain act. An injunction can be either temporary or permanent.

IN-LAW SUITE

A small apartment added to an existing home. The addition normally included sleeping, eating, and bathing facilities.

INN

A public facility where meals, lodging, and related services are provided to all who conduct themselves properly and who are ready and able to pay for the services received.

INNER CITY

The part of an urban area comprising the center part of the city. This area normally contains the *central business district (CBD)* as well as other commercial uses. In addition, particularly in older cities, the inner city houses many of the city's poor residential population. (*See* **Concentric Circle Theory**)

INNOCENT PURCHASER

One who purchases or acquires an interest in real property with the belief that the title is clear and there are no liens or encumbrances against the property. (*See* **Constructive Notice**)

INNOVATIVE FINANCING TECHNIQUES

Various types of financing made available as a result of changes in economic and social conditions. As conditions and needs change, new and flexible financing techniques have been introduced by lenders. The increase in loan-to-value ratios and the introduction of graduated payment mortgages are examples of such action.

IN PERSONAM

Legal proceeding against a person. (*See* **In Rem**)

IN REM

Legal proceeding against a specific object or thing. For example, when a mortgagee forecloses on a mortgage the proceeding is in rem, in that it is taken against the property, specifically to have the property sold in order to repay the outstanding debt.

INSIDE LOT

Any lot located between the corner lots on a specific block. Generally, inside lots have less value than outside lots.

INSPECTION

A visit to and examination of the subject property. For example, many sales contracts have a clause inserted which states: "Purchaser represents that an inspection satisfactory to purchaser has been made of the property, and purchaser agrees to accept the property in its present condition except as may be otherwise provided in the description of the property above."

INSPECTION CERTIFICATE

A certificate issued by a mortgage banker or correspondent representing a lender that the property being used to secure a loan has been personally inspected and meets the minimum requirements as set forth in the loan agreement.

INSTALLMENT LAND CONTRACT

(*See* **Contract for Deed**)

INSTALLMENT PAYMENT

One payment of principal and interest, required as a periodic payment on a mortgage loan.

INSTALLMENT SALE

A method of selling real estate in which the payment of capital gains taxes on the profit is postponed. A transaction automatically qualifies under the installment sales method if payments of the gross sales price are spread over two or more years. Gross sales price includes cash received, mortgages of the seller that are assumed or taken by the buyer, and any other property or property rights given to the seller. This method permits the seller to defer paying capital gains taxes on a pro rata basis until installments are actually received. As each installment payment is made, a portion of that payment is treated as interest, a portion as a capital gain, and a portion is not subject to any kind of tax.

INSTALLMENT TO AMORTIZE ONE

The periodic payment necessary to retire a one dollar loan with interest computed on the declining loan balance.

INSTITUTE OF REAL ESTATE MANAGEMENT (IREM)

An organization organized to promote and encourage professionalism in real estate property management. The institute is affiliated with the National Association of Realtors. IREM sponsors various education programs, publishes and distributes numerous publications, and awards the professional designation *Certified Property Manager (CPM)*. The mailing address is 430 North Michigan Avenue, Chicago, Illinois 60611; (312) 661-1930.

INSTITUTIONAL LENDER

A financial institution such as a commercial or mutual bank, savings and loan association, or insurance company that invests deposits or customers' money into mortgages. Some institutional lenders maintain and service their loans while others sell their mortgages to investors and reinvest the proceeds into more mortgages. Since such lenders are investing other people's money, institutional lenders are tightly regulated by both federal and state laws and regulations.

INSTITUTIONAL LOAN

A loan secured from an institutional lender.

INSTRUMENT

A written legal document setting forth the rights and liabilities of the parties to the instrument.

INSURABLE INTEREST

The relationship to the object or the person to be insured that one must show in order to take out an insurance policy. In order to collect damages through an insurance policy, a person would have to prove that he or she had an insurable interest at the time the loss was suffered. (*See* **Insurance**)

INSURABLE TITLE

Title to real property that is of sufficient nature to cause a title insurance company to agree to insure the title. (*See* **Title Insurance**)

INSURABLE VALUE

The highest reasonable value that can be placed on property for hazard insurance purposes.

INSURANCE

A means by which one party shifts the risk of a certain loss or disastrous event to another party. This is done through a contract called a *policy*, and with a certain payment called a *premium*. The party assuming the risk, an insurance company, normally insures many parties against the same risk and is therefore able to predict the number of losses likely to occur. The individual being insured needs this service because he or she cannot accurately predict the probability of loss. Quite often the purchaser of real estate has little choice concerning insurance. If there is a third party providing any part of the financing, the funds will not be made available until the borrower can show that adequate insurance coverage has been obtained. The same is generally true for someone leasing property. A common covenant in the lease agreement calls for the lessee to maintain a certain amount of insurance on the property. In most states, insurance companies who desire to adjust their rates must submit a request supported with data to the state department of insurance or the insurance commissioner. State insurance laws typically require that rates be adequate, not excessive or unfairly discriminatory. This does not mean that every insurance company must offer the same coverage and charge exactly the same rates. Many factors enter into how much a certain amount of coverage will cost. One thing is the loss experience of the insurance company. This refers to how much money the insurance company has paid out for damages to property and people. If this loss experience is increasing, then the company will want to charge more to provide that type of coverage. The material used to construct the improvement is also important. Rates for an all-brick house will normally be less than for an all-wood house. Further, the fire rating or classification of the jurisdiction is important. This rating is based on the amount of fire protection available in the jurisdiction. Obviously the more perils insured against, the higher the cost. The amount of coverage purchased also affects the cost. It would stand to reason that a person insuring a house for $30,000 would not pay as much as someone purchasing $90,000 coverage. The cost of insurance is also affected by the deductible clause. If the insured chooses $100 deductible, for example, the insured is responsible for all losses up to that amount.

Many property owners find that even though they had adequate coverage when the policy was initially purchased, as a result of inflation their property is seriously underinsured. This can be true even though the owner has the property insured for the amount of its current market value. It is the replacement cost, not the market value, that should determine how much insurance coverage is carried. Most homeowner's policies contain a clause which states that if damage occurs, be it full or partial loss, the total replacement cost will be paid by the insurance company, provided that the property is insured for a certain percentage of the replacement cost, usually 80 percent. If the house is insured for less than the stated minimum, then in case of damage, the insurance company will pay the larger amount of either (1) the cash value of the damaged property (replacement cost minus depreciation) or (2) a percentage of the replacement cost (a ratio of the insurance carried to 80 percent of the current replacement cost).

Example: A house is insured for $60,000, but its current replacement cost is $100,000. If the owner suffers a $40,000 loss, the insurance company will normally pay only 75 percent (the $60,000 carried is 75 percent of what should be carried) of any loss, up to a maximum of $60,000 for a total loss.

Particularly for an older home, the owner might find little relationship between the replacement cost and the fair market value. Insurance companies provide a general formula for deriving the replacement cost of a home, derived by multiplying the total base cost by a location multiplier. A business package policy is available for the owner of an apartment building, office building, or store. Such a policy offers the same type of advantages to the business owner as the homeowner's policy offers to the homeowner. This policy is cheaper than separate policies and can be adapted to the particular needs of the individual.

INSURANCE COVERAGE

The total amount of insurance protection carried.

INSURANCE RATE

The ratio of the insurance premium to the amount of insurance coverage. For example, a homeowner's policy costing $500 and providing $50,000 of coverage would have a rate of $1 per hundred ($500/$50,000).

INTANGIBLE PROPERTY

Personal property rights, such as contractual rights, legal claims, patents, or trademarks, as compared to tangible property which refers to objects and physical things. The law recognizes intangible property to the extent that in many cases these rights are subject to taxation by the state.

INTANGIBLE TAX

A tax levied by some states against intangible property such as mortgages and bonds.

INTENSITY OF DEVELOPMENT

The amount of floor space over a given area of land. (*See* **Floor Area Ratio**)

INTEREST

The sum paid for the use of money. Also, the degree of rights in the ownership of land.

INTEREST ESCALATION

Increasing the interest rate on a loan at one or more intervals during the life of the loan. (*See* **Escalator Clause**)

INTEREST-ONLY MORTGAGE

A balloon mortgage that requires installment payments of interest only with no amortization. (*See* **Amortized Loan, Term Mortgage**)

INTEREST RATE

Rate of return on a principal amount. The rate is normally stated as an annual percentage, for example, ten percent.

INTEREST RATE RISK

The probability that market interest rates will change, thus affecting the value of an investment that bears a stated fixed rate.

INTERIM FINANCING

A short-term loan (six months to three years) normally made to provide funds for the construction of a building. Interim financing, also known as a *construction loan*, normally carries a variable interest rate tied to the prime rate. *Permanent financing*, in turn, is used by the builder/developer to "take out" the interim financing. (*See* **Permanent Financing, Takeout Commitment**)

INTERMEDIATE THEORY STATES

A state statute recognized in a few jurisdictions whereby in case of default on a mortgage, title is said to pass to the mortgagee (lender). (*See* **Lien Theory State, Title Theory State**)

INTERMINGLING

(*See* **Commingling of Funds**)

INTERNAL RATE OF RETURN (IRR)

The rate at which discounted returns from an investment equal the cost of the investment. Internal rate of return, a technique used to compare various investment alternatives, is also known as *discounted cash flow*. (*See* **Present Value**)

INTERNATIONAL ASSOCIATION OF ASSESSING OFFICERS (IAAO)

An international group of real estate professionals who specialize in the property tax assessment of real estate. The association publishes various material and conducts numerous seminars to aid in the assessment of property. The association is located at 1313 East 60th Street, Chicago, Illinois 60637; (312) 947-2069.

INTERNATIONAL CITY MANAGEMENT ASSOCIATION (ICMA)

ICMA is a professional organization whose membership is comprised of municipal executives of local governments. The mailing address is 1120 G Street, N.W., Washington, D.C. 20005; (202) 626-4600.

INTERNATIONAL CONFERENCE OF BUILDING OFFICIALS (ICBO)

ICBO is an organization whose members consist of city, county, and state governments. It is involved in the promotion of the *Uniform Building Code* and publishes various documents related to the safety of life and property in buildings. The mailing address is 5360 South Workman Mill Road, Whittier, California 90601; (213) 659-0541.

INTERNATIONAL REAL ESTATE FEDERATION (FIABCI)

FIABCI, a French acronym for International Real Estate Federation, is an international association of real estate professionals from member countries throughout the world. Members of FIABCI are specialists in brokerage, property management, counseling, development, appraisal, and financing. Educational courses and seminars are offered around the United States to instruct members on the basic knowledge and skills necessary to compete successfully in the growing international real estate market. Information on membership and services available can be obtained by contacting: FIABCI-USA, 777 14th Street, N.W., Washington, D.C. 20005; (202) 383-1167.

INTERNATIONAL RIGHT OF WAY ASSOCIATION

A professional association comprised of individuals involved in the acquisition of real estate. The association awards the designation *IR/WA* which requires competency in four areas: (1) negotiation, (2) law, (3) engineering, and (4) appraisal. The address is Suite 515, 9920 LaCienega Blvd., Inglewood, California 90301; (213) 649-5323.

INTERPLEADER

Legal action undertaken by a third party to determine rights that exist between two or more other parties.

INTERPOLATION

The process of deriving a value that is known to lie between two given amounts.

INTERSTATE LAND SALES FULL DISCLOSURE ACT

A federal act which makes it unlawful to offer land for sale in interstate commerce unless certain information has been filed with the *Department of Housing and Urban Development (HUD)*. In addition, certain disclosures must be made to prospective purchasers. Violation of the act may lead to fine, imprisonment, or both.

INTERVAL OWNERSHIP

(*See* **Time Sharing**)

INTESTATE

Dying without first making a will. (*See* **Descent**)

IN THE PIPELINE

A loan application, rezoning request, or proposed subdivision development currently going through the approval process. The period of time needed to get it "through the pipeline" can be relatively short as well as somewhat lengthy.

INTRINSIC VALUE

The true or inherent value of something not dependent upon special features or variables which would make its market value different. (*See* **Value**)

INVALID

Without legal force; not binding.

INVESTMENT

The outlay of money for income or profit; property acquired for income or profit.

INVESTMENT ADVISOR

An individual or firm employed for a fee to give investment counseling and advice. Investment advisors are often used by real estate investment trusts, life insurance companies, and foreign investors to assist in determining the type and amount of real estate in which to invest.

INVESTMENT ANALYSIS

An examination of investment property that considers its suitability for the unique situation of a particular investor.

INVESTMENT APPETITE

Characteristics of an investment that are desired by a particular investor.

INVESTMENT PROPERTY

An asset such as real estate acquired for income or profit as compared to an asset acquired for business, trade, or personal use.

INVESTMENT VALUE

The worth of investment property to a specific investor.

INVESTMENT YIELD

The internal rate of return on an investment.

INVESTOR

One who acquires investment property.

INVOLUNTARY LIEN

An encumbrance against property such as a tax lien or judgment without the owner's consent. In contrast a *voluntary lien*, such as a mortgage, attaches to the property with the consent of the owner. (*See* **Lien**)

INWOOD FACTOR

A multiplier used by appraisers/investors to value an ordinary annuity. Named after William Inwood, this technique provides a means by which an income stream can be converted into present value. The method is also known as *level annuity capital recovery*.

INWOOD, WILLIAM

An English architect (1771-1843) who is credited with originating the use of present worth factors to capitalize or discount to present worth a stream of level income.

IREM

(See **Institute of Real Estate Management**)

IRONCLAD AGREEMENT

An agreement worded in such a way that the parties to it have no legal basis for not carrying out the terms and conditions of the agreement.

IRR

(See **Internal Rate of Returns**)

IRREVOCABLE

Not capable of being changed.

IR/WA

(See **International Right of Way Association**)

J FACTOR

A factor used in income property analysis to derive the change in net operating income that is required to realize a certain equity yield rate.

JACOBS, JANE

A writer who, in her book *The Economy of Cities*, provides examples of the importance of external economies of scale to the manufacturing efforts of a particular area.

JOINT AND SEVERAL LIABILITY

A situation in which a creditor may sue one or more of the parties separately, or all of them together. For example, partners are jointly and severally liable for the debts and obligations incurred by the partnership. As such, one partner could find that he or she is being sued by a creditor for a partner's portion of a debt.

JOINT TENANCY

A concurrent ownership by two or more persons with the *right of survivorship*. This form of ownership is recognized by all but a small handful of states. Upon the death of a joint tenant, the interest does not pass to the joint tenant's heirs or devisees, but to the other joint tenant(s). Effectively, when a joint tenant dies, his or her interest is automatically extinguished. As a result of this, no interest exists which may be passed on after death by will. Likewise, no dower or curtesy can attach. Further, all unforeclosed liens of one of the joint tenants placed on the land are extinguished. The same result occurs to any easements or leases which were granted by one of the joint tenants without the conveyance by the other joint tenants. Because no interest passes after death, there is no need for probate; the surviving tenant(s) retain the property. If two or more tenants die simultaneously, who receives the property if no joint tenant(s) survive? These rights are controlled by state law. Most states have passed the *Uniform Simultaneous Death Act* which defines how the property interests would be allocated. This form of co-ownership is not favored by the courts. In order to create such an ownership form, the conveying deed must be clear and specific and ordinarily must specify the right of survivorship. Also, in order to create this form of ownership, four unities were required under common law and still are essential in many states. These are the unities of time, title, interest, and possession.

The unity of *time* states that all interests of the joint tenants must have been acquired at the same moment.

Example: Jay owns Blackvalley in severalty. He married Barbara and wishes to hold Blackvalley as joint tenants with his wife. In order to do this, Jay must convey the property to some third party known as a *straw man* or nominee who in turn reconveys the property "to Jay and Barbara as joint tenants with right of survivorship and not as tenants in common." Some states have modified the rule that a person cannot grant property to himself and would allow Jay to directly create the joint tenancy without the process of using a nominee.

The unity of *title* states that the joint tenancy interests were created in a single conveying instrument. This means that if a joint tenant sells his or her interest to a third party, the joint tenancy is terminated in relation to the third party. If originally two joint tenants owned the property and one of these conveyed his or her interest to a third party, a tenancy in common would be created. If there were more than two joint tenants, the conveyance by one tenant of his or her interest would not terminate the right of survivorship among the remaining tenants as to their interest but would create a tenancy in common only insofar as the purchaser was concerned.

Example: Mary, Kris, and Fred own Hillystreet as joint tenants. Kris sells an undivided one-third in Hillystreet to Sam. Mary and Fred remain joint tenants in two-thirds of Hillystreet while Sam holds one-third interest as a tenant in common. If Sam were to die, his interest would pass on to his heirs or devisees and if he left no heirs or devisees, the interest would pass to the state by escheat. However, if either Mary or Fred were to die, the survivor would automatically acquire the deceased's interest.

The unity of *interest* states that each joint tenant must have the same estate and an equal fractional share in the property.

Example: Jim conveys Prettyshore to Jack and Pam in joint tenancy. Jim specifies Jack is to have 60% interest in the property and Pam is to have 40% interest. Despite Jim's attempt to create a joint tenancy, all he was able to create would be a tenancy in common.

The unity of *possession* is the right of each tenant to the possession and use of the whole property. A tenancy in common has only the unity of possession. If one of the four required unities is destroyed, the joint tenancy is terminated as described above unless state law specifies otherwise. A joint tenant may sell his or her share without the consent or permission of the other joint tenants. If a creditor forecloses on a lien, this would terminate the joint tenancy except as described above when more than two joint tenants are involved. In some states which recognize title theory mortgages, a conveyance of a mortgage would terminate the joint tenancy unless all of the joint tenants joined in the conveyance. This rule, however, would not apply in most lien theory states.

JOINTURE

A freehold estate created for the life of a wife and to take effect upon the death of her husband. Under common law, such a provision as jointure was made prior to marriage and was made in lieu of dower. (*See* **Dower**)

JOINT VENTURE

An agreement by two or more individuals or entities to engage in a single project or undertaking. Joint ventures are used in real estate developement as a means of raising capital and spreading risk. For all practical purposes a joint venture is similar to a general partnership. However, once the purpose of the joint venture has been accomplished, the entity ceases to exist.

JUDGMENT

The final legal determination of rights between disputants, such as a mortgagor and a mortgagee, by a court of competent jurisdiction.

JUDGMENT CREDITOR

The party who gains under a judgment. (*See* **Judgment Lien**)

JUDGMENT DEBTOR

The person burdened by a judgment. (*See* **Judgment Lien**)

JUDGMENT LIEN

The charge upon the property of a debtor resulting from the decree of a court entered in the judgment docket. Once a certified abstract of the court judgment is recorded, it becomes a lien upon all of the judgment debtor's real and personal property within the jurisdiction. The lien may be suspended by posting a bond until the time for final appeal has expired or an appeal has been turned down by the appellate court. This abstract is recorded in a judgment docket kept by the county clerk or other public official which is arranged alphabetically according to the names of judgment debtors. The abstract places a cloud on the title of all real property owned by the judgment debtor for the statutory time of the judgment lien or until the lien is satisfied. When a judgment is a lien on all the property of the judgment debtor, it is called a *judgment in personam* as contrasted to a *judgment in rem*, which applies only to a specific property. The statutory time period is set by state law, in most states ten years.

JUDICIAL FORECLOSURE

A means of selling property through a court procedure to satisfy a lien. (*See* **Foreclosure**)

JUNIOR LIEN

An encumbrance second in priority to a previously recorded lien or to a lien to which the encumbrance has been subordinated.

JUNIOR MORTGAGE

A mortgage which has a lower priority or lien position than a first mortgage. A third or even a fourth mortgage is also classified as a junior mortgage. What establishes a mortgage as being a junior mortgage is that it was recorded after the first mortgage was recorded and thus its lien position is inferior to the first mortgage. (*See* **Second Mortgage, Subordination Clause**)

JURISDICTION

The extent of authority of a court to render legal decision over person or subject matter.

JUST COMPENSATION

Fair and reasonable compensation to both owner and the public when property is taken for public use through *condemnation*. Protection is provided to property owners under the U.S. Constitution for the taking of land. The Fifth Amendment provides that "just compensation" must be made. (*See* **Condemnation, Eminent Domain**)

KEY LOT

A parcel of land that because of its location must be acquired in order to assemble several parcels into one large parcel. The key lot may be a corner lot or it could be an interior lot. (*See* **Plottage**)

KICKBACK

Payment made to someone for referral of a customer or business. Generally speaking, kickbacks are illegal. The reason is that, unlike a commission, a kickback is made without the customer's knowledge; thus, the referral could have been made without the customer's best interest at heart. Secret kickbacks to a lender from a provider of a service are specifically prohibited by the *Real Estate Settlement Procedures Act.*

KICKER

The right of a mortgage lender or other investor to share in income, in addition to principal and interest receipts. Also known as *equity-kicker* and *lender participation.*

KINNARD, WILLIAM N.

A real estate appraiser credited with use of the term "most probable use" which is defined as the use to which land and building would most likely be put. Kinnard is the author of *Income Property Valuation.*

KIOSK

A small freestanding structure located in a shopping center or mall from which merchandise is sold. The type of products marketed would include film, flowers, ice cream, or any item that is uniform in nature so that it can be purchased with little or no shopping. Typically, the tenants of these operations pay a substantially high rent based on a percentage of sales. (*See* **Percentage Lease**)

L

LAND

The earth's surface, the space beneath which extends to the center of the earth, and the space above, which extends to the skies. *Real property, real estate,* and *realty* are terms which may be used interchangeably. These terms refer to land and the improvements both "on" and "to" the land. Further, it refers to all man-made objects and articles permanently attached to the land. (*See* **Real Estate**)

LAND ACQUISITION LOAN

A loan made for the purpose of securing title to a parcel of land as compared with a construction loan which is used to finance improvements on the land. Since unimproved land normally does not generate any income, land acquisition loans are considered riskier than some other types of loan and thus may carry a high rate of interest.

LAND BANK

Land acquired for the purpose of holding with the intention of developing or using the land at some points in the future. Governmental units sometimes acquire land and place it in a land bank in order to preserve the land in its natural state or to prevent commercial development of the land.

LAND BUILDING RATIO

The proportion of total land space to the gross building area. (*See* **Floor Area Ratio**)

259

LAND CAPACITY

The ability of land to economically absorb inputs of capital and labor. Determining the capacity of land is the first step in deriving *highest and best use*. (*See* **Highest and Best Use**)

LAND CONTRACT

(*See* **Contract for Deed**)

LAND DESCRIPTION

A description of a parcel of real estate. Land descriptions appear in listing agreements, sales contracts, deeds, mortgages, leases, notes, and other instruments involving rights and interests in real estate. (*See* **Legal Description**)

LAND DEVELOPMENT

The steps taken to prepare raw land so that improvements can be made on the land. Necessary steps normally include clearing and grading of the land plus the installment of streets, curbs, gutters, and lines for water, sewer, gas, and electricity.

LAND DEVELOPMENT LOAN

A loan acquired by a developer to cover the cost incurred during the stages of developing a tract of land. The interest rate is normally tied to the prime rate, for example, prime plus two. (*See* **Construction Loan**)

LAND ECONOMICS

A social science which studies the relation of people to the utilization and distribution of land and to the creation of real estate products.

LANDED HOMES ASSOCIATION (LHA)

A concept of ownership which allows for fee ownership in a single family detached house and the land surrounding the house. In addition, the owner voluntarily or mandatorily owns an interest called a *participation membership* in a homeowner's association which owns a package of amenities such as a club house, swimming pool, golf course or other property. The LHA concept is a hybrid ownership form which takes elements of condominium ownership, cooperative ownership, and ownership in severalty.

LAND EFFICIENCY

A qualitative measure referring to how factors of production (labor, capital, and management) can be combined with land to generate the greatest possible income from the land. (*See* **Highest and Best Use**)

LAND GRANT

A gift of land by the government.

LAND LEASE

(*See* **Ground Lease**)

LANDLOCKED

Reference to a piece of land that belongs to one person and is completely surrounded by land belonging to another person(s). Thus, the only way the landlocked piece can be reached is by crossing over the land of another. Access to such land will normally be by an *easement by necessity*. (*See* **Easement**)

LANDLORD

The owner or *lessor* of leased property who through either a written or oral agreement has agreed to lease the property to another party known as a tenant or *lessee*. (*See* **Landlord-Tenant Relationship**)

LANDLORD-TENANT RELATIONSHIP

A relationship between an owner of property and a renter of that property through a lease agreement. The landlord (*lessor*) gives the right to the tenant (*lessee*) to use and have exclusive possession, but not ownership, of the real estate for a period of time, either definite or indefinite, in consideration for the payment of rent. The interest that the tenant has is a nonfreehold estate, also known as a *leasehold*. The landlord's interest is referred to as a *leased fee*. A leased fee interest includes both the right to receive the contract rent and the *reversion*, the right to repossession of the realty at the end of the term.

LANDMARK

A marker, tree, stream, or some other object set on the boundary line of two adjoining parcels of land to establish the boundaries of the land. The term also refers to a parcel of land or a building which has historical significance. (*See* **Monument**)

LAND POOR

A situation in which a person owns a large quantity of unimproved land and has little, if any, cash due to the fact that the land is not generating any income.

LAND RESIDUAL TECHNIQUE

A method of estimating the value of land through the capitalization of income used when the value of the land is not known and when the building can be valued based on its replacement cost.

LANDSCAPE ARCHITECT

A person trained and experienced in designing the site features such as gardens, vegetation, and topography on a real estate project.

LANDS, TENEMENTS, and HEREDITAMENTS

The technical term for describing real property, which would include the land, all improvements on and to the land, and any rights and interests that may exist in the land.

LAND TRUST

A devise whereby property is transferred to a trustee under a trust agreement.

LAND USE

The specific zoning classification of a parcel of land such as residential, industrial, commercial, or agricultural.

LAND-USE INTENSITY

A part of a zoning ordinance that establishes various density requirements for land such as floor area ratios, setbacks, and minimum open space. (*See* **Floor Area Ratio, Planned Unit Development**)

LAND-USE MAP

A map showing types and intensities of various land uses.

LAND-USE REGULATIONS

Controls and limitations imposed by governments over the use of land. Examples would include zoning, building codes, housing codes, and subdivision regulations. Such regulations are imposed by local governments by virtue of their police power. (*See* **Police Power**)

LARGE LOT ZONING

(*See* **Exclusionary Zoning**)

LATE CHARGE

A financial charge made to a borrower for failing to pay a loan installment on time. Such a charge is normally not made until after a stated grace period such as ten or fifteen days. The penalty is not considered interest but rather payment to a lender for the time and inconvenience resulting from the payment not being made on time.

LATENT DEFECTS

Defects in the structure such as a crack in the foundation, or failure of mechanical equipment, or a faulty air conditioner occurring during the winter months, of which the owner has no knowledge or which could not easily be detected by an inspection of the property. Knowledge by either the seller or broker of such defects must be made available to a buyer, with failure to do so being grounds to void the contract. (*See* **Fraud, Misrepresentation**)

LATERAL AND SUBJACENT SUPPORT

The right of a landowner to have his or her land supported by the land of adjoining landowners. This is a nonpossessory right recognized by law which means that a landowner may not excavate his or her land in such a manner as to cause an adjoining property owner's land to subside or collapse.

LAW DAY

The due date of an obligation. Under English common law a borrower had to pay off a mortgage debt on or before law day. If the debt were not paid by that time, the lender automatically acquired title to the property and the borrower lost all legal claims to the property.

LAWFUL OBJECT

(*See* **Legality of Object**)

LAW OF NUISANCE

A legal concept of ownership which states that a property owner may not use his or her property in such a manner as to interfere with the reasonable and ordinary use of an adjoining property owner.

LEAGUE OF NEW COMMUNITY DEVELOPERS

An organization comprised of developers of new towns and communities which seeks both private and public support of new communities.

LEAPFROG DEVELOPMENT

Land development that takes on a "checkerboard" pattern as certain parcels are skipped or "leapfrogged" during the development process.

LEASE

An agreement by which a landlord (*lessor*) gives the right to a tenant (*lessee*) to use and to have exclusive possession but not ownership of realty for a period of time in consideration for the payment of rent. A lease creates rights and liabilities between the landlord and tenant and operates both as a conveyance of a property interest and as a contract between the landlord and tenant. As a result, rights and liabilities between the two parties are defined by both property law and contract law principles.

Because a lease is both a conveyance of an interest in land and a contract, it must meet certain minimum legal essentials in order to be valid. These essentials depend on whether the lease is oral and whether it falls within the ambit of the state's statute of frauds and therefore must be in writing. The essentials of a valid lease are described below:

1. In order to have a valid lease, the parties to the lease must have *contractual capacity*.

2. A valid written lease should contain an *agreement to let and take*. This agreement states the conveyance by the landlord to the tenant.
3. A *sufficient description* of the realty demised by the lease is essential.
4. The *term* of the lease should be specified.
5. The lease should indicate the *consideration*.
6. If the *purpose* or consideration of the lease is illegal, the lease is considered to be void.
7. A *statement of the rights and duties* of the respective parties should be included in the written lease.
8. The *signature* of the landlord is essential to a valid written lease.
9. Where required to be valid, the lease should be *executed and acknowledged*.
10. If a lease exceeds a statutory term as it does in some states, the instrument must also be *recorded* in order to be valid.

Both the lessor and lessee may transfer their respective interests in a lease to a third person, unless prohibited by the terms of the lease. The lessor may sell, assign, or mortgage the leased fee interest. Conveyance is taken subject to the rights of the lessee unless the lessee has agreed to subordinate the rights. The lessee may transfer the leasehold interest either by assignment or by sublease. If the lessee parts with the entire estate, retaining no interest, the transfer is called an *assignment*. If the lessee retains a reversion, the transfer is called a *sublease*. In a sublease the sublessor has a *sandwich lease* and no direct legal relationship is created between the landlord and the sublessee. A sublease is really an estate within an estate. The lessee becomes a sublessor and a landlord tenant relationship is established between the sublessor and the sublessee. Since the sublessor can only convey the rights which he or she has, the sublease is effectively bound by any limitations in the main or underlying lease. The sublessor remains primarily liable to the landlord for rent and the performance of all covenants.

Leases may be terminated by (1) expiration of the term, (2) notice, (3) surrender and acceptance, (4) occurrence of certain contingencies, (5) breach of covenant, (6) merger, (7) eviction, and (8) suit for possession.

Expiration of Term: An estate for years terminates on the expiration of the term. The term is considered expired on midnight of the last day of the term specified in the lease.

Notice: An estate from year to year, a tenancy at will, and a tenancy at sufferance expire by giving appropriate notice as defined in the lease agreement, by statute, or by common law.

Surrender and Acceptance: Surrender and acceptance terminates a lease either by mutual agreement or by operation of law. Surrender and acceptance occurs by mutual agreement if the lessee offers to terminate the lease, which is the "surrender," and the lessor agrees to the offer, which is the "acceptance." Surrender is distinguished from mere *abandonment*. A lessee may not just walk away from a lease and hope to escape legal liability. A lessor does not show acceptance by entering on the realty in order to protect it after abandonment. The landlord may attempt to lease the property for the best terms that he or she can get in order to mitigate damages, and to sue the breaching lessee for the actual injury suffered. Surrender and acceptance, however, will occur by operation of law if the landlord takes unqualified possession of the property and gives a new lease without reservation.

Occurrence of Certain Contingencies: The lease may specify several contingencies which serve to terminate the lease. Other events beyond the control of either party may also serve to terminate the lease. For example, destruction of the premises, if no covenant to repair by the lessee exists, would serve to terminate the lease. Likewise if a mortgage which was recorded prior to the lease is foreclosed, the lease is terminated. It should be noted that the foreclosure of mortgages of the leased fee recorded subsequent to the lease have no effect on the lease. The lessee merely gets a new landlord. Provisions may also be included to terminate the lease upon sale of the leased fee to a third person or by bankruptcy of either party. Some courts recognize the doctrine of *commercial frustration*. Commercial frustration occurs if the purpose of the leasehold cannot be effectuated. For example, if the purpose of the leasehold were to sell beer, and the tenant is unable to procure a license, some courts may allow this lease to be terminated for hardship. This approach, however, is in the minority.

Breach of Covenant: Breaches of implied or express covenants may terminate the lease. While there is not implied warranty as to the condition of the premises as an ordinary rule, some exceptions exist which would allow the lessee to terminate the lease. If a new building is being constructed and is not finished when the lease is signed, or if the building is not fit for occupancy when it is completed, the lessee may terminate the lease. Likewise, if the landlord allows the condition of the premises to materially change after the lease is signed but before delivery of possession, the tenant may terminate the lease. If the tenant uses the property for unauthorized purposes or breaches other covenants which are expressed in the lease, the landlord may call for a *forfeiture* and declare the lease to be terminated. Courts construe forfeiture strictly. A landlord must be acting in good faith when using this power in enforcing covenants and conditions in the lease.

Merger: If the lessee acquires the leased fee interest, the leasehold and the leased fee interest are merged and the lease is terminated. This is also true if the lessor somehow acquires the leasehold. The doctrine of merger states that when two estates or two legal instruments are brought together under one ownership, the inferior right or interest merges into the superior right or interest.

Eviction: Eviction is any action by the landlord which interferes with the tenant's possession or use of the leased premises in whole or in part. *Actual eviction* is a material breached by the landlord of any covenants or any other act which wrongfully deprives the tenant of the possession of the premises. A *partial eviction* occurs when the tenant loses possession of part of the premises. If an actual eviction occurs the tenant may bring a suit to recover possession or for damages. Where a partial eviction occurs the tenant is freed from the obligation to pay rent until he or she regains full possession of the premises. *Constructive eviction* occurs when the tenant's use of the premises is substantially disturbed or interfered with by the landlord's actions or failure to act where there is a duty to act. For example, if the premises become unfit for occupancy because of the landlord's failure to maintain heat in the winter, or to repair elevator service in a high-rise building, or to exterminate insects and vermin, the tenant may vacate the premises within a reasonable time and be freed from any further obligations to pay rent. In order to have constructive eviction, the tenant must give up possession.

Suit for Possession: A suit for possession is sometimes referred to as an *actual eviction by law*. When a tenant unjustifiably retains possession of the land this is called *unlawful detainer*. A suit for possession is a court suit to regain lawful possession of the leased premises. After a hearing the judge issues a writ of possession which is executed by the sheriff. Procedure and terminology differ slightly from jurisdiction to jurisdiction. Possession of the premises may not be a sufficient remedy if the tenant still owes rent. Common law provided remedies called *distress* or *distraint* which allowed the landlord to seize the tenant's property on the premises and to sell or hold the property to satisfy a claim for rent. Today, a court action is required. Many states give the landlord a lien on the personal property. Often in the lease, a *cognovit* or *confess judgment clause* is included. This clause authorizes the landlord's lawyer to appear in the name of the tenant and to confess judgment to the court allowing the landlord to recover delinquent rent, court costs, and attorney's fees. In many cases several tenants seek to lease one housing unit, common office or commercial space. A clause for *joint and several liability* is often included. This allows the landlord to sue any and all of the tenants in the case of a default on the lease.

LEASEBACK
(*See* **Sale and Leaseback**)

LEASED FEE
The landlord's interest in leased property.

LEASED FEE MORTGAGE
A loan secured by the landlord's interest in the property. (*See* **Leasehold**)

LEASEHOLD
The interest that a tenant has in the property by virtue of a lease. A leasehold and a leased fee are valuable property rights which may under certain circumstances be sold, assigned, or mortgaged.

LEASEHOLD IMPROVEMENTS
Fixtures and other improvements to leased property, made by or for a specific tenant.

LEASEHOLD MORTGAGE
A mortgage secured entirely by the tenant's (*lessee's*) interest in a parcel of real estate. The mortgage is a type of secondary financing since it is subordinate to the landlord's (*lessor's*) fee interest. Insurance companies and some commercial and savings banks are the primary sources for this type of loan.

LEASEHOLD VALUE

The value of a lease present in those instances where the market rental value (*economic rent*) is higher than the rent established by the lease (*contract rent*). For example, if a 20-year lease required an annual payment of $1,000 on a building with a market rental value of $2,000, the value of the leasehold would be $2,000 minus $1,000 or $1,000 per year. Capitalizing the difference at an appropriate rate would determine the leasehold value of this particular lease.

LEASE INSURANCE

Insurance available to a landlord that protects against loss in income due to the tenant(s) not paying rent. Such coverage is normally available only for commercial real estate.

LEASE OPTION

(*See* **Lease with Option to Buy**)

LEASE PURCHASE AGREEMENT

An arrangement between the lessor and the lessee whereby part of the rent payment is applied toward the purchase price, and when the prearranged total amount has been received by the owner (lessor), title is transferred to the lessee.

LEASE WITH OPTION TO BUY

A lease which includes a clause or statement giving the tenant (lessee) the right to buy the property at a predetermined price. Part or all of the rent being paid during the period of the option may go toward part of the purchase price. (*See* **Lease, Option**)

LEGACY

A gift of personal property by a will; a bequest.

LEGAL AGE

The age at which a person attains full capacity to enter into binding contracts. In most states the legal age or *age of majority* is eighteen.

LEGAL BENEFIT

Consideration which occurs when one receives a promise, act, or forbearance to act to which he or she was not legally entitled. The benefit may or may not have any real monetary value. (*See* **Consideration**)

LEGAL CAPACITY

Recognition which the law gives that a person has the ability to incur legal liability or acquire legal rights.

LEGAL DESCRIPTION
A description of a parcel of real estate complete and specific enough so that a competent civil engineer or surveyor could locate the exact boundaries of the property. (*See* **Lot and Block, Metes and Bounds, Monument, Government Survey Method**)

LEGAL DETRIMENT
Occurs when one does something that one is not obligated to do or gives up a legal right. It may be noted that promises to refrain from criminal, tortious, or immoral conduct are not detriments because everyone already has a general duty to society to avoid this kind of activity.

LEGAL ENTITY
Any person, proprietorship, partnership, copartnership, or corporation which has the legal capacity to enter into an agreement or contract.

LEGAL GUARDIAN
(*See* **Guardian**)

LEGAL INTEREST
The highest rate of interest that may be charged as prescribed by law.

LEGAL LIFE ESTATE
An interest in real property that is limited to the life of someone and exists by operation of law when a certain status such as marriage is achieved. Legal life estates include *curtesy*, *dower*, and *homestead*. (*See* **Curtesy, Dower, Homestead Exemption**)

LEGALITY OF FORM
(*See* **Statute of Frauds**)

LEGALITY OF OBJECT
An essential element of a contract that must be present for a contract to be valid and enforceable. The law will not enforce a contract in which either the consideration or object is illegal or against public policy.

Example: Karen pays a member of the city council $1,000 to "fix" a zoning hearing so that her property is zoned commercial. The council member takes the money but then refuses to help her with the rezoning matter. Karen brings a suit to recover the $1,000 she paid. The court refuses her recovery because the money was paid for an illegal purpose.

LEGAL NAME
The name of an individual consisting of a given or baptismal name and a surname or family name.

LEGAL NOTICE

Notice which is required by law to be given for a specific purpose or in a particular instance. For example, prior to a public auction of property in which a lender has foreclosed, proper legal notice of the foreclosure would have to be given by the lender.

LEGAL RESIDENCE

The place which is the permanent home and domicile. In many states a person must be a legal residence of that state prior to applying for a real estate broker's or salesperson's license.

LEGAL TITLE

Title that is complete and perfect in regard to the apparent right of ownership. (*See* **Title**)

LENDER

The entity from which money is borrowed.

LENDER PARTICIPATION

(*See* **Kicker**)

LESSEE

The party to whom property has been leased. The interest that the tenant has is a nonfreehold estate, also known as a *leasehold*. (*See* **Lease**)

LESSOR

The party who leases property. The landlord's interest is referred to as a *leased fee*. A leased fee interest includes both the right to receive the contract rent and the *reversion*, the right to repossession of the realty at the end of the term. (*See* **Lease**)

LESS THAN FREEHOLD ESTATE

Estates in possession generally referred to as *leaseholds*. Also known as *nonfreehold estates*, such interests are considered to exist for a definite period of time or successive periods of time until termination by notice.

LET

To lease property.

LETTER OF COMMITMENT

(*See* **Loan Commitment**)

LETTER OF CREDIT

A written agreement by a lender on behalf of a customer that the lender will honor drafts drawn by a third party against the account of the customer.

LETTER OF INTENT

The written preliminary agreement between two parties who intend to enter into a contract at some future time. For example, the owner of a building and a potential tenant may tentatively agree to the terms of a lease and put their intentions into writing prior to entering into a formal lease agreement.

LEVEL ANNUITY

A series of periodic receipts or payments that are each equal in amount.

LEVEL ANNUITY CAPITAL RECOVERY

(*See* **Inwood Factor**)

LEVEL-PAYMENT MORTGAGE

A method of loan repayment in which the dollar amount of each payment is the same. Each payment consists of both interest and principal. Interest is paid on the outstanding balance as of that date and the remainder of the payment goes toward reducing the principal. (*See* **Amortization**)

LEVERAGE

Use of borrowed capital to finance the purchase of real estate or other assets. Leverage is a technique of magnifying risks and returns on an investment through the use of borrowed financing. To illustrate the use of leverage, consider a project costing $10,000 which produces an income of $1,200 after expenses. If the investment is purchased completely with equity dollars, it would earn a rate of return of 12% on equity. What would happen to this rate of return if the investor could borrow money costing 9% at a 90% loan-to-value ratio? The effect of this financing on the rate of return is as follows:

Revenues after expenses	$1,200
Interest on loan	
(9% on $9,000)	- 810
Return	$ 390

Rate of return on equity invested:
$390/$1,000 = 39%

As the simple example illustrates, the investor has magnified the rate of return substantially by using leverage. Using borrowed money at this same loan-to-value ratio, an investor could control ten similar investments costing $10,000 instead of just one. However, a high loan-to-value ratio is not always beneficial since it carries with it risks to both the equity and debt positions. In the previous illustration, assume the revenue after expenses dropped to $800. The return would be 8% to the all-equity investor but minus 1% to the leveraged investor.

LEVY

To assess or tax, such as to collect property tax.

LIABILITY INSURANCE

A type of insurance that protects one party against liability or losses suffered by a third party. For example, a landlord may have a liability policy to insure against losses or injuries suffered by a tenant.

LIBER

Latin word for "book". When deeds, promissory notes, subdivision regulations, and other legal instruments dealing with real estate are recorded in the public land records, they are assigned a liber volume and *folio* (page) number. Anyone desiring to examine the instruments can then locate the specific book and page in the public records.

LICENSE

A personal privilege to go upon the land of another. A license is a personal property right and may be created orally. An attempt to create an easement orally would be treated as the creation of a license. A license does not run with the land and unlike an easement, which is more or less a permanent right, a license is mere authority to enter upon land for a particular purpose and is usually temporary. Without a license a person who enters upon land without authority would be considered a trespasser and would be liable in damages to the landowner. The owner of the land who grants the license is called the *licensor* and the recipient of the privilege is called the *licensee*. The licensor may revoke the license at will. Examples of licenses include: tickets to theaters, ball games, and concerts; the right to hunt, fish, or ski on someone's land; the rental of a parking space; and the rental of camp sites.

LICENSEE

One who has the legal personal privilege to go upon the land of another. The term is also used to denote anyone, either a broker or salesperson, licensed to broker real estate.

LICENSING EXAMINATION

A written examination administered by a real estate commission to test a potential real estate broker's or salesperson's understanding of real estate principles and practices. Each state requires an examination be given prior to the issuance of a license, and that a minimum passing score is required. Some states use the *Real Estate Licensing Examinations* prepared by the *Educational Testing Service*. Other states use the *ACT Multistate Examination* or the *Real Estate Assessment for*

Licensure Program (ASI) while some employ real estate examination specialists within their own state or from colleges and universities to write the examination questions. The examinations are given periodically. State requirements vary as to how often the examination can be taken by someone who has previously failed all or part of the examination. *(See* **License Laws***)*

LICENSE LAWS

Laws enacted by every state to oversee the licensing and regulations of persons engaged in real estate brokerage and related activities. Early in the 20th century various states began to recognize the need for regulating the activities of certain participants engaged in real estate. In 1913 the National Association of Real Estate Boards, predecessor to the National Association of Realtors, took a strong position encouraging each state to enact statutes for the regulation of certain real estate activities. States began enacting real estate license laws, and today every state has some form of regulation. Anyone desiring to become a real estate licensee must be familiar with the license laws in his or her particular state. For those practitioners involved in real estate activities in other states or jurisdictions, an understanding of the laws and statutes in those locations is also important.

The power to enact and enforce real estate license laws is provided for under the police power reserved by implication to each state by the Constitution of the United States. While laws and statutes differ from jurisdiction to jurisdiction, the purpose of the real estate license law is the same, namely *to protect the public* rather than to merely produce revenue. The licensee must know what is required in protecting the public in real estate transactions. A first step in this direction is to acquire a copy of the real estate laws from the appropriate real estate regulatory body *(See* **Appendix C***)*.

Many states have structured their rules and regulations after a model real estate license law published by the *License Law Committee* of the *National Association of Realtors* in cooperation with the *National Association of Real Estate License Law Officials (NARELLO)*. Certain uniformities from state to state do exist. The more common provisions in the real estate laws cover such topics as: (1) definitions, (2) who must be licensed, (3) real estate commission, (4) issuance of license, (5) refusal, suspension, or revocation of license, (6) hearing procedures, and (7) numerous additional provisions.

LIEN

A legally recognized right to enforce a claim or charge on the property of another for payment of some debt, duty, or obligation. A lien may be created voluntarily, such as by the giving of a mortgage, or it may be created involuntarily, such as by the imposition of a mechanic's lien. The lien may be *specific (in rem)* in that it attaches to a particular property, or it may be *general (in personam)* in that it attaches to all property owned by an individual. This right may be enforced by the judicial sale of a person's property if the claim or charge which the property secures is not satisfied. A lien is a type of *encumbrance* on property. An encumbrance is any interest in the land of another which in some manner burdens or diminishes the value of property. Because liens diminish the use of land or quality of title, where they exist there may be problems with the marketability and insurability of title.

There are three classifications of liens which indicate the legal basis of their creation: (1) contractual liens, (2) statutory liens, and (3) equitable liens. *Contractual liens* are created by agreement of parties. A common example of a contractual lien is a mortgage which is given to secure the debt represented by a promissory note. A *statutory lien* is created when requirements specified in state law are fulfilled. For example, when a judgment is issued by a court against a person, a lien attaches over all of that person's property which is the legal effect specified by state statute. An *equitable lien* is created when justice and fairness would require a court of equity to declare that such a lien exists or when the conduct of parties would imply that a lien was intended. For example, if a tenant in common made necessary repairs to a house which was in danger of collapse and in violation of the housing code, an equitable lien would attach to the other co-tenant's undivided interest for a proportionate share of the expenses. The person who owns the lien is called the *lienor* while the person whose property is burdened by the lien is called the *lienee*. The principal kinds of specific liens are mortgages, mechanic's, and materialman's liens, tax liens, and special assessments. The principal kinds of general liens are judgment liens, liens of creditors on decedent's estate, and federal and state tax liens.

What happens when two or more liens attach to the same property? Which lien has priority in a foreclosure action? This is important when insufficient proceeds are generated in a foreclosure sale to satisfy all liens. If a senior lienholder is the party bringing the foreclosure action, all junior liens are extinguished at the sale. But when a junior lienholder brings a foreclosure action, the property is sold subject to all existing senior liens. In order to determine the priority of liens, the reader should be familiar with the treatment of three basic rules in each state.

RULE ONE: What is the priority of tax liens and special assessments in a state? In most states specific liens and special assessments take priority over all private liens no matter when the private liens have attached. This helps explain why many mortgage lenders require that property taxes be paid in advance into an escrow account or that some mortgages make nonpayment of property taxes and special assessments a default of the mortgage.

RULE TWO: Priority of all other liens, except for specific statutory exceptions such as mechanic's liens, are defined by the state's recording statute. The general rule is that the lien which is first recorded is superior to all subsequent liens. This is usually true unless the lienholder recording first had actual or constructive notice of a prior claim. The reader should be familiar with the distinction between actual notice and constructive notice. *Actual notice* is the actual knowledge that a person has about the existence of a particular fact. For example, Sally tells Ken that she sold her house to David. Ken has actual notice of the sale to David. *Constructive notice* is the knowledge that the law presumes a person has about a particular fact, irrespective of whether the person knows about the fact or not. Any information which is recorded properly in the public records or announced in an official legal newspaper is constructive notice on every person in the world.

RULE THREE: Irrespective of the rule of priorities established by the state's recording statute, in some states subsequent recorded mechanic's liens may nevertheless still have priority.

In addition to the three rules which have been described, the reader should note that priority liens can be recorded by contract, that is, a subordination agreement by a senior lienholder; or by operation of law, that is, order by a court in bankruptcy for certain kinds of priorities.

LIENEE

The person whose property is burdened by the lien.

LIENOR

The person who owns the lien.

LIEN THEORY STATE

A state which recognizes a legal doctrine by which a mortgage merely creates a lien right in the mortgagee (lender) with the mortgagor (borrower) retaining title to the property. In contrast a *title theory state* holds that a mortgage actually conveys title to the lender subject to the debt being satisfied. When the debt is satisfied title will automatically pass back to the borrower.

LIFE ANNUITY

The right of an individual to receive periodic payments until death.

LIFE ESTATE

(*See* **Conventional Life Estate**)

LIFE ESTATE PUR AUTRE VIE

A type of life estate in which the term of the estate is measured by the life or lives of one or more third persons. An example of this is: Joe conveys some land to Sam for the life of Mary; when Mary dies, Sam's life estate is terminated. It should be noted, however, that Sam's death would not terminate the estate so long as Mary were alive. The estate in this case would belong to Sam's heirs.

LIFE INSURANCE COMPANIES

A primary source of lending for income-producing property, particularly permanent financing. Life insurance companies play an important role as providers of capital for real estate both from a mortgagee's (lender) standpoint and from an equity (owner) standpoint. Unlike the savings and loan association or the commercial bank, which normally deal directly with the borrower, the 2,300 life insurance companies typically do their lending through local correspondents, either mortgage brokers or mortgage bankers. Life insurance companies normally specialize in large-scale projects and mortgage packages. Historically, between 30 and 35% of their assets have been invested in mortgages. Life insurance companies receive their money through the payment of premiums by their policy-holders, and since both the inflow of premiums and the outflow of claim payments can be predicted with reasonable accuracy, life insurance companies are able to invest in those assets yielding higher returns but less liquidity than is available to either banks or associations. For their real estate investments this normally means long-term commercial and industrial financing. While life insurance companies have historically invested in residential mortgages, this form of investment has continued to become a smaller and smaller percentage of their portfolio. Few life insurance companies presently originate residential mortgages. All life insurance companies are state chartered since there is no federal agency which issues charter. The result is less regulation in most states than is true for either S&Ls or banks. Less regulation generally results in liberal lending patterns which leads to the funding of a wide variety of real estate projects. Over 90% of the life insurance companies are stock companies; however, the majority of the industry's assets are held by mutual companies.

LIFE TENANT

The holder of a life estate.

LIGHT INDUSTRY

A type of classification used in zoning ordinances to denote land uses which do not generate the noise, odor, or fumes generally associated with heavy industrial uses. Examples of light industries include small assembly plants and food processing centers.

LIKE-KIND PROPERTY

Property which qualifies for a tax-free exchange. (*See* **Tax-Free Exchange**)

LIMITED COMMON ELEMENTS

Those portions of a condominium jointly owned by all unit owners but under the exclusive control or possession of only some of the owners. Limited common elements may include enclosed courtyards, balconies, shutters, and other features which may lie outside the description of an individual unit but are under the exclusive control of a percentage of the owners. (*See* **Condominium**)

LIMITED LIABILITY

Legal protection from the liabilities of an organization. The primary advantage to a limited partnership form of ownership, so popular in real estate syndications, is the limited liability protection guaranteed to the limited partners. Thus, under the worse scenario, the limited partners can lose no more than their original investment. The general partner remains liable for the liabilities of the partnership.

LIMITED PARTNER

A partner in a business venture whose liability to creditors is restricted to the money which he or she has invested in the partnership. A limited partnership consists of at least one *general partner*, who may under certain circumstances be a corporation, and at least one limited partner. A limited partner has no control over the day-to-day management of the partnership and is essentially a passive investor. Dangers in limited partnership shares include the fact that they are classified as securities, and unless an exemption exists their sale must be registered with the SEC. Further, many states apply the state securities law or "blue sky" law to the sale of limited partnership shares. Broadly defined, a security is any property interest whereby one commits money or accepts liability for the purpose of making a profit from the efforts of another. The broadness of this definition suggests that legal counsel be hired if there is any doubt if a security is involved. A limited partnership can also be defined as an association by the Internal Revenue Service; the entity is then taxed as a corporation. The IRS may declare the entity an association if a limited partnership meets a majority of the following tests:

1. *Continuity of life.* If the entity lasts indefinitely this is considered to be a corporate characteristic.
2. *Centralization of management.* This is by definition a characteristic of a limited partnership since management is left up to the general partner.
3. *Limited liability.*
4. *Free transferability of interest* or share of ownership.

LINEAL

A direct line descendant, as from grandfather to father, father to son.

LINEAL FOOT

A measurement denoting one foot or twelve inches in length as contrasted to a square foot or a cubic foot.

LINE OF CREDIT

The maximum amount of money that a customer of a bank may borrow without further need for approval. By establishing a prearranged line of credit one does not have to go through the normal steps and delays associated with borrowing money.

LINE-OF-CREDIT MORTGAGE

A loan in a second lien position established to provide cash to the borrower on an as-needed and on-going basis. In recent years homeowners have used this type of loan as a source of cash for medical expenses, education, and consumer purchases. The interest rate charged is normally an adjustable or variable rate and is only charged on the outstanding balance, not on the total line of credit. As a result of the *Tax Reform Act of 1986*, such loans, also known as *home equity loans*, have become very popular, primarily due to the fact that interest paid by the borrower is completely tax deductible.

LISTING   277

LINE OF NAVIGATION
(*See* **Harbor Line**)

LINKAGE
The proximity of a parcel of land to a supporting land use. Linkage refers to the *time* and *distance* necessary to reach the supporting facility. If the retail store is too far away from its customers, they will be attracted to a nearer store, or a nearer store will be developed to intercept the customer. (*See* **Situs**)

LIQUID ASSETS
Cash and other assets which can easily and quickly be converted into cash.

LIQUIDATED DAMAGES
An agreed-to sum of money which will be paid one party to a contract if the contract is breached by the other party. (*See* **Contract**)

LIQUIDITY
The ease with which an asset may be converted into cash.

LIS PENDENS
A notice filed in the public records for the purpose of serving constructive notice that title or some matter involving a particular parcel of real property is in litigation. Any person who acquires property under a notice of lis pendens will take it subject to any adverse judgment which may result.

LISTING
An employment agreement between an owner of property and a real estate broker authorizing the broker to find a buyer for the property and defining the duties and rights of the parties. Listing contracts are classified into the following categories: (1) *open listing,* (2) *exclusive agency listing,* (3) *exclusive right to sell listing,* (4) *net listing,* or (5) *multiple listing.*

Even in states which permit oral listing agreements, it is nevertheless a good idea to enter into a written contract. This precaution may help prevent misunderstanding, disagreements, and litigation in the future. Further, written listing contracts help define duties and rights on the part of both the broker and owner and may be entered into evidence to prove these obligations in a court of law. In states which require written listing contracts, the following elements should generally be included: the name of the parties; description of the property; sales price; terms of sale if other than cash; duration of the listing; type of listing, be it open, exclusive agency or exclusive right to sell; amount of commission and how and when it will be paid; special stipulations concerning earnest money deposits; multiple listing arrangements and other special conditions or covenants. Some states have specific elements which must be included in order to permit the broker to receive the commission. For example, many states require that a definite expiration date be specified on the listing contract. If a date is not specified, the broker will not be permitted to recover a commission. Since generally it is the broker who prepares the contract, any ambiguity will be construed against the broker in a dispute. It is important, therefore, that the listing contract be carefully and precisely prepared. If the broker has any question as to the proper wording of a provision, a competent real estate lawyer should be consulted. Since the broker is a party to the listing agreement, preparation of a prepared form would not be deemed as practicing law without a license. This rule does not apply to sales contracts. A broker is generally restricted to mechanically filling blanks in a prepared form. Any other work should be delegated to a licensed attorney. (*See* **Exclusive Agency, Exclusive Right to Sell Listing, Multiple Listing, Net Listing, Open Listing**)

LISTING AGENT

A real estate salesperson who acquires the listing on a particular parcel of real estate. This person may or may not be the person who actually sells the property. Listing agents generally receive 25 percent of the total commission if and when the property sells; they would receive more if they were also responsible for the sale.

LITTORAL LAND

Land bordering a lake, ocean, or sea.

LIVERY OF SEIZIN

The process of transferring title to land under common law. This phrase is derived from the Old French term "livrer" which means "to deliver" and from the term "saisine" which refers to the "taking of possession." A ceremony called *livery in deed* occurred under common law when a grantor (owner) and a grantee (purchaser or donee) physically entered on the land and in the presence of witnesses, the grantor handed to the grantee a piece of turf, a branch, a key, or some other symbol representing the land to be transferred. In making the symbolic delivery, the grantor also stated before the witnesses the intent to make a present transfer and indicated the description of the land and the extent of the estate which was being conveyed. By the end of the twelfth century, it became common to write down the occurrence of the property transfer in a document which came to be known as the deed. In the seventeenth century, the statute of frauds was passed which required that any interest in land be conveyed by a deed. Many of the terms and legal requirements in modern conveyancing are based on these feudal origins.

LOAN CLOSING

The point in time when the lender disburses the funds and the borrower executes the necessary legal documentation such as recording of the deed and mortgage.

LOAN COMMITMENT

A contractual agreement from a lender to finance a certain amount of the purchase price on a particular parcel of real estate. The commitment may be a firm commitment, in which case the borrower is assured of getting the loan provided certain conditions are met (such as the completing of a building for a commercial loan). Residential loans are often given as conditional or qualified commitments, with the loan being assured assuming a satisfactory credit report is obtained and an acceptable title examination is made.

LOAN CONSTANT

(*See* **Mortgage Constant**)

LOAN CORRESPONDENT

A mortgage broker or mortgage banker who negotiates and services loans for lenders or investors. The correspondent normally receives a loan origination fee from the borrower and a percent of each mortgage payment for servicing the loan. (*See* **Loan Origination Fee, Mortgage Banker**)

LOAN COVERAGE RATIO

(*See* **Debt Coverage Ratio**)

LOAN ORIGINATION FEE

A charge incurred by a borrower to cover the administrative costs of the lender in making a loan. The amount is typically stated as a percentage of the loan, for example, one percent.

LOAN PACKAGE

A document delivered to the escrow agent or closing attorney covering the legal documentation and settlement procedures necessary for a transfer of title to take place. The package includes the abstract of title, survey, termite inspection, and deed, as well as the settlement statement. (*See* **Closing**)

LOAN PROCESSING

The steps taken by a lender to complete a loan transaction once the loan application has been approved. For real estate loans the steps would include a credit report, verification of employment and gross income, appraisal report, title examination, and various other documentation. (*See* **Closing**)

LOAN SUBMISSIONS

A set of papers and documentation submitted to a lender by someone who would like to borrow money to purchase or construct a particular real estate project. Included in the package would be a credit report, financial statements, feasibility and market studies of the property, plat, cost analysis of the project, and other such information that will assist the lender in determining whether or not a loan should be made.

LOAN-TO-VALUE RATIO

The relationship between the amount of money borrowed and the appraised value of the property. For example, a $40,000 loan on property valued at $50,000 would represent an 80% loan-to-value ratio. In recent years this ratio has continued to increase, due largely to higher prices, which has resulted in people having to borrow a higher percentage of the purchase price. Historically, loan-to-value ratios for residential property have been higher than for commercial or income-producing property.

LOCAL ADJUSTMENT FACTOR

A factor used to recognize construction cost variations found in different cities in the United States. The average city is 100%; high-cost areas exceed 100%; low-cost areas are below 100%.

LOCAL (IMPROVEMENT) ASSESSMENT

A tax levied against property to pay for such improvements as roads and sidewalks that will directly benefit the owners of the assessed property.

LOCATION

A particular surface on earth that is defined by legal description. (*See* **Situs**)

LOCATION, LOCATION, LOCATION

A commonly used phrase to denote the "three" most important factors in determining the success of a real estate project. (*See* **Situs**)

LOCATIONAL OBSOLESCENCE

(*See* **Economic Obsolescence**)

LOCKED-IN INTEREST RATE

A guaranteed interest rate quoted by a lender that is good from the time the quote is made until the loan is closed. Historically, during periods of little inflation, lenders were apt to guarantee a quoted rate for a lengthy period of time as a means of making the loan. However, during the 1970s and 1980s when it became impossible to forecast very far into the future, lenders got away from locking themselves into a guaranteed rate. Today, most lenders, while agreeing to make a loan, do not lock in the interest rate until the closing is ready to take place.

LOCUS SIGILLI

Latin meaning, "in place of the seal." Following the signature line on certain legal documents the letters *L.S.* sometimes appear in place of the actual seal of the corporation or person signing the document.

LOG HOME

A type of housing structure which uses some type of wooden log as the exterior material of the structure. Such housing received limited popularity among home buyers in the 1970s after energy costs increased significantly. Today, a number of national and regional companies offer log homes as well as kits for the construction of such units.

LONG-LIVED ASSETS

Components of a building that have a relatively long useful life, such as the foundation and framework.

LONG-TERM CAPITAL GAIN

The gain realized from the sale or exchange of a capital asset held for more than one year.

LONG-TERM FINANCING

A mortgage covering a period of time of ten years or more. In contrast, short-term financing such as a construction loan, covers a much shorter period of time. (*See* **Permanent Financing**)

LONG-TERM LEASE

A lease covering a period of ten years or more. (*See* **Ground Lease**)

LOSS FACTOR

The difference, expressed in percentage, between the rentable area of a building and the usable space in the building. For example, a building with 10,000 square feet of rentable space and 8,500 square feet of usable space has a loss factor of 15 percent (10,000 - 8,500 = 1,500 /10,000). The loss factor is a quick and easy means by which a prospective tenant can compare two possible rentals which may rent for the same dollars per square foot but which may have quite different loss factors.

LOSS PAYEE

The person named in an insurance policy as the one to be paid in the event of damages to the property.

LOT

A parcel of land having frontage on a road or street.

LOT AND BLOCK

A method of land description based on reference to a particular lot and block number recorded in the public records. Also referred to as the *recorded plat method*, this means of land description is frequently used after land has been subdivided into building lots. When a land developer subdivides a tract of land, a surveyor's plat map is recorded in the public records of the jurisdiction where the land is located. The subdivision plat contains a great deal of information regarding the intended use of the land being subdivided. Included in the plat map are the boundaries of each parcel of land. The boundary description is by metes and bounds or by rectangular survey. Each parcel of land is assigned a lot number and each group of contiguous lots is given a block number. Streets in the subdivision are identified in the tract itself is given a name. A directional arrow and scale will also be included. Easements will also be identified. If an easement lies completely within one lot, it is normally shown by dotted lines; if the easement lies along the boundary of a lot, the boundary line appear as a solid line.

Once the plat is recorded in the public records, any future reference to a particular lot within the subdivision will be by lot and block description. Consider the following lot and block description in a deed: Being known and designated as Lot No. 24 as shown on Subdivision Plat of Block 1, of "Loch Raven Village," which Plat is recorded among the Land Records of Carrol County in Liber C.H.K. No. 13, Folio 122. The improvements thereon being known as No. 1738 Aberdeen Road. By referring to this particular book and page number in the land records (book 13, page 122), a copy of the surveyor's plat map could be examined and Lot 24 of Block 1 could be identified. As this particular piece of property is conveyed from one party to another, reference to the plat will be made in the same way.

LOT BOOK

(*See* **Plat Book**)

LOT LINE

A term used to denote the line which is the boundary for a parcel of land known as a lot.

LOVE AND AFFECTION

Consideration which is considered sufficient when a gift is made. For example, a deed of land from father to son could be supported by love and affection. However, when valuable consideration is necessary, love and affection is not considered adequate. (*See* **Consideration**)

LOWBALL OFFER

An offer to purchase that is significantly less than the other offers being made. Such an offer, if accepted, allows the buyer to acquire the property at a price that appears to be below market value. (*See* **Market Value**)

L.S.

An abbreviation for *locus sigilli*, meaning in place of a seal.

LTV

(*See* **Loan-To-Value Ratio**)

MACKAYE, BENTON

Author of *The New Exploration: A Philosophy of Regional Planning* which established numerous regional planning fundamentals that are still in use today. In addition, Mackaye was instrumental in the planning of the Appalachian Trail Highway System.

MAI

Member, Appraisal Institute. A professional designation awarded by the American Institute of Real Estate Appraisers to persons who have met minimum education, experience, and demonstration requirements in the areas of valuation and appraisal. (*See* **American Institute of Real Estate Appraisers**)

MAINTENANCE

The act of keeping a building in general repair. Lack of proper maintenance will result in a loss in value. (*See* **Deferred Maintenance**)

MAINTENANCE COSTS

The expenditure necessary to keep a building and grounds in general repair. Such costs appear on an income statement as an operating expense and are the responsibility of the property manager. While maintenance costs vary greatly from property to property, there is some degree of uniformity with like-like properties. As such, investors and lenders often examine the history of maintenance costs as an indication of how a specific property has been maintained.

MAINTENANCE FEE

Payment made by the unit owner of a condominium to the homeowner's association for expenses incurred in the maintenance and upkeep of the common areas. The fee is ordinarily collected monthly and failure to pay can lead to liens being placed on the individual unit, attachment, and foreclosure. (*See* **Condominium, Homeowner's Association**)

MALL

Part of a retail shopping area set aside for pedestrian traffic.

MANAGEMENT AGREEMENT

An employment contract between the owner of real estate and a property management firm that agrees to oversee the management of the property. As is true in any business agreement, the property manager or management firm and the owner of the property should enter into a formal contract. The management contract should include the responsibilities specified in the employment agreement, the term and period of the contract, the management policies to be followed, the power and authority of the property manager, and the compensation for the management services. Normally, a property manager's compensation is an agreed-upon percentage of gross income. The range can vary from a very small amount, perhaps one percent on a large structure, to as much as ten or fifteen percent on a single-unit house. (*See* **Property Management**)

MANAGEMENT FEE

The agreed-upon compensation paid to a property management company for managing a real estate project. The fee is usually based on a percentage of gross income. (*See* **Management Agreement**)

MANAGEMENT PLAN

A written report of what the property management company hopes to accomplish and how it intends to do so. Before assuming the management of a piece of property, a long-range plan should be developed. However, before the plan can be developed, an analysis has to be made of the owner's objectives. Certainly, the property manager has to be confident that these objectives can be met. A physical inspection of the property itself has to be made, and the property manager needs to understand existing market conditions regarding competition rental structures and operating expenses.

MANUFACTURED HOUSING

A housing unit primarily constructed in a plant or factory prior to transporting it to the lot where it is set. Manufactured housing can be delivered in various stages of production which offers the purchaser the flexibility of buying the "shell" up to and including purchase of a completely finished unit. Cost per square foot for manufactured housing is normally considerably less than comparable costs for stick-built structures.

MANUFACTURED HOUSING INSTITUTE

This trade organization represents the manufacturers and dealers of mobile and modular homes throughout the United States. The institute's headquarters is 1745 Jefferson Davis Highway, Arlington, Virginia 22301; (703) 979-6620.

MARGINAL LAND

Land which for one or more reasons is incapable of producing much income given the costs that would be incurred to produce the income. Examples of deficiencies would include poor access, steep terrain, inadequate drainage, and odd-shaped lots.

MARGINAL PRODUCTIVITY

(See **Contribution, Principle of**)

MARGINAL TAX BRACKET

The rate of federal income tax that will apply to the next increment of taxable income.

MARGINAL UTILITY

The addition to total utility of the last unit of a resource. (See **Increasing and Decreasing Returns, Principle of**)

MARINA

A docking and servicing for boats and equipped to provide repair service, gasing, and supplies.

MARKET

The economic function of bringing buyers and sellers together through the price mechanism.

MARKETABILITY STUDY

(See **Feasibility Study**)

MARKETABLE TITLE

Title to property which is free from reasonable doubts or objections and which the courts would compel a purchaser to accept under the terms of a sales contract. (See **Abstract of Title, Chain of Title**)

MARKETING PLAN

A report detailing the means by which a parcel(s) of real estate will be sold. The plan, if developed properly, will identify the target market establish how and when the property will be shown and, generally, cover the total marketing of the property. Such a plan, while it may be used for a single parcel such as a home, is very commonly used in association with timesharing and second home sites. The marketing plan should be developed prior to the property being available for purchase.

MARKET DATA APPROACH

A technique used to estimate value by comparing similar properties. This method is used when there is an active market and where reasonable comparables can be identified.

MARKET PRICE

The amount of money actually paid in a transaction.

MARKET RENT

The rental income that a property is likely to command in the current market. Market rent may be either higher or lower than what the property is actually renting for under the terms of a lease. (*See* **Contract Rent**)

MARKET RENTAL RISK

The probability that market rental rates will change, affecting the value of a property that is subject to fixed rent.

MARKET VALUE

The price in terms of cash or its equivalent upon which a willing buyer and a willing seller will agree, where neither is under any undue pressure and both are typically motivated, have adequate knowledge, and are acting in their own best interest. This concept of value assumes that there is sufficient activity in the marketplace to generate enough buyers and sellers so that no one of them controls the price. Each party is also acting in his or her best interest and is fully informed as to market conditions. Finally, individual financing and taxation consequences are not considered, the property is exposed on the market for a reasonable period of time, and the seller is capable of conveying marketable title. Market value is an ideal standard which is very seldom achieved in real-world real estate markets; nevertheless, this is ordinarily the objective of most appraisals. (*See* **Fair Market Value**)

MASS APPRAISING

Simultaneously appraising a large number of parcels of real estate. Such a technique is sometimes done by appraisal firms employed by a local government to reappraise property for the purpose of determining assessment values for property tax purposes. (*See* **Market Data Approach**)

MASTER AND SERVANT RELATIONSHIP

A relationship between two people in which the employer is liable for actions or wrongdoings on the part of the employee. In a *principal-agent relationship*, the test to determine if a principal will be liable for the actions of an agent is whether the agent is a *servant* or an *independent contractor*. If the principal and agent are in a master-servant relationship, the law will impose *vicarious liability* on the master for torts committed by the servant while in the scope of the master's employment. Vicarious liability means that the master will be civilly liable to injured third persons even though the master did not personally commit the tort. The doctrine which allows a third person to recover is called *respondeat superior* or "let the master answer." An employer, however, is not generally liable for torts committed by an independent contractor. An independent contractor, unlike a servant, is not subject to the control of the person with whom the contract is made. A master has the right to control the physical activities of a servant in the performance of the duties of employment, whereas an independent contractor contracts for particular results and retains control and discretion over how such results will be accomplished. The distinction between servant and independent contractor is also important from the perspective of who is responsible for paying federal withholding taxes and social security. Independent contractors are responsible for paying their own taxes. The distinction is also important in the application of state worker's compensation laws. A real estate broker working for a principal is considered to be acting as an independent contractor. A typist or clerk in a broker's office is generally considered to be a servant of the broker. The test to be applied is whether the employer has the right to control the method and mode of service. Salespeople working for a broker can be either servants or independent contractors. Which status a salesperson has depends on the method of compensation and the agreement between the broker and salesperson as to the broker's right to control activities. Some state licensing laws specify that a salesperson is essentially a servant under the control of the broker.

MASTER DEED
(See **Condominium Declaration**)

MASTER PLAN
A program for the future development of a community which serves as the guidelines for capital expenditures.

MASTER POLICY
An insurance policy that covers a number of parcels of real estate rather than one parcel, as is normally covered with an insurance policy. *(See* **Insurance**)

MATERIAL BREACH
A violation of a contract of such nature or importance that the innocent party may rescind the contract as well as recover damages. *(See* **Contract**)

MATERIAL FACT
Any fact which, if known, would affect the judgment of one or more of the parties to a transaction. *(See* **Contract**)

MATERIALMAN'S LIEN

(See **Mechanic's and Materialman's Liens**)

MATURITY

The date when a note or negotiable instrument is due and payable.

MAXIMUM LOAN AMOUNT

The largest dollar figure in terms of how much money can be borrowed under a specific government program, such as a subsidized housing program or an FHA project.

MBS

(See **Mortgage-Backed Securities**)

MEANDER LINES

A measurement used in surveying to denote the boundary line of a stream showing the natural course of the stream.

MEAN HIGH TIDE

The average of all the high tides as calculated over a long period of time.

MEAN SEA LEVEL

A frame of reference assumed to be at zero elevation used in the surveying of land. Elevations above zero elevation are positive and those below zero elevation are negative.

MEASUREMENTS

Certain standards of measurement are needed in working with the dimensions of land. The following measurements are commonly used:

Linear Measurements

1 foot (ft.)	= 12 inches (in.)
1 yard (yd.)	= 3 feet (ft.)
1 mile	= 1,760 yds. = 5,280 ft.

Square Measurements

1 sq. ft.	= 144 sq. in.
1 sq. yd.	= 9 sq. ft.
1 acre	= 43,560 sq. ft.

Land Surveying Measurements

1 sq. acre	= 208.71 ft. on each side
1 section	= 1 sq. mile = 640 acres = 1/36 township
1 township	= 36 sections = 36 sq. miles = 23,040 acres
1 minute (')	= 60 seconds (")
1 degree (°)	= 60 minutes (')
1 quadrant	= 90 degrees (°)
1 circle	= 360 degrees (°)

MECHANIC'S AND MATERIALMAN'S LIENS

Statutory liens levied on property by persons who are not compensated after providing labor (mechanic) or material (materialman) for the improvements to the property. Both types of liens are commonly referred to as mechanic's liens. The mechanic's lien is justified on the equitable theory that work or materials provided by contractors add to the value of the improvements and increase the value of the land. Because of this theory, work and materials must become permanently attached or incorporated into the land or improvements. For example, if a materialman provides lumber which is merely stored in a warehouse, no specific lien would attach to the land on which the warehouse stands. Likewise, if a property owner hires workers to build a fence on only one of his two lots, the workers may not levy a lien on both lots, but only on the lot on which they built the fence. Some states permit those who rent out construction equipment used on the property to also levy a lien, others do not. (*See* **Lien**)

MEETING OF THE MINDS

A mutual agreement or assent between the parties as to the terms and conditions of a contract. To form a contract there must be a "meeting of the minds." (*See* **Contract**)

MEGALOPOLIS

A heavily populated urban area that runs continuously through numerous cities. An example would be the Eastern Seaboard of the United States starting with Washington, D. C., and continuing through Baltimore, Philadelphia, New York and Boston.

MENACE

A threat of force or improper action against a person or property in order to induce a party to act.

MERCHANTABLE TITLE

(*See* **Marketable Title**)

MERGER

The absorption of one thing into another. In contract law, for example, the oral discussions that take place between a potential buyer and seller merge into the written sales contract and thus the sales contract takes precedent over previous oral discussions. In real property law when a lesser estate is acquired by someone holding a greater estate, the lesser estate is immediately merged. For example, if Bill has an easement over John's property and later Bill acquires John's property, the easement is terminated by merger since the dominant and servient estates have come under one ownership.

MERIDIANS

Imaginary lines running north-south which intersect with base lines to form the reference points in the government survey method of land descriptions. (*See* **Government Survey Method**)

METER

The basic unit of measuring length in the metric system. A meter equals 39.37 inches.

METES AND BOUNDS

A method of land description in which the dimensions of the property are measured by distance and direction. This method is the primary means of legally describing land in some twenty states. To correctly use this method there must be a definite starting point. This starting point must be one that can be located by future surveyors, thus it is necessary that it be as precise as possible. Physical evidence of this point, referred to as a *monument,* is often an iron pipe set in concrete which in turn can be and often is referenced to a permanent reference point such as a *bench mark.* Bench marks are bronze discs permanently placed and precisely identified by government survey teams. Monuments, both natural and artificial, also include fences, rivers and streams, trees, wooden stakes and road intersections. However, none of these is as precise as bench marks. Once the *point of beginning (POB)* on the property has been established, *boundary lines* are identified and described until the land being surveyed has been "completely enclosed." Boundary lines measure *distance* and *direction.* Where two boundary lines cross, referred to as a *corner,* a monument is often used to identify the intersection. Distance is stated in terms of feet, normally to the nearest hundredth (for example, 212.65). Direction is given by its bearing, which shows the direction of one object with respect to another object. The bearing of a boundary line is the *acute angle* (an angle of less than 90 degrees) the line makes with a *meridian* (an imaginary line running north to south extending from the North Pole to the South Pole). In land description, the bearings are identified with reference to the *quadrants* on a compass and are expressed in terms of *degrees, minutes,* and *seconds.* A circle contains 360 degrees, 1 degree contains 60 minutes, and each minute contains 60 seconds. The circle is divided into four quadrants, each containing 90 degrees. The quadrants are identified by their boundary lines, namely Northeast

(NE), Northwest (NW), Southeast (SE), and Southwest (SW). For each boundary line set in a metes and bounds description, the distance of the line, the direction of the line, and the monument used to mark the end of the distance should be clearly and precisely stated in the legal description. The following is an example of a metes and bounds description:

Beginning for the same at pipe set on the north side of Charles Street, distance South 85° 08' 16" East 430.50 feet measured along the north side of said Charles Street from the east side of Mt. Royal Avenue and running thence for new lines of division through the property now or formerly owned by John Smith the three following courses and distances; namely North 15° 10' 12" East 224.60 feet to a pipe set, North 82° 54' 38" East 315.00 feet to a pipe set on the north side of said Charles Street and then binding on the north side of said Charles Street North 85° 08' 16" West 332.45 feet to the place of beginning. Containing 80,313.23 square feet or 1.8437 acres of land, more or less. All courses and distances in the above descriptions are referred to the true meridian as adopted by the Orange County Survey Control System.

This particular description was based on "walking" around the property in a clockwise direction. While it is common to describe land this way, the description would be perfectly acceptable had the direction been counterclockwise. In the example above a description based on a counterclockwise direction would result in changing the "N" directions to "S", the "E" to "W," with the degrees, minutes, and seconds remaining unchanged. The distances between points are not changed as a result of changing direction. While it does not matter in which direction you travel, the important point is to "close the circle."

METROPOLITAN AREA

The land in and around a city. The area may cross both county and state lines, as for example, Washington, D. C., which includes parts of Virginia and Maryland.

MIDDLEMAN

A person who brings parties together for the purpose of entering into a contract such as the borrowing of money to finance a real estate project. Normally, the middleman is paid a fee, often referred to as a finder's fee, if and when the parties enter into an agreement. (*See* **Mortgage Banker**)

MILE

A measure of length equalling 5,280 feet, 1,760 yards, 1,609 kilometers, or 8 furlongs. Such a measurement is a statute mile, whereas a nautical mile contains 6,080 feet.

MILITARY CLAUSE

A clause included in a lease of residential property which allows the tenant to terminate the lease without penalty if and when the tenant is transferred to another location.

MILKING A PROJECT
(See **Bleeding a Project**)

MILL

One-tenth of one cent. Property taxes in many jurisdictions are stated in mills.

MILLAGE RATE

A tax rate stated in tenths of a cent. For example, a millage rate of 150 mills on property assessed at $100,000 would result in a property tax of $1,500 ($100,000 x .150). *(See* **Tax Rate)**

MINERAL DEED

A conveyance by an owner of the subsurface rights to his or her property while reserving the surface and air rights to the property.

MINERAL LEASE

An agreement entered into by an owner permitting another party to explore for and, if found, extract minerals in consideration of the payment of a rent or royalty.

MINERAL RIGHTS

The right to share in the sale of minerals that may be extracted from one's land.

MINIMALL

A shopping area consisting of small specialty stores and absent of any anchor tenants, such as one of the national retailers.

MINIMUM-GUARANTEED PERCENTAGE LEASE

A type of percentage lease that provides the lessor (landlord) a minimum rent regardless of the amount of sales. The minimum guarantee is referred to as a "floor," referring to the fact that the rent cannot fall below that amount. *(See* **Percentage Lease)**

MINIMUM LOT SIZE

A provision of a zoning ordinance stipulating the minimum dimensions of a lot necessary for the construction of a building, for example, two-acre lots for each residence. *(See* **Zoning)**

MINIMUM PROPERTY STANDARDS

Minimum construction and location requirements that must be met before the *Federal Housing Administration (FHA)* will underwrite a loan for residential property. *(See* **Federal Housing Administration)**

MINIMUM SETBACK REQUIREMENTS
(See **Setback Requirement(s)***))*

MINIMUM RENT
The least amount of rent due from a tenant under a lease with a varying rental schedule.   For example, in a percentage lease the lessor (landlord) normally receives a percentage of gross sales as the rental for the property.   The lease may also include a fixed guaranteed minimum which is due from the tenant regardless of total sales.   Thus, the landlord is assured of a certain amount of rent even during periods of low sales.   *(See* **Percentage Lease***)*

MINIWAREHOUSE
A one-story structure partitioned into individual units for use by individuals and businesses to store personal belongings.   Individual units are normally rented on a month-to-month basis with the rent charged varying with the unit size.   Units vary in size from 50 or 60 square feet up to 500 square feet.

MINOR
An infant or person who has not attained the age of majority and thus does not have the legal capacity to be bound by most contracts. Most contracts entered into by a minor are *voidable* at the minor's option. However, a minor may choose to *ratify* a contract after achieving the age of majority. A minor or infant is bound to pay the reasonable value of necessities. Necessities include food, shelter, and clothing which are appropriate for a person in the minor's station of life.

MIP
(See **Mortgage Insurance Premium***)*

MISDEMEANOR
An offense or crime lower or less than a felony. *(See* **Felony***)*

MISNOMER
Mistake in name. Normally, when a mistake in name occurs in a deed a *correction deed*, also known as a *deed of confirmation,* is used to correct the error.

MISREPRESENTATION
An innocent or negligent misstatement of a material fact detrimentally relied upon by an innocent party. If a person makes a misrepresentation and later learns of the mistake, a duty then arises to inform the person who is detrimentally relying on the misrepresentation. Failure to do so is *fraud.* *(See* **Fraud***)*

MISTAKE
An unintentional error or misunderstanding. Certain kinds of mistakes are

grounds for rescinding a contract; others are not. Mistakes are classified as *unilateral* or *mutual*. A unilateral mistake is a mistake of a material fact involving a contract made by just one of the parties. If only one of the parties is mistaken as to a material fact, the mistake is not a defense unless the other party is chargeable with knowledge of the mistake. Whether or not the mistake is chargeable is judged by a "reasonable man" standard; that is, whether a reasonable person would believe that the other party made a mistake.

Example: Seale sends a bid of $11,000 to construct a warehouse for Chap. He meant to send a bid of $110,000. Chap, who received other bids ranging from $90,000 to $120,000, would have to reasonably believe that a mistake had been made. If, however, Seale had sent a bid of $100,000 instead of $110,000, Chap could not be chargeable with the knowledge of the mistake.

A mutual mistake occurs when both parties in a contract are mistaken as to the same material fact. This is grounds for rescission. For example, Kathy and Hilda enter into a contract for the purchase of Kathy's office building not knowing at the time that the building had been destroyed in a fire. Both made a mistake as to the existence of the subject matter.

MIXED-USE COMMERCIAL PROJECT

A real estate development that contains two or more different uses all intended to be harmonious and complementary. An example would include a high-rise building with retail shops on the first two floors, office space on floors three through ten, apartments on the next ten floors, and a restaurant on the top floor.

MLS

(*See* **Multiple Listing Service**)

MOBILE HOME

A manufactured unit constructed on a chassis and wheels and designed for permanent or semi-attachment to land.

MOBILE HOME LOAN

A loan acquired for the purchase of a mobile home. Certain lenders, although not all, make loans on mobile homes. Typically, the amount financed is for much less than the average residential loan, and the amortization period is much shorter, perhaps seven to ten years, even though longer terms are available under both FHA and VA financing. The amortization period is usually shorter since, unlike a permanent home, a mobile home normally depreciates in value, and thus, the lender wants to be repaid over a shorter period of time. A fear of some lenders is that since mobile homes are not permanently affixed to the land, the security for the loan, the mobile home, can be moved by a dishonest borrower. Thus, not all lenders make mobile home loans.

MOBILE HOME PARK
A parcel of land zoned and developed for use by occupants of mobile homes.

MODEL HOME
A house built and used by a builder to demonstrate quality of construction, floor plans, styles, and amenities that are to be available in other homes available for sale by the builder. Quite often a builder will construct one or more model homes at the entrance to a subdivision. Once the other homes have been built and sold, the model homes are placed on the market and sold as residences.

MODULAR HOUSING
A form of housing in which construction of the unit takes place at a factory, followed by the assembling of the house on the building site. Cost per square foot is considerably less due in part to the design which allows for little waste of materials and provides efficiency during construction.

MONEY MARKET
The short-term financial market which brings together investors who wish to invest in assets maturing in a short period of time and users of capital who wish to raise funds by selling short-term instruments. Treasury bills and commercial paper are examples of money market instruments.

MONTH-TO-MONTH TENANCY
(*See* **Periodic Tenancy**)

MONUMENT
Physical evidence, either natural or manmade, which has been established as the boundary(s) for a parcel of land. Land is sometimes described by monuments which serve to identify the boundaries of the subject parcel. This method, while quite common in older descriptions in rural areas, relies on the use of both natural and artificial monuments. Land description by monuments is considered less exact than a description by metes and bounds since the boundaries used are sometimes something not permanent, for instance, a river bed or a pile of rocks. Oftentimes reference is made to land owned by someone else, for instance, a neighbor's farm.

The following is an example of a monuments description: Beginning at a point marked by an iron pipe on the south side of State Highway 31E approximately eight miles west of Dycusburg and at the beginning of a fence row marking the land of John Smith; then along the fence line in a southerly direction for 935 feet to an oak tree marking the land of Elbert Jones; thence in a westerly direction for 1750 feet to Mansker Creek; thence along the creek bed of Mansker Creek in a northerly direction for 900 feet to the right-of-way of State Highway 31E; thence easterly along the right-of-way line of State Highway 31E for approximately 1700 feet to the point of beginning, containing 36.5 acres more or less.

MORATORIUM

In regard to the development of land, a temporary suspension or delay in the granting or approval of building permits, sewer and water hookups, or rezoning requests. Such action may be initiated by a local government to allow time for a comprehensive growth management study which will be used to assist in formulating future growth plans.

MORE OR LESS

Used in the legal description of land to denote that the total acreage given in the description is an approximation. For example, a legal description may read "_____, containing 500 acres more or less." Inclusion of these words allows for slight differences which may arise; for example, the exact acreage may be 499 acres or 501 acres. However, the use of "more or less" in a legal description does not insure the validity of the description if substantial differences exist between the actual dimensions and what has been included in the description.

MORTGAGE

An interest created by a person in regards to a particular property to secure the payment of a debt or performance of some other obligation. This interest may be a lien or a conditional title interest subject to defeasance when the debt is paid or the obligation fulfilled. A borrower who gives a mortgage is called a *mortgagor* and the lender who receives the pledge is called the *mortgagee*. It is important to realize that the mortgage is given by the borrower, not the lender. The term "mortgage" is derived from the Old French term "mort" meaning dead and "gage" meaning pledge. Thus, when a mortgage note is paid off, the pledge is cancelled or becomes dead.

Real estate financing involves two separate obligations, one represented by the *promissory note* or the *bond*, the other by the mortgage or some similar security instrument. The promissory note is the primary financing obligation in which the borrower promises to pay back a sum of money borrowed. This is the main evidence of the actual debt and is a personal obligation of the borrower. The mortgage is the secondary financing obligation in which the borrower or mortgagor agrees to pledge property to secure the debt represented by the note. The requirements for a valid mortgage are very similar to the requirements of a valid deed since both instruments convey an interest in land and must stipulate requirements necessary to permit recordation. A valid mortgage instrument should provide for the following:

1. There must be a written instrument involving a mortgagor and a mortgagee, each having contractual capacity. These parties must be identified in the instrument. Where the mortgagor is a co-owner of the property to be pledged, or where curtesy or dower rights are recognized, the co-owner(s) or spouse should also be identified and join in the mortgage.
2. The property interest being pledged must be specified. For example, if the mortgagor only possesses a leasehold, this leasehold must be described.
3. A legal description of the property must be included.

4. Words of conveyance should be used which are compatible with either the title theory or lien theory which prevails in the state where the property is located. These words are often referred to as the mortgaging clause.
5. A statement of the obligation should be included. This can be done by referring to the obligation in the promissory note or bond. In order to preserve the confidentiality of the transaction, financial information such as the interest rate is seldom included on the mortgage instrument, but it is included on the note, which is ordinarily not recorded. It should be made clear that the mortgage is being given to secure payment of a debt or some other obligation. Without a debt or some other obligation there can be no mortgage.
6. Any promises or covenants must be included. Such covenants might include a prepayment clause or an acceleration clause. In addition, a mortgage instrument may contain several other kinds of clauses.

MORTGAGE-BACKED SECURITIES
Securities purchased by investors that are secured by mortgages. Such securities are also known as *pass-through securities* since the debt service paid by the borrower is passed through to the purchaser of the security.

MORTGAGE BANKER
A financial middleman who, in addition to bringing borrower and lender together, makes loans, *packages* them, and sells the packages to both primary and secondary investors. If a mortgage banker is not financially strong enough to package the loan, financial help is sought from a lender, typically a commercial bank. The bank becomes a *warehouse* for mortgage money, and the mortgage banker draws on these funds until payment is received from the investors. Usually the mortgage banker continues to service the loan (collect debt service, pay property taxes, handle delinquent accounts, etc.) even after the loan has been packaged and sold. For this management service a small percentage of the balance paid to the investor goes to the mortgage banker. Obviously, the success of the mortgage banker depends upon the ability to generate new loans. In some geographic areas mortgage bankers are the primary source for financing real estate. All mortgage bankers try to stay in constant touch with investors and are aware of changing market conditions and lender requirements. Quite often the loan origination fee or finder's fee charged the borrower is more than offset by a lower interest rate from a lender not directly accessible to the borrower. Mortgage bankers are involved in both commercial and residential financing and also carry out related activities, such as writing hazard insurance policies, appraising, and investment counseling. As with mortgage brokers, mortgage bankers are regulated by state law.

MORTGAGE BANKERS ASSOCIATION OF AMERICA (MBA)
The Mortgage Bankers Association of America is the primary trade organization of the mortgage bankers and brokers in the United States. The association

provides numerous seminars and publications for its membership and sponsors the designation *CMB (Certified Mortgage Banker)*. The headquarters is 1125 15th Street, N.W., Washington, D.C. 20005; (202) 861-6500.

MORTGAGE BOND PROGRAM

A means of providing financing for real estate through the proceeds of issuing tax-exempt bonds. Since the bonds are tax-exempt, the interest rate paid when the bonds are sold is less than other bond rates. This, in turn, means that the money made available to the ultimate borrowers will be at a below-market rate of interest. (*See* **Housing Finance Agency**)

MORTGAGE BROKER

A person who brings together a user of capital (borrower) and a supplier of capital (lender) and in return is paid a *finder's fee*. A finder's fee equal to one percent or so of the amount borrowed is normally paid by the borrower. Thus, the financial success of the mortgage brokerage firm depends upon the ability to locate available funds and to match these funds with creditworthy borrowers. Certain sources of funds, particularly insurance companies, do not always deal directly with the person looking for capital; rather, they work through a mortgage broker. Thus, if you wish to borrow from certain lenders you would need to go through a mortgage broker. Normally, the mortgage broker is not involved in servicing the loan once it is made and the transaction is closed.

MORTGAGE COEFFICIENT

A multiplier used in certain income property appraisal techniques to compute a capitalization rate. In the *Ellwood Technique* for appraising property the mortgage coefficient is designated by the symbol "C."

MORTGAGE COMMITMENT

An agreement whereby a mortgage lender agrees to fund a certain mortgage loan and a borrower agrees to comply with its requirements.

MORTGAGE CONSTANT

The relationship between annual mortgage loan requirements and the initial mortgage loan principal, expressed as a decimal or percentage, for level-payment mortgage loans. For example, a $100,000 loan which requires a total annual payment of $11,000 would have a mortgage constant of .11, or 11 percent. The mortgage constant is also referred to as a *loan constant.*

MORTGAGE CORPORATION, THE

(*See* **Federal Home Loan Mortgage Corporation**)

MORTGAGE CORRESPONDENT

A person authorized to represent a financial institution in a particular geographic area for the purpose of placing loans. (*See* **Mortgage Broker**)

MORTGAGE DISCOUNT
(See **Discount Points***)*

MORTGAGEE
A lender who receives a pledge of property to secure a debt. *(See* **Mortgage***)*

MORTGAGEE IN POSSESSION
A lender or creditor who has taken over property after default for the purpose of collecting rents and conserving the property until foreclosure.

MORTGAGE-EQUITY TECHNIQUE
A technique for estimating the value of income-producing property based on the sum of the mortgage principal added to the discounted present value of the forecasted cash flow and the reversion to equity.

MORTGAGE FORECLOSURE
(See **Foreclosure***)*

MORTGAGE GUARANTY INSURANCE CORPORATION (MGIC)
A private insurance company which insures a certain percentage of a conventional loan, thus reducing the lender's risk on a high loan-to-value ratio. MGIC, or "MAGIC" as it is commonly known, was established in 1957 to offer a borrower on a conventional loan what FHA offers on its insured loans. *(See* **Private Mortgage Insurance***)*

MORTGAGE INSURANCE
(See **Private Mortgage Insurance***)*

MORTGAGE INSURANCE COMPANIES OF AMERICA
A trade association comprised of the nation's private mortgage insurance companies. The address is 1615 L Street, N.W., Washington, D.C. 20006; (202) 785-0767.

MORTGAGE INSURANCE PREMIUM (MIP)
The charge paid by the borrower to cover the cost of a mortgage insurance policy under an *FHA* insured mortgage. The insurance policy provides protection for all or a certain percentage of the loan amount to the lender in case of default by the borrower. Historically the premium was paid each month as part of the mortgage payment; but, in recent years it has been paid either in cash at closing or financed and repaid as part of the total amount borrowed.

MORTGAGE INTEREST DEDUCTION
An allowable tax deduction for persons who itemize their federal and state

income tax returns. Interest paid on a mortgage loan(s) up to the cost of one's home plus the cost of any improvements is deductible. Any interest on debt above that amount is not deductible unless used for medical expenses, education, or home improvements.

MORTGAGE LIFE INSURANCE

A decreasing-term life insurance policy purchased by a borrower which will pay off the outstanding balance in the event of the death of the borrower (mortgagor). The premium is paid as part of the monthly mortgage payment.

MORTGAGE LOAN SERVICING

The process of collecting periodic mortgage payments and escrow funds, paying property taxes and insurance, and overseeing the administration of a loan over its life.

MORTGAGE LOAN UNDERWRITING

The process of reviewing an application for a loan and making a recommendation as to the desirability and risk of the lender making the loan. The underwriting process is an integral part of the lending process.

MORTGAGE NOTE

(*See* **Promissory Note**)

MORTGAGE PORTFOLIO

The total of all mortgages held by a lender.

MORTGAGE REQUIREMENT

(*See* **Debt Service**)

MORTGAGE SECURITIES POOL

A technique by which securities backed by the value of specific real estate mortgages are issued in the financial market for investment purposes. Such securities, because they are mortgage-backed, are more marketable and generally are issued with a lower rate of interest than if no such backing existed.

MORTGAGE VALUE

The value of an asset for purposes of securing a mortgage loan. The term is also used to denote the market value of a mortgage loan.

MORTGAGING OUT

Acquiring 100 percent of the funds necessary to acquire or develop a project; thus, the buyer/developer does not have to put up any up-front cash and has no equity in the property.

MORTGAGOR

A borrower who pledges property through a mortgage to secure a loan. (*See* **Mortgage**)

MOST PROBABLE SELLING PRICE

The likely price a property will bring, given current market conditions, buyer and seller motivations, and the financing terms that are likely to be employed.

MOTEL

A facility which offers lodging for the general public.

MOTHER HUBBARD CLAUSE

(*See* **Anaconda Mortgage**)

MULTIFAMILY HOUSING

A structure consisting of housing units for a number of different family units. Quite often zoning ordinances require a special zoning classification for multifamily housing.

MULTIPLE DWELLING

A structure containing more than two units designed for accommodating households.

MULTIPLE LISTING SERVICE (MLS)

A marketing service in which many brokers pool all of their listings and establish procedures for sharing commissions. Generally, multiple listing services (MLS) require that property owners sign an exclusive agency or exclusive right to sell listing with participating listing brokers in order to have access to the marketing pool.

MULTIPLE REGRESSION

A mathematical technique used in estimating the amount of value for a subject property based on known variables and prices for comparable properties.

MULTIPLIER

A rate to be multiplied by an amount. (*See* **Gross Rent Multiplier**)

MUNICIPALITY

A local government, commonly referred to as a city or town.

MUNICIPAL ORDINANCE

A law or rule such as a zoning ordinance or building code enacted by a municipality for the purpose of conducting the affairs of the municipality.

MUNIMENTS OF TITLE

Written evidences of title such as a deed which an owner of land possesses and could use to prove his or her title to the land. (*See* **Title**)

MUTUAL ASSENT

The combination of the offer and acceptance which together form the terms of a contract. (*See* **Contract**)

MUTUAL RESCISSION

A means of discharging a contract by which each party agrees to release the other party in exchange for his or her own release.

MUTUAL SAVINGS BANKS

A primary source of financing real estate for residences. Located primarily in northeastern states, the mutual savings banks are an important supplier of real estate financing. As their name indicates, these banks are owned by their depositors, who receive interest on their deposits. All mutual savings banks are state chartered and typically are less regulated than their closest financing relative, the savings and loan association. The percentage of their assets invested in real estate mortgages is less than the average S&L, although a higher percentage of their total mortgage portfolio is FHA and VA loans. Most mutual banks have a relatively larger percentage of their mortgage loan portfolio invested in multi-family mortgages. Mutual banks also make personal loans and interstate loans, which can result in capital being moved from surplus areas to deficit areas. Over two-thirds of the mutual banks maintain membership in the FDIC. The remaining ones are insured by state savings insurance agencies. These state agencies exercise authority over both the type of investments and the amount of their assets mutual banks can invest in particular types of real estate.

NAA

(See **National Apartment Association**)

NAAO

(See **National Association of Assessing Officers**)

NAHB

(See **National Association of Home Builders**)

NAIFA

(See **National Association of Independent Fee Appraisers**)

NAMED INSURED

The person named in an insurance policy as the one protected.

NAMSB

(See **National Association of Mutual Savings Banks**)

NAR

(See **National Association of Realtors**)

NAREB

(*See* **National Association of Real Estate Brokers**)

NAREIT

(*See* **National Association of Real Estate Investment Trusts**)

NARELLO

(*See* **National Association of Real Estate License Law Officials**)

NARRATIVE APPRAISAL

The final report compiled by an appraiser stating his or her opinion of value based on data and the appraisal method(s) used in deriving the estimate of value. (*See* **Appraisal**)

NATIONAL APARTMENT ASSOCIATION (NAA)

NAA membership consists of builders, owners, and suppliers of apartment complexes. The mailing address is 1111 14th Street, N.W., Washington, D.C. 20005; (202) 842-4050.

NATIONAL ASSOCIATION FOR COMMUNITY DEVELOPMENT

This organization seeks to promote community development and to preserve community concepts in cities throughout the United States. The mailing address is 1424 16th Street, N.W., Washington, D.C. 20036; (202) 293-7587.

NATIONAL ASSOCIATION OF ASSESSING OFFICERS (NAAO)

An organization comprised of people employed at the local and state level as property assessors.

NATIONAL ASSOCIATION OF CORPORATE REAL ESTATE EXECUTIVES (NACORE)

NACORE is a nonprofit association of real estate executives representing commerce, industry, and government. The association provides numerous programs and seminars for its members. The mailing address is Suite 8, 471 Spencer Drive, South, West Palm Beach, Florida 33409; (407) 683-8111.

NATIONAL ASSOCIATION OF COUNTIES

This association serves as a liaison between county governments and other levels of government. The headquarters is at 440 1st Street, N.W., Washington, D.C. 20001; (202) 393-6226.

NATIONAL ASSOCIATION OF HOME BUILDERS (NAHB)

The National Association of Home Builders serves as the primary voice of the housing industry. NAHB offers the designation *Professional Builder* in addition to providing numerous services to its membership. The association is located at 15th & M Streets, N.W., Washington, D.C. 20005; (202) 822-0200.

NATIONAL ASSOCIATION OF HOME MANUFACTURERS (NAHM)

An association which represents the interest of the industrialized housing industry. NAHM's mailing address is 1619 Massachusetts Avenue, N.W., Washington, D.C. 20036; (202) 822-0200.

NATIONAL ASSOCIATION OF HOUSING AND REDEVELOPMENT OFFICIALS (NAHRO)

NAHRO is a professional association which provides an opportunity for private and public officials to exchange ideas in an effort to provide decent living environments for all Americans. The mailing address is 2600 Virginia Avenue, N.W., Washington, D.C. 20037; (202) 333-2020.

NATIONAL ASSOCIATION OF HOUSING COOPERATIVES

This association provides information and research on housing cooperatives to persons involved with cooperatives. The mailing address is 2501 M Street, N.W., Washington, D.C. 20037; (202) 887-0706.

NATIONAL ASSOCIATION OF INDEPENDENT FEE APPRAISERS (NAIFA)

The National Association of Independent Fee Appraisers was founded in 1961 as a non profit professional society of real estate appraisers. Members of the association are comprised of full-time professional real estate appraisers and others in related fields such as real estate, banking, construction, governmental agencies, and savings and loan associations. NAIFA awards three designations: (1) *Member (IFA)*, (2) *Senior Member (IFAS)*, and (3) *Appraiser/Counselor (IFAC)*. The mailing address is 7501 Murdoch Avenue, St. Louis, Missouri 63119; (314) 781-6688.

NATIONAL ASSOCIATION OF MUTUAL SAVINGS BANKS (NAMSB)

The major trade organization representing the mutual savings institutions in the United States. The mailing address is 200 Park Avenue, New York, NY 10017; (212) 973-5432.

NATIONAL ASSOCIATION OF PENSION FUNDS

A trade association which represents the interests of the pension fund industry. The mailing address is 1150 Connecticut Avenue, Suite 500, N.W., Washington, D.C. 20036; (202) 457-1049.

NATIONAL ASSOCIATION OF REAL ESTATE BROKERS (NAREB)

The nation's oldest, largest, and most effective minority-oriented trade organization. The group was formed in 1947 and is represented through its national office in Washington, D.C., and through approximately 50 state associations and local boards. The designation *REALTIST* is awarded to its membership. The mailing Address is 4324 Georgia Avenue, N.W., Washington, D.C. 20011; (202) 289-6655.

NATIONAL ASSOCIATION OF REAL ESTATE INVESTMENT TRUSTS (NAREIT)

A trade association headquartered in Washington, D.C., representing the real estate investment trust (REIT) industry. The association serves as a spokesman for the REIT industry and publishes various studies and reports dealing with real estate investment trusts. The mailing address is 1101 17th Street, N.W., Washington, D.C. 20036; (202) 785-8717.

NATIONAL ASSOCIATION OF REAL ESTATE LICENSE LAW OFFICIALS (NARELLO)

Founded in 1929, the National Association of Real Estate License Law Officials (NARELLO) is a group of real estate license law officials from the United States, Canada, the Virgin Islands, and Guam which regulates more than 2 million real estate licensees. More than 200 members, who are full-time regulatory agencies of the member jurisdictions, commissioners, or board members, make up the individual membership of NARELLO. NARELLO maintains several committees to study the real estate field and examine potential problem areas. The headquarters is located at P. O. Box 129, Centerville, Urah 84014; (801) 298-5572.

NATIONAL ASSOCIATION OF REALTORS (NAR)

The largest and best-known real estate organization in the world, with a current membership in excess of 700,000. Active brokers who maintain membership in the association may use the term *REALTOR*, and their salespersons hold membership on a *REALTOR-ASSOCIATE* status. There is a recent trend for boards to provide only one class of membership to both brokers and salespersons, whereby all board members are REALTORS, and the REALTOR-ASSOCIATE classification is eliminated. The organization is represented through state associations and 1,780 local boards. Of particular interest are three features of the organization. First, membership in the National Association of Realtors requires a person to subscribe to the organization's *Code of Ethics*, which is a strict guide of ethical practice and serves as a guideline for practitioners. Second, the association participates actively as a spokesman for the real estate industry and maintains a full-time staff headquartered in Washington, D. C., to provide testimony on important real estate related issues before Congress and various regulatory agencies. Third, the association provides extensive educational programs through its nine professional institutes, societies, and councils. The address is 430 North Michigan Avenue, Chicago, Illinois 60611; (312) 440-8000.

NATIONAL ASSOCIATION OF REGIONAL COUNCILS (NARC)

An association which provides assistance to voluntary associations of local governments regarding planning, economic forecasting, and land uses. NARC is headquartered at 1700 K Street, N.W., Washington, D.C. 20006; (202) 457-0710.

NATIONAL BANK

A commercial bank chartered and supervised by the U. S. Comptroller of the Currency, as compared to state banks which are chartered by a particular state. If a bank is nationally (federally) chartered the word "national" appears in its name, and the bank must maintain membership in the *Federal Reserve System*. Nationally chartered banks are also required to maintain membership in the *Federal Deposit Insurance Corporation (FDIC)*.

NATIONAL CENTER FOR HOUSING MANAGEMENT, INC. (NCHM)

The National Center for Housing Management, Inc., was created to provide leadership in aiding the country to meet its housing management and training needs. The center works with both private and public agencies in areas related to housing management. The address is 1275 K Street, N.W., Washington, D.C. 20005; (202) 872-1717.

NATIONAL COMMITTEE AGAINST DISCRIMINATION IN HOUSING

A civil rights organization engaged in research and monitoring the enforcement of fair housing laws. This group works with federal, state, and local agencies in matters dealing with fair housing. The mailing address is 1425 H Street, N.W., Washington, D.C. 20005; (202) 783-8150.

NATIONAL ENVIRONMENTAL POLICY ACT (NEPA)

Federal legislation enacted by Congress in 1969 which created the *Council on Environmental Quality (CEQ)* and the *Environmental Protection Agency (EPA)*. In addition, the act also established the requirement for *Environmental Impact Statements (EIS)*.

NATIONAL FLOOD INSURANCE PROGRAM

A federal program enacted by Congress in 1968 intended to provide insurance coverage for those people suffering both real and personal property losses as a result of floods. To encourage the buying of flood insurance, any property located in a flood area cannot be financed through a federally regulated lender unless flood insurance is purchased.

NATIONAL FOREST PRODUCTS ASSOCIATION

An association representing the interest of the forest products industry. The mailing address is 1250 Connecticut Avenue, N.W., Washington, D.C. 20036; (202) 463-2700.

NATIONAL HOUSING AND ECONOMIC DEVELOPMENT LAW PROJECT

A legal service center providing research and assistance in cases involving housing. The center is located at 2313 Warren Street, Berkeley, California 94704; (415) 548-9400.

NATIONAL HOUSING CONFERENCE, INC.

This conference provides information and assistance for various housing programs. Various research publications dealing with housing topics are available upon request. The mailing address is 1126 16th Street, N.W., Washington, D.C. 20036; (202) 223-4844.

NATIONAL HOUSING REHABILITATION ASSOCIATION

An association comprised of companies involved in the development and management of low-income housing. The association is located at 1726 18th Street, N.W., Washington, D.C. 20009; (202) 328-9171.

NATIONAL INSTITUTE OF FARM AND LAND BROKERS (NIFLB)

One of the affiliates of the National Association of Realtors whose members are directly involved in land development and brokerage of agricultural land. The professional designation *AFLB, Accredited Farm and Land Broker*, is awarded to qualified members.

NATIONAL INSTITUTE OF REAL ESTATE BROKERS (NIREB)

(*See* **Realtors National Marketing Institute**)

NATIONAL LEAGUE OF CITIES (NLC)

The National League of Cities has as its objective the improvement of the quality of life in the nation's cities. NLC serves as a spokesperson for cities and projects that are of concern to cities. The address is 1301 Pennsylvania Avenue, N.W., Washington, D.C. 20004; (202) 626-3000.

NATIONAL LEASED HOUSING ASSOCIATION

This association offers assistance to those persons involved in the Section 8 Leased Housing Program. The Association is located at 2300 M Street, N.W., Washington, D.C. 20037; (202) 785-8888.

NATIONAL REALTY COMMITTEE

A spokesman for those individuals and entities involved in taxation and development of real estate. The headquarters is located at 230 Park Avenue, New York, NY 10017; (212) 697-1750.

NATIONAL RURAL HOUSING COALITION

This coalition seeks to voice the opinions of the rural poor in matters of concern to them. Numerous research publications are available upon request. The address is 2001 S Street, N.W., Washington, D.C. 20009; (202) 483-1504.

NATIONAL SAVINGS AND LOAN LEAGUE
A trade organization for both state and federally chartered savings and loan associations. The address is 1101 15th Street, N.W., Washington, D.C. 20005; (202) 331-0270.

NATIONAL SOCIETY OF EXCHANGE COUNSELORS (SEC)
Membership in the National Society of Exchange Counselors consists of brokers and investors specializing in real estate investment and exchanging.

NATIONAL SOCIETY OF REAL ESTATE APPRAISERS
A professional real estate organization whose members are involved in the appraisal of real estate. The society awards three designations: (1) *Residential Appraiser (RA)*, (2) *Certified Real Estate Appraiser (CRA)*, and (3) *Master Real Estate Appraiser (MREA)*. The mailing address is 1265 East 105th Street, Cleveland, Ohio 44108; (216) 795-3445.

NATURAL AFFECTION
The feeling that naturally exists between close relatives such as a parent and child or a husband and wife. In law, such is regarded as *good consideration* and may appear in a deed when property is being transferred.

NATURAL MONUMENT
An object such as a river, shore, or beach which exists as it was placed by nature. Such objects are used to denote boundaries in the description of legal boundaries. (*See* **Monument**)

NAVIGABLE WATERS
Waters which have a channel sufficient to allow navigation by commercial vessels. (*See* **Riparian Rights**)

NECESSARIES
Articles such as food, shelter, and clothing which are required for sustaining life. While contracts entered into by infants (minors) are voidable at the infant's option, an infant is bound to pay the reasonable value of necessities.

NEGATIVE AMORTIZATION
Periodic repayment on a loan that results in an increase in the outstanding balance. Negative amortization, while uncommon in real estate lending, results from the interest on a loan accruing at a faster rate than it is being repaid. The difference is added to the existing outstanding balance which then accrues interest at whatever rate is being charged.

NEGATIVE CASH FLOW

A situation which may arise with income-producing property in which gross rental income is less than operating expenses plus debt service. (*See* **Cash Flow**)

NEGATIVE COVENANT

(*See* **Restrictive Covenant**)

NEGATIVE EASEMENT

An easement which limits the use of the land by its owner due to the effect that the use may have on the land of another. (*See* **Dominant Estate, Easement, Servient Estate**)

NEGATIVE LEVERAGE

The condition experienced when expenses incurred to repay an interest-bearing debt exceed the financial benefits of assets that were acquired with the borrowed money. Such a situation, also known as *reverse leverage*, is illustrated below:

Example: An income producing piece of property which cost $1,000,000 has an annual net income of $100,000; thus, an investor who purchases the property without the help of borrowed money will realize a 10% return on investment ($100,000/$1,000,000). Assume that a 75% loan ($750,000) is acquired and that the interest rate is 12%. The annual interest is $90,000 ($750,000 x .12). Thus, the yield to the investor is only 4% ($10,000/$250,000). Negative leverage has occurred. (*See* **Leverage**)

NEGOTIABLE INSTRUMENT

A written instrument such as a check or promissory note which can be legally transferred from one party to another by either endorsement or delivery.

NEIGHBORHOOD

A homogeneous grouping of residential buildings within customarily accepted geographic boundaries.

NEIGHBORHOOD LIFE CYCLE

The growth, maturity, decline, and potential for renewal phases of the life of a neighborhood.

NEST EGG

A savings of money which is often used as a down payment on real estate.

NET

The balance remaining after subtracting expenses from income. (*See* **Net After Taxes, Net Income**)

NET AFTER TAXES

Income remaining after all expenses, including state and federal income taxes, have been deducted from the income received.

NET BEFORE TAXES

Income remaining after all expenses except state and federal income taxes have been deducted from the income received.

NET ESTATE

The remaining portion of an estate after deduction of legal expenses incurred in the settlement of the estate.

NET INCOME

In accounting and taxation, income after all expenses or deductions. (*See* **Net Operating Income (NOI)**)

NET INCOME MULTIPLIER

A number which when multiplied by the net operating income (NOI) of a project gives an estimate of the market value of the property. The net income multiplier is used by real estate analysts and investors as a quick indicator as to how the net income of a given project for sale compares to the NOI of other properties that have sold. (*See* **Gross Rent Multiplier**)

NET INCOME RATIO

The ratio of net operating income (NOI) to effective gross income (EGI). (*See* **Effective Gross Income, Net Operating Income**)

NET LEASABLE AREA (NLA)

The part of the total area leased that is used exclusively by a tenant, normally excluding such areas as hallways and washrooms.

NET LEASE

A lease that imposes on the lessee (tenant) an obligation to pay such costs as the real estate taxes, special assessments, insurance premiums, cost of repairs, maintenance, and operating costs as agreed to between the parties to the lease. A net lease does not ordinarily include the cost of debt service which was placed on the property by the lessor (landlord). The lessor receives a fixed amount which may be treated as an annuity because, in a pure net lease, the lessor is not encumbered by an expense associated with the property. The terms, "net," "net, net," and "net, net, net" are often used in real estate markets. The number of "nets" indicates that the lessee is assuming more and more of the expenses. For example, the "net" lease may include only an obligation by the tenant to pay increases in property taxes, insurance and maintenance while the lessor pays all other costs from the rental payment received. A "net, net, net" lease may include an obligation by the tenant to pay all expenses except debt service. The degree of "netness" is subject to negotiation by the parties to the lease. (*See* **Triple Net Lease**)

NET LISTING

A type of listing contract in which the broker agrees to sell the property in order to achieve a net price to the owner and anything received above the net price is the broker's commission. A net listing may be an open, exclusive agency, or exclusive right to sell listing. The feature which distinguishes this listing is the method of compensation to the listing broker. For example, if a property has a net listing for $25,000 and it sells for $35,000, the broker is entitled to a $10,000 commission. If, however, the property sells for $25,000, the broker is entitled to nothing. Because of the potential for conflict of interest, many state licensing laws prohibit a true "net" listing contract. (*See* **Listing**)

NETNESS

A colloquial term used to indicate the degree to which expenses have been subtracted from income. (*See* **Net Operating Income**)

NET OPERATING INCOME (NOI)

The remaining income from property after operating expenses have been subtracted from the gross income received from the property. Net operating income is what is left over to pay the owner's profit and debt service.

NET PRESENT VALUE

The value of an income stream and/or reversion at a given discount rate, less the original investment cost. For example, assume an income-producing building can be purchased for $100,000. The building is expected to generate the following amount of net income: (1) Year 1, $22,000; (2) Year 2, $22,000; (3) Year 3, $25,000; (4) Year 4, $20,000; (5) Year 5, $20,000. At the end of the fifth year the building can be sold for $80,000. The net present value of this income stream and reversion, assuming a 16% discount rate, would be calculated as follows:

Year	Income	Present Value Factor (16%)	Amount at Present Value
1	$22,000	.8621	$ 18,966
2	$22,000	.7432	16,350
3	$25,000	.6407	16,018
4	$20,000	.5523	11,046
5	$20,000	.4761	9,522
5	$80,000	.4761	38,088
			$109,990

$109,990 - $100,000 = $9,990
The Net Present Value at 16% would be $9,990

NET SALE CONTRACT
(*See* **Net Listing**)

NET SPENDABLE INCOME
(*See* **Cash Flow**)

NET WORTH
Total assets minus total liabilities; also known as *equity*.

NET YIELD
An investment's return after all costs of operation have been deducted.

NEW PROPERTY
Property improvements, the original use of which commences with the taxpayer.

NEW TOWN
A planned community offering a complete mix of various residences, shopping facilities, employment opportunities, and recreational facilities. Quite often the new town, or *planned city* as it is also known, is built on previously undeveloped land located close to an existing metropolitan area. Examples of such developments include Reston, Virginia (near Washington, D.C.), Columbia, Maryland (near Baltimore), and Peachtree City, Georgia (near Atlanta).

NEW TOWN IN TOWN
A new town planned and constructed within an existing city. Such a development offers the advantage of a new town yet has the added feature of proximity to the large city. Roosevelt Island in New York City is an example of such a project.

NEXT OF KIN
The person(s) most nearly related by blood to a deceased person.

NIBD
Net Income Before Depreciation (*See* **Net Operating Income**)

NIFLB
(*See* **National Institute of Farm and Land Brokers**)

NINETY-NINE YEAR LEASE
A long-term lease for unimproved land whereby the tenant acquires full use and possession without having to purchase the property. All rental payments, commonly known as *ground rent*, are tax deductible. (*See* **Ground Lease**)

NIREB

(*See* **National Institute of Real Estate Brokers**)

NLA

(*See* **Net Leasable Area**)

NO DEAL, NO COMMISSION CLAUSE

A clause sometimes included in a listing contract which states that a brokerage commission will be paid if and only when title actually passes from seller to buyer. Normally, the broker has earned the commission when a *ready, willing, and able* buyer has been found.

NOI

(*See* **Net Operating Income**)

NOMINAL CONSIDERATION

Consideration which bears no relationship to the actual consideration or value of a contract. In the conveyance of real estate, a deed will often state "ten dollars and other good and valuable consideration" rather than the actual selling price. (*See* **Consideration**)

NOMINAL INTEREST RATE

The rate of interest stated in a contract which may or may not be the effective interest rate charged the borrower. Also known as the *face rate* of interest. For example, if discount points are charged, then the lender's effective interest rate is higher than the nominal interest rate. (*See* **Annual Percentage Rate, Discount Points**)

NOMINEE

One who has been designated to represent or act for another.

NONASSUMPTION CLAUSE

A clause inserted in some mortgages prohibiting a buyer of property from assuming an existing mortgage on the property without consent of the lender. Such consent may be given for a fee and a possible jump in the interest rate if the rate on the existing mortgage is below the prevailing interest rate. The clause is also known as a *due on sale clause*.

NONBASIC INDUSTRY

In economic base analysis, a service or support industry. In contrast, a *basic industry* denotes economic activity that generates income from outside the area such as by the selling of goods produced. Normally, for every basic industry in a town or region a certain number of nonbasic industry jobs are needed. (*See* **Economic Base Analysis**)

NONCOMPETITION CLAUSE

A clause frequently found in commercial leases prohibiting a party to the lease from operating a business at or near the leased property which would be in direct competition with a business operated by the other party to the lease. The clause, for example, may prohibit the landlord from leasing space in a retail shopping center to a food store when there is another food store already in the center. Likewise, a tenant who had signed a lease to operate a record store could be prohibited from opening up another such store in or nearby the shopping center. (*See* **Percentage Lease**)

NONCONFORMING USE

A pre-existing use of land which does not conform to the present zoning ordinance. Quite often when a zoning district is created, some uses may exist which are not consistent with the zoning ordinance. A nonconforming use may ordinarily remain; however, certain restrictions are usually imposed. For example, the property owner may not expand a nonconforming use. If a building which is nonconforming is destroyed or damaged to a significant degree, the owner may not replace or repair it. (*See* **Variance, Zoning**)

NONCORPOREAL PROPERTY

Property which does not entitle the owner to possession although it may include a right to use. Noncorporeal rights include future interests such as reversions and remainders, easements, licenses, rents, and liens.

NONDISTURBANCE CLAUSE

A clause found in some mortgages on income-producing property stating that the lender (mortgagee) will not terminate the leases of those tenants who pay their rent in the event that the lender forecloses on the borrower (landlord). If such a clause was not included, any tenant whose lease was signed after the property was mortgaged could find the lease terminated as a result of foreclosure. (*See* **Foreclosure**)

NONEXCLUSIVE LISTING

(*See* **Open Listing**)

NON-PERFORMANCE

Failure or neglect to perform an act or obligation stipulated by an agreement.

NONRECOURSE LOAN

A type of loan in which the borrower (mortgagor) is not personally liable for payment of the debt if the value of the property securing the loan is less than the amount necessary to repay the loan. (*See* **Deficiency Judgment**)

NONRESIDENT

One whose primary residence is in another state. In real estate licensing law some states permit a nonresident broker or salesperson to acquire a nonresident license for the purpose of carrying out brokerage functions in the nonresident state.

NORMAL WEAR AND TEAR

The physical wearing out of property that occurs with normal use. A tenant is not responsible for loss in value resulting from normal wear and tear. Neither can a landlord keep part or all of a security deposit for such loss. What is considered to be normal wear and tear is generally a function of how the property is used and the time period over which it is used. For example, an apartment rented to the same tenant for five years would be expected to have carpets that needed cleaning and walls that needed painting.

NOTARY PUBLIC

A person with the authority to administer oaths and take acknowledgments.

NOTE

A signed legal instrument acknowledging the existence of a debt and the promise to repay the debt. (*See* **Promissory Note**)

NOTHING DOWN

A real estate purchase that consist of 100% financing. Most real estate transactions, especially residential purchases, involve some down payment but it is legally possible to finance a home through the Veterans Administration with nothing down.

NOTICE

Knowledge or information which a person has if he or she actually knows (*actual notice*) and/or has enough information available to ascertain the information (*constructive notice*).

NOTICE OF PENDENCY

(*See* **Lis Pendens**)

NOVATION

A mutual agreement substituting a new debt or obligation for an existing one. For example, if the purchaser of a house desires to assume an existing mortgage and the lender agrees to the assumption, a novation is executed, in which case the original borrower is no longer obligated to repay the loan and the buyer now becomes legally liable for payment of the debt. If an assumption of a mortgage is made and the lender does not agree to a novation then both the seller and the buyer are liable and the lender has recourse against both of them in case of default. (*See* **Assumption of Mortgage**)

NUISANCE

Any action or inaction which is harmful or injurious to another person or interferes with the reasonable and expected use of another person's property. (*See* **Law of Nuisance**)

NULL AND VOID

Invalid and unenforceable.

NUNCUPATIVE WILL

An oral will which a terminally ill person declares before qualified witnesses. This type of will must, however, be reduced to writing within a statutorily prescribed time period in order to be admitted into probate. (*See* **Devise**)

OBLIGATION BOND

A bond signed by a mortgagor (borrower) for an amount greater than the loan amount. Such a bond creates a personal obligation on the part of the borrower and assures the lender of recourse in case of nonpayment of property taxes and insurance or past due interest on the mortgage.

OBLIGEE

The person, such as a lender or creditor, to whom someone else is obligated under a contract.

OBLIGOR

Someone, such as a borrower or mortgagor, who owes a duty to perform under a contract.

OBSOLESCENCE

A loss in value due to a decrease in the usefulness of property caused by decay, changes in technology, people's behavior patterns and tastes, or environmental changes. *(See* **Economic Obsolescence, Functional Obsolescence***)*

OCCUPANCY

Physical possession and use of real estate.

OCCUPANCY AGREEMENT
(*See* **Proprietary Lease**)

OCCUPANCY PERMIT
A permit required under the building codes of many local governments which indicates that the property passes a final inspection. The permit indicates that all applicable building codes have been met and that the structure is suitable for occupancy.

OCCUPANCY RATE
The ratio of the space rented to the total amount of space available for rent. A 50-unit apartment complex in which 40 units are currently rented has an occupancy rate of 80 percent (40:50).

OFFER
A promise conditioned upon some requested or asked for act or promise. An offer demonstrates intent by one party to form a contract with another party. In order to be effective, an offer must contain three essential elements:

1. An offer must be an expression of *present contractual intent*. This means that an advertisement or any other preliminary negotiation could not, as a general rule, be an offer.

Example: John writes the following words to Bob: "I might be interested in selling my house for $53,000." Is this an offer which Bob can accept? No. John has merely expressed a desire to sell his house. He did not express intent to be presently bound. Contrast with these words: "I will sell you my house for $53,000." This phrasing suggests present contractual intent.

2. An offer must be *definite and certain* in terms. Ordinarily an offer must include, either expressly or by implication, the following:

    A. Identification of the parties to the contract
    B. Description of the subject matter
    C. Time for performance
    D. Price

It should be noted that the law will allow a reasonable time for performance unless the phrase *time is of the essence* is included which requires strict performance of all time obligations. The reader must also be aware of *illusory offers*. Illusory offers are those which do not really bind the offeror to any real commitment.

Example: "I offer to purchase your house for $100,000 subject to my finding acceptable financing." Since the offeror may personally determine what is or is not "acceptable" financing and this is not measured by any objective standard, there is no effective way to bind the offeror.

3. An offer must be *communicated* to the offeree. An offer ordinarily can only be effective when the offeror *volitionally* (voluntarily) communicates the offer.

Example: Gene signs a written offer to purchase Tom's house for $74,000. Gene has not determined whether or not to make the offer and leaves it on his own desk. If Tom were to come into the office while Gene was out to lunch,

Tom could not accept the offer if he happened to see it lying on the desk. However, if Gene inadvertently included the offer with a number of other documents he mailed to Tom, his mailing would be considered volitional and a person receiving the offer would be reasonably entitled to accept it. It should be noted that only Tom or an authorized agent of Tom's could accept the offer. The rule is that only the person (or persons) to whom an offer is made is empowered to accept the offer. However, if an offer is made to the public, as in a reward offer, then anyone who performs as requested by the offer may accept. When an offer is communicated to the offeree, this creates a power to bind the offeror to a contract. The offeree exercises this power through a timely and appropriate acceptance.

OFFER AND ACCEPTANCE

Two of the necessary components for forming a contract. Together, offer and acceptance are referred to as *mutual assent* and if supported by legally sufficient consideration, a contract is formed. (*See* Contract)

OFFEREE

The person to whom an offer is made.

OFFEROR

The person who makes an offer.

OFFER TO SELL

Any attempt, either verbal or in writing, to induce or encourage someone to acquire an interest in property.

OFFICE BUILDING

A structure used primarily for the carrying on of business.

OFFICE OF INTERSTATE LAND SALES REGISTRATION

An agency within the *Department of Housing and Urban Development (HUD)* which has the responsibility for enforcing the *Interstate Land Sales Full Disclosure Act*. (*See* **Interstate Land Sales Full Disclosure Act**)

OFFICE PARK

A parcel of land designed and developed to provide for a number of separate or attached office buildings. Normally located in suburban areas such as next to a beltway surrounding a metropolitan area, office parks are intended to provide the users with the facilities necessary to carry on normal business. Such facilities include ample parking, a well-designed road system, landscaping, restaurants and hotel facilities, and an adequate supply of labor.

OFFICIAL MAP

The land-use control used by local governments to designate and reserve private land for street widenings, new streets, parks, and other public improvements.

OFF-SITE COSTS

The costs of improvements that service a particular lot or development, but that are not located directly on the lot. For a residential subdivision, examples would include the costs of sewage treatment facilities, streets, and streetlights.

OFF-SITE IMPROVEMENTS

Physical improvements that affect the use and value of a parcel of land, but are not located directly on the lot. For a residential subdivision, examples would include streets, street lights, and curbs.

OIL AND GAS LEASE

A right given by an owner (lessor) to another (lessee) for the purpose of extracting oil and or gas from the land. An oil and gas lease normally runs for a specific number of years and payment to the owner is in the form of a royalty based on a percentage of the oil or gas taken from the land.

ONCE A MORTGAGE, ALWAYS A MORTGAGE

A legal rule which states an instrument originally intended as a mortgage cannot at some later date be converted into another instrument such as a deed by either a clause in the instrument or an agreement between the parties.

ONE-HUNDRED PERCENT FINANCING

Action taken by a developer or investor which results in all of the cost or the purchase price being financed with borrowed money and thus the developer/investor does not have any equity in the property. Also known as *mortgaging out*, the ability to arrange such financing is generally more prevalent with new construction since the loan-to-value ratio will be based on the value of the property rather than on the cost of the project. For example, an office building which cost $1 million could have a value of $1.5 million. A permanent loan based on a two-thirds loan-to-value would provide the developer $1 million, in which case the developer would have one-hundred percent financing.

ONE-HUNDRED PERCENT LOCATION

The particular area or spot in the business district of a city considered to be the best or prime location. The location might be an intersection, a square block or a portion of the business or shopping district. Normally such a location demands the highest rents in the area.

ONE-THIRD, TWO-THIRD RULE

An appraisal rule of thumb stating that the first one-third of a standard lot nearest the street contains half of the total value while the rear two-thirds of the lot contains the other half of the value. While this is only a rule of thumb, it can be useful for appraisers in the valuation of land being condemned through eminent domain.

ON OR ABOUT

The designation of an approximate date without a firm commitment to a precise date. Real estate sales contracts may include a sentence stating "closing to occur on or about June 1" in which case June 1 would be the approximate closing date rather than the exact date.

OPEN AND NOTORIOUS

Action by one party on the land belonging to someone else sufficient to notify the owner that such a use may result in transfer of title through adverse possession. (*See* Adverse Possession)

OPEN-END MORTGAGE

A loan containing a clause which allows the mortgagor (borrower) to borrow additional money at some point in the future without rewriting the mortgage. The money which may subsequently be loaned will carry whatever the current rate of interest is at the time the money is loaned. By writing such a mortgage, the lender eliminates the time and paper work normally spent in processing and approving a loan.

OPEN HOUSE

A marketing technique commonly used by real estate brokers to show residential property by having it available to the public during particular hours, such as from 1:00 to 5:00 Sunday afternoon. During the open house the broker or a representative is at the house and is available to show the property and answer any inquiries made by prospective buyers.

OPEN LISTING

A type of listing agreement in which more than one broker may be employed to sell the property and the owner pays a commission only to the broker who is the efficient and procuring cause of the sale. This listing is also known as a *simple listing* or a *general listing* and the owner is not obligated to pay anyone a commission if the owner personally sells the property. Such a listing is often used by builders and developers who agree to pay a sales commission to any broker who sells a house or lot in their subdivision.

OPEN MORTGAGE

A mortgage written without a *prepayment clause* and which thus can be repaid in part or in full at any time during the term of the loan without the borrower having to pay a prepayment penalty. Some mortgages are written so that the borrower can only prepay 20 percent of the outstanding balance per year for the first five years, otherwise a prepayment penalty is imposed.

OPEN SPACE

Land which has not had improvements such as buildings and other structures added to it. Such land is often left in a subdivision by a developer for recreational use and enjoyment by those who buy lots in the development and as such the land is *dedicated* to and maintained by either the subdivision or the local government. (*See* **Greenbelt**)

OPERATING EXPENSE RATIO

The relationship of operating expenses to potential gross income or effective gross income. This ratio may vary with each type of property. However, it can be used by an appraiser/ investor to compare a particular property with similar-use properties. For apartment buildings the ratio generally falls between 35% and 45%; however, it may be as high as 50% if the landlord is responsible for paying all utilities. Office buildings which are expensive to maintain can have ratios exceeding 50%, while property leased under a net or net, net agreement will have a very low operating expense ratio.

OPERATING EXPENSES

Periodic expenses of operating income-producing property other than debt service and income taxes. Operating expenses are those directly related to the level of occupancy and usage of the building. These can include management fees, maintenance, ground maintenance, utilities, supplies, legal fees, accounting fees, and other such costs. These expenses when subtracted from gross income equal net operating income. (*See* **Net Operating Income**)

OPERATING INCOME

(*See* **Net Operating Income**)

OPERATING LEVERAGE

The effect of increasing gross income while maintaining expenses at a fixed or semi-variable rate. (*See* **Leverage**)

OPERATION OF LAW

The application of established rules of law upon a particular fact situation. For example, a principal-agent relationship will be terminated through operation of law by such things as expiration of term, death of either party, destruction of the subject matter, or material change in circumstances.

OPINION OF TITLE

(*See* **Attorney's Opinion Of Title**)

OPM
(See **Other People's Money)**

OPPORTUNITY COST
The economic principle that a prudent investor would pay no more for a particular piece of property than for equally attractive substitutes, whether those substitutes are real estate or other investments that promise to offer equal financial benefits and the same risk. *(See* **Capitalization Rate)**

OPTION
A right, given for consideration to a party *(optionee)* by a property owner *(optionor)*, to purchase or lease property within a specified time at a specified price and terms. An option is an offer which, because it is secured by consideration, cannot be revoked. An option may be assigned to another person who may exercise the option. This is an exception to the rule that only the offeree may accept an offer. Assignment is not effective if the option itself prohibits the assignment or if the terms are dependent on the personal credit of the original option holder. An option is irrevocable by the optionor and will not be extinguished by death or insanity of either party. *(See* **Acceptance, Offer)**

OPTIONEE
The holder or receiver of an option.

OPTIONOR
One who gives an option to another.

OPTION TO PURCHASE LEASED PROPERTY
A right given to a tenant in a lease to buy the property within a specified period of time either at a predetermined price or at a price to be mutually agreed upon at a later date. In some instances if the tenant exercises the option then the rent paid up to that time is applied toward the purchase price.

ORAL CONTRACT
An agreement that is unwritten or only partially written and thus depends in whole or in part on spoken words of the parties to the contract. In order to be enforceable any contract involving an interest in land must be in writing. *(See* **Statute of Frauds)**

ORDINANCE
A rule or statute enacted by the legislative branch of a local government. Examples of ordinances directly affecting real estate include building codes, housing codes, and occupancy regulations.

ORDINARY ANNUITY

A series of equal periodic receipts or payments, receivable or payable at the end of each period. For example a triple-net lease covering an extended period of time would be treated as an ordinary annuity.

ORDINARY INCOME

Income stemming from regular and recurring sources as contrasted with capital gains or tax-free cash flow. Ordinary income includes wages and other compensation, interest and dividends, rents and royalties, alimony, pensions, and proceeds from life insurance in excess of premiums paid (excluded if received because of death of the insured).

ORDINARY WEAR AND TEAR

(*See* **Physical Deterioration**)

ORIGINAL EQUITY

The cash down payment applied to purchase property.

ORIGINATION FEE

The dollar amount charged by a lender to cover the time and expenses incurred in arranging a loan. The fee covers such expenses as credit check, employment verification, and appraisal of the property. Normally the origination fee is stated as a percentage of the loan amount, for example, one percent. If the loan is either FHA or VA, the loan origination fee cannot exceed one percent.

OSTENSIBLE AUTHORITY

Authority which a third person can reasonably assume that an agent has on the basis of actions or inactions of the principal. This is so despite the fact that the agent may not have actual authority. A third person may justifiably rely on appearances and is not bound by secret instructions of the principal to the agent. Consider the case where John delivers a car to Honest Joe, a used car dealer. Honest Joe is instructed to sell the car for no less than $1,000. Honest Joe sells the car for $750 to Pam. Joe had apparent authority to sell the car at any price from the viewpoint of a innocent third party purchaser. John therefore cannot refuse to deliver title to Pam despite the fact that Honest Joe failed to obey his instructions.

OTHER PEOPLE'S MONEY

The use of someone else's money in the purchase of real estate. The higher loan-to-purchase ratio, the more other people's money is being used, and thus, the higher the leverage.

OUTBUILDING

An accessory structure such as a tool shed or storage barn that serves the main building or structure on the land.

OUTLOT (OUTPARCEL)

A small parcel of land in a shopping center development that is excluded from the mortgage in order to permit the developer to sell or lease the parcel and thus not be in violation of the mortgage.

OVERAGE INCOME

Percentage rent based on retail sales, in addition to a base rent. *(See* **Percentage Lease**)

OVERALL CAPITALIZATION RATE

(See **Direct Capitalization**)

OVERALL RATE OF RETURN

The mathematical rate obtained by dividing net operating income by the selling price or value of income-producing real estate. *(See* **Capitalization Rate**)

OVERBUILDING

A market condition in which new construction continues even as current supply exceeds current demand. Since real estate markets are not pure competitive markets, periods of oversupply as well as periods of undersupply occur. Quite often a period of overbuilding occurs following a time of undersupply.

OVERFLOWED LANDS

Land that is covered by nonnavigable water.

OVERIMPROVEMENT

An improvement to land which results in the land not being able to obtain its highest and best use. Overimprovement occurs when an owner combines more factors of production with the land than can be profitably employed. For example, a fifty-story hotel in the middle of nowhere would be an overimproved parcel of land. *(See* **Highest and Best Use**)

OVERRIDE

The part of a real estate sales commission that goes to the sales manager or other management personnel.

OWNER

The person who has ownership or title to property.

OWNER FINANCING

(See **Seller Financing**)

OWNER-OCCUPANT

A home in which the owner also resides in the structure. The majority of homes in the United States are owner occupied. Quite often a condition for a loan approval is a requirement that the borrower occupy the home.

OWNERSHIP IN SEVERALTY

(*See* **Severalty**)

P

PACKAGE MORTGAGE

A real estate loan which in addition to real property covers certain personal property items and equipment. Quite often the sale of real property includes certain items and equipment as part of the sales price. Rather than acquiring separate mortgages on each of these items, the buyer can, through the use of a package mortgage, finance both the real property and the personal property. In residential real estate, a builder might include a stove, refrigerator, dishwasher, or air conditioner in the sales price. For commercial real estate, certain equipment or furniture is often included in the sales price. The advantage to the purchaser is that these items can be financed over a much longer period and at a much lower interest rate than if a separate financial instrument was used. For the builder or seller these items often serve as inducements used in finalizing the sale.

PAPER

A term used to denote a promissory note or mortgage taken by the seller as part of the sales price rather than receiving the entire sales price in cash. For example, a house sells for $80,000 with $20,000 down and the seller agrees to finance the remaining $60,000 by taking back a mortgage. The $60,000 is known as "paper" and the seller may either keep the note and collect interest and principal or sell the paper to an investor.

PAPER PROFIT

The increased value of real estate during the time the real estate is being held. If and when the property is sold, the paper profit becomes realized profit.

PARABOLIC FORMULA

A formula used by some real estate appraisers in years past to enable them to better estimate the value of land. The formula, while not used today, was a substitute for the popular 4-3-2-1 Rule, still used today by some in estimating the value of land. (*See* **Depth Table**)

PARAMOUNT TITLE

Title to property which is better or superior to any other alleged title to the same property. (*See* **Title**)

PARCEL

A part or portion of a piece of land.

PARKING RATIO

The relationship between the number of available parking spaces and the rentable square feet in a commercial real estate project. Most zoning ordinances have a minimum parking ratio for various types of commercial property.

PAROL

Verbal; not in writing. (*See* **Parol Evidence Rule**)

PAROL CONTRACT

An oral contract as compared to one that is in writing.

PAROL EVIDENCE RULE

An evidence rule of law which says that oral agreements which modify the subject matter of a written contract will be inadmissible in a court of law for the purpose of contradicting what is written in the contract.

PARTIAL EVICTION

That which occurs when the tenant loses possession of part of the premises he or she is leasing. When a partial eviction occurs, the tenant is freed from the obligation to pay rent until he or she regains full possession of the premises. (*See* **Constructive Eviction**)

PARTIAL INTEREST

A less than fee simple interest in real property. (*See* **Fee Simple**)

PARTIALLY AMORTIZED MORTGAGE

A method of loan repayment in which the balance of the outstanding loan is not zero at maturity and thus a *balloon payment* is required. (*See* **Amortization**)

PARTIALLY DISCLOSED PRINCIPAL

A principal in a principal-agent relationship whose identity is not known to the third person, but the third person knows that he or she is dealing with an agent. When an agent is representing a partially disclosed principal, the agent is considered to be liable under the contract. However, the third person and the agent may agree to limit the agent's personal liability. Partially disclosed principles exist in real estate, but they are not common. (*See* **Agency**)

PARTIAL RELEASE CLAUSE

A clause sometimes found in a mortgage which provides that upon payment of a certain amount of the outstanding loan the lien is removed from part of the property used as security for the loan. Such a clause is commonly found in the mortgage covering the development of a subdivision. The developer borrows money to finance the purchase of the land and to pay for the cost of developing the lots. As certain lots are developed the developer would like to sell them and then develop additional lots. By having a partial release clause included in the mortgage, specific lots can be released to the developer as the loan is repaid. Otherwise, the total amount borrowed would have to be repaid before any of the lots could be released. (*See* **Blanket Mortgage**)

PARTIAL TAKING

Under eminent domain, the taking of part of an owner's property for public purposes. Compensation to the owner must not only include payment for the part taken but also payment for any damage to the remaining part of the property. (*See* **Eminent Domain**)

PARTICIPATION

Sharing in income and/or ownership.

PARTICIPATION MORTGAGE

A type of mortgage that provides the *mortgagee* (lender) with a certain percentage of cash flow beyond the fixed rate of interest paid by the *mortgagor* (borrower). An example would be an insurance company that loans an investor $1,000,000 at 12 percent interest over 10 years for the purchase of an income-producing property valued at $1,500,000. In addition, the lender receives 25 percent of the before tax cash flow, and thus has an equity position in the building. The 25 percent of cash flow is known as an *equity kicker*, *kicker*, or *sweetener* and is used by the lender as a hedge against inflation as well as to increase the overall yield of the loan.

The term has other meanings in real estate finance. Another use of the word is when more than one mortgagee lends on a real estate project, such as with a large commercial project. For example, 25 savings and loan associations may pool part of their funds to finance a large land development project. Another type of participation mortgage has more than one borrower being legally liable for the repayment of a mortgage, such as with a cooperative apartment.

PARTICIPATION SALE CERTIFICATE

Securities sold by the *Federal Home Loan Mortgage Corporation* to finance the purchase of mortgages from approved lenders. (*See* **Federal Home Loan Mortgage Corporation**)

PARTITION

The dividing of real estate held by two or more people which results in each of the parties holding individual or severalty ownership.

PARTNERSHIP

An association of two or more persons for the purpose of carrying on a business. Under common law a partnership was not considered to be an entity which could own property. Title was held in each of the partner's individual names. Most states have passed the *Uniform Partnership Act* which permits a partnership to own property in its own name. No individual partner owns a direct specified interest in property so held. The property is limited to use for partnership business and the partner's property right is in a fractional share of the partnership which is specified in the partnership agreement. No partner may sell his or her partnership interest without consent of the other partners. If a partner dies or goes bankrupt, title to real property passes to the other partners who have a duty to pass the value of the partner's interest to the heirs or devisees of the deceased.

PARTY WALL

A wall constructed on the boundary line between two parcels and which is intended to serve to support structures on each of the two parcels.

PASSIVE INVESTOR

A person who invests money but does not have any control over the day-to-day management of the operation. An example is a *limited partner* whose liability is restricted only to the money which he or she has invested in the partnership.

PASS-THROUGH SECURITY

A security issued by the *Government National Mortgage Association* which provides for the interest and principal paid on a mortgage to pass through to the holder of the security.

PATENT

A grant or conveyance of land from the federal or a state government to an individual. Most title in land stems from grants given by the government of this country and before territory was acquired by this government from governments such as England, France, Spain, or Mexico.

PATENT DEFECT

A defect that is recognizable and visible to a person through a casual inspection. In contrast, a *latent defect* is one that is hidden and, thus, not visible by inspection.

PATIO HOME

(*See* Zero Lot Line)

PAYBACK PERIOD

The time necessary for the cash flow generated from a project to equal the initial amount invested. Payback can be computed on either a before-tax or an after-tax basis and can be based on the entire property or just on equity invested.

PAYEE

The creditor on a promissory note. (*See* **Promissory Note**)

PAYOR

The debtor on a promissory note. (*See* **Promissory Note**)

PEAK-HOUR TRAFFIC

The one hour in a twenty-four hour period when the most vehicles or pedestrians pass over or through a particular location.

PENSION FUND

An institution that invests its assets and uses the proceeds to pay retirement benefits to its members. Pension funds are one of the newer sources available for financing real estate. Whereas these funds historically were invested in stocks and bonds, the recent growth of pension funds has meant new outlets have had to be found for their investments. This growth plus the favorable yield available through real estate investments has resulted in active participation in financing real estate projects. Besides making mortgage loans, pension funds also own real estate. The majority of all their real estate activity is done through mortgage bankers and mortgage brokers.

PENTHOUSE

An apartment or room built on the roof of a building. Normally such a structure is large in comparison to other apartments in the building and commands a significantly higher rental payment. In addition, the term also denotes a structure located on the roof of a building to store or cover mechanical or electrical equipment used in the operation of the building.

PENT UP DEMAND

The desire for real estate resulting from a period of little, if any, supply and or little ability to purchase because of high interest rates.

PER AUTRE VIE

(*See* **Life Estate Pur Autre Vie**)

PERCENT (PERCENTAGE)

A mathematical term which means per hundred or parts of a hundred. Percent is denoted by the sign "%."

Examples: 35% = 35/100 = .35 150% = 150/100 = 1.50

Many of the mathematical problems such as commissions and interest rates which have to be worked by people engaged in real estate activities involve percentages.

To change a percent to a decimal, place a decimal point two places to the left and drop the percent sign.

Examples: 15% = .15   118% = 1.18   1% = .01

To change decimals to percent the procedure is reversed. Move the decimal point two places to the right and add a % sign.

Examples: .32 = 32%   2.15 = 215%   1 = 100%

To change percents to fractions, divide the percent quantity by 100, drop the percent sign and reduce the answer to the lowest terms.

Examples: 50% = 50/100 = 1/2   300% = 300/100 = 3

PERCENTAGE CASH FLOW

The annual before-tax cash flow of an income-producing property divided by the equity invested in the property. Percentage cash flow is also called *cash-on-cash return*, *current yield*, and *equity dividend rate*, and provides a measure of the current performance of a project to the equity investment. Some investors determine the minimum required rate of cash return and then use this to estimate the price to pay for the investment. (*See* **Cash Flow**)

PERCENTAGE LEASE

A lease whereby the *lessor* (landlord) receives a percentage of the gross sales or net profits as part or all of the rental payment for the lease of the property. Percentage leases are commonly used in shopping centers and merchandising activity uses and, thus, allow the lessor to share in the locational value of a particular property. The percentage lease may also include a fixed guaranteed minimum. Normally percentage leases are based on gross sales because the term "profits" is ambiguous and often leads to dispute and litigation. A lessor ordinarily requires that a provision be included in the lease to allow for an inspection of the lessee's books in order to ensure that the correct rent amount is paid. Percentage leases often include a restriction as to the type of activity which must or must not be carried out on the premises. In some cases the percentage lease contains a *recapture clause* which allows the lessor to take back the realty if the property does not generate a certain minimum of gross receipts.

Example: Mark agrees to pay a rent of 6% of the gross sales with a guaranteed minimum of $400 rent each month for the rent of a key store. If the key store receives $7,500 in sales in May, what is the rent owed? The answer is $7,500 x .06 = $450. (*See* **Net Lease**)

PERCENTAGE RENT

Rent based on a percentage of a retail tenant's sales, usually in addition to a base rent. Also known as *overage* or *overage income*.

PERCH

A land surveying measurement 16.5 feet in length. Also referred to as a *rod* or *pole*.

PERCOLATION TEST

A test used by developers/engineers to determine a particular tract of land's ability to absorb and drain water. Normally a percolation test is required by local governments prior to the issuance of building permits.

PERFECTING TITLE

The steps taken to remove title defects. (*See* **Abstract of Title**)

PERFORMANCE

The fulfillment or completion of a legal obligation such as a contract, according to its terms and conditions. (*See* **Contract**)

PERFORMANCE BOND

A bond given by someone such as a contractor to guarantee the completion of a construction project within a specified period of time. Also known as a *completion bond*, a bond normally costs approximately one percent of the construction cost and can only be obtained by contractors who have a good construction record.

PERIODIC TENANCY

A leasehold estate which is automatically renewed for successive periods until proper notice to terminate is given by either the landlord or the tenant. If the lease term is for more than one year, the term upon renewal is considered by most states to be for one year. Where no term is specified, the manner and time that the rent is paid establishes the term by implication. For example, if the rent is paid quarterly, the implication is that the term is from quarter to quarter. What is proper notice to prevent renewal of the term? Ordinarily, this is specified by the lease itself, or where the lease is silent, by statute. As with an estate for years, death of either the lessor or lessee does not terminate a periodic tenancy. This type of leasehold is also referred to as an *estate from year to year* or an *estate from period to period.*

PERMANENT FINANCING

A long-term loan secured by real estate. The permanent loan is used by a developer to repay the construction loan. Whereas a construction loan is typically short term, permanent financing normally covers ten years or more. Permanent financing will either be fully or partially amortized through periodic mortgage payments. Since the payment will be paid from the income generated from the project, the lender can make the amount borrowed contingent upon a certain amount of the available space being leased prior to closing the loan transaction. For instance, the developer of a shopping center might be able to borrow $2,000,000 if 80% of the available space is leased but only $1,600,000 if 70% of the space is leased. This could result in a gap in the capital needed for financing. (*See* **Gap Financing**)

PERMISSIVE WASTE

Occurs if the lessee (tenant) or mortgagor (borrower) fails to properly maintain and repair the premises, thus allowing the improvements to deteriorate beyond normal wear and tear in a manner which impairs the rights of owners or lenders having interests in the real property.

PERMIT

A written document which allows a person to do something, such as a building permit issued by a local government.

PERPETUITY, IN

Forever; something perpetual such as an income stream expected to continue without end.

PERSONAL PROPERTY

Things which are movable and not annexed to or part of the land. Also known as *personalty* and *chattels*, personal property, as distinguished from real property, is one of the two ways property is classified. Personal property also applies to objects such as trees which have been severed or separated from the real property. (*See* **Fixture, Real Property**)

PERSONAL RESIDENCE

The place where an individual resides, normally referred to as his or her *home.*

PERSONALTY
(*See* **Personal Property**)

PETITION
A written application to a court or a board requesting action on some matter over which the board has authority. For example, a land owner can petition the zoning board for a change in the landowner's zoning classification.

PHYSICAL DETERIORATION
A reduction in the usefulness or attractiveness of property and thus a loss in value due to impairment of its physical condition. For example, physical deterioration consists of all wear and tear, from a leaky faucet to structural decay. (*See* **Cost Approach**)

PIGGYBACK LOAN
A loan that involves two lenders but only one mortgage. The two lenders do not have to participate on an equal basis. For example, on a $1 million loan, one lender could supply $600,000 and the other lender $400,000. In such an instance the $400,000 is not a second mortgage since both loans are secured by the same mortgage.

PITI
An acronym for the four monthly payments required under many real estate loans; namely *principal, interest, taxes*, and *insurance*. In residential financing it is common for the lender to require payment of all four each month. Principal and interest payments are retained by the lender while tax and insurance payments are held by the lender in escrow until the annual taxes and insurance premiums are due. At such time the payments are made by the lender from the monthly payments collected from the borrower.

PLANNED UNIT DEVELOPMENT (PUD)
A type of exception or special land use permitted under many modern zoning ordinances allowing a mixture of different land uses or densities. Traditional zoning practices place different uses into separate districts. However, the Planned Unit Development or *Community Unit Plan (CUP)* gives a developer flexibility in mixing various uses and densities. For example, a PUD could permit cluster-housing development with large open spaces. A traditional zoning ordinance would require separate housing on separate lots. The PUD technique allows for more efficient land-use planning and permits residents some of the advantages of condominium ownership by providing a recreational amenity package and reduced maintenance requirements. (*See* **Condominium, Zoning**)

PLANNING
A process undertaken by governmental units for developing a guide for the

future. The process is based on the scientific method and depends on the collection of facts, analysis, the weighing of alternatives, and the selection of goals. Local governments receive authority to engage in land-use planning from enabling legislation enacted by the state. Some states provide this power as part of the home rule powers in the municipal charter or state constitution. Most states have passed enabling legislation based on the *Standard City Planning Enabling Act* which was developed by the U.S. Department of Commerce in 1927. The enabling act provides for the creation of a planning commission or board. This commission is usually a board of citizens, often including real estate brokers, architects, lawyers, business people, and others, who advise local government officials and legislators on planning matters. In passing a zoning ordinance the planning commission usually recommends whether or not an ordinance should be approved by examining the proposed change and weighing its impact on the community on the basis of planning criteria. The planning commission's powers are usually limited, with the actual planning being handled by professional planners in the planning department and with final authority resting with the legislative body of the local government.

PLANNING COMMISSION

A local, state, or regional governmental agency which determines long-range plans and objectives for the physical growth of an area.

PLANS AND SPECIFICATIONS

The detailed design and description of all the work that is to be done in the construction of a building.

PLAT

A map showing the specific location and boundaries of land that has been subdivided into individual lots. Normally included in the plat is the identification and location of roads, public easements, and dedicated land. In addition, each lot is assigned a number so that the lot can be easily identified when it is sold.

PLAT BOOK

A group of plats located in the public records of a jurisdiction identifying the location, size, and owners of various parcels of real estate.

PLATTED LAND

Land that has been subdivided with each lot within the subdivision numbered and the land recorded as a subdivision.

PLEDGE

The putting up of property as security for a debt. Even though the creditor does not have title to the property, provisions do exist which allow the creditor to sell the property when the borrower is in default.

PLEDGED ACCOUNT MORTGAGE
(See **Flexible Loan Insurance Program**)

PLOT
(See **Plat**)

PLOTTAGE
The combining of two or more lots into a single ownership with the result that the value of the assembled site is worth more than the sum of the values of the individual sites. For example, the total value of a square block combined under ownership in the commercial district of a metropolitan area could be substantially greater than the total value of the land divided into 10 parcels, each owned by a different person.

PMI
Abbreviation for *private mortgage insurance*. *(See* **Private Mortgage Insurance**)

POCKET LICENSE CARD
Physical evidence of a real estate broker or salesperson license issued by the state regulatory agency and carried by the licensee. Such a card is not considered to be the license, which generally is required to be displayed at the licensee's place of business.

POCKET LISTING
A listing acquired by a real estate broker or salesperson that is not made available to other licensees within the same firm or other members of a *multiple listing service*. Thus the other licensees cannot sell the property and therefore cannot share in the sales commission. Real estate firms strongly discourage such a practice and multiple listing services normally require that any listing acquired by one of its members must be brought to the listing service within a stipulated period of time, such as forty-eight hours. *(See* **Multiple Listing Service**)

POINT
One percent (1%). *(See* **Discount Points**)

POINT OF BEGINNING
The starting point used to describe land by the metes and bounds method. This starting point must be one that can be located by future surveyors; thus, it is necessary that it be as precise as possible. Physical evidence of this point, referred to as a *monument*, is often an iron pipe set in concrete. *(See* **Metes and Bounds**)

POLICE POWER

The inherent right of the state to regulate for the purpose of promoting health, safety, welfare, and morality. Police power gives the state the right to impose certain restraints on human conduct which are reasonably necessary in order to safeguard the public interest. This right is the basis of zoning, the official map, building codes, and subdivision regulations. When the state uses the police power it is not required to compensate a property owner for any loss in property values as a result of the regulation. However, a policy power regulation must be reasonable and must apply equally to all similar property. If a police power regulation is too restrictive or arbitrary, it may violate the due process and equal protection clauses of the U. S. Constitution. In addition, the Fifth Amendment contains a clause stating: "... nor shall private property be taken for a public use without just compensation." The U. S. Supreme Court has ruled that, while property may be regulated under the police power without requiring state compensation, if the regulation goes too far, the state must apply its powers of eminent domain and pay just compensation. It is up to the courts to decide if a regulation is too extensive in its restrictions on property rights. (*See* **Building Codes, Subdivision Regulation(s), Zoning**)

POLICY

In insurance, the name given to the contractual agreement entered into between the insurance company and the person insured.

POOL OF MORTGAGES

A number of mortgages gathered or "pooled" together by a lender for the purpose of selling them in the secondary mortgage market. By pooling the mortgages and selling them, the lender is able to turn existing loans into cash and thus, in turn, the lender can make additional loans.

POOR MAN'S WILL

A situation in which all of the property owned by a husband and wife is under a *joint tenancy* or *tenancy by the entirety* form of ownership with the *right of survivorship*. Thus, upon the death of either husband or wife, the interest automatically passes to the remaining spouse. Because no interest passes after death, there is no need for probate; the surviving tenant retains the property. (*See* **Joint Tenancy, Tenancy By The Entirety**)

POPULATION DENSITY

The number of people located within a specific area.

PORTMAN, JOHN

An architect and developer noted for his use of open space and modern design. Famous for his hotels, Portman developed "space for people" which he believed should be unencumbered by traditional physical and structural constraints.

Portman's success has proven that exciting design can create an atmosphere that will be readily accepted by consumers in the marketplace. His hotels are located in major cities throughout the United States as well as in other cities throughout the world.

POSITIVE CASH FLOW

The amount of cash remaining from a real estate investment when the net income of the project is greater than the total of the operating expenses plus the mortgage payment(s). Not all real estate projects generate a positive cash flow and, in fact, many projects have a negative cash flow, which is the result of net income being less than operating expenses plus mortgage payment(s).

POSSESSION

The control, either actual or constructive, of real estate. (*See* **Adverse Possession, Constructive Notice**)

POSSIBILITY OF REVERTER

The right retained by the granting party (grantor) when a *fee simple determinable* interest in land is granted. (*See* **Fee Simple Determinable**)

POTENTIAL GROSS INCOME

Gross receipts that would be collected if all available rental units were leased and all rents due were paid by tenants. Due to vacancies and an allowance for bad debts, the actual rent collected, referred to as *effective gross income*, is normally less than potential gross income. (*See* **Net Income**)

POWER OF ATTORNEY

A written instrument giving a person the authority to act on behalf of another person. Such authority can be either general or specific. (*See* **Attorney in Fact**)

POWER OF SALE

A clause normally included in a mortgage or deed of trust giving the lender (mortgagee or trustee) the legal right, upon default by the borrower, to sell the property at public auction. The proceeds of the sale are used to repay the debt plus any legal fees incurred by the lender and any surplus must be given to the borrower. The power of sale also gives the lender the legal right to convey title to whomever purchases the property at public auction. (*See* **Foreclosure**)

PREMISES

The introductory section of a deed. Ordinarily, the premises contains the date that the deed is signed, identifies the parties to the deed, recites the consideration, and contains a granting clause, the legal description, any reservations or exceptions, the recital, any subject to clauses, and the conveyance of the appurtenances. (*See* **Deed**)

PREMIUM

The dollar payment made by the insured to the insurance company for an insurance policy. (*See* **Insurance**)

PREPAID EXPENSES

Payments made for future charges before the expense is due. Normally rent is paid in advance as are insurance premiums. In some jurisdictions, property taxes are also paid in advance in which case the seller would be credited at closing for that portion of the prepaid expenses which has not yet become due. (*See* **Closing**)

PREPAID INTEREST

Interest paid before it is due.

PREPAYMENT CLAUSE

A clause in a mortgage or deed of trust which permits the borrower to pay, without penalty, the outstanding loan amount before the due date of the loan.

PREPAYMENT PENALTY

The dollar amount levied against a borrower by a lender for paying off a loan before its maturity date. The purpose of having such a penalty is to permit the lender to recover part of the interest that would have been earned had the mortgage not been prepaid. While such a penalty is illegal in some states, other states permit it but limit both the amount of penalty that can be charged and the time period during which the penalty can be imposed. A typical prepayment penalty would read as follows: "If the mortgage debt is paid before maturity and the aggregate amount of all prepayments made in any one year exceeds 20 percent of the original principal amount of the loan, three months' interest, at the then current rate specified in this mortgage on the part of the aggregate amount of such access, shall be paid to the mortgagee as consideration for the acceptance of such prepayment, provided that no such charge may be imposed after the expiration of five years from the date of the original loan." (*See* **Mortgage**)

PREPAYMENT PRIVILEGE

The right given by a lender to a borrower to pay off all or part of a debt without financial penalty before the maturity date of the loan. Such a mortgage is known as an *open mortgage*. In contrast, a *closed mortgage* is one in which there is no prepayment privilege. (*See* **Prepayment Penalty**)

PRESALE

A technique used by a builder/developer in which houses or condominium units are sold prior to their actual construction. By preselling these units the developer is better able to borrow construction money since the lender is assured that these units, if completed, will be sold. In addition, presales also allow the developer an opportunity to market the unsold units as "only a few remaining units" or "Phase I now completely sold out." As an inducement to purchase prior to construction, buyers are often quoted a presale price that may be lower than the price quoted once construction is completed.

PRESCRIPTION
A means of acquiring title to property through open and continuous use. (*See* **Adverse Possession, Prescriptive Easement**)

PRESCRIPTIVE EASEMENT
An interest in the property of another obtained through the open, notorious, hostile, and continuous use of the land for a statutory period of time. (*See* **Adverse Possession, Easement**)

PRESCRIPTIVE TITLE
(*See* **Adverse Possession**)

PRESENT VALUE
The value in today's dollars of an income stream and/or reversion at a given discount rate. Since money has a time value, one dollar to be received in the future is worth less than one dollar now. How much less? The amount of discount or present value depends upon two things: (1) the time span between the cash outflow and inflow, and (2) the necessary rate of interest or discount. For example, at a 12% rate of discount, $1,000 expected to be received one year from now has a present value of $892.90. Had the $1,000 not been expected until two years from now, the present value would have been $797.20. (*See* **Present Worth of One Factor**)

PRESENT WORTH (VALUE) OF AN ANNUITY
The value, at a specified discount rate, of a stream of level cash flows or payments. (*See* **Present Worth of an Annuity Factor**)

PRESENT WORTH OF AN ANNUITY FACTOR
The value, at a specified discount rate, of a stream of cash flow having $1.00 payable or receivable at the end of each period. Listed below are the appropriate factors given various time periods and interest rates or discounts.

Present Worth Annuity Factors (Annual)

Year	5%	10%	15%	20%
1	.9524	.9091	.8696	.8333
2	1.8594	1.7355	1.6257	1.5278
3	2.7232	2.4869	2.2832	2.1065
4	3.5460	3.1699	2.8550	2.5887
5	4.3295	3.7908	3.3522	2.9906

Using the table, the present value of $1.00 received each year for five years when discounted at a 10% rate is $3.79. The same $1.00 per year when discounted at 20%, has a present value of only $2.99. While present worth factors are normally stated in terms of $1.00, the factors can be used to calculate present value of any annuity. For example, the present worth of $500 per period for five years using a 10% discount rate is $1,895.40. ($500 x 3.7908) (*See* **Present Worth of One Factor**)

PRESENT WORTH OF ONE FACTOR

The present value, at a specified discount rate, of $1.00 to be received at the end of a specified period. Listed below are the appropriate factors given various time periods and interest rates or discounts.

Present Value of One Factor (Annual)

Year	5%	10%	15%	20%
1	.9524	.9091	.8696	.8333
2	.9070	.8264	.7561	.6944
3	.8638	.7513	.6575	.5787
4	.8227	.6830	.5718	.4823
5	.7835	.6209	.4923	.4019

Using the table, the present value of $1.00 received one year from now when discounted at a 10% rate is $.9091 or $.91. The same $1.00 when discounted at 20% is worth only $.83. As is the case with the present worth of an annuity factor, the present worth of one factors are stated in terms of present worth of $1.00. Thus, to calculate the present worth of an amount greater than $1.00, the factor is multiplied by the specific amount. For example, $500 due in 5 years when discounted at 15%, has a present value of $246.15 ($500 x .4923). The same $500 if discounted at 5% would have a present value of $391.75 ($500 x .7835). (*See* **Present Worth of an Annuity Factor**)

PRETAX INCOME

The cash flow generated from income-producing real estate prior to the payment of federal income taxes.

PREVENTIVE MAINTENANCE

Periodic work and upkeep performed on and to property in order for the building and equipment to function as they should. Examples would include painting, changing filters on a cooling system, and the oiling of equipment.

PRICE

An amount, usually expressed in terms of money, paid for property. While the price or amount paid may be equal to value and/or cost, such is not always the case. Consider, for example, the family moving to another city who must sell their house. They may, particularly if they have already bought another house, be forced to accept a price much lower than for what a comparable property recently sold. Conversely, consider the buyer who is able to finance all of the purchase price with a low-interest loan and, thus, is willing to pay more than would have been paid had the purchase been made entirely with cash. *(See* **Cost, Value)**

PRIMA FACIE

All the proof necessary in a lawsuit to justify a legal decision unless the proof is rebutted or disproved.

PRIMARY FINANCING

The loan that has first legal priority. *(See* **First Mortgage)**

PRIMARY MORTGAGE MARKET

The financial market where loans are made directly from the lender to the borrower. In contrast, the secondary mortgage market consists of lenders who sell existing mortgages to investors who invest in such mortgages. *(See* **Secondary Mortgage Market)**

PRIME CONTRACTOR

(See **General Contractor)**

PRIME RATE

The interest rate charged by a lender to its financially strongest customers. Normally, the prime rate serves as the base or minimum interest rate from which other interest rates are derived. For example, a builder with a good credit rating might be charged "prime plus two," which means that the interest on the loan will be two percentage points above the prime rate. For another builder, the rate might be "prime plus four." In either case, a change in the prime rate results in a change in the interest rate paid by the borrower.

PRIME TENANT

A tenant who leases a significant portion of a building's leasable space, typically at least 25 percent. In the case of a shopping center, such a tenant may be a national retail chain, while for an office building the prime tenant may be a commercial bank or a large law firm. There are instances where a building has more than one prime tenant.

PRINCIPAL

One who directs or authorizes another to act for and in the place of the principal in regard to relations with third persons. The person acting on behalf of the principal is known as an *agent* and the principal is bound by the acts of the agent when the latter is operating within the scope of the agent's authority. In a real estate transaction, the principal is the person who hires a real estate broker (the agent) to sell his or her property.

The term *principal* also is used to denote money or capital. For example, the principal payment on a mortgage refers to the amount paid toward reducing the original loan. (*See* **Agent**)

PRINCIPAL-AGENT RELATIONSHIP

(*See* **Agency**)

PRINCIPAL BROKER

The licensed broker in a real estate firm who is, according to the state licensing law, responsible for the activities of all licensees, both brokers and salespersons, licensed to operate within the firm. (*See* **Broker**)

PRINCIPAL MERIDIAN

The primary measuring line used in the *Rectangular Survey* or *Government Survey Method* of land descriptions. There are 36 principal meridians used to describe land in the United States. Some of these are designated by names, others by numbers. (*See* **Government Survey Method**)

PRINCIPAL RISK

The possibility that the resale price of an investment will be less than was originally forecast. (*See* **Risk Rate**)

PRIOR APPROPRIATION SYSTEM

A system of water law used in most of the western states based on water scarcity. Under this system a water right is a separate legal right apart from the ownership of land. It is determined on a hierarchy which is based on the priority of the time a claim was established. The first claim has priority over all other subsequent claims. If any water remains after the first claimant or appropriator has received his or her share, the second appropriator receives his or her share and so on until the water supply is exhausted. This system is subject to administrative control by state agencies, and by the federal government where federal water is involved.

PRIORITY

Having legal precedence over others, such as a first mortgage in contrast to a second mortgage. In such a case, the priority determines which creditor receives first payment in case of foreclosure. (*See* **Lien**)

PRIVATE MORTGAGE INSURANCE

A mortgage insurance policy written to insure a portion of a mortgage. An insured conventional loan is one which is insured by a private (nongovernmental) insurance company. The establishment of FHA-insured loans and VA-guaranteed loans resulted in higher loan-to-value ratios and longer amortization periods than lenders were willing to offer under conventional financing. As the costs of housing continued to increase year after year, some means of providing protection against loss of high loan-to-value conventional mortgages was needed. Thus, in 1957, the *Mortgage Guaranty Insurance Corporation (MGIC)*, or "MAGIC" as it is normally referred to, established a private mortgage insurance program (PMI) for approved lenders. MGIC offered the lender quicker service and less red tape than FHA. Today private mortgage insurance companies insure more loans than both FHA and VA. Unlike FHA which insures the whole loan, PMI insures only the top 20% or 25% of the loan, and the insurer normally relies on the lender to appraise the property. While the majority of PMI loans are for 90% loan-to-value, coverage does extend to a maximum of 95%. On a 90% loan, the borrower is normally charged one-half of 1% at closing and one-fourth of 1% of the outstanding balance each year thereafter. With a 95% loan, the rate is normally 1% of the loan at closing plus 1/4% of the outstanding balance each year the insurance is carried. Since only the top portion of the loan is covered, once the loan-to-value drops below a certain percentage, the lender may terminate the coverage, and, thus, the insurance premium is no longer charged to the customer. In case of default, the insurance company can either pay off the loan or let the lender foreclose and pay the loss up to the amount of insurance coverage.

PRIVATE PROPERTY

Real estate owned by an individual in contrast to *public property*, which is owned by government, be it local, state, or federal.

PRIVITY OF ESTATE

The relationship that exists between individuals who have an interest in the same land, such as a lessor and lessee or mortgagor and mortgagee.

PROBATE

The process of proving a will before a duly authorized court or person. (*See* **Devise**)

PROCURING CAUSE

The direct action that results in the successful completion of some objective. In real estate brokerage, the term is used to denote the action(s) by a broker that results in the owner selling his or her property. Under an open listing agreement, the broker who can show that he or she was the procuring cause is normally the one entitled to the sales commission. (*See* **Agency, Open Listing**)

PRODUCERS COUNCIL

This council represents manufacturers of quality building products. The mailing address is 1717 Massachusetts Avenue, N.W., Washington, D.C. 20036.

PROFIT A' PRENDRE (PROFIT)

The right to remove something from the land of another. Rights to remove gravel, water, minerals, coal, gas, oil, timber, and game are considered to be profits. Ordinarily, a profit a' prendre is created and terminated the same way as an easement. A profit is considered to be a real property right.

PRO FORMA STATEMENT

A financial statement used to project anticipated revenues and expenses for a real estate project. The information is based upon assumptions regarding the operation of the property.

PROGRESS PAYMENTS

A method used by lenders in the financing of construction loans in which dollars are released to the general contractor at predetermined stages of construction. In turn, the general contractor pays subcontractors and suppliers of materials for the work and materials provided. *(See* **Construction Loan**)

PROJECTION PERIOD

The forecast holding period for an investment under consideration.

PROMISEE

One to whom a promise is made. *(See* **Promissory Note**)

PROMISOR

One who promises to perform a certain act(s). *(See* **Promissory Note**)

PROMISSORY NOTE

A written promise to pay back a specified sum of money at specified terms and at a specified time. The primary evidence of a debt is the *promissory note* or *bond*. The main distinction between a promissory note and a bond is that the bond is under seal. Without a valid promissory note or bond giving evidence to a debt, a mortgage is no good. A mortgage is only good so long as a debt exists. If the note is paid off or in some other fashion cancelled, the mortgage will also be cancelled. However, it should be noted that, in some areas of the country, a common practice is to incorporate both the promissory note and the mortgage into one legal document. Conceptually these are legally two different instruments. The borrower is a person who has an obligation to pay a debt; thus, the borrower is also referred to as the *obligor*. The lender is referred to as the *obligee*. If an obligor defaults on the obligation, the lender may bring a personal suit against the borrower. If insufficient money exists to pay off the judgment, the lender may move against the security pledged by the mortgage. The mortgage is usually referenced in the promissory note or bond. In order for a promissory note or bond to be valid, it must meet certain requirements:

1. There must be a *written* instrument.

2. Both the obligor and obligee must have *contractual capacity*.

3. There must be a *promise* or covenant to pay a *sum certain* by the obligor.

4. The *terms of payment* as well as the interest rate must be specified. There is ordinarily no right to prepay a promissory note unless this privilege is specified in the note itself or in the mortgage. A lender has a contractual right to expect that the money lent will be fully invested for the time specified. A *prepayment privilege clause* may provide for a small penalty if the privilege is exercised.

5. A clause providing for what constitutes *default* must be specified. It is advisable to include an *acceleration clause* in either the note or in the mortgage. An acceleration clause states that upon default all of the principal installments come due immediately. If an acceleration clause is not included, then the obligee must bring a separate suit each time another installment is due. In a thirty-year mortgage note payable in monthly installments, conceivably 360 separate suits would be required to collect all of the installments.

6. The note or bond must be properly *executed*.

7. The instrument must be voluntarily *delivered* by the obligor and *accepted* by the obligee.

PROPERTY

Anything in which there is ownership. The law classifies property as real, personal, and mixed. Property is also classified as tangible and intangible. (*See* **Bundle of Rights, Law of Nuisance, Personal Property, Real Property**)

PROPERTY DESCRIPTION

(*See* **Legal Description**)

PROPERTY MANAGEMENT

The activities associated with the advertising, leasing, and maintenance of rental property. The person(s) responsible for carrying out these functions is known as a *property manager*. Property management as a specialized field of real estate has grown rapidly in recent years. Reasons for employing a professional manager to manage property have been the growth in multi-ownership forms, the increase in absentee ownership and in size of projects, the proliferation of housing laws and regulations, the requirements of lending institutions, and the more competitive real estate markets. Property management has become a highly specialized field, and owners of property find that the cost of employing a property manager is more than offset by total dollars saved by efficient management.

Each property has unique features that require both knowledge and expertise if the property is to be managed correctly. The demand for office space has continued to increase in most urban areas. As more and more office buildings are added to the supply, an owner needs someone who can market space and at the same time maintain good owner-tenant relationships. Industrial properties, either warehouses or manufacturing facilities, have unique management problems which need to be solved by someone familiar with this type of property. Shopping centers, small retail stores, and residential properties also need efficient property management.

There are two primary objectives of property management, which are interrelated. The first objective is to generate for the owner the highest net operating income over the economic life of the property. Thus, potential income, vacancy allowances, and operating expenses are of great concern since they determine what the net operating income will be. Secondly, the property manager strives to maintain and, if possible, enhance the owner's capital investment in the property.

Neither objective can be met without considering the effect of one objective on the other. Net income can possibly be increased in the short run by cutting back on maintenance and repair. However, over the long run, such an approach will result in both a decrease in net income and a lessening of the property's value. Likewise, more than an adequate amount can be spent on operating expenses through poor management. This can also result in a decrease in net income. (*See* **Property Management**)

PROPERTY MANAGER

A person employed by the owner of real estate to advertise the property, negotiate leases, collect rents, maintain the property, and perform other services necessary to protect the owner's investment. There are generally three levels on which the managers of property can be involved:

The Property Manager: This person can be a member of a real estate brokerage office who oversees the management of a number of different properties for various owners. However, in large urban areas it has become quite common for persons to establish property management firms specializing only in the management of property.

The Building Manager: This person can be employed either by a property management firm or, as often is the case, directly by the owner of a building. Such a person is involved in the management of only one building and is generally hired on a straight salary basis.

The Resident Manager: The resident manager is an employee of the property management firm and is its representative on the premises. Such a person could be the building superintendent or the manager of an apartment complex. If the latter, the resident manager normally lives on the premises. This person is also normally employed on a straight salary basis.

As is true in any business agreement, the property manager or management firm and the owner of the property should enter into a formal contract. The management contract should include the responsibilities and obligations of both parties. Responsibilities specified in the employment agreement should include the term and period of the contract, the management policies to be followed, the power and authority of the property manager, and the compensation for the management services. Normally, a property manager's compensation is an agreed-upon percentage of gross income. The range can vary from a very small amount, perhaps one percent, on a large structure, to as much as ten or fifteen percent on a single-unit house.

There are a number of functions required of a good property manager. For purposes of discussion, the more important ones are classified as follows: (1) management plan, (2) budget preparation, (3) leasing space, (4) collecting rent, (5) keeping accurate records, (6) maintenance, and (7) tenant-owner-manager relations.

Management Plan: Before assuming the management of a piece of property, a long-range plan should be developed. Such a plan should include what the management company hopes to accomplish and how it intends to do so. Before the plan can be developed, analysis has to be made of the owner's objectives. Certainly the property manager has to be confident that these objectives can be met. A physical inspection of the property itself has to be made, and the property manager needs to understand existing market conditions regarding competition, rental structures, and operating expenses.

Budget Preparation: Once a definite management plan has been established, a budget for each property must be carefully prepared. The budget should contain an estimate of the total income and expenses to be incurred in the operation of the project. For the property manager the budget can serve as a guide to how successfully the management plan is being carried out. The owner will want to know the projected budget to see if the return on investment desired can be obtained and if not, what can be done to obtain it.

Leasing Space: An important function of the property manager involves attracting and selecting tenants. It is usually the responsibility of the property manager to select those tenants who fit into the overall management plan. For residential real estate, such as an apartment complex, the lease agreement normally follows a standard form and typically does not provide for *concessions* to be made. A concession is a service offered by the owner to a tenant that results in the actual rent paid being less than the rent specified in the lease.

Example: An office 100 x 75 feet rents for $6.00 per square foot. If a tenant will sign a five-year lease, rent will only be charged for the first four years.

Rent Calculation: 100 x 75 x $6.00 = $45,000 per year or $3,750 per month. With Concession: $45,000.00 x 4 = $180,000/5 = $36,000 per year or $3,000 per month.

Reasons for offering concessions to tenants might include the desire to attract *anchor tenants* such as a national chain store or the desire to "rent up" a certain amount of available space prior to the actual completion of the building. Even though less common than with commercial buildings, apartment complexes sometimes offer concessions. Examples would include such things as free membership in a private club or a twelve-month lease for eleven month's rent.

Collecting Rent: If tenants have been properly selected and the lease agreements clearly worded, the collection of rents is a much easier task. If not stated in the lease, rent payments are due on the last day of the leasing period. However, both the amount of rent and the due date are normally stated very clearly in the lease agreement. Rent payments are typically stated as being due on the first of the month, payable in advance. It is important for the property manager not to let tenants become delinquent in the payments since a steady gross income is needed both to meet the expenses of the building and to return a positive net income to the owner.

Keeping Accurate Records: The means by which records are kept vary from manager to manager and from property to property. The most important thing is that the records kept should be accurate, precise, easy to understand, and complete. They should present to the owner a clear picture of what happened with both income and expenses during the particular accounting period. A common practice is to present a monthly statement to the owner.

Maintenance: Neither of the two objectives of property management can be met without proper physical maintenance. Included in the maintenance function will be a certain amount of repair work such as fixing doors and repairing air conditioners. Also included will be preventive maintenance which involves the periodic inspection of both the building and the equipment. The property manager's maintenance responsibility also encompasses purchasing supplies, managing maintenance personnel and overseeing any service contracts such as pool cleaning or window washing services.

Tenant-Owner-Manager Relations: The property manager is employed by the owner and as such is a representative or agent of the owner in dealing with third parties. Thus, the property manager has certain duties to the owner. At the same time, the property manager must also deal with tenants who are expecting to receive the services called for in the lease agreements. To many tenants, especially in residential complexes, the property manager is the only contact the tenant has with the owner. In fact, the tenant may not even know who owns the building. Therefore, the property manager must form a good business relationship with both the owner and the tenants to meet the objectives of property management.

PROPERTY OWNER'S ASSOCIATION

(*See* **Homeowner's Association**)

PROPERTY REPORT

A document that must be made available to potential purchasers of subdivided lots that come under the *Interstate Land Sales Full Disclosure Act*. A would-be purchaser must be furnished a copy of the report at least 48 hours prior to signing a sales contract and failure on the part of the developer to provide such information may lead to fine or imprisonment.

PROPERTY RESIDUAL TECHNIQUE

A form of the income approach to valuing income-producing property that estimates the present value of property by combining the present value of forecasted income with the present value of the forecasted resale proceeds. (*See* **Building Residual Technique, Land Residual Technique**)

PROPERTY TAX

A tax imposed by government against real and/or personal property. While many local jurisdictions tax personal property such as automobiles, property taxes on real property are levied by all local jurisdictions and are the main source of revenue for most local governments. A tax on property is referred to as an *ad valorem tax.* That is, the tax is based on the value of the property, so two different parcels of property with the same assessed value have the same ad valorem tax. Likewise, similar properties with different assessed values do not have the same property tax. The total amount of property tax due on a parcel of land and its improvements is determined only after the completion of certain steps. Whereas the property tax process varies somewhat from jurisdiction to jurisdiction, these same basic steps are followed by all jurisdictions levying a property tax.

First, the taxing jurisdiction prepares a budget which shows the expected expenditures over a period of time, normally a fiscal year. How these expenditures will be appropriated for public education, capital improvements, road maintenance, and so forth, is also shown on the budget. Once this budget is determined, the sources of revenue must be identified and estimated as to their total contribution. By subtracting sources of revenue (sales tax, income tax, federal revenue, license fees, and others) from the projected total expenditures, the taxing jurisdiction knows how many dollars must be generated through the taxation of property.

The next step in the process is for the tax assessor to appraise each parcel of property and to assign an *assessed value* to the property. While various appraisal methods are used, property is normally assessed at some percentage of *full market value.* Full market value is the price a willing seller will accept and a willing buyer will pay at arms-length negotiating where neither are under undue pressure.

Almost all taxing jurisdictions contain certain exempt property such as property owned by federal, state, and local governments, and property used by certain groups such as churches, hospitals, and educational institutions. The total assessed value of these exempt properties must be subtracted from the total assessed value of all property before the tax rates are determined. A tax rate is calculated by dividing the total amount of revenue needed by the total assessed value of all taxable property within the taxing jurisdiction. This tax rate or, in some jurisdictions, *millage rate* is then multiplied by the assessed value of each parcel to give the amount of tax due on each parcel. In order to use the millage rate to calculate taxes it is important to remember that 1 mill is one-tenth of 1 cent or $1/$1,000 of assessed value.

Consider the following example of finding a tax rate:

Budget	$ 20,000,000
Revenue from other sources	- 6,000,000
Property tax revenue needed	$ 14,000,000
Total taxable assessed value	$350,000,000

Tax rate = $14,000,000/$350,000,000 = .04

Tax rate = 4 percent

        = $4 per $100 of assessed value

        = 40 mills per dollar (a mill is one-tenth of 1 cent)

Residential fair market value	$60,000
Assessed at 50%	$30,000
Tax rate	$4 per $100

Tax due = $30,000/$4 per $100 = $1,200

Once the tax bill on property is received, the owner of record has a certain period in which to challenge the assessed value. This statutory period is normally 15 days to 6 months. If a protest is filed within this period the property owner is given the opportunity to present reasons why the assessment is incorrect. The procedure involves either meeting with the tax assessor or appearing before a local appeals board or board of equalization whose job is to listen to each complaint and then decide if indeed the property has been incorrectly assessed. If the property owner is still dissatisfied, many jurisdictions provide a tax court which periodically reviews those cases not settled by the appeals board or board of equalization. The tax is billed and is due normally within a stated period of time. Unpaid property taxes become specific liens superior to private liens. Unpaid taxes beyond the grace period allowed by a jurisdiction can result in the selling of that property at public auction to satisfy the tax lien.

PROPRIETARY LEASE

A lease used in a cooperative apartment in which the tenant makes a capital contribution to the corporation through the purchase of stock and in turn receives a lease giving the tenant the right to occupy a certain apartment unit. (*See* **Condominium, Cooperative**)

PRO RATA

In proportion.

PRORATION

The division of expenses and/or income between the buyer and seller of property as of the date of settlement. The closing of a real estate transaction occurs on a particular date. Certain expenses incurred by the buyer and seller involve charges shared by both which are divided according to contractual agreement. Other expenses, however, are on-going and must be divided at the time of closing to cover the separate time periods over which the buyer and seller actually own the property. Examples are property taxes, water bills, and possibly property insurance. To prorate it is necessary to divide correctly these expenses (or income in certain instances) between the buyer and seller. In prorating the seller incurs these expenses up to and including the day of closing and likewise is credited with rents received, if applicable, up to and including the day of closing.

Consider the following example: A house is purchased and closing takes place February 17. The annual property tax bill of $324, which is due January 1 of each year, has not been paid for either the current calendar year or the previous calendar year. How much should be debited to the seller at closing?

Step 1: Previous tax year due = $324
Step 2: Current year:
Monthly tax = $324/12 = $27.00
Daily tax = $27/30 = $.90

Step 3: January   30 days
       February <u>17</u> days
               47 days x $.90 = $42.30

Step 4: Total tax due: $324 + $42.30 = $366.30

As noted, prorating is also necessary for dividing income generated by the property. To illustrate, consider the following: Mr. Hubbard is selling his 12-unit apartment complex to Mr. Carn. Each unit rents for $250 per month and the rent, paid in advance, was collected for each unit by Mr. Hubbard on the first day of the month. How much of this rent will Mr. Carn be credited at closing if closing is April 21?

Step 1: Rent collected = $250 x 12 = $3,000
        Daily rent = $3,000/30 = $100

Step 2: Amount due Mr. Carn: 9 days x $100/day = $900

PROSPECT

A person who appears to be interested in buying a particular piece of real estate.

PROSPECTING

The soliciting of customers such as action by a real estate broker to secure new listings.

PROSPECTUS

A written statement made available to potential investors that describes the potential and expected operation of a real estate investment opportunity.

PUBLIC PROPERTY (LAND)

Land owned by local, state, or federal government as compared to private property, which is owned by an individual.

PUBLIC PURPOSE

A purpose or service which is reasonably expected to be provided by the government. The objective of a public purpose is to provide for the health, safety, morals, security, and well-being of all inhabitants. Examples in which there is a public purpose include zoning, building codes, and fire and police protection. (*See* **Eminent Domain, Zoning**)

PUBLIC RECORD

Information which a governmental unit such as a city or county is required to keep in order to carry out its official duties. Such records are available for public inspection and are normally indexed in such a manner that specific information sought by someone can be found. Examples include the recording of deeds and subdivision plats and information regarding the assessment of land for purpose of collecting property tax.

PUBLIC SALE

A sale of property by auction that is open to anyone wishing to attend. Such a sale may be the result of a property owner not paying the property tax due on his or her property. In such a case, the local government will hold a public sale in order to raise the tax due on the property. (*See* **Property Tax**)

PUBLIC UTILITY EASEMENT

The taking of an interest in land by a public utility in order to install power lines, gas line pipes, or other such things for the purpose of providing services to the population.

PUD

(*See* **Planned Unit Development**)

PUFFING

To exaggerate or make claims regarding a particular situation. Such a claim is an opinion and since it is not made as fact, the person making the statement cannot be held as having misrepresented the truth. For example, a real estate broker may refer to a house as having "a gorgeous yard" in which case he or she is merely puffing. If, however, the broker had said "this house has the largest yard in the city" and the yard was not, in fact, the largest, the broker would have been misrepresenting the truth. (*See* **Fraud, Misrepresentation**)

PUNITAVE DAMAGES

The court-awarded compensation received by an injured party as punishment against the party who caused the grief or aggravation. (*See* **Actual Damages**)

PUR AUTRE VIE

(*See* **Life Estate Pur Autre Vie**)

PURCHASE AND LEASEBACK

The simultaneous buying of property and leasing it back to the seller. (*See* **Sale and Leaseback**)

PURCHASE CAPITAL

Amounts used to acquire property.

PURCHASE MONEY MORTGAGE

A loan given by the seller to the buyer to cover all or part of the sales price. Normally such a loan is used when the buyer is assuming an existing mortgage and does not have the money necessary to buy out the owner's equity. In such a case the owner, by agreeing to a purchase money mortgage, receives his or her money at some point or at various points in the future rather than at closing. In recent years, the term *owner financing* has been used to denote such an activity and has been particularly popular in times of high interest rates. Generally, a seller is more apt to finance part or all of a sale at an interest rate substantially below what would be available through a lending institution.

PURCHASER

The person in a sales transaction who is buying the item being sold. In real estate transactions, the purchaser is often referred to as the buyer.

PYRAMID ZONING

A type of zoning ordinance in which the land uses allowed in the more restricted zone classifications are permitted in the less restricted zone classifications. (*See* **Zoning**)

QUALIFIED ACCEPTANCE

An acceptance of an offer subject to a condition or conditions which must be met. Since new conditions are included, a qualified acceptance is a rejection of the original offer and thus is a *counteroffer*. (*See* **Acceptance, Counteroffer, Offer**)

QUALIFIED FEE ESTATE

A legal interest in land which is subject to a limitation(s) placed on the estate by the owner. For example, a qualified fee could be created "to First Church so long as the land is used exclusively for religious purposes." The two most important kinds of qualified fees are: (1) *fee simple determinable* and (2) *fee simple subject to a condition subsequent*. (*See* **Fee Simple, Fee Simple Determinable, Fee Simple Subject to a Condition Subsequent**)

QUANTITY SURVEY METHOD

A method of estimating reproduction cost for appraisal purposes by totaling the cost of each individual part to be used in construction and the cost of labor per part, plus additions for indirect costs. (*See* **Cost Approach**)

QUANTUM

The duration or length of an estate or interest in land such as "an estate for life."

QUARTER SECTION

An area of land measuring 2,640 feet on each side (one-half mile) and containing 160 acres. Such a measurement is part of the *Government Survey Method*. (*See* **Government Survey Method**)

QUASI CONTRACT

A legal obligation imposed by law where there is unfair or unjust reward to one party.

QUIET ENJOYMENT

The legal right of an owner to use and enjoy property without interference of possession by someone with a superior title.

QUIET TITLE ACTION

Action by a court to remove a cloud or claim that has been placed on title to property.

QUITCLAIM DEED

A deed which conveys only what present interest a person may have in a particular property without making any representations or warranties of title. Such a deed is useful in clearing up doubtful claims such as possible dower rights or disputed liens. A person giving a quitclaim deed releases and waives all present rights, and if the grantor has good and merchantable title, this is what is conveyed. If the grantor actually has no interest in the property, no interest is conveyed. However, if the grantor later acquires good title to the property previously conveyed by a quitclaim deed, the grantor keeps it; it is not automatically passed on to the grantee. (*See* **Deed**)

R-1 ZONE

A residential zoning classification that limits the use of land to single-family homes within a defined geographic area. (*See* **Zoning**)

R-2 ZONE

A residential zoning classification that permits duplexes, and in some jurisdictions, triplexes and quadraplexes within a defined geographic area. (*See* **Zoning**)

R-3 ZONE

A residential zoning classification that permits apartment buildings and multi-family housing within a defined geographic area. (*See* **Zoning**)

RADIUS

The distance from the center of a circle to its perimeter. Radius is used in the *metes and bounds method* of legal description to describe a curved boundary line.

RANGE

A land description measurement used in the *Government Survey Method* consisting of a strip of land located every six miles east and west of each principal meridian. (*See* **Government Survey Method**)

RATCLIFF, RICHARD U.

A post-World War II urban economist and appraiser noted for his writings in the area of capitalization theory. In his book, *Modern Real Estate Valuation*, Ratcliff expressed concern over some of the traditional ways in which income-producing property had been appraised and offered suggestions as to how capitalization theory could be better applied.

RATE OF INTEREST

The rate at which borrowed money earns money. Rate of interest is used in real estate finance and investment decisions.

RATE OF RETURN

A percentage relationship between the investment price or equity invested and the composite returns, normally net income.

RATIFICATION

The approval of a previously authorized act performed on behalf of a person which gives the act validity and legally binding effect. For example, the owner of a home may, by his or her actions, ratify the act(s) of a real estate broker acting as an agent resulting in the selling of the home. (*See* **Agency**)

RATIFY

To confirm or approve. Most contracts, including real estate contracts, are voidable on the part of a minor, which means that the minor may disaffirm the contract any time before achieving the age of majority. However, a minor may choose to ratify a contract after achieving majority and thus be bound by the conditions of the contract. (*See* **Contract**)

RAW LAND

Land that has not been graded and made ready for the construction of improvements. Also known as *unimproved land*.

READY, WILLING, AND ABLE

A phrase used to denote the capacity and intent of a potential buyer of real estate. Unless there is agreement to the contrary in the listing contract, a broker is normally entitled to a sales commission when a buyer is found ready, willing, and able to purchase the property on the exact terms specified by the seller. "Ready and willing" denote a buyer who is agreeable to the terms and conditions set by the seller, while "able" refers to the ability of the buyer to meet the financial conditions as set by the seller.

REAL ESTATE

Land and all improvements made both "on" and "to" the land. Improvements "on" the land refer to such things as buildings, while improvements "to" the land denotes such things as clearing, building of roads, and the laying of sewers. Real estate provides the basis of shelter and privacy for the individual and the family. It is also the basis for work and commercial activities. Food and mineral resources are extracted from real estate. Cities are formed by complex and interrelated real estate decisions.

REAL ESTATE AGENT

A term commonly used to refer to a real estate salesperson who is licensed to work on behalf of a real estate broker. For example, an owner might say, "I listed my house with Susan Jones, an agent for First Realty." (*See* **Salesperson**)

REAL ESTATE ANALYST

A real estate consultant normally employed by a client to advise as to the economic and financial feasibility of a particular land use. Real estate analysts are involved in market analysis, feasibility studies, and highest and best use studies. The analysis may also include valuation and appraisal assignments.

REAL ESTATE BOARD

An organization in a specific geographic area whose membership consists primarily of licensed real estate brokers and salespersons. In the early 1900s local real estate boards joined forces to form the *National Association of Real Estate Boards*, today known as the *National Association of Realtors*. Today, this organization is represented through state associations and 1,800 local real estate boards. (*See* **National Association of Realtors**)

REAL ESTATE BOND

A negotiable instrument issued by a person or an entity, such as a *Real Estate Investment Trust (REIT)*, which is secured by a collective mortgage on all or a specified portion of the issuer's property. (*See* **Real Estate Investment Trust**)

REAL ESTATE BROKER

(*See* **Broker**)

REAL ESTATE COMMISSION

The state regulatory body or agency whose duty is to carry out the provisions of the real estate licensing law in that particular state. Under certain conditions real estate commissions also have the authority to refuse, suspend or revoke licenses for just cause provided constitutional due process is afforded the applicant or licensee. In a few states the commission is created as a separate department of real estate. However, in most states the real estate commission is part of some centralized licensing body such as the Department of Licensing and Regulation. The real estate commission is comprised of persons called *commissioners*, normally appointed by the governor for specific terms, who act as a governing or policy-making body of the commission. The actual number of commissioners varies from state to state. Some states require the commissioners to be licensed as either real estate brokers or real estate salespersons; other states require a certain number of the commissioners specifically not to be engaged either directly or indirectly in the real estate business. Quite often the state is divided into areas or districts and the commissioner representing a particular area must have been and continue to be a resident of that area. In some states the commissioners are paid an annual salary while in others they receive expenses incurred in traveling to meetings, etc. In many jurisdictions, the commissioners annually elect from among their group a chairperson who serves as such for that year.

A chief administrative officer, referred to as an executive director, director, executive secretary, secretary, or administrator, is employed to do all other things deemed necessary to carry out the duties of the real estate commission. This person will be someone who possesses a broad knowledge of the generally accepted practices in the real estate business and will be well informed as to the real estate license laws in that state. The chief administrator's staff will include assistants, investigators, education directors, clerical staff, and others. The commission or department of real estate meets periodically in public session, and anyone has the right to appear and be heard. Accurate accounting records of fees collected and expenses incurred must be kept. Funds collected by the commission are normally deposited into the state treasury.

REAL ESTATE DEVELOPMENT

The process of converting an undeveloped tract of land into a parcel(s) ready for construction. Real estate development includes all types of land. For example, the process could take the form of a developer acquiring a 100-acre tract of land from a farmer, subdividing the large parcel into one-half acre tracts, putting in roads, curbs, gutters, sewers, and water mains, and then selling the individual lots to either builders or private individuals who in turn construct houses on the lots. Real estate development can also involve commercial property such as the development of a large shopping district, or industrial property such as an industrial park.

REAL ESTATE EDUCATORS ASSOCIATION (REEA)

A professional association established for and by real estate educators. Membership in the association comes from colleges and universities, private schools, real estate organizations, boards and associations, as well as regulatory agencies. The purpose of REEA is to promote educational and professional standards of competence and performance among all real estate practitioners as well as to facilitate communication and cooperation among all those concerned with any aspect of real estate education. REEA awards the designation *Designated Real Estate Instructor (DREI)*. The mailing address is Suite 1200, 230 North Michigan Avenue, Chicago, Illinois 60601; (312) 372-9800.

REAL ESTATE INVESTMENT TRUST

An organized association whereby individual investors pool their funds for the purpose of investing in real estate. The real estate investment trust, or *REIT*, is a creature of both state and federal tax law. A REIT is created in the form of a business trust. If the tax requirements are met, it provides for a pass through of income without double taxation. Further, it has the added advantage of limited liability to the investor and ease in the transfer of shares. However, the value of a REIT share is based on the capability of the management and the quality of the investments. Many people suffered significant financial losses during the 1973-1975 recession because of incompetent management, poor investments, and a bad real estate climate. Some REITs fared well and were able to weather the economic downturn. In order to qualify for a pass through of income, the trust must have at least 100 investors, no five persons may own more than 50% of the beneficial title, 90% of the income received must be from passive sources such as mortgage interest or rentals, 75% of the income must be from real estate investments, and the trust must distribute 90% of its annual income to the beneficiaries. Significant disadvantages to the REIT include no pass through of capital losses or net operating losses and the requirement that assets be managed by an independent contractor.

REAL ESTATE MARKET

The mechanism by which rights and interests in real estate are sold, prices set, supply adjusted to demand, space allocated among competing alternate uses, and land-use patterns set.

REAL ESTATE MORTGAGE INVESTMENT CONDUIT (REMIC)

A tax-exempt vehicle used as a mechanism for issuing multiclass pass-through securities. REMIC's were created by the *Tax Reform Act of 1986*.

REAL ESTATE SALESMAN (SALESPERSON)

(*See* **Salesperson**)

REAL ESTATE SECURITIES AND SYNDICATION INSTITUTE (RESSI)

A professional institute affiliated with the National Association of Realtors whose members are involved in the marketing and management of real estate securities. The institute awards two professional designations: (1) *CRSM (Certified Real Estate Securities Marketer)* and (2) *CRSS (Certified Real Estate Securities Sponsor)*. In addition, RESSI publishes numerous pamphlets and reports on matters dealing with real estate securities.

REAL ESTATE SETTLEMENT PROCEDURES ACT (RESPA)

In 1974 Congress passed the Real Estate Settlement Procedures Act (RESPA), which took effect in June 1975 and covers most mortgage loans made for one- to four-unit residential property. While RESPA does not set limits on the charges lenders can levy in closing a loan, it does require the lender to provide the loan applicant with pertinent information so that the borrower can make informed decisions as to which lender to use in financing the purchase.

Information booklet: When a person submits an application or when a lender prepares a written application, RESPA requires the lender to give the applicant a copy of a booklet prepared by the *U. S. Department of Housing and Urban Development (HUD)* entitled *Settlement Costs and You*. If the booklet is not made available by the lender on the day of the application, it must be mailed to the applicant within three business days after the application is filed. Part One of the booklet describes the settlement procedures, the various services the buyer needs, and information on the borrower's rights under RESPA. Part Two explains each item in the settlement statement and gives sample forms for the borrower to use in making cost comparisons.

Good faith estimates: When someone applies for a loan the lender must also provide good faith estimates of the settlement costs that will likely be incurred in financing the property. If this estimate is not provided at the time of application, it must be mailed within three business days. The estimates given are supposed to be based on the lender's experience in making such loans but they may change due to changing market conditions. The final costs incurred at closing may not be exactly the same since the lender's good faith estimate is not a guarantee.

Lender designation of settlement-service providers: Some lenders use particular closing attorneys, title examination companies, title insurers, and other settlement-service providers. Where this occurs RESPA requires the lender to provide the borrower with the name, address, and telephone number of each provider, the specific service each firm provides, and an estimate of charges the borrower can expect to pay. Also, the lender must specify if the provider has a business relationship with the lender. The lender is prohibited from receiving secret kickbacks from a provider of a service.

Disclosure of settlement cost: One day before the scheduled closing the borrower has the right under RESPA to inspect the *Uniform Settlement Statement* which gives an itemized account of all fees charged by the lender. While some of the fees to be incurred at closing might not be known, the lender must make available those charges he or she knows will be levied. Even though the borrower might choose to waive the right to examine the settlement statement, it must be mailed at the earliest practical date.

REALITY OF CONSENT

Mutual agreement between the parties to a contract regarding the terms and conditions of the contract. In order for a contract to be valid and enforceable, there must be reality of consent or, as is often stated, a "meeting of the minds." Contract law deals with the fulfillment of reasonable expectations of the contracting parties. A person who is forced or tricked into a contract cannot normally achieve reasonable expectations. The law will give relief to an innocent party in cases where fraud, misrepresentation, certain kinds of mistakes, duress, menace, or undue influence caused one or more of the parties to a contract not to freely give consent. Contracts induced without reality of consent are normally voidable at the option of the innocent party but valid as to the wrongdoer. (*See* **Contract**)

REAL PROPERTY

The aggregate of rights, powers and privileges inherent in the ownership of real estate. Property rights and interests are analogous to a *bundle of sticks*. Each stick represents a different right or interest. The distinction between real and personal property is important for several reasons. First, in a transfer of real estate, all objects which are classified as real property go to the purchaser and all objects classified as personal property stay in the ownership of the seller unless contractual provisions specify differently. Proof of ownership and sale is different depending on whether an object is real property or personal property. If a person dies, the law in the person's state of residence controls the disposition of personal property, but the law where the real property is located controls its disposition. Finally, the taxes levied on real and personal property differ.

REALTIST

The designation awarded to its membership by the National Association of Real Estate Brokers. *(See* **National Association of Real Estate Brokers***)*

REALTOR

A registered trademark of the National Association of Realtors. The term may only be used by brokers and salespersons who hold active membership in the association. *(See* **National Association of Realtors***)*

REALTOR-ASSOCIATE

The designation used by real estate salespersons who are members of the National Association of Realtors. *(See* **National Association of Realtors***)*

REALTORS LAND INSTITUTE (RLI)

The Realtors Land Institute is a professional organization affiliated with the National Association of Realtors. Membership consists of people involved in the marketing and brokerage of land. Previously known as the Farm and Land Institute, the organization awards the professional designation *AFLM (Accredited Farm and Land Member)*. The mailing address is 430 North Michigan Avenue, Chicago, Illinois 60611; (312) 329-8200.

REALTORS NATIONAL MARKETING INSTITUTE (RNMI)

An affiliate of the National Association of Realtors whose members specialize in the marketing of real estate. The institute awards three designations: (1) *CRS (Certified Residential Specialist)*, (2) *CRB (Certified Residential Broker)*, and (3) *CCIM (Certified Commercial Investment Member)*. RNMI publishes numerous textbooks and pamphlets on real estate marketing and related topics. The Institute was formerly known as the National Institute of Real Estate Brokers (NIREB). RNMI's headquarters is 430 North Michigan Avenue, Chicago, Illinois 60611; (312) 670-3520.

REALTY

A term used to refer to land and the improvements on and to the land. The terms realty, real estate, and real property are often used interchangeably to refer to land and improvements. (*See* **Real Estate**)

REAPPRAISAL LEASE

A lease that includes a provision for periodic reevaluation of property, the rent to be set as a percentage of the appraised value.

Example: If Joe agrees to pay Nancy 12% of the fair market value of Nancy's property each year, with the property being appraised every three years, and if the property is worth $100,000 at the beginning of the term and found to be valued at $250,000 three years later, how much will Joe owe for the first three years? He will owe $100,000 x .12 or $12,000 per year. How much will he owe the second three years? $250,000 x .12 or $30,000 per year. Disputes often occur over the fair market value of the real estate involved with a reappraisal lease. Provisions are often made for an appraisal by professional appraisers and if a dispute occurs, the matter is to be resolved in *arbitration*. Arbitration is a procedure for resolving disputes out of court.

REASSESSMENT

A change in the assessed value of property for ad valorem tax purposes. (*See* **Property Tax**)

RECAPTIVE CLAUSE

A provision found in some percentage leases giving the landlord the legal right to terminate the lease and take back possession of the property if the tenant fails to maintain a minimum sales level. (*See* **Percentage Lease**)

RECAPTURE OF DEPRECIATION

(*See* **Depreciation Recapture**)

RECAPTURE RATE

The annual rate at which capital invested in a declining-value asset is recovered through the income provided by the asset. Also known as *rate of return* of the investment.

RECEIPT

Written acknowledgment that money or something else of value has been received. In real estate sales contracts a clause acknowledging receipt of the deposit is often included as part of the contract.

RECEIVER

A court-appointed person who is charged with preserving a property, collecting rents, and doing anything necessary to maintain the property's condition. The appointment of a receiver is normally the result of either bankruptcy or foreclosure action against a person or property belonging to that person.

RECEIVER CLAUSE

A clause included in some mortgages which permits, in case of default, the appointment of a receiver. *(See* **Receiver***)*

RECIPROCITY

The recognition that some states give whereby a licensee of one state can be involved in real estate transactions in other states. Certain states have *full reciprocity* agreements with other states; some states have *partial reciprocity* agreements. Jurisdictions allowing reciprocity have strict requirements as to the licensee's place of business, maintaining an active license, splitting of fees, and other licensing regulations.

RECONCILIATION

In appraisal, the adjustment process whereby comparables are adjusted to the subject property. *(See* **Appraisal Process***)*

RECONVEYANCE DEED

A deed used to transfer title to property back to the original owner. When a deed of trust is used, the borrower conveys title to the property to a third party (trustee) who holds title for the lender (beneficiary). Once the debt on the property has been fully repaid, the trustee reconveys title to the property back to the borrower by means of a reconveyance deed. *(See* **Deed of Trust***)*

RECORD(ED) PLAT

A land description map describing the geographic boundaries of each lot in a subdivision. Normally the map is located in the public land records and is referenced when lots in the subdivision are sold.

RECORDATION

The act of filing a document in the public land records thereby giving *constructive notice* to the world of the existence of the document and its contents. State recording acts are designed to provide a means of protecting persons who acquire an interest in real estate by permitting them to give constructive notice to the whole world as to the existence of that interest. This also gives subsequent purchasers protection from secret, unrecorded claims on the property by cutting off those claims when the land is acquired by a bona fide purchaser who pays value without notice of these adverse claims. Thus, in most cases a person who wishes to preserve a claim or interest in property must record or file an appropriate instrument as required by state law. This rule does not apply to persons in possession of property such as a tenant under a short-term lease. Any evidence of possession which can be determined by reasonable physical inspection of the property also serves as constructive notice. It is therefore always advisable to inspect land before purchase to determine if such unrecorded interests as prescriptive easements burden the property. *(See* **Chain of Title***)*

RECORD TITLE

The legal claims to real estate as evidence by recorded instruments on file in the records of the county (or city) where the land is located. *(See* **Constructive Notice, Title***)*

RECOURSE LOAN

A loan in which the promissory note allows the lender to take legal action against the borrower personally in case of default. Such a loan means that in addition to securing the loan with a mortgage on the property, a borrower may also have his or her personal assets used to satisfy the outstanding debt on the property. *(See* **Deficiency Judgment***)*

RECOVERY FUND

A fund established in some states for payment to persons who have suffered loss as a result of wrongful actions by licensed brokers and salespersons in that state. Any person injured by any action of a licensee arising out of a real estate transaction may recover compensation from the fund. The normal procedure would be for a complaint to be filed with the real estate commission, followed by an investigation, hearing, and, possibly, the awarding of compensation in the amount of the actual loss.

RECTANGULAR SURVEY

A method of land description used in approximately thirty states and based on imaginary lines of longitude *(meridians)* and latitude *(base lines)*. *(See* **Government Survey Method***)*

REDEMPTION PERIOD

The legal right of a borrower to make good on a defaulted loan within a statutory period of time and thus regain the property. *(See* **Equity of Redemption***)*

REDEVELOPMENT

The replacing of deteriorated and vacated property in an urban area with new structures on the land and new improvements to the land. Quite often the redevelopment is funded through a local, state, or federal agency. In recent years, however, many cities have been part of redevelopment projects through a cooperative agreement with a private developer.

REDLINING

An illegal practice of refusing to provide services such as mortgage money or insurance in certain defined geographic areas due to the belief that loans or insurance underwriting in the area would be of high risk. (*See* **Federal Fair Housing Act of 1968**)

REDUCTION OF MORTGAGE CERTIFICATE
An instrument issued by the mortgagee (lender) stating the outstanding balance, interest rate, and maturity date on an outstanding loan. In a situation where a person is taking property subject to or assuming a mortgage, it is useful to find out how much remains unpaid on the principal balance. Once issued, a reduction of mortgage certificate bars the issuer (lender) from pleading any subsequent defenses that the principal stated is incorrect.

REENTRY
The right of a landlord to repossess leased property following the violation by the tenant of the terms and conditions in the lease. (*See* **Lease**)

REEVALUATION LEASE
(*See* **Reappraisal Lease**)

REFERRAL
A client in a real estate dealing who has been reached as a result of a recommendation or action on the part of another person. (*See* **Finder's Fee**)

REFINANCE
To repay one or more existing mortgage loans by simultaneously borrowing funds through another mortgage loan. An increase in the value of property or a decrease in interest rates are common reasons why a borrower may decide to refinance the loan(s).

REGIONAL SHOPPING CENTER
An enclosed retail shopping area consisting of a large amount of floor area, normally between 200,000 square feet and 1,000,000 square feet. The center normally includes national retail stores as well as regional and local chains. The marketing of the stores is normally done to a population of at least 250,000 people.

REGISTERED LAND
Land registered in the public land records through the *Torrens System*. (*See* **Torrens System of Title Registration**)

REGULATION B
A regulation enacted by the *Federal Reserve System* to define the obligations and procedures of the *Equal Credit Opportunity Act*. (*See* **Equal Credit Opportunity Act**)

REGULATION Q

A regulation originally issued by the *Federal Reserve System* which established the maximum interest payments that can be paid on savings accounts by commercial banks and thrift institutions. In recent years, Regulation Q has been fazed out as part of the *Depository Institutions Deregulation and Monetary Control Act of 1980.*

REGULATION Z

A regulation issued by the *Federal Reserve System* to implement the *Truth-in-Lending Act.* (*See* **Truth-in-Lending Act**)

REHABILITATION

The restoration and renovation of an older or distressed building for the purpose of improving the use that can be made of the building.

REINVESTMENT RATE

The interest rate at which the cash flows from income-producing property, particularly the portion of the cash flows that represent a recovery of capital, are presumed to be invested.

REIT

(*See* **Real Estate Investment Trust**)

REJECTION

A refusal of an offer by the offeree, the person to whom the offer is made. A rejection has the legal effect of extinguishing the offer. (*See* **Acceptance, Offer**)

RELEASE CLAUSE

(*See* **Partial Release Clause**)

RELICTION

An increase in the amount of land due to the permanent withdrawal of a river or sea. (*See* **Accretion**)

REMAINDER ESTATE

A future interest in real estate which is created simultaneously with the granting of an estate of limited or potentially limited duration. For example, Don conveys his land to Knox for life and then to F.J. and his heirs. In this case, F.J. has a remainder estate in the land conveyed to Knox.

REMAINDERMAN

The person who has a future interest in a life estate once the present estate terminates. (*See* **Remainder Estate**)

REMAINING ECONOMIC LIFE

The estimated number of remaining years of usefulness of a structure or component. (*See* **Economic Life**)

REMIC

(*See* **Real Estate Mortgage Investment Conduit**)

REMISE

To release or give up. Normally the wording in a *quitclaim deed* used to express the intentions of the grantor include "_____ to remise, release, and quitclaim." (*See* **Quitclaim Deed**)

REMODELING

Activity undertaken to change the appearance and function of a building.

RENEGOTIABLE RATE MORTGAGE (RRM)

A type of rollover mortgage whereby the interest rate is adjusted to prevailing rates at fixed time intervals. The RRM, following guidelines set by the Federal Home Loan Bank Board, is actually a series of short-term loans issued for terms of three to five years each but secured by a long-term 20- or 30-year mortgage that carries a mortgage rate adjusted every three to five years in accordance with a national index. The interest rate could, for exemple, change by only one-half of a percentage point per year for each short term with a maximum increase or decrease of five percentage points. A loan with an original rate of 15 percent, for example, could go as high as 20 percent or as low as 10 percent. The lender cannot refuse to renew the loan at the end of one of the loan periods. However, after the end of the first renewal term, there is no prepayment penalty, and the borrower can pay off the loan and seek another loan with a different lender. There are also no penalties for partial prepayment on renegotiable rate mortgages.

RENEWAL OPTION

A provision included in some lease agreement that gives the tenant (lessee) the right to extend the time period covered by the lease. The renewal option is specific as to the conditions of the option such as the time period involved and the amount of the rent. If the tenant chooses not to exercise the option and renew the lease, the landlord (lessor) cannot force the tenant to renew. Renewal options are particularly common in commercial leases.

RENT

Payment made by a tenant to a landlord for the use of real estate owned by the landlord. If not stated in the lease, rent payments are due on the last day of the leasing period. However, both the amount of the rent and the due date are normally stated very clearly in the lease agreement. Rent payments are typically stated as being due on the first of the month, payable in advance.

RENTABLE AREA

The amount of space in a building available for rent as measured by the distance from the inside finish of the outer walls of the building or from the glass line if at least 50 percent of the outer building is glass.

RENTAL POOL

An agreement between owners of rental property, such as a resort condominium unit, whereby the owners make their units available for rent and in return receive a portion of the rental income. The amount of rent received by each owner is determined by a formula based on what percent of the total units rented consist of a particular owner's unit. In resort areas a rental pool agreement is often included as part of the sale of condominiums and is used as a marketing tool in the sale of such condominiums. (*See* **Condominium**)

RENT CONCESSION

(*See* **Concession**)

RENT CONTROL

Limitations imposed by state and local authorities in certain parts of the country as to how much rent can be charged by the landlord and what percentage increase can be levied. While rent control is often popular among tenants, such action has often resulted in abandonment of existing units by the owners as well as little desire on the part of investors to build additional units within rent control areas.

RENTER'S INSURANCE

An insurance policy available to renters that insures the contents and personal property of the renter. Since a renter does not own either the dwelling or other private structures on the property, the dwellings are not insured by the renter's insurance policy. (*See* **Insurance**)

RENT ESCALATION

Adjustment of rent by the owner to reflect changes in either the cost of maintaining the property or the cost of living index. Such escalation clauses have become common in rental agreements particularly in times of high inflation and high interest rates. There are several ways a landlord may maintain flexibility to adjust the rentals received from the property to cope with inflation and changes in the market value of the property. One strategy is to enter only into short-term leases of three to five years. At the end of each term the lessor may reset the rental payments to whatever the market will pay. This approach calls for close management on the part of the lessor and takes the chance of high vacancy rates in periods of oversupply in the marketplace. The lessee might be reluctant to make significant improvements or to risk loss of good will in short-term leases. Another strategy is to provide for automatic adjustment by a provision in the lease itself.   Leases which provide for flexibility within the lease provisions may be classified into the following categories: (1) *graduated leases*, (2) *index leases*, and (3) *reappraisal leases*.   (*See* **Graduated Lease, Index Lease, Reappraisal Lease**)

RENT INSURANCE

Insurance available to a landlord that protects his or her investment against loss due to fire or other perils which result in the space being unavailable for rent and thus the tenant not being liable for paying rent.   Such insurance is normally written as a rider on the fire insurance policy carried by the landlord.

RENT MULTIPLIER

(*See* **Gross Rent Multiplier**)

RENTUP

The period of time following the completion of construction or renovation that it takes to rent the space to a predetermined occupancy level.   A common provision in a permanent loan on income-producing property is that the developer must reach a predetermined "rentup" before the permanent loan is made.   In addition, the amount of the loan can also be influenced by the amount of rentup. For example, a developer seeking a two million dollar loan may have to show that 85 percent of the rentable space has been leased before a permanent lender will make a commitment for the two million dollars.   A rentup of only 75 percent, for example, may mean a commitment for only 1.8 million dollars by the permanent lender.

RENUNCIATION

The action by a person to abandon a right or interest acquired without transferring the right to someone else.   For example, a spouse could renunciate his or her interest received through a will and claim a statutory share if one is provided.

REPLACEMENT COST

The current cost of constructing a new building having utility equivalent to that of the subject property being appraised, but built with modern materials and techniques and designed in accordance with current tastes and standards.   (*See* **Cost Approach, Reproduction Cost**)

REPLACEMENT RESERVE

A fund established to replace assets when they wear out.   Such a reserve is particularly appropriate when an owner has property in use that has an expected short life such as the carpeting, stoves, and refrigerators in an apartment building.

REPOSSESSED PROPERTY

Action taken by a landlord or creditor to regain legal possession of property as a result of the nonpayment of rent or debt or breach of some condition or covenant. (*See* **Foreclosure**)

REPRODUCTION COST

The current cost of constructing an exact duplicate of the property being appraised. (*See* **Cost Approach, Replacement Cost**)

RESALE PRICE

The gross selling amount of an asset at the end of the investment holding period.

RESALE PROCEEDS

Resale price minus selling expenses, closing costs, and unpaid debts on the property at resale.

RESCISSION OF CONTRACT

Legal action taken to repeal a contract either by mutual consent of the parties to the contract or by one party when the other party is in breach of the contract.

RESERVATION

A provision added to the premise of a deed by the grantor creating a right or interest in the property that is to be retained by the grantor. For example, the grantor might wish to keep a life estate and could thus state "Don conveys the described property to Robert reserving a life estate for Don in the property." Similarly, an *exception* is an exclusion of a specified portion of property previously described in a deed. For example, "Joe conveys a 100-acre tract of land to Jim except for a half-acre family graveyard (legal description of the graveyard is included)." (*See* **Deed**)

RESIDENCE

One's place of abode. A person may have more than one residence, such as a city home and a vacation home. In contract, however, you can only have one *domicile*, which means living in a particular location with the outward intent of making that place your permanent home.

RESIDENTIAL MEMBER (RM)

A professional designation awarded by the American Institute of Real Estate Appraisers. Persons holding this designation are deemed as having skills and expertise necessary in appraising single-family property.

RESIDENTIAL RENTAL PROPERTY

Property from which 80 percent or more of the gross rental income is rental income from dwelling units.

RESIDENT MANAGER

A person employed, normally on a straight salary basis, to manage a building. Such a person could be the building superintendent or the manager of an apartment complex. If the latter, the resident manager normally lives on the premises. (*See* **Property Management**)

RESIDUAL

Left over. Real estate is said to be residual in that its value is dependent on how much compensation (income) is left after the other factors of production have been compensated. (*See* **Highest and Best Use, Value**)

RESIDUAL TECHNIQUES

Various appraisal techniques used to estimate the value of improvements or land, given net operating income and a known value and income requirement for the improvements or the land. (*See* **Building Residual Technique, Land Residual Technique, Property Residual Technique**)

RESORT CONDOMINIUM

A building located in a recreational or resort location that has been set up as a condominium form of ownership. Units within the structure are sold for recreational and leisure use and in turn may be placed in a *rental pool* for rent to nonowners. (*See* **Condominium, Rental Pool**)

RESPA

(*See* **Real Estate Settlement Procedures Act**)

RESPONDENT SUPERIOR

A legal doctrine which means "let the master answer." In agency law the test is to determine if a principal is liable for the actions of an agent or whether the principal and agent are also in a *master-servant relationship.* If so, the law imposes vicarious liability on the master (principal) for torts (legal wrongdoings) committed by the servant (agent) while in the scope of the master's employment. (*See* **Agency**)

RESSI

(*See* **Real Estate Securities and Syndication Institute**)

RESTRAINT ON ALIENATION

A limitation included in the conveyance of property intended to restrict or limit the transfer of the property. Such restraints may be unenforceable such as a *fee tail* estate which restricts the conveyance of title to the descendants of the grantee.

RESTRICTION

A limitation on the use of real estate. Such a limitation can be created through a *restrictive covenant* included in a deed or lease. (*See* **Restrictive Covenant**)

RESTRICTIVE COVENANT

A private limitation placed on the use that can be made of real estate. Such limitations are normally included in a deed and by using them it is possible to limit the land-use activities that are permitted, to limit height and density of structures, to require minimum floor area ratios, and other such restrictions. Restrictive covenants can be used by an individual to accomplish the same things that zoning and subdivision regulations accomplish for local governments. If there is a conflict between a restrictive covenant and a zoning restriction, the more restrictive of the two applies. (*See* **Deed**)

RETIRE A DEBT

To pay off the remaining balance on a mortgage. Whether a borrower can pay the debt early may be limited by conditions set forth in the mortgage. (*See* **Prepayment Privilege**)

RETURN ON EQUITY

The internal rate of return on initial equity based on the cash flow of the property. Also known as *cash flow return* and *cash-on-cash return*.

REVALUATION LEASE

(*See* **Reappraisal Lease**)

REVENUE STAMPS

(*See* **Documentary Stamp**)

REVERSE ANNUITY MORTGAGE

A financing arrangement whereby a lender pays the borrower a fixed annuity or periodic payment based on a percentage of the property's value. The loan is not repaid until the property is sold or upon death of the borrower at which time it is settled through normal probate procedures. In recent years this financial arrangement has been used by older people who have little or no debt on their property and can thus use the annuity payment to supplement their income.

REVERSE LEVERAGE

The financial condition experienced when expenses incurred to repay an interest-bearing debt exceed the financial benefits of the assets that were acquired with the borrowed money. Also known as *negative leverage*. (*See* **Leverage**)

REVERSION

A *future interest* a person has in property which is created when a grantor conveys an estate of lesser duration or interest than he or she presently has. Two examples follow:

Susan, a fee simple owner of ten acres, grants the property to Beth for ten years. Upon the expiration of the ten-year term, the ten acres will automatically revert to Susan.

Wayne, who has a life estate in Greenacre, grants a life estate to Paul. If Wayne should die first, Paul's life estate would automatically terminate, but if Paul died first, Wayne would reacquire possession.

REVERSIONARY INTEREST

The future interest a person has in property after present possession is terminated. (*See* **Reversion**)

REVERSIONARY LEASE

A lease scheduled to take effect at some time in the future upon the expiration of an existing lease.

REVERSION FACTOR

The mathematical present worth of one factor applied to the resale proceeds of property to convert the resale price into a present value. In numerous financial tables, the reversion factor appears as column four in a six column table. (*See* **Reversion Value**)

REVERSION VALUE

The projected value of property at the end of the expected holding period. That value when multiplied by the appropriate present worth factor can be converted into the current value of the reversion or future interest.

REVOCATION

The nullification of an offer to contract by the person (offeror) making the original offer.

REZONING

An amendment or change to the zoning map. Ordinarily, requests for rezonings are heard by a zoning board which is appointed at the local government level. The zoning board considers recommendations of the planners and listens to citizen groups. Recommendations of the zoning board are made to the legislative body of the local government who in turn makes the final decision. If the rezoning will create hazards or adversely affect surrounding properties, it will ordinarily be turned down. (*See* **Zoning**)

RIGHT OF FIRST REFUSAL

The right to have the first opportunity to buy real estate when the property becomes available. In rental property the lease may contain a provision giving the tenant the first opportunity to buy the property if and when the owner decides to sell. (*See* **Cooperative**)

RIGHT OF REDEMPTION

The ability given by statute to reacquire one's property after a foreclosure sale by paying any outstanding mortgage debt, interest and necessary legal fees. Also known as *statutory redemption*, the right of redemption period in those states that recognize it is usually from six months to two years. This right should not be confused with *equity of redemption* which exists in every state and is the right to redeem ones property up to the foreclosure sale. (*See* **Foreclosure**)

RIGHT OF REENTRY

The future interest retained by a grantor when a *fee simple subject to a condition subsequent* is created. (*See* **Fee Simple Subject to a Condition Subsequent**)

RIGHT OF SURVIVORSHIP

The legal right of a survivor to the property of a deceased person. Both *joint tenancy* and *tenancy by the entirety* provide for the right of survivorship which means that upon the death of one of the parties the legal interest of that party does not pass to the tenant's heirs but rather to the remaining tenant(s). (*See* **Joint Tenancy, Tenancy by the Entirety, Tenancy in Common**)

RIGHT OF WAY

The legal right of one person to cross over the land belonging to someone else. Such a right may be either private (allowing a neighbor to cross over one's property to access a river or stream) or public (use of public roads to reach a public park) and can be created either by contractual agreement or through continued use. (*See* **Easement**)

RIPARIAN RIGHTS

The right of a landowner whose land is next to a natural watercourse to reasonable use of whatever water flows past the property.

RISK-FREE RATE

The interest rate available on investments having the least risk, such as short-term U. S. Treasury obligations and liquid deposits insured by an agency of the U. S. Government.

RISK RATE

The rate of return on an investment that is necessary to attract capital or the rate of earnings perceived to be commensurate with the risk. People may wonder why certain investments such as a bank account pay five percent while others such as real estate often pay 25 percent or more. For example, if both Investment A and Investment B are expected to pay $100 each year in dividends, why are the two investments not selling for the same price? The answer is that investors pay a premium for certainty. If they are uncertain that Investment A will pay the promised $100 dividend but are more sure Investment B will, Investment B will sell for a higher price. The lack of certainty on the part of the investor is based on perception of risk in the investment. The riskier the investment, the less the investor is willing to pay for it. Risk has two sides: the upside, which is the possibility of gain, and the downside, which is the possibility of loss. Generally, more attention is paid to the downside; i.e., loss of original investment or failure by the investor to realize the promised gain. Gamblers and speculators tend to emphasize the upside risk; i.e., the chances of gaining greater profits than expected.

The general equation for valuing return from an investment is expressed as follows:

$$V = I/R$$

where $= V =$ Value, $I =$ Income, $R =$ Rate of Capitalization

The greater the risk perceived, the higher the *capitalization rate*. As the capitalization rate increases, the value of the income stream is reduced.

Example: If an investor examines two investments, each of which pays $100 dividends annually, and determines that one is safe and should be capitalized at six percent, while the other is marginally safe and should be capitalized at eight percent, how much should be offered for each?

Safe Investment:	$V = I/R$	$V = \$100/.06$	$V = \$1,666.67$
Marginal Investment:	$V = I/R$	$V = \$100/.08$	$V = \$1,250$

RM

A professional designation, *Residential Member*, awarded by the American Institute of Real Estate Appraisers.

ROD

A lineal measure equaling 5.5 yards or 16 1/2 feet.

ROLLOVER MORTGAGE

(*See* **Renegotiable Rate Mortgage**)

ROUSE, JAMES W.

A real estate developer noted for his concepts of planned cities and urban development. Rouse is known for the development of Columbia, Maryland, a planned community located between Washington, D.C. and Baltimore, Maryland. In addition, he has overseen the development of numerous shopping centers and inner city developments throughout the United States, most notably the Inner Harbor in Baltimore and Faneuil Hall in Boston.

ROW HOUSE

A form of residential housing in which the units are attached with a common wall. Such housing, very common in northeastern cities (particularly Baltimore), normally has similar architectural style and design and the cost of construction is generally less per square foot than that for detached housing.

RULE OF 72

A financing rule of thumb used to estimate the time period necessary to double the value of an asset subject to compounding. The formula to determine the period is:

$$\frac{72}{\text{Annual Growth Rate}} = \text{Years Necessary to Double}$$

For example, an asset growing at six percent per year would double in 12 years (72/6 = 12), while one growing at ten percent per year would double in less than 8 years (72/10 = 7.2).

RULE OF 78

A financing method used by some lenders to compute the amount of unearned finance charge to be refunded on a loan that is repaid before its maturity date. The '78' is used because the summation of 1 through 12 equals 78; thus on a one-year loan, the creditor retains 12/78 of the total finance charge for the first month, 11/78 for the second, 10/78 for the third and so forth down to the twelfth month at which time 1/78 would be earned. If a borrower repaid a loan after four months, the creditor has earned 42/78 (12 + 11 + 10 + 9) of the total finance charge and the borrower would be entitled to 36/78 (8 + 7 + 6 + 5 + 4 + 3 + 2 + 1) of the finance charge.

RUN WITH THE LAND

Rights or limitations such as deed restrictions, easements and covenants which are part of the ownership of land and thus are not terminated when title is transferred but rather remain in effect from owner to owner.

RURAL HOUSING ALLIANCE

The Rural Housing Alliance provides information and assistance to groups seeking to provide housing for low-income families in rural areas. RHA is located at 1346 Connecticut Avenue, Washington, D.C. 20036; (202) 659-2800.

"R" VALUE

A measurement of insulation's resistance to heat transfer.

SAFE RATE

A rate of return on investment that can be earned through relatively risk-free investments.

SALE AND LEASEBACK (SALE-LEASEBACK)

A technique used by owners of property as a means of raising capital. The process involves the simultaneous selling and leasing back of the property, usually through a net lease. The advantages to the seller include the freeing of capital previously tied up in the project and the inclusion of the rental payment as a legitimate operating expense for income tax purposes. For the investor, the rental payment represents a return on investment and any depreciation for tax purposes or increases in value due to market conditions accrue to the investor.

SALE OF PERSONAL RESIDENCE BY ELDERLY

A provision in the federal income tax law which allows for a forgiveness of $125,000 in capital-gains taxes for taxpayers 55 years or older who sell their principal residence. To qualify, a taxpayer must be at least 55 years old on or before the date of the sale. The house must have been the principal residence in at least three of the five years preceding the sale. If married, only one spouse must be 55 years old, but both must join in making the election. If filing separately, each spouse is only allowed half the exclusion or $62,500.

SALES CONTRACT

An agreement by which the buyer and seller agree to the terms and conditions of a sale. (*See* **Contract**)

SALESPERSON

A person licensed by a state real estate commission to perform on behalf of any licensed real estate broker any act or acts authorized to be performed by the broker. This is the person often carelessly or casually referred to as an *agent*. (*See* **Broker**)

SALES PRICE

The actual price agreed to by the purchaser and seller. Also referred to as *gross price*, the sales price is generally more than the seller actually receives since both the sales commission and all the seller's closing costs are subtracted before determining the *net sales price* realized by the seller.

SALVAGE VALUE

The expected worth of a piece of property at the end of its economic life.

SAM

(*See* **Shared Appreciation Mortgage**)

SANDWICH LEASE

A lease agreement created when a lessee (tenant) sublets the property to another person, thus creating a *sublessor-sublessee relationship*. The person in the "sandwich" is a lessee to one party and a lessor to another party.

SATISFACTION OF MORTGAGE

A written release issued by a *mortgagee* (lender) stating that a mortgage has been paid in full.

SAVINGS AND LOAN ASSOCIATION (S&L)

A primary supplier of mortgages, lending primarily on single-family residential real estate. While savings and loan associations (S&Ls) are not the largest financial intermediary in terms of total assets, historically they have been the most important source of funds in terms of the dollars made available for financing real estate. S&Ls have sustained large asset growth in recent years, and currently the total assets of the 3,000+ associations is second only to commercial banks. Traditionally, they have been the largest supplier of single-family, owner-occupied residential permanent financing although S&Ls are not limited solely to this type of financing. Savings and loan associations also make home-improvement loans and loans to investors for apartments, industrial property, and commercial real estate. An S&L is either federally or state chartered. Approximately 40 percent of the S&Ls are federally chartered. If federal, the association must be a member of the

Federal Home Loan Bank System (FHLBS), and its funds must be insured by the *Federal Savings and Loan Insurance Corporation (FSLIC)*. All federally chartered S&Ls are mutually owned (owned by depositors) and the word "federal" must appear in their title. State chartered S&Ls can be either mutually owned or stock associations. In a stock association, individuals buy stock which provides the equity capital. State chartered associations have optional membership in both the FHLBS and FSLIC. In some states these lenders are known as *building and loan associations* or *cooperative banks*.

SAVINGS BANKS
(*See* **Mutual Savings Banks**)

SCARCITY
An economic principle which when used to explain real estate markets states that while there is no physical shortage of land in the United States, there are occasional shortages of economically useful land at particular locations. In the short term the supply of usable land is inelastic, which means that little if any increase in quantity can be made. Therefore, possessors of key locations may have a monopolistic advantage. Over the long term, other land may be modified and brought into the effective supply. However, it should be noted that, even though there are millions of acres of land in the United States, urban land accounts for only about 2 percent of the total.

SCENIC EASEMENT
An easement created for the purpose of preserving a certain view or to prevent any construction on a particular site so as to preserve the land in its natural state. (*See* **Easement**)

SEAL
An impression in wax or paper to signify the formality of the execution of a legal instrument. In earlier times the signature of a grantor had to be under seal, particularly in times when many people were unable to sign their own name. Today, however, many states recognize the initials *L.S.*, which means "in place of the seal;" or the word, "seal," as a substitute. Other states have no requirement for a seal unless a corporation is the grantor.

SEASONED MORTGAGE
A loan made a number of years ago and in which the borrower has been timely and consistent in payment of the mortgage.

SECOND
A quantitative measurement used in the metes and bounds legal description method represented by the symbol '"'. An angle N 30° 10' 5" E would be read as "North thirty degrees, ten minutes, 5 *seconds* East." (*See* **Metes and Bounds**)

SECOND MORTGAGE

A mortgage that is second in priority because of the time of recording the mortgage or of the subordination of the mortgage. (*See* **Junior Mortgage**)

SECONDARY FINANCING

A loan secured by a junior mortgage on property. In recent years, for example, as interest rates and selling prices have continued to rise, many buyers have had to borrow money over and above the amount secured through the first mortgage. Such additional financing often comes in the form of a *purchase money mortgage* by which the seller agrees to take back part of the sales price in the form of a junior mortgage. (*See* **Junior Mortgage**)

SECONDARY MORTGAGE MARKET

The means by which existing first mortgages are bought and sold. The secondary mortgage market provides a lender with an opportunity to sell a loan before its maturity date. The availability of funds for financing real estate is affected by economic conditions both local and national. The result is that at certain times or in certain geographic locations little or no capital is available for mortgages; consequently, few if any loans are made. From the viewpoint of the lender another problem is that real estate loans can be highly illiquid; thus, the supplier of funds can have a difficult time converting loans into cash. For these reasons, the need exists for some means by which a lender can sell a loan prior to its maturity date. The secondary mortgage market attempts to meet these needs. Capital can be made available during times of tight money and at capital-deficient locations. By selling mortgages in the secondary mortgage market, a lender can convert existing mortgages into cash which can, in turn, be used to fund new mortgages. Likewise, an investor in the secondary mortgage market can buy existing mortgages, pay the seller a small servicing fee and avoid the time and expense of originating and servicing the loans. (*See* **Federal Home Loan Mortgage Corporation, Federal National Mortgage Association, Government National Mortgage Association**)

SECONDARY MORTGAGE MARKET ENHANCEMENT ACT OF 1984

Federal legislation that enhanced the development of the private mortgage securities markets, amended federal securities laws and preempted certain state laws.

SECTION

A quantitative measurement of land used in the *Government Survey Method* equal to one mile square, containing 640 acres. There are 36 sections in a *township*. (*See* **Government Survey Method**)

SECURITY DEPOSIT

A sum of money held by a landlord from a tenant for the purpose of securing the performance of the terms of the lease by the tenant for such things as the payment of rent and repair of damages caused by the tenant.

SEED MONEY
(See **Front Money***)*

SEE-THROUGH BUILDING
A building characterized by a high vacancy rate, perhaps 100 percent, and thus, you can "see" through it.

SEISIN (SEIZIN)
Possession of land by someone holding a freehold estate in the land. *(See* **Covenant of Seisin***)*

SELF-AMORTIZING MORTGAGE LOAN
A mortgage loan that requires level annual payments adequate to meet interest requirements and fully repay the principal over its term. *(See* **Amortization***)*

SELLER FINANCING
A loan made by the owner of property to the purchaser to cover part or all of the sales price. While common with both residential and commercial real estate, seller financing, or owner financing as it is also called, becomes a very popular means of "making the deal work" when interest rates are high. During such times, the purchaser who is unable to qualify for a loan from a traditional lender often turns to the seller and makes an offer to purchase contingent upon seller financing. *(See* **Purchase Money Mortgage***)*

SELLER'S MARKET
An economic situation in which demand is greater than supply. The result is greater opportunities for owners who may find someone willing to offer the asking price or even a figure greater than the asking price. During times of high demand, particularly in local markets, stories appear regarding the owner who had "five offers above the asking price" before the property was put on the market. In contrast, a *buyer's market* refers to a situation in which demand is less than supply at which time the advantages shift to the buyer.

SELLING AGENT
A real estate licensee who finds the purchaser in a transaction even though the agent did not actually list the property for sale. The majority of residential listings, particularly in metropolitan areas, become part of a *multiple listing service (MLS)* which establishes a working and legal relationship between the licensee who listed the property and all other members of the MLS. By selling the property, the selling agent is entitled to a certain agreed-to percentage, normally 50 percent, of the real estate commission. *(See* **Multiple Listing Service***)*

SEMENOW, ROBERT W.

Author of *Questions and Answers on Real Estate*, a comprehensive sourcebook for answering problems encountered in the real estate brokerage business. Semenow served for many years as the executive vice-president of the *National Association of Real Estate License Law Officials (NARELLO)*.

SEMIANNUAL

Twice a year at six-month intervals.

SEMIDETACHED HOUSING

A dwelling whereby one of the outside walls is shared with an adjoining unit of similar style and size.

SENIOR MORTGAGE

(*See* **Mortgage**)

SENIOR REAL ESTATE ANALYST (SREA)

A professional real estate designation awarded by the Society of Real Estate Appraisers to persons who have met minimum education and experience requirements related to real estate value and investment analysis.

SENIOR REAL PROPERTY APPRAISER (SRPA)

A professional real estate designation awarded by the Society of Real Estate Appraisers to persons who have met minimum education and experience requirements related to the valuation and appraisal of income-producing property.

SENIOR RESIDENTIAL APPRAISER (SRA)

A professional real estate designation awarded by the Society of Real Estate Appraisers to persons who have met minimum education and experience requirements related to the valuation and appraisal of residential property.

SEPARATE PROPERTY

Property individually owned by either husband or wife during the time of marriage, as opposed to property jointly owned by husband and wife. (*See* **Community Property**)

SERVICING FEE

The periodic (monthly or annual) payment made by the purchaser of a mortgage to the mortgage banker who originally made the loan for servicing the loan. The fee, which varies from one-fourth to one-half percent of the outstanding loan balance, covers the administrative costs of servicing such as collection and payment of property taxes and property insurance premiums. (*See* **Mortgage Banker**)

SERVICING (THE LOAN)

The periodic, normally monthly, collection of mortgage interest and principal repayment and other mortgage-related expenses, such as property taxes and property insurance. (*See* **Servicing Fee**)

SERVIENT ESTATE

The property or parcel of land which is burdened by an easement. (*See* **Easement**)

SETBACK REQUIREMENT(S)

The distance, normally measured in feet, back from the street or property line upon which no permanent improvements such as a building can be met. Setback requirements may be publicly imposed through zoning ordinances or privately imposed through deed restrictions or covenants.

SETTLEMENT

The closing of a real estate transaction at which time prorations and adjustments are made between buyer and seller for the purpose of concluding the transactions. (*See* **Closing**)

SETTLEMENT BOOK

A booklet given by a lender to an applicant for a residential loan entitled *Settlement Costs and You*. The book describes the settlement procedures, the various services the buyer needs, and information on the borrower's rights under the *Real Estate Settlement Procedures Act*. (*See* **Real Estate Settlement Procedures Act**)

SEVERALTY

Individual ownership of real estate. The word severalty or *several* in property law means separate or severed. It should not be confused with the normal usage of the word "several" which means many. Owning land in severalty means owning an estate or other interest in the land by separate or individual right. An individual who is the sole owner of property has exclusive right to the estate without sharing the ownership of the estate with another. The person who owns the estate in severalty is the only one required to sign a deed to convey title, unless an additional signature is required to release some curtesy, dower, or homestead right which might be recognized in a particular state. It is also possible, however, for an estate to be owned in some type of concurrent or multiple ownership.

SEVERANCE

Action that results in the removal or separation of something from the land. For example, the cutting of trees results in those trees being *severed* from the land.

SEVERANCE DAMAGE

The loss in value to the remaining tract or parcel of land resulting from a partial taking of land through the power of *eminent domain*. (*See* **Eminent Domain**)

SHAKEOUT

The activities taking place in a real estate market during bad financial times. Since real estate markets are unique, one segment of the market, (for example, office buildings) may be going through tough times while another segment, such as single-family residential, is in the midst of a boom period. The shakeout often results in marginal projects going under as well as poorly-financed developers and builders leaving the market.

SHARED APPRECIATION MORTGAGE (SAM)

A mortgage in which the lender shares in the appreciation or increased value of the real estate. Under such an agreement, the lender receives a part of the gain realized from a sale of the property and in exchange the lender typically reduces the interest rate on the loan. In the event the property is not sold by a predetermined date, a provision is normally included in the mortgage which provides for an independent appraisal of the property by a third party. The value estimated by the appraisal is then used to determine the amount of gain due the lender by the borrower.

SHELL LEASE

A type of lease arrangement under which the lessee (tenant) rents the shell of a building and agrees to make the necessary interior improvements such as wiring and plumbing, walls, painting, and carpeting.

SHERIFF'S DEED

A deed given to a buyer when property is sold through court action in order to satisfy a judgment for money or for foreclosure of a mortgage.

SHERIFF'S SALE

A forced sale of property, the proceeds of which are used to satisfy the unpaid claims of the debtor. The legal conveyance of any property sold during the sale will be done by a *sheriff's deed*.

SHORT RATES

An insurance concept relating to the fact that the insured party under an insurance policy has the right to cancel a policy at any time. Written or oral notice must be received by the insurance company, and any unused part of the premium is refunded. However, the refund is normally less than the straight pro rata charge since upon cancellation insurance companies calculate the used portion based on short rates. Short rates are higher than pro rata charges and thus the percentage refunded is not the same as the percentage of the unused term of the coverage.

SILENT PARTNER

A participant in a partnership whose name is unknown to the public but who nevertheless shares in the proceeds of the partnership.

SIMPLE INTEREST

Interest earned only on the initial principal, not on the accrued interest.

SINGLE-FAMILY RESIDENCE

A housing unit designed and maintained for occupancy by only one family. Zoning ordinances as well as subdivision regulations often limit the use that can be made of certain land to that of single-family residences.

SINKING FUND

Periodic deposits of money into an account that, with its interest earnings, will be used to replace assets or to retire loans. For example, an owner of a 10-unit apartment building estimates the refrigerators, valued at $500 each, will have to be replaced in 7 years. Thus $5,000 will be needed. In order to accumulate the necessary fund, the owner, assuming a 10 percent compounded annual return, would need to deposit $527.03 ($5,000 X .105405) each year in order to accumulate the necessary $5,000. In this example the .105405 is the sinking fund factor.

SIR

A professional designation denoting *Specialist in Industrial Realty.* The designation is awarded by the Society of Industrial and Office Realtors, a professional affiliate of the National Association of Realtors. (*See* **Society of Industrial and Office Realtors**)

SITE

The location or place of a plot of ground set aside for a particular type of land use.

SITUS

A term used to refer to the economic location of a particular parcel of land. Economic location is an important factor in determining the success or failure of real estate. The importance of location is due largely to the fact that individuals need specific types of land for specific uses at specific places. A decision as to whether or not a particular parcel will be used is dependent upon how that parcel fits into the land use pattern. For example, the success of a retail store is dependent on how near it is to where the customers live or shop. (*See* **Linkage**)

SLUM

A part or section of a city or town generally inhabited by the very poor. Such an area is normally characterized by a large amount of deteriorated housing, poor public facilities, absentee ownership, and a high incidence of crime.

SMMEA

(*See* **Secondary Mortgage Market Enhancement Act of 1984**)

SNOB ZONING

(*See* **Exclusionary Zoning**)

SOCIETY OF INDUSTRIAL AND OFFICE REALTORS (SIOR)

An affiliate of the National Association of Realtors whose members specialize in the brokering and marketing of industrial and office space. Active members of the society, which in 1986 changed its name from Society of Industrial Realtors to reflect office property brokerage and marketing, are experienced professionals who have a minimum of seven years of industrial or office property sales experience and have met a minimum volume of business requirements. They are trained to match buyers and sellers of unusual and complex industrial and office properties. The society awards the professional designation, *S.I.R.*, a specialist in industrial real estate. The mailing address is 430 North Michigan Avenue, Chicago, Illinois 60611; (312) 440-8000.

SOCIETY OF REAL ESTATE APPRAISERS (SREA)

A professional real estate organization whose members specialize in valuation and market analysis. Society membership now exceeds 16,000 members in the United States, Canada, and the Caribbean. It is the largest independent association of professional real estate appraisers and analysts in North America. Each of these members is pledged to uphold the high standards of professional practice and conduct established by the society and to perform all assignments under the constraints prescribed by the society's code of ethics.

The society awards three professional designations, each having a different set of requirements. The designations are:

Senior Residential Appraiser (SRA). A person who specializes in the appraisal of residential properties. These may include single family homes, condominiums, townhouses, and multi-family structures up to four units.

Senior Real Property Appraiser (SRPA). This designation is intended for those members who have chosen to expand the practice of appraisal to income producing properties. The training and educational program necessary to achieve this designation instructs the member in the appraisal of both residential and income producing real estate.

Senior Real Estate Analyst (SREA). A Senior Real Estate Analyst is an SRA or SRPA whose practice has expanded to encompass all forms of appraisal as well as analytical assignments. Advanced education and experience are only two of the qualifications necessary for this designation. In addition, analysts must demonstrate capability in investment analysis, marketability studies, and feasibility studies.

The society sponsors numerous seminars dealing with appraisal and related topics. The mailing address is 645 North Michigan Avenue, Chicago, Illinois 60611; (312) 346-7422.

SOFT MARKET

A market situation in which there are few buyers and thus those that do exist are apt to find a great deal of supply given the limited demand.

SOLE OWNERSHIP

(*See* **Severalty**)

SOUTHERN BUILDING CONGRESS INTERNATIONAL, INC.

This group provides assistance and information to local governments in their building code administration. The headquarters is 3617 8th Avenue South, Birmingham, Alabama 35222; (205) 591-1853.

SPECIAL AGENT

A person limited in authority to transact a single business affair or a specific series of business affairs or to perform restricted acts for a principal. Ordinarily, a real estate broker is construed to be a special agent. A person dealing with a special agent must inquire as to the scope of the agent's actual authority. (*See* **Agency**)

SPECIAL ASSESSMENT

An assessment levied against property by a local jurisdiction when property receives a special benefit which differs significantly from the benefit that the public at large receives. For example, if a government widens a road adjoining the property, or builds sewers, sidewalks, or a nearby neighborhood park, the owners of property benefiting from this action may be required to pay a special assessment. The assessment will ordinarily be levied on the proportionate benefit to the property and not as a percentage of the value of the property.

Example: The city constructs a sidewalk costing $1,500 in front of three lots of similar size. The lots have houses costing $50,000, $80,000, and $120,000, respectively. How much will each lot be assessed? Since each lot benefited equally from the sidewalk, each lot would have a $500 special assessment imposed. (*See* **Property Tax**)

SPECIAL LIEN

A claim against a particular piece of property. Examples of special liens include mortgages, mechanic's and materialman's liens, property tax liens, and special assessments. In contrast, a general lien is a claim against all of one's property, both personal and real, such as a federal income tax lien. (*See* **Lien**)

SPECIAL USE PERMIT

A means by which an individual is legally permitted to make use of a parcel of land that is an exception to the zoning ordinances. For example, a subdivision that is zoned single-family residential may permit the use of certain parts of the land for a country club/golf club. A special use permit differs from a *variance* which is a violation of the zoning ordinance that has been authorized by the governing body. (*See* **Variance**)

SPECIAL WARRANTY DEED

A deed in which the seller (grantor) warrants only against defects of title that have occurred after the grantor acquired title. Because sellers are often reluctant to assume the risk of title defects which may have occurred prior to their acquisition of the title, they will limit their liability by giving a special warranty deed rather than a general warranty deed. The special warranty deed does not contain the covenant of warranty of title. Instead, the grantor will warrant against defects that have occurred after the grantor acquired title. Language is usually used that the grantor warrants only against lawful claims on the title which occurred "by, from, through or under" the grantor. The grantor is warranting that he or she did not encumber the property, but makes no representations as to what may have happened prior to the time of his or her ownership. As is true with a general warranty deed, if the grantor with a special warranty deed has conveyed defective title and later acquires good title, this good title passes to the grantee *automatically* by operation of law. (*See* **Deed, General Warranty Deed**)

SPECIFIC LIEN

(*See* **Special Lien**)

SPECIFICATION

A legal remedy by which a court of law can order a contract to be performed as agreed to by the parties to the contract. Such remedy is available when the subject of the contract is a unique good. Since by definition all real estate is considered unique, the remedy of *specific performance* is available to both the purchaser and seller of real estate in case one of the parties attempts to default on the contract. The term is also used to denote written instructions and information made available to the contractor of a building detailing the type of construction, material to be used, and details as to building design, etc. (*See* **Contract**)

SPECULATIVE BUILDER

A person who constructs or builds real estate without having a definite purchaser or tenant under contract at the time construction begins. The builder begins the construction with the opinion that due to the location of the property, quality of construction, and/or general business conditions a purchaser or tenant will step forward prior to completion of the project. Speculative building is particularly common in the housing industry, especially during times of low interest rates and increases in the demand for housing. In contrast, a *contract builder* has entered into a contract with someone to build or construct a structure for them.

SPECULATOR

A person who acquires title or legal control of real estate with the belief that due to changing market conditions the property can be sold at a future date for more than what was initially invested. Such action is particularly common in viable real estate markets where cities or communities are growing rapidly and the direction of growth is toward a particular part of the city.

SPENDABLE INCOME

(*See* **After-Tax Cash Flow**)

SPILLOVER EFFECT

The economic impact felt by one parcel of land as a result of changes or modifications of other parcels. Such changes can be the result of both private and public expenditures. Consider, for example, the impact of building a freeway interchange next to a parcel of land, or the impact of an adjoining property owner developing a large shopping center. These modifications and the resulting spillover effect will in all likelihood change the highest and best use of the surrounding real estate. (*See* **Highest and Best Use**)

SPLIT COMMISSION

(*See* **Splitting Fees**)

SPLITTING FEES

The means by which a person shares compensation with one or more other persons. Generally, a licensed real estate broker can split a commission with any other licensed real estate broker or with any salesperson licensed on his or her behalf. Splitting fees with salespersons licensed through other brokers without going through the licensed broker is illegal, as is splitting a fee or making compensation to any unlicensed person for assisting in the transaction.

SPOT ZONING

A rezoning of a particular parcel of land to a zoning classification which is significantly different from the adjoining properties. Generally, spot zoning involves a relatively small parcel of land. Such action has normally not been favored by the courts unless it can be shown that such action is in line with the general comprehensive master plan of the jurisdiction. (*See* **Zoning**)

SPREADING AGREEMENT

An agreement by a *mortgagor* (borrower) to place additional property under the provisions of an existing mortgage. The purpose of such action is to give the *mortgagee* (lender) additional security for a loan. (*See* **Mortgage**)

SQUARE-FOOT METHOD

A technique used to estimate the total cost of construction in which the total number of square feet to be constructed is multiplied by a cost per square foot figure to derive total cost. Builders and architects have some idea as to what a particular type of construction will cost on a square-foot basis, given the quality of construction desired, the type of materials to be used, and the manner in which construction will take place. By having a cost per square foot available to them, the estimate of total construction cost is obtainable. (*See* **Cost Approach**)

SQUATTER

A person who is occupying the land of another without legal title or authority to do so. (*See* **Squatter's Right**)

SQUATTER'S RIGHT

The legal right of a person who is in adverse possession of the land belonging to another. Such a person is referred to as a *squatter* and may under certain conditions acquire legal title to the land through the open, actual, notorious, and continuous use of the land. (*See* **Adverse Possession**)

SRA

An appraisal designation denoting *Senior Residential Appraiser (SRA)*, awarded by the Society of Real Estate Appraisers. Membership is intended for professionals who specialize in the appraisal of residential properties including single family-homes, condominiums, townhouses, and multi-family structures up to four units. (*See* **Society of Real Estate Appraisers**)

SREA

An appraisal designation denoting *Senior Real Estate Analyst (SREA)* awarded by the Society of Real Estate Appraisers. An SREA is an SRA or SRPA whose practice has expanded to encompass all forms of appraisal assignments as well as analytical assignments such as market feasibility studies. (*See* **Society of Real Estate Appraisers**)

SRPA

An appraisal designation denoting *Senior Real Property Appraiser (SRPA)*, awarded by the Society of Real Estate Appraisers. Membership consists of those professionals who have expanded their appraisal practice to include the appraisal of income-producing properties. (*See* **Society of Real Estate Appraisers**)

SRS

A real estate designation denoting *Specialist in Real Estate Securities*. The SRS designation is awarded by the Real Estate Securities and Syndication Institute (RESSI), an affiliate of the National Association of Realtors.

SR/WA

A designation denoting *Senior Right of Way Agent*. The designation is awarded by the International Right of Way Association.

STAKING

A means by which the geographic boundaries of a parcel of land are identified by placing stakes in the ground at the boundary points. (*See* **Survey**)

STAMP TAX

The dollar cost of stamps which in some jurisdictions are required to be affixed to certain legal documents such as deeds prior to recordation in the land records. (*See* **Documentary Stamp**)

STANDBY COMMITMENT

An agreement between a real estate lender and a builder whereby the lender stands ready to make a certain loan amount available to the builder for a specified period of time. Normally, a fee for making such a commitment is charged by the lender to compensate the lender for the risk and legal liability in committing funds to the builder. Normally, the fee is forfeited if the funds are not borrowed.

STARTER HOME

The first home purchased by someone.

STATEMENT OF RECORD

A written document that must be filed with the *Department of Housing and Urban Development (HUD)* by a developer of 50 or more lots who intends to market the lots through any means of interstate commerce. Registration is required under the *Interstate Land Sales Full Disclosure Act*. In addition, certain disclosure must be made to prospective purchasers. Violation of the act may lead to fine or imprisonment.

STATUTE

A law enacted either by Congress (federal statute) or by a state government (state statute).

STATUTE OF FRAUDS

A state law which requires that certain contracts must be in writing and contain certain essential elements in order to be enforceable. A statute of frauds has been adopted in some form by every state. The original statute of frauds was passed by the British Parliament in 1677 in order to prevent fraud and perjuries. Certain types of transactions are so important to human activities that many people have incentive to lie, or these transactions are for such a long period that people forget. In order for courts to enforce these categories of contracts a sufficient memorandum must be present. The statute applies only to executory oral agreements. Fully executed contracts are not within the statute. Where there has been performance on one side which would lead to injustice or fraud if the other side did not perform, the courts may nevertheless compel performance. While the provisions of the statute of frauds differ somewhat from state to state, the following three types of contracts are important from the viewpoint of real estate transactions:

1. *Contracts for the sale of an interest in land.* Ordinarily, contracts involving land sales, leases, mineral rights, air rights, easements, and similar rights must be in writing. In some states oral contracts for leases of a certain duration are enforceable. Where there has been partial performance in a real estate sales agreement, the courts will ordinarily enforce an oral contract where the purchaser has gone into possession, paid part of the purchase price and made improvements to the property.

2. *Contracts which cannot be performed within one year.* A contract for a lifetime employment would be enforceable in most states because the employee could conceivably die within one year. Some states, however, include lifetime contracts specifically within their statutes of frauds.

Example: Neil orally agrees on December 1, 1989, to lease his farm to Bonnie on December 15, 1990, for the period of thirty days. This contract is not enforceable because, although the lease is for only thirty days, the commencement of the lease is more than one year away.

3. *Contracts for the sale of goods in excess of a statutory amount, typically $500.* This provision does not, however, apply to contracts for services even if the service involves providing materials worth more than the statutory amount.

Example: Dick orally agrees to build a house on Dudley's land for $70,000. This oral agreement is enforceable since it is for services rather than for the sale of goods.

In order to satisfy the statute of frauds, a writing or memorandum must contain the following essential elements:

1. Identity of the contracting parties
2. Description of the subject matter
3. The terms and conditions of the contract
4. The consideration
5. The signature of the party to be charged or an authorized agent. Some states may require both parties to sign the contract in order for it to be enforceable. (*See* **Contracts**)

STATUTE OF LIMITATIONS

The period of time limited by statute within which certain court actions may be brought by one party against another. The period of time varies from state to state as well as between the various types of action.

STATUTORY FORECLOSURE

(*See* **Foreclosure**)

STATUTORY LIEN

A lien created by legislation establishing the requirements that must be fulfilled before the lien may be levied. (*See* **Lien**)

STATUTORY PERIOD OF REDEMPTION

A statutory period of time enacted in some states in which the borrower (mortgagor) can redeem the property after foreclosure by paying the outstanding debt, interest, and legal fees. The statutory periods that exist usually extend from six months to two years and should not be confused with *equity of redemption*, which is the legal right of the mortgagor to redeem the property up to the time of foreclosure. While a statutory period of redemption is recognized in only a few states, equity of redemption is recognized in every state. (*See* **Foreclosure**)

STAYING POWER

The financial wherewithal to survive less than favorable economic conditions.

STEERING

The illegal practice of channeling prospective home purchasers or renters into homogeneous neighborhoods and actively directing them away from neighborhoods of different racial or ethnic composition. For example, if a real estate broker intentionally fails to make a house available to a prospect because of the prospect's race, sex, religion, color, national origin, handicap, or because there are children in a family, the broker is in violation of the law and may be found guilty of steering. The prospect, not the person showing the property, is entitled to choose which neighborhoods are suitable. (*See* **Federal Fair Housing Act of 1968**)

STEP-UP LEASE

A lease agreement which provides for periodic increases in the rental payment during the term of the lease. For example, in a five-year step-up lease, the rental may be $1,000 per month for the first two years, $1,200 for the next two years and $1,400 for the last year. The rentals can be gross or net payments as agreed to by the landlord (lessor) and tenant (lessee). Step-up leases are also known as *graduated leases*. (*See* **Lease**)

STRAIGHT-LINE METHOD OF DEPRECIATION

A method of computing depreciation for income tax purposes in which the difference between the original cost and the salvage value is deducted in even installments over the depreciable life of the asset. For example, if original cost is $150,000 and the salvage value is $30,000, then the depreciable basis ($150,000-$30,000) when divided by the estimated useful life, for example 20 years, would give an annual straight-line depreciation of $6,000.

STRAIGHT TERM MORTGAGE

(*See* **Term Mortgage**)

STRAW MAN

Someone who purchases property on behalf of another so as to conceal the identity of the true owner. A person who purchases on behalf of another is sometimes referred to as a *nominee.*

STREET ADDRESS

An easy and quick way of identifying a parcel of land. To have mail delivered or to find a house that has been advertised being "For Sale" normally require no more exact legal description than this method. However, this is not a formal method since it does not identify the exact boundaries of the subject land, nor does it indicate the quantity of land being described. This method should only be used to give the location of the land rather than as a precise legal description. In addition to being an informal method, street names and addresses can be unclear or confusing, particularly in large urban areas. "House For Sale--1520 Washington." Is that the house on Washington Avenue or the one on Washington Street? Is that 1520 North Washington or 1520 South Washington? Furthermore, streets are sometimes renamed and renumbered. This method is best used as an additional means of locating property. For example, the wording "____ and more commonly known as 1738 Aberdeen Road," or "____ the improvements being known as No. 1149 Kirkland Avenue" often appear in a sales contract or deed following the use of a more formal method. (*See* **Legal Description**)

STRICT FORECLOSURE

A type of mortgage foreclosure in which the mortgagee (lender) acquires all of the legal interest in the property without having to sell the property. This kind of foreclosure is not favored in this country because the mortgagor (borrower) loses all equity invested in the property. Most states have *foreclosure by sale* in which the pledged property is sold at public auction with the proceeds used to pay off the debt and any remainder being returned to the mortgagor after a deduction of costs. (*See* **Foreclosure**)

STRIP CENTER

A commercial/retail use of land characterized by adjoining buildings that are narrow in depth relative to their length. Neighborhood shopping centers normally take the form of a strip center. Such centers often have a grocery store or a retail discount center as the anchor (main) tenant as well as other retail outlets such as a drug store, shoe store, beauty salon, etc.

SUBAGENT

A person appointed by an agent to assist the agent in performing some or all of the tasks of the agency. In real estate brokerage transactions, a subagency relationship is often created through a multiple listing service where there are two brokers involved. First, there is the broker who has signed an agreement with the seller to list the property. The seller has agreed to pay a commission to the broker if the property sells. This broker is referred to as the *listing broker* and is clearly working as an agent for the seller. Secondly, there is the broker who may have been showing a buyer various properties in the community. Usually a buyer has approached this broker and asked to be shown properties for sale in the market. In most cases there has been no agreement between the second broker and the would-be buyer to pay a fee or commission. The normal assumption is that this broker, also known as the *selling broker*, will be paid by the seller. If the buyer had agreed to pay a fee, then the broker would be known as a *buyer's broker* and would, therefore, be an agent for the buyer. However, since the seller is paying the fee, the selling broker does not work for the buyer. He or she is, in fact, a subagent of the seller. (*See* **Agency**)

SUBCHAPTER S CORPORATION

A small business corporation that has elected to be treated for income tax purposes as a partnership and, thus, can avoid the liability of double taxation incurred by a corporate form of ownership.

SUBCONTRACTOR

A person employed by the prime or general contractor to carry out part of a contractual agreement as in the construction of a building. Examples would include electricians, plumbers, painters, and carpenters who are paid by the general contractor to complete the various components of the finished product.

SUBDIVIDE

To divide or separate into smaller parcels such as dividing a large tract of unimproved land into lots suitable for building. (*See* **Subdivision**)

SUBDIVIDER

A landowner or developer who divides a tract or parcel of land into smaller parcels for the purpose of making the smaller tracts available for development. The subdivider may do nothing but plat the tracts and provide minimum amenities or improvements such as roads and sewer, or he may ready the lots for development and then actually construct the improvements on the lots. (*See* **Subdivision**)

SUBDIVISION

A parcel of land that has been divided into two or more smaller lots. An example would include a 500-acre tract that has been platted and made ready for the building of homes. The subdivision has been recorded in the land records of the county where the land is located and is available for individuals to purchase the lots and or builders to purchase the lots and in turn construct houses on the lots.

SUBDIVISION REGULATION(S)

A local ordinance that establishes various minimum standards that must be met before a subdivision will be approved for development. These standards relate to the size of lots, width of the streets, curbing, lighting, drainage, and other improvements. If a developer wishes to turn the streets and public areas over to the local government for it to maintain, minimum construction-quality standards must be met before the local government will accept responsibility.

SUBJECT TO MORTGAGE

A real estate transaction in which the grantee (purchaser) takes over the existing mortgage payments from the grantor (seller) but assumes no personal liability on the mortgage. When a mortgage is taken *subject to*, the purchaser can walk away from the mortgage and lose nothing but the equity already invested. If, however, the purchaser *assumes* the mortgage, he or she becomes personally liable on any deficiencies occurring in a foreclosure sale. In both situations the original borrower is liable to the lender unless specifically released in a *novation*. (*See* **Mortgage**)

SUBLEASE

A lease agreement in which the lessee (tenant) transfers some of the interest in the leased property to a third party (sublessee) but retains some reversionary interest for himself or herself. In a sublease the sublessor has a *sandwich lease* and no direct legal relationship is created between the landlord and the sublessee. A sublease is really an estate within an estate. The lessee becomes a sublessor and a landlord-tenant relationship is established between the sublessor and the sublessee. Since the sublessor can only convey the rights which he or she has, the sublessee is effectively bound by any limitations in the main or underlying lease. The sublessor remains primarily liable to the landlord for rent and the performance of all covenants. (*See* **Assignment, Lease**)

SUBLESSEE

The tenant under a sublease who has subleased from someone who in turn is a lessee (tenant) of the owner of the property. (*See* **Sublease**)

SUBLESSOR

A lessee (tenant) who leases part of his or her interest to a third party (sublessee) but retains some interest in the property. (*See* **Sublease**)

SUBMARGINAL LAND

Land that because of location, topography, or some other defect is economically not viable for development. (*See* **Situs**)

SUBMORTGAGE

A situation in which a mortgagee (lender) borrows money from a third party and pledges a mortgage he or she is holding as security for the borrowed funds. (*See* **Mortgage**)

SUBORDINATION CLAUSE

A clause which may be included in a mortgage agreement in which the mortgagee (lender) agrees to permit a later-acquired mortgage to have legal priority. Such a clause is often included in a *purchase money mortgage* used in the acquisition of acreage property requiring a later construction or development loan. For example, a developer agrees to purchase 500 acres from a landowner for $100,000 down and a purchase money mortgage (owner financing) of $2,000,000 for the remainder of the purchase price. The developer may have paid a slightly higher price to induce the landowner to *subordinate* his legal position to an $8,000,000 loan secured by a mortgage being issued by a commercial bank. Thus, the commercial bank is in a first lien position and the landowner is in a junior (second) mortgage position. (*See* **Mortgage**)

SUBORDINATED GROUND LEASE

A land (ground) lease in which the rent payment due from the lessee to the lessor is subordinated to the debt service owed by the lessee to the mortgagee (lender). Normally, a ground lease contains such a clause in that without such a clause it may be more difficult to construct improvements on the land. A lender, without a subordination agreement by the lessor of the land, will only consider the value of the leasehold in making the loan, while with a subordinated ground lease the lender will consider the full value of the property. (*See* **Ground Lease**)

SUBROGATION

The substitution of one person into another person's legal position in reference to a third person. For example, insurance companies commonly include a subrogation clause which means that in case of an actual loss, this clause prevents the insured from collecting both from the insurance company and from the third party who actually caused the damage. When the insurance company pays the insured, any rights the insured may have to sue the party at fault will be assigned to the insurance company. The insurance company may then, if it so chooses, take legal action against the third party to collect what was paid to the insured.

SUBSCRIPTION AND PURCHASE AGREEMENT

The sales contract used in the sale of a condominium unit which must contain all of the elements of a real estate contract. Many states provide for a ten to fifteen day *cooling off period* which allows a purchaser to change his or her mind and rescind the purchase agreement. (*See* **Condominium**)

SUBSIDIZED HOUSING

A grant of money or credit to a tenant for the purpose of making housing available to that person who otherwise would not be able to financially afford the rental payment. The payment may go directly to the landlord and may include all or a portion of the market rent of the property.

SUBSTANDARD HOUSING

Housing that due to physical defects does not meet current housing codes. (*See* **Housing Code**)

SUBSTITUTION, PRINCIPLE OF

An economic principle which states that the maximum value of a parcel of real estate is set by the cost of acquiring an equally desirable substitute. For example, a house would not sell for $200,000 if equally desirable substitutes were available with no costly delay for $150,000. (*See* **Value**)

SUBSURFACE EASEMENT

The permission granted by a landowner to allow someone else to make use of below-ground space. Example would include such things as the laying of a gas line, digging of tunnels, or addition of a sewer line. (*See* **Easement**)

SUBURB

A developed area located in close proximity to a central city. The suburb may serve as the residence of people working in the central city as well as an area that has employment opportunities within itself.

SUCCESSION

The legal transfer of a person's interest in real property under the laws of descent and distribution. If a person dies without a will (*intestate*) his or her real estate will pass directly to the person's heirs as defined by the state law in which the real estate is located, subject to the debts of the decedent. A court in the state where the decedent lived will appoint a person called an *administrator* to dispose of the property of the estate. The administrator will collect the assets of the estate, pay debts, and distribute the remainder. The administrator is usually required to put up a bond and may sell that real property which is necessary to pay off the estate's debts if the sale of personal property produces insufficient proceeds. The real estate remains charged with debts of the estate until the state's statute of limitations has expired. States have different rules as to who receives property of the decedent. For example, depending on the state, a wife might receive half the property, the same share as the children, a dower's share, or the entire property. (*See* **Testate**)

SUFFERANCE

The passive consent given to someone as a result of no action. (*See* **Tenancy at Sufferance**)

SUFFICIENT CONSIDERATION

The value which the law finds necessary in order to support the creation of a binding contract. (*See* **Consideration, Contract**)

SUIT

A court action to enforce a legal claim or right.

SUPERADEQUACY

A feature of a building which is not fully valued by the marketplace. For example, if a house had a marble sink with 24-karat gold faucets, the market would probably not add the cost of the sink and faucets to the value of the home. The sink would be referred to as a superadequacy. (*See* **Cost Approach, Value**)

SUPPORT DEED

A deed conveyed by a grantor to another person in consideration for an agreement to take care of the grantor for life.

SURETY BOND

A bond issued by a company guaranteeing the performance or action of someone such as a contractor or builder. Surety bonds involve three parties: (1) the principal, the individual or company on whose behalf the surety bond is issued; (2) the obligee, the owner person assured of performance; and (3) the surety, the company issuing the surety bond.

SURFACE RIGHT

The legal right to use or occupy the surface of land. The owner of land may convey the surface rights to someone else and retain the subsurface or mineral rights.

SURPLUS FUNDS

The money obtained at a foreclosure sale over and above the amount necessary to pay the outstanding liens against the property. (*See* **Foreclosure**)

SURRENDER

The giving back of an interest in an estate to the person who has the reversion or remainder interest. An example of surrender would be the giving up of the lease by the lessee (tenant) to the lessor (landlord) prior to the expiration of the leasing term. In the case of a lease, surrender by the lessee and acceptance by the lessor terminates the lease either by mutual agreement or by operation of law. Surrender and acceptance occurs by mutual agreement if the lessee offers to terminate the lease, which is the surrender, and the lessor agrees to the offer, which is the acceptance. Surrender is distinguished from mere *abandonment*. A lessee may not just walk away from a lease and hope to escape legal liability. A lessor does not show acceptance by entering on the realty in order to protect it after abandonment. The landlord may attempt to lease the property for the best terms that he or she can get in order to *mitigate* (minimize) damages, and to sue the breaching lessee for the actual injury suffered. Surrender and acceptance, however, will occur by operation of law if the landlord takes unqualified possession of the property and gives a new lease without reservation.

SURVEY

The process by which the precise physical boundaries of a parcel of land are measured. Legal descriptions appear in listing agreements, sales contracts, deeds, mortgages, notes, and other instruments involving rights and interests in real estate. When land is conveyed from one party to another, the instrument of conveyance needs to contain a *legally sufficient description* of the parcel. Courts have interpreted this to mean that property is sufficiently described if a competent civil engineer or surveyor could locate the subject property given the land description.

SURVEYOR

A person sufficiently trained to locate and record the exact physical boundaries of a parcel of land. When property is conveyed from one party to another it is important to identify positively the exact boundaries of the property so that there is no doubt where the property lies in relation to all other parcels. To accomplish this task a survey is made. A surveyor physically inspects and measures the property. The precise measurements are included in the deed used to transfer ownership of the property.

SURVIVORSHIP

The living of one or more persons after the death of another person(s). In real estate ownership survivorship occurs when one or more owners in a joint tenancy or one of the parties in a tenancy by the entirety survives or outlives the deceased tenant(s). (*See* **Joint Tenancy, Right of Survivorship, Tenancy by the Entirety**)

SUSPENSION

A temporary stop or forced inactivity against someone. In the real estate brokerage business, a real estate commission has the power to suspend the license of a broker or salesperson. During the time of suspension, the suspended licensee is legally barred from performing any of the activities or services which require a real estate license. (*See* **Real Estate Commission**)

SWEAT EQUITY

A contribution to the value of real estate in the form of labor provided or services rendered. Sweat equity is normally associated with someone who purchases property that needs work, perhaps is below acceptable building code standards and normally has a market value below that of property that is not in disrepair. The purchaser, by performing some of the repair work personally, can increase the value and in turn, the marketability of the property, and is thus contributing sweat equity to the property.

SWEETENER

Something added to a deal to make it more attractive to an investor or lender. A lender making a commercial loan may require the developer/owner to pledge a certain part of the income generated by the project as partial payment to the lender over and above the debt service. The income generated by the sweetener serves to increase the lender's rate of return.

SWING LOAN

A loan, normally short term, used by an owner to purchase real estate pending the sale of another property. Normally, the loan is repaid from the owner's equity if and when the previous property sells.

SYNDICATION

An arrangement by which two or more people are assembled for the purpose of raising equity capital for purchasing real estate or other types of investments. Normally, the more desirable income-producing properties available are too expensive for the average investor to purchase alone. Therefore, in order to purchase such properties, it is common for investors to combine their resources and establish some form of multiple ownership arrangement such as a corporation, cooperative, condominium, tenancy in common, or partnership. Individuals who establish and sell shares in these ownership arrangements are called *syndicators*. The syndications formed by these individuals are usually classified as *securities* by federal law.

SYNDICATOR

A person who establishes and sells shares in a *syndication*. (*See* **Syndication**)

TACKING

A legal doctrine that allows a person who is in adverse possession of property belonging to another to add or "tack" his or her time of possession on to previous adverse possessors so as to establish the statutory time needed to claim title to the property through adverse possession. The term is also used to explain the action of a third mortgage holder who acquires the first mortgage on the property and adds or "tacks" the third mortgage amount to the first mortgage, and thus, has a superior lien position to the existing second mortgage holder. (*See* **Adverse Possession, Mortgage**)

TAKE BACK A MORTGAGE

Action by the seller of property to provide some or all of the permanent financing for the sold property by "taking back a mortgage" against the property. (*See* **Purchase Money Mortgage**)

TAKEDOWN

The receiving of funds by a borrower such as a developer or builder against a line of credit or construction loan secured from a lender. Normally, the full amount to be loaned under a construction loan is committed by the lender, but the actual disbursement is dependent upon the progress of the construction. Thus, as the project is completed, the developer/builder "takes down" part of the loan commitment. (*See* **Construction Loan**)

TAKEOUT COMMITMENT

An agreement by a permanent lender to provide the permanent financing for a real estate project when a certain event occurs, normally the completion of the project. Since construction loans are considered high risk loans, a construction lender often requires a standby or takeout commitment from a permanent lender. In turn, the permanent lender may require a certain percentage of the project to be preleased before the permanent financing is provided. The takeout commitment assures the construction lender that permanent financing will be available to repay the construction loan if the project is completed and other conditions are met. (*See* **Construction Loan**)

TAKING

To acquire or receive property. For example, under the power of *eminent domain* land may be acquired by a public agency, such as the city or state, from a private owner. (*See* **Eminent Domain**)

TANDEM PLAN

A special mortgage assistance program of the *Government National Mortgage Association (GNMA)*, by which it purchases high-risk, low-yield mortgages at current market-yield rates. In turn, these mortgages are sold, quite often to the *Federal National Mortgage Association (Fannie Mae)*, and the difference in the cost of purchasing the loans and the yield as a result of selling them is absorbed by the agency as a subsidy for the housing industry. (*See* **Federal National Mortgage Association, Government National Mortgage Association**)

TANGIBLE PROPERTY

Objects and other physical things which may be either real or personal property. (*See* **Personal Property, Real Property**)

TAXABLE VALUE

(*See* **Assessed Value**)

TAXATION

The right of government to require contribution from citizens to pay for government services.

TAX BASE

The total tax-assessed value of all the real property in a particular taxing jurisdiction. (*See* **Property Tax**)

TAX BRACKET

The rate or percentage on which a taxpayer pays taxes on income above a certain amount. Normally, the tax brackets differ for individuals as income changes whereas the rate applied to corporations may be constant regardless of changes in income.

TAX CERTIFICATE

A document given to the purchaser of property at a tax sale (auction) which entitles the holder of the certificate to a *tax deed* at the end of the statutory tax redemption period. (*See* **Tax Deed**)

TAX DEED

A deed issued by a government acting as grantor when property is sold to satisfy delinquent taxes. After an owner's property is sold at public auction, he or she normally has a statutory period of time in which to pay the delinquent property taxes and interest and reclaim title to the property. (*See* **Tax Lien**)

TAX-EXEMPT PROPERTY

Real estate that is not subject to assessment for property tax purposes due to the way in which it is being currently used or due to who owns the property. Property used for educational, charitable, or religious purposes is normally exempt from property taxes.

TAX-FREE EXCHANGE

A legal method of deferring capital gains taxes by exchanging one qualified property for another qualified property. When real estate for investment or for production of income is exchanged for *like-kind property*, a tax-free exchange can take place. Generally, exchanges of real estate for other real estate meets the like-kind test, but any additional property included is called *boot* and is subject to taxation. Examples of boot include cash, mortgages or other liabilities assumed by one of the parties for the other, or any other property such as machinery or art objects. Where a tax-free exchange takes place, the adjusted basis of each property follows the taxpayer. For example, assume that John owns Springdale with an adjusted basis of $50,000 and Ann owns Valleyview with an adjusted basis of $37,000. Assuming they exchange properties, what will John's basis in Valleyview be? Assuming no boot passes hands, John's basis will be $50,000 in Valleyview since in a tax-free exchange the basis follows the taxpayer, not the property. If there is boot, the gain of the party receiving the boot will be taxed to the extent of the booth received.

TAX LIEN

A lien imposed against real property by a governmental agency which may foreclose on the property for payment of the lien. For example, local governments have the right to assess and collect taxes on real property located within the taxing jurisdiction. A failure to pay these taxes can result in the levying of a tax lien which, in most states, is prior and senior to all other liens, even those which pre-existed the tax lien. If the lien is not satisfied within the time period specified at law, the taxed property may be sold at a tax sale. The defaulting taxpayer will be sent a tax sale notice advising of the impending sale. This gives the taxpayer an opportunity to appeal and state a defense or to pay the tax. If the tax is still not paid, the property will be put up for sale at a public sale.   The purchaser at auction will be given a *tax certificate* which will entitle the holder of the certificate a tax deed or a treasurer's deed at the end of the tax redemption period.   The tax redemption period is the time, usually two to seven years, that the defaulting taxpayer has to make good on the tax owed to the purchaser plus interest and legal fees.   The interest may run as high as 18 percent, although generally it is much lower, and is usually payable semi-annually.   Rules differ in each state.   If the property is not redeemed by the end of the redemption period, the holder of the certificate will be entitled to receive a quitclaim deed from the taxing jurisdiction. In some states this deed is considered to be very weak evidence of title, while in other states it is considered to be very acceptable evidence of title.   Instead of just taking such a deed, the holder of the certificate may wish to foreclose on the tax lien in a judicial proceeding to cut off all other claims on the property.   Where a city provides water and other utilities, a water charge or other charge may be levied on the property.   The legal effect, if the charge is not satisfied by the taxpayer, is the same as if it were a tax lien.

TAX MAP

A scaled drawing of the property in a taxing jurisdiction showing the exact location of property, dimensions, and the amount of the assessed value of each parcel of property within the taxing jurisdiction.

TAX RATE

The percentage or rate applied to the assessed value of property to determine the amount of tax due.   Tax rates vary from taxing jurisdiction to jurisdiction and are stated in one of two ways.   First, the rate may be stated in units of per one hundred of assessed value which in the case of a tax rate of $1.50 would mean the taxes due on the property would be $1.50 for each $100 of assessed value.   Second, the tax rate may be stated in terms of a *millage rate*.   A mill is one-tenth of one cent and, thus, a millage rate of 30 mills would mean a tax of $3.00 per $100 of assessed value.   (*See* **Property Tax**)

TAX ROLL

Public records that identify each parcel of land in the taxing jurisdiction, the owner of record, and the assessed value of each parcel for tax purposes.

TAX SALE

Action by a taxing jurisdiction to sell the property at public auction when taxes levied against the property have not been paid within a statutory period of time. (*See* **Tax Certificate, Tax Deed**)

TAX SHELTER

A means by which a taxpayer can legally shield or reduce income or gain from tax liability.   Certain real estate investments, in addition to cash flow, also have the ability to shelter income beyond the income generated by the project. A portion of income from an investment may be sheltered by artificial losses, whereas income from another investment may be tax free except for certain minimum tax requirements resulting from the investor's total tax situation.

Example: Assume an investor owns an apartment complex with annual net operating income of $720,500, interest of $480,000 and depreciation of $270,000. The result would be:

Net operating income	$720,500
- Interest	- 480,000
- Depreciation	- 270,000
Taxable income	($29,500)

Thus, in terms of this particular project, the taxable income is negative, specifically -$29,500. That does not mean the project is losing money, as the before-tax cash flow is still positive:

Net operating income	$720,500
- Debt service	- 587,296
Before-tax cash flow	$132,204

Rather, the income generated by this project has been sheltered.

TDR

(*See* **Transfer of Development Rights**)

TEASER RATE OF INTEREST

A relatively low and thus attractive rate of interest offered by a lender on an adjustable rate mortgage during the first few years of the loan.

TECHNI-COOP, INC.

An organization of existing federally assisted cooperatives. The mailing address is 1010 Washington Boulevard, Stamford, Connecticut 06901; (203)327-9605.

TENANCY

A tenant's legal interest in real property. A tenancy may be created either by title or by lease. Examples of tenancy by title include tenancy in common, joint tenancy, and tenancy by the entirety. Tenancies created by lease would include tenancy for years, tenancy from period to period, tenancy at will, and tenancy at sufferance.

TENANCY AT SUFFERANCE

A tenancy which is created when one is in wrongful possession of realty even though the original possession may have been legal. A tenant at sufferance is treated as a *licensee*. He or she is not a trespasser and the landlord has a duty not to injure that person. However, if the landlord accepts rent, this converts the tenancy to either a periodic tenancy or a tenancy at will, depending on the circumstances. A tenancy at sufferance may occur when a tenant holds over from an estate for years. Such a tenancy may also be created when a mortgagor continues to possess realty after foreclosure, or if a spouse of a deceased life tenant continues to occupy the property after the realty has passed to a remainderman. In some states advance notice is required to dispossess a tenant at sufferance if the original possession was legal. (*See* **Tenancy at Will**)

TENANCY AT WILL

The possession of real estate belonging to another with their permission for an indefinite period of time which can be terminated by either the lessor (owner) or lessee (tenant). Under common law, a tenancy at will was for an indefinite period which could be terminated by either the lessor or lessee at any time. No advance notice was required. Today, this has been modified by statute in most states. A tenant has no right to dispose of the leasehold, and the death of either will terminate the tenancy. In those agricultural leases which are tenancies at will, if the lease is terminated unexpectedly, the tenant may enter on the land after the expiration of the term to harvest the crops. This is referred to as recovering the *emblements*.

TENANCY BY THE ENTIRETY (ENTIRETIES)

A special form of joint tenancy, limited to husband and wife, which places all of the legal ownership of the tenancy into the marital unit. In addition to the four unities which are required for the creation of a joint tenancy, there must also be the *unity of person* which is created by the marriage contract. The property which is held in a tenancy by the entirety is owned as a whole by the husband and wife and not in undivided shares. There is no individual interest which may be conveyed, and the tenancy cannot be terminated without the consent of both. The public purpose for this form of concurrent ownership is to help preserve the assets of the family unit. Both parties must sign any conveyances in order to make them legally effective. If the husband and wife are divorced, the unity of person is broken, and the tenancy changes into a tenancy in common with each party having an undivided half interest. While the unity of person is intact, there can be no action for partition by one of the two parties. (*See* **Joint Tenancy**)

TENANCY FOR LIFE

An interest in land for either the life of the holder of the tenancy or for the life of someone else. (*See* **Life Estate**)

TENANCY FOR YEARS

The use or possession of land for a definite period of time. Such an interest is the most common type of leasehold in real estate and is unique in that it has a specified beginning and ending to the term. Although the leasehold is called an *estate for years*, it may in fact be for a shorter time. The term may be one month, one week, or even one day. In most states if the term is less than one year, it may be created by oral agreement. Some states permit leaseholds for less than three years to be created orally. During the term of this lease, a tenant has a right to possess, control, enjoy, and dispose of the property rights. If the tenant were to die during the term of the leasehold, the property interest would pass to the tenant's estate. If the tenant retains possession of the property after the expiration of the term, this is referred to as *holding over*. The landlord has the option to treat the holdover tenant as a trespasser and proceed to dispossess him or her from the property, or he may elect to treat the term of the lease as renewed, thereby converting the leasehold into a periodic tenancy, or in some states into a tenancy at will.

TENANCY FROM YEAR TO YEAR

A leasehold interest in the land of another where no definite term has been established, and the lease is automatically renewed for the same term unless one of the parties to the lease gives proper notice to the other party. This type of leasehold is also referred to as a periodic tenancy or an estate from period to period. If the lease term is for more than one year, the term upon renewal is considered by most states to be for one year.

Example: If Jan signs a lease for a five-year period with an automatic renewal provision, then at the end of the term, if Jan has failed to give proper notice to terminate the lease, the tenancy will automatically renew for an additional term of one year.

Where no term is specified, the manner and time that the rent is paid establishes the term by implication. For example, if the rent is paid quarterly, the implication is that the term is from quarter to quarter. What is proper notice to prevent renewal of the term? Ordinarily, this is specified by the lease itself, or where the lease is silent, by statute. Under common law, where a lease term was for less than one year, notice had to be given at least one period in advance. If the lease was for one year or more, six months' advance notice was considered sufficient. Despite notice, if the tenant held over by even one day past the expiration of the term, the courts under common law construed this as a renewal of the lease for another term. As with the estate for years, death of either the lessor or lessee does not terminate a periodic tenancy.

TENANCY IN COMMON

A form of concurrent ownership of real estate where two or more persons hold separate legal title in the same property through the *unity of possession*. This form of ownership is recognized in all states except for Louisiana, which recognizes a statutory estate with essentially the same legal effect. In a tenancy in common, each co-owner has an undivided fractional interest in the land and a right to use the whole property. No tenant may exclude a co-owner from any portion of the property. Each co-owner may own a different fractional interest. For example, Beth, Sally, and Janet may own Greenacres as tenants in common with Beth having a 60% interest, Sally a 30% interest, and Janet a 10% interest. Each co-owner may transfer his or her interest to a third party without the consent of the other co-owners. Upon death of one of the co-owners or co-tenants, that person's interest is passed on to his or her heirs or devisees. In those states that have dower or curtesy, these rights attach to the deceased co-tenant's interest. If there is any doubt what kind of co-ownership was intended, states today favor the creation of a tenancy in common unless the grantees are husband and wife. In the latter case, those states recognizing tenancy by the entirety would presume the co-ownership to be a tenancy by the entirety unless the deed or will specified otherwise.

TENANCY IN PARTNERSHIP

A form of multiple ownership in which the property is held in a lawful business venture. Under common law, a partnership was not considered to be an entity which could own property. Title was held in each of the partner's individual names. Most states have passed the *Uniform Partnership Act* which permits a partnership to own property in its own name. No individual partner owns a direct specified interest agreement. No partner may sell his or her partnership interest without consent of the other partners. If a partner dies or goes bankrupt, title to real property passes to the other partners who have a duty to pass the value of the partner's interest to the heirs or devisees of the deceased. A disadvantage of a general partnership is that each general partner is jointly and severally liable for the expenses and claims against the partnership. Unless care is taken by providing appropriate provisions to the contrary in the partnership agreement, the death or bankruptcy of one of the general partners will terminate the partnership. Further, many states apply a usury ceiling to the borrowings of the partnership.

One method whereby the problem of personal liability may be solved is by creating a *limited partnership*. A limited partnership consists of at least one general partner, who may under certain circumstances be a corporation, and at least one limited partner. A limited partner has no control over the day-to-day management of the partnership and is essentially a passive investor. The limited partner's liability is restricted only to the money which he or she has invested in the partnership.

TENANCY IN SEVERALTY

(*See* **Severalty**)

TENANT

One who holds or has the legal right to occupy the property belonging to someone else. The legal relationship established between a tenant and the owner of the land (landlord) is created by *lease*. A lease is an agreement by which a landlord (lessor) gives the right to the tenant (lessee) to use and to have exclusive possession but not ownership of the realty for a specified period of time in consideration for the payment of rent. The interest that the tenant has is a nonfreehold estate, also known as a *leasehold*. The landlord's interest is referred to as a *leased fee*. A leased fee interest includes both the right to receive the contract rent and the *reversion*, the right to repossession of the realty at the end of the term. A leasehold and leased fee are valuable property rights which may, under certain circumstances, be sold, assigned, or mortgaged. (*See* **Lease**)

TENANT CONTRIBUTION(S)

Expenditures made by the tenant over and above the contract rent in regard to the expenses of the property such as maintenance expenses.

TENANT'S FIXTURES

Items which have been attached to the leased property but which can be dismantled and taken away by the tenant during the term of the lease. (*See* **Fixture**)

TENANT'S RIGHT OF FIRST REFUSAL

The right of a tenant to purchase property from the owner in the event the owner decides to sell the property. Such a right is normally included in the lease agreement and, thus, allows the tenant to match any offer the owner may have from an interested third party. By having such a provision in the lease, the tenant is assured that he or she will at least be able to purchase the property rather than having someone else purchase it from the owner.

TENEMENT

The right of ownership of real estate held by a person.

TENEMENT HOUSE

A type of residential rental property characterized with minimum health and sanitary features and normally occupied by low-income families.

TERM

A fixed period of time, such as the term or length of a mortgage or lease.

TERM MORTGAGE (STRAIGHT TERM)

A method of borrowing money in which interest only with, no amortization of the principal, is paid during the time of the loan. At maturity, the entire original principal is due and payable. Prior to the Great Depression of the 1930s, the straight-term or term mortgage was the common means of financing residential real estate. Typically, term mortgages covered short periods of time (three to five years) and there was normally little intent by either the borrower to repay the principal or the lender to demand payment of the principal. The original amount borrowed was either extended for another term at an agreed upon interest rate or the borrower would negotiate with a new lender and pay off the old loan. However, as a result of financial conditions during the Depression and the *National Housing Act of 1934*, which among other things established the Federal Housing Administration, term mortgages became less popular. Borrowers during the Depression were unable to pay the principal when it became due. Because of the tightness in the money supply, lenders were unable to roll these loans over, and thus had to foreclose. Over a million families lost their homes during this time. The failure of the money market led to the creation of the Federal Housing Administration and increased usage of the amortized mortgage. Today, term mortgages are generally used only in the financing of land and construction.

TERMINATION OF AGENCY RELATIONSHIP

The end or conclusion of a principal-agent relationship. Normally a real estate broker is employed through a principal-agent relationship and, as such, the legal relationship established through the agency can be terminated in a number of ways. Among the ways in which the agency relationship can be terminated are the following:

Performance: An agency relationship will ordinarily be terminated when the purpose of the relationship has been completed. Thus, when a broker has been employed to sell a house, the agency would normally expire when the broker procured a qualified buyer. In an open listing where several brokers are employed, the agency relationships and authority of all brokers are extinguished when one of the brokers finds a buyer who signs a contract or if the owner sells the property.

Mutual agreement: Both parties may agree to rescind the agency contract.

Discharge: An agency relationship may be terminated at any time by the principal unless it is an agency coupled with an interest. The broker's only recourse for a wrongful termination is to sue for breach of contract. This rule is true even if the parties had agreed that the agency would be irrevocable for a specific period of time. In a case of wrongful discharge, the general rule is that the broker will only be entitled to recover for damages actually sustained, such as the cost of advertising and promoting the property. In some jurisdictions the measure of damages is the commission which might have been earned, but most jurisdictions will not award anything in excess of actual damages except as a punitive measure. In order to limit the damages, the discharge must be made in good faith. If a broker is discharged when a sale is imminent, the broker will be entitled to the full commission. Unilateral act of the principal or the principal's death may not terminate an agency coupled with an interest. This kind of agency occurs when a person is given powers to secure the performance of a duty owed or to protect some proprietary interest. It must be supported by consideration.

Example: Alan lends Ellwood $100,000 to help purchase twenty-five acres of lakefront property in the mountains. At the same time, Alan is given an exclusive right to sell lots which will be subdivided from the tract of land. Alan is also given a 20% equity interest in the development and is told that his loan will be repaid from the proceeds of the sales. In this case Alan has an agency coupled with an interest. His interest is both a debt and an equity interest in the subject matter of the agency.

Resignation: An agent may resign at any time. If the resignation is wrongful the agent will be liable for breach of contract. When the agent resigns he or she no longer has authority to bind the principal.

Abandonment: The agent may abandon the agency without explicitly resigning. Inactivity for a prolonged or unreasonably long period of time would suggest abandonment and thereby termination of the agent's authority.

Breach of agency duties: While not all breaches of an agency contract necessarily terminate an agency relationship, there are circumstances where the agent's authority is suspended or even terminated. Such breaches generally involve loyalty or fidelity. An unfaithful and disloyal agent cannot be acting with actual authority to bind the principal. A contract entered into for the principal would not be valid unless the agent is also exercising apparent authority in relation to innocent third parties.

Expiration of term: The agency relationship expires at the end of a specified term. If no term is specified, it expires at the end of a reasonable period.

Death of parties: Death of either the principal or agent automatically terminates the agency relationship. The reader is advised to beware of situations in which a complicated transaction is involved which includes a death of either the principal or agent without notice to parties to the transaction. The entire transaction may also be terminated. The exception to the rule of automatic termination is an agency coupled with an interest.

Insanity or bankruptcy: Insanity or bankruptcy of either party will automatically terminate the agency relationship as a general rule. In the former case the party would not have mental responsibility, whereas in the latter case the party would not have financial responsibility. It should be noted that the bankruptcy of the agent does not always terminate the relationship when the subject matter of the agency is in no way related to the agent's financial responsibility or if the parties established the relationship in contemplation of the agent's bankruptcy.

Change in law: Where the purpose or consideration of the agency contract becomes illegal because of a change in the law, the agency is terminated.

Destruction of the subject matter: If the subject matter of the agency is destroyed, the relationship is also terminated. For example, if a listed house burns down before a buyer is procured, the brokerage agency is terminated. However, it should be noted that if the broker's right to a commission was vested by the broker's having previously performed as stipulated in his employment contract, the agent would still be entitled to a commission even if the house had burned down before closing. This rule would not apply if the commission was contingent on the closing actually occurring.

Material change in circumstances: If the subject matter of the agency changes materially or is affected by a material change, the authority of the agent may be cancelled. For example, if after a property had been listed at a certain price, gold was discovered on the land causing the property value to change dramatically, this would be construed as a material change in circumstances. The authority of the broker to find a buyer at the listed price would be cancelled.

TERMITE CLAUSE

A provision appearing in most sales contracts obligating the seller to have the property inspected for termites or termite damages prior to the time title to the property is delivered and accepted. Normally, the seller is required to have some proof that property inspection has been made, such as a certificate of inspection from an approved termite company.

TERMITE INSPECTION

A physical inspection of a structure by a licensed person to determine whether the building and grounds are inhabited by termites or vermin. (*See* **Termite Clause**)

TESTATE

To die having left a will, in contrast to *intestate* which refers to having died without leaving a will. (*See* **Devise**)

TESTATOR

A person who has made a will. (*See* **Devise**)

TESTATRIX

A woman who has made a will. (*See* **Devise**)

TESTIMONIUM CLAUSE

A clause found in a deed or instrument of conveyance containing the execution, attestation, and acknowledgment of the deed. (*See* **Deed**)

TFTV

(*See* **Total Financing-to-Value Ratio**)

THIN EQUITY

A situation in which the total outstanding debt on a parcel of property just about equals the property's current market value. (*See* **Equity**)

THIRD MORTGAGE

A mortgage that has an inferior lien position to both a first mortgage and a second mortgage. Any mortgage against property that is not in a first lien position is often referred to as a junior mortgage, regardless of whether the mortgage is a second, third, or fourth mortgage. (*See* **Mortgage**)

THIRD PARTY

A person who may be affected by the terms of an agreement but who is not a party to the agreement.

THOMPSON, WILBUR R.

An urban economist who believed that the economy and success of a city can be measured by three factors: affluence, equity and stability. Thompson is the author of *Urban Economics*.

TIER

A row of townships running in an easterly and westerly direction and comprising a geographical area six miles wide. This measurement is used in the *rectangular survey method* of legal descriptions.

TIGHT MARKET

A market condition in which the demand for rental space equals or exceeds the current supply.

TIME IS OF THE ESSENCE (TIME IS THE ESSENCE OF CONTRACT)

A phrase often included in a contract that requires punctual performance of all obligations in the contract. If such a clause is included and the obligation(s) is not performed, the failure to perform is a breach of the contract. (*See* **Contract, Specific Performance**)

TIME-PRICE DIFFERENTIAL

A method by which the owner of property charges one price for an all-cash sale and a higher price if payments for the property are to be made over time through an installment sales agreement. The difference between the two prices is the time-price differential.

TIME SHARING

A form of condominium ownership in which the purchaser owns the property for a certain specified time interval. Time sharing has become very common in selling off ownership units in recreational properties. It involves a separation of individual units from common areas just like the conventional condominium regime. However, the time share adds an additional fragmentation. It allows an individual to own a certain specified time interval.

The attractiveness of the time-share unit depends on the location of the property, the level of amenities offered, and the season. Consider a family who wishes to take a vacation in the same location and at the same time each year. This family may find a time-share unit or *interval ownership* a very useful idea. A promoter usually divides the right to use a time-share unit into 52 weekly time intervals. A purchaser may buy as many time intervals as desired. Normally, the intervals are priced according to the season. For example, a time-share condominium in a ski resort may cost more for a week during the winter than during the summer. The purchaser will pay a fixed price for the time-share unit, which can be financed by the developer or a lender. In addition, there is usually an annual maintenance fee that is assessed for each time interval purchased. By purchasing such an interval, the owner will have the right to occupy the space for the same week each year for as long as the time share was purchased. Some time-share units are purchased in fee simple, and the right to use these units will continue indefinitely. In other instances, the purchaser buys a right to use for a set time period. Many rights to use last no longer than 25 years, after which time the property reverts back to the original developer. To make the time interval more attractive, some promoters have joined a vacation pooling arrangement with developers of other time-share projects. A purchaser in one project can decide to use a time interval in another project by paying a registration fee and making his or her time interval available for the use of someone else. For example, a person who owns a time-share interval in Hawaii may decide not to use the unit that year and instead use someone else's time interval in Paris, France or in Houston, Texas. (*See* **Condominium**)

TIME VALUE OF MONEY

A finance theory based on the idea that since money is normally assumed to earn interest, a dollar received today is considered to be more valuable or have more present value than a dollar received a year from today.

TIME ZERO

The beginning of the first period in a projected period of time. Time zero is necessary to properly and correctly undertake cash flow analysis for income-producing property.

TIMING AND SEQUENCING CONTROLS

A technique developed by local governments which limits the growth of a community to the capital improvements budget available to the local government. Such control is one of many designed by local governments to slow growth down or redirect growth to other communities. In recent years there has been a reluctance of local governments to accept growth for the sake of growth.

TITLE

The legally recognized evidence of a person's right to possess property. By being able to transfer title, real property gains economic value and permits land to be used efficiently as a factor of production. The ways in which title to real property is transferred may be classified as: (1) voluntary conveyance, by *deed*, (2) transfer by *devise* or *descent*, (3) transfer by *adverse possession*, (4) transfer by *accession*, and (5) transfer by *public action* or by *operation of law*. (*See* **Adverse Possession, Deed, Title Insurance**)

TITLE ABSTRACT

(*See* **Abstract of Title**)

TITLE COMPANY

A company which examines the public records to determine the marketability of an owner's title to real property. (*See* **Abstract of Title, Title Insurance**)

TITLE EXCEPTION

A section of a title insurance policy which lists all discovered defects and encumbrances against which the company will not insure the marketability of the title. This section of the title policy is sometimes referred to as *Schedule B*. If the noted defects are satisfactorily corrected by obtaining proper releases, the company may remove the exception from this schedule. (*See* **Title Insurance**)

TITLE INSURANCE

An insurance policy that protects the named insured against loss or damage due to defects in the property's title. This type of protection extends not only to negligent errors and omissions by the title examiner but also to hidden or unknown defects in title prior to the date of the title policy. In addition to indemnification of losses, the title insurance company also promises to pay the cost of defending a lawsuit brought about because of alleged defects in title insured by the policy. Title insurance involves the payment of a single premium at the time that the coverage is purchased. Premiums vary from company to company but usually range between $3.50 to $5.00 per $1,000 of coverage. This premium is in addition to the costs of the title examination itself. The protection is for the face amount of the policy or the insured's interest, whichever is the lesser sum. In general there are two types of title insurance policies: (1) the *owner's policy* and (2) the *mortgagee's policy*. Many lenders require a borrower to take out a title policy in favor of the lender at the time a loan is made for the principal amount of the loan. As the principal is amortized, the maximum coverage on the policy is also reduced. Even though the owner may pay the premium on the mortgagee's policy, in the event of loss due to a title defect, the owner's equity interest is not protected. In addition, after indemnification is made to the mortgagee, the insurance company, by right of subrogation, may be able to place a lien on the property unless the owner also has title insurance coverage with the same company. This coverage can be acquired under an owner's policy for a small additional premium which is paid at the same time the mortgagee's policy is purchased. This protection is personal to the named insured and subsequent heirs, and the policy is not transferable. The mortgagee's policy, however, may be transferred by assignment.

As with other contracts, care should be taken to read a title insurance policy to determine exactly what kind of coverage is being purchased. A title insurance policy is usually divisible into five sections, discussed below.

Agreement to Insure: The agreement to insure specifies what the title insurance company agrees to do in case of loss sustained due to defects in title. This agreement is entered into after the company has examined title and has satisfied itself that the risk of loss is minimal. The company is under no obligation to insure title which it deems to be uninsurable due to unexplained breaks in the chain or other serious clouds on title. After the search, the company issues a preliminary binder which indicates the company's willingness to insure subject to stated exceptions. These exceptions may be due to defects which can be cleared prior to issuing the final policy.

Description of the Subject Matter: This section describes the estate or interest being insured. For example, the policy may be issued to protect the interests of a lessee having a long-term leasehold which will be improved with a costly building. A sufficient legal description of the land is included plus identification of any improvements on the land. This section of the policy is sometimes referred to as Schedule A.

Exceptions: This section, sometimes referred to as *Schedule B*, lists all discovered defects and encumbrances against which the company will not insure. If these defects are satisfactorily corrected by obtaining proper releases, the company may remove the exception from this schedule. The process of removing defects is called perfecting title.   In addition, each policy contains standard exceptions. Included are any facts that a survey would disclose, rights of parties in possession, facts that physical inspection of the property would reveal, any unrecorded tax liens and special assessments, any unrecorded mechanic's liens, and any losses sustained by planned government action, such as zoning restrictions or actions taken pursuant to the power or eminent domain. Some of these exceptions may be left out by agreement of the insured and the insurer. For example, if the company is provided with a survey taken by a licensed surveyor, the company may broaden the coverage to include protection against encroachments or other such defects that a survey would be expected to reveal.

Conditions: This is a set of stipulations which must be met before the company is required to pay indemnification.   Conditions may include the right of the company to step in and defend a lawsuit and the requirement that they reach final adjudication. Another requirement may be the company's right of subrogation, a right to step into the legal position of the insured. Any waiver of a person's rights against those persons responsible for the loss by signing releases could damage the company's right to subrogation and acts as a defense against the company being required to pay indemnification.   Another condition might be the right of the company to take over the property at a fair appraised price if it pays out money exceeding a certain amount to cover a loss.

Endorsements: In addition to the standard coverage, an insured may wish to purchase additional coverage for an extra premium. The amount and cost of this additional coverage is subject to negotiation and agreement between the insurer and the insured. For example, a mortgagee may wish to have an endorsement which will extend coverage for any subsequent loss of priority of lien by any unrecorded mechanic's lien which is later properly filed.

TITLE REGISTRATION

(*See* **Torrens System of Title Registration**)

TITLE SEARCH

A physical examination of the public land records to determine the extent to which someone has legal interest in a parcel of land. The search is normally performed by someone experienced in searching title such as a title abstractor or a title insurance company. (*See* **Abstract of Title, Title Insurance**)

TITLE THEORY STATE

States in which a legal doctrine considers the mortgagee (lender) to actually have title to the mortgaged property, as opposed to merely having a lien, and the mortgagor to have equitable title in the property. Mortgages used in title theory states contain a *defeasance clause* which states that when a certain condition is met (repayment of the financial obligation), title will automatically pass back to the borrower. In contrast, most states are referred to as *lien theory states*. In lien theory states a mortgage merely creates a lien right in the mortgagee with the mortgagor retaining the title to the property. (*See* **Mortgage**)

TITLE UPDATE

A search of the land records immediately prior to the time of closing or settlement for the purpose of bringing up to date a previous title examination or search. In many instances a financial institution may have previously made a loan on a parcel of land at which time a title search was performed. If the current owner wants additional funds or if a new owner is attempting to finance the purchase, the lender may accept a title update rather than having a complete title search performed. (*See* **Abstract of Title**)

TO HAVE AND TO HOLD

(*See* **Habendum Clause**)

TOPO

Shortened form of the term *topography*.

TOPOGRAPHIC MAP

A map of a parcel of land showing the changes in elevation of a surface area through the use of contour lines.

TOPOGRAPHY

A description of the surface features of a parcel of land such as changes in elevation, height of mountains, and location of rivers.

TORRENS SYSTEM OF TITLE REGISTRATION

A legal system recognized in some jurisdictions in which title to land is registered. The system, named after Sir Robert Torrens, who developed the system in Australia in 1857, operates parallel to the more conventional system of title transfer and recordation. The Torrens System is very similar to the system of registering automobile titles, in that the person who owns title to land registers the title and the title is represented by a certificate of registration called a *Torrens Certificate*. For any liens or encumbrances to have validity, they must appear on an original certificate of title kept by the registrar of titles in the jurisdiction. In states that recognize the Torrens System, a property owner initially has the option to record title conventionally or to register title under the Torrens System. Once the option is taken to register the title, only a court order can remove the title from registration. All subsequent transfers and other dealings involving the title must take place through the registrar's office, or the transaction will have no validity against innocent third parties. Under the Torrens System, title does not pass until it is properly registered and a new original certificate issued to replace the cancelled old one; thus, a deed is not effective in passing title when it is delivered and accepted as it is under the conventional system. Once title is registered, all prior liens are cancelled and all title defects removed. Title becomes absolute in the name of the registered owner. Because of this serious legal consequence, each state has developed an elaborate procedure for the initial title registration. (*See* **Abstract of Title, Title Insurance**)

TORT

A civil wrong for which the law allows an injured party to recover damages from a wrongdoer.

TOTAL FINANCING-TO-VALUE RATIO

The sum of the outstanding balance of the first mortgage and the original amount of the second mortgage divided by the current market value of the property.

TOWN HOUSE

A type of dwelling normally consisting of two or more floors and connected to an adjoining unit by a common wall. Quite often the legal form of ownership of such a unit is a condominium in which the owner of the town house has fee simple title to the space under roof and has interest in the land and outside area through a tenancy in common form of ownership with the other town house owners. (*See* **Condominium**)

TOWNSHIP

A physical division of land used in the *government (rectangular) survey method* of land description. A township is a 6-by-6 mile area containing 36 sections, each section equal to 1 mile square. (*See* **Government Survey Method**)

TRACK RECORD

The results or outcome of a investment indicator or developer's previous undertakings or projects. Potential investors as well as lenders often look to past projects as an indication of the person's ability to make the projected undertaking a success.

TRACT

An area of land. The term, while it may apply to any amount of space, is normally used to refer to a large geographic area.

TRACT HOUSE(S)

A house or group of houses produced in mass and situated along a street or road one next to the other. The term became popular in the 1950s when national builders constructed houses in mass similar in size, design, and price, and developed large subdivisions of such homes.

TRACT INDEX

A means by which records of title to land are indexed in the public records. Under a tract index a separate page is kept for each tract of land in a particular jurisdiction. All instruments involving a particular tract are indexed on the page for that tract. Another method of indexing, referred to as the grantor-grantee or cross index, has two sets of indexes, one for each party to an instrument. These indexes are kept in alphabetical order for each year. Because each jurisdiction has its own peculiarities in keeping and indexing records, the job of title examination is often left to professionals who are called *title examiners* or *abstractors*. (*See* **Abstract of Title**)

TRADE AREA

A defined geographic area from which a particular business attracts the majority of its customers. The potential trade area of a certain location is of importance to a real estate developer/lessor who is attempting to put together a particular type of shopping or retail outlet and needs to know from where customers will be attracted.

TRADE FIXTURE(S)

Personal property used in a business venture which has been attached or annexed to the real property by the lessee (tenant). Trade fixtures are removable by the tenant prior to the expiration of the lease term or a reasonable time thereafter. If not removed, these items become property of the lessor (landlord). (*See* **Fixture**)

TRADING ON THE EQUITY

A means of increasing the rate of return on an owner's equity by borrowing part or all of the purchase price at a rate of interest less than the expected rate of return generated on the net income of the property. (*See* **Leverage**)

TRAFFIC COUNT

The number of vehicles or people moving past a particular location during a specific period of time. Traffic counts are used in conjunction with market feasibility studies in determining the likelihood that a particular location for some land use will have enough traffic to make the project successful.

TRAILER PARK

(*See* **Mobile Home Park**)

TRANSFERABILITY

One of the elements necessary for real estate or any economic good to have value. Transferability is the ability to transfer legal rights to real estate. If legal rights could not be transferred from one person to another, no value could result. (*See* **Value**)

TRANSFER OF DEVELOPMENT RIGHTS (TDR)

A method of regulating the use that can be made of land by allowing the owner to transfer certain rights that he or she has in a particular parcel to other land and, thus, enhancing or increasing the use to which the second parcel can be put.

TRANSFER OF TITLE

The conveyance of the legal right to land from one party to another. (*See* **Title**)

TRANSFER TAX

A charge levied against the legal transfer of land that must be paid prior to the title being recorded in the public land records. Prior to January 1, 1968, there was a requirement for U.S. revenue stamps on deeds at the rate of $55 per $500. Since the end of this requirement, some states have passed their own requirements for revenue stamps and transfer taxes.

TRESPASS

Illegal or wrongful entry upon the property belonging to someone else.

TRIPLE A TENANT

(*See* **AAA Tenant**)

TRIPLE NET LEASE

A net, net, net lease which means that in addition to normal rent, the lessee (tenant) is paying certain expenses associated with the on-going operation of the property. Such expenses would normally include property taxes, insurance, and maintenance. (*See* **Net Lease**)

TRIPLEX

A building consisting of three separate units and designed to be occupied by three different households. Most legislation intended to protect consumers is often referred to as "including one- to four-unit residential property." Such wording would include triplex units as well as duplexes and quadriplexes.

TRUST

A legal relationship under which title to property is transferred to a person known as a *trustee* who has control over the property and must manage it for another person known as a *beneficiary*. (*See* **Beneficiary, Deed of Trust, Trustee**)

TRUST DEED
(See **Deed of Trust***)*

TRUSTEE
A person who holds title and control over property for another person known as a *beneficiary*. A state's trust deed act specifies who may act as a trustee. Some states have created the office of public trustee, while others allow individuals, such as attorneys or brokers, or entities, such as title insurance companies or savings and loan associations, to serve in that capacity. *(See* **Deed of Trust***)*

TRUSTEE'S DEED
A conveyance of property by a trustee of property under his or her trust.

TRUSTEE'S SALE
A sale conducted by a trustee once a default of a deed of trust has occurred foreclosing the borrower's interest in the property. *(See* **Foreclosure***)*

TRUST FUND
Money or anything of value received by a real estate broker to be held in escrow. Licensing law requires a real estate broker to establish an escrow account to be used for holding all funds entrusted to him or her by any party with whom the broker is dealing. As an example, when someone makes an offer on property, the offer normally includes a cash (check) deposit which, if the offer is accepted by the owner, will be placed in the broker's trust fund where it will remain until either closing occurs or some other event occurs which would require the broker to dispense of the deposit. A real estate broker is in violation of state licensing law if he or she *commingles* monies being held in a trust account with his or her personal account.

TRUSTOR
The person who creates a trust and gives the instructions to the trustee. *(See* **Beneficiary, Deed of Trust, Trust***)*

TRUTH-IN-LENDING ACT (REGULATION Z)
The common name given to the *National Consumer Credit Protection Act* which became law July 1, 1969. Regulation Z, published by the Federal Reserve System to implement this law, requires lenders to make meaningful credit disclosures to individual borrowers for certain types of consumer loans. The regulation also applies to all advertising seeking to promote credit. This advertising is required to include specific credit information. Consumers are given information on credit costs both in total dollar amounts and in percentage terms. The intent of Congress was to assist consumers (residential, non-investment customers) with their credit decisions by providing them with specific information. It should be noted that the law merely requires disclosure and does not attempt to establish minimum interest

rates or other charges.

To whom does Regulation Z apply? :   Regulation Z applies to a person (or business) who is classified as a creditor. A creditor is one who regularly extends consumer credit that is either subject to a finance charge or is payable in more than four installments. The phrase "regularly extends" means that a person or firm has been engaged in five or more transactions in the past calendar year. Regulation Z also requires that the note signed by the consumer be payable on its face to the creditor. In other words, Regulation Z applies only to actual extenders of credit and not arrangers of credit. Thus, if a real estate broker or salesperson helps arrange creative financing to sell a house, the broker or salesperson would not have to comply with Regulation Z disclosure requirements.

What transactions are covered? : All real estate lending transactions involving consumers are covered by Regulation Z. Except for real estate transactions, all credit extended in five or more installments and not in excess of $25,000 for personal, family, household, or agricultural purposes is covered by the regulation. The regulation does not apply to credit extended to nonnatural persons such as corporations or governments, to credit extended for business and commercial purposes, or for credit transactions with an SEC-registered broker for trading in securities and commodities. The regulation applies to new loans, refinancing, or consolidation of loans. However, an assumption of a loan by a new borrower is exempt. Notice that Regulation Z applies to consumer real estate transactions. Would a loan to renovate an apartment building be covered by the regulation? Since an apartment building is normally a business to collect rents from tenants, this would not be deemed a consumer transaction. Thus, the loan would be exempt from Regulation Z reporting requirements.

What information must be disclosed? : The law requires a lender to make several types of credit information disclosures. Two important disclosures include the finance charge and a disclosure of the following: interest, finder and origination fees, discount points, service charges, credit report fees and other charges paid by the consumer directly or indirectly which are imposed as an incident to the extension of credit. Certain fees which are not in fact additional finance charges are exempt. These charges may include various title examination fees, escrow requirements, and appraisal fees. To determine the charges which are covered or exempt, Regulation Z should be examined by anyone extending credit to consumers. (Note: This includes brokers, professionals, and craftsmen as well as financial intermediaries unless exempt.) The *APR* (annual percentage rate) is the yearly cost of credit stated to the nearest one-eighth of 1 percentage point in regular transactions and the nearest one-fourth of 1 percentage point in irregular transactions. A transaction is irregular if repayment is in uneven amounts or the loan is made in multiple advances. The APR is usually different from the contract or nominal rate of interest and includes the impact on the effective rate from discount points and other charges. The calculation of the APR is complex and involves the use of actuarial tables which are available from the Federal Reserve System and member banks.

Example: Tom borrows $1,000 from Ken which is repayable in one payment at the end of the year. The loan is to finance a real estate purchase. They agree to a contract rate of 10% plus four discount points. What is the APR?

> Actual amount borrowed: $1,000 - $40 (discount points) = $960
> Amount to be paid back: $1,000 + $100 (contract interest) = $1,100
> Actual interest: $1,100 - $960 = $140
> APR: $140 / $960 = 14.58%

This calculation would differ depending on the term of the loan and the amortization period. If the interest is collected in the beginning, the APR could be twice the contract rate. If the loan involves variable payments, then the creditor must disclose how the payments may change, including the index that is being used, limitations on increases, and an example illustrating how payments would change in a given increase. In addition to the finance charge and the APR, anyone extending credit must also disclose such information as the number, amount, and time that the installments are due, description of the penalties and charges for prepayment, and the description of the security which is used as collateral. If a personal dwelling is used as collateral, as in refinancing or using a second mortgage to obtain equity, a consumer has three business days to rescind (cancel) the credit transaction. This right or rescission does not apply to credit which was used to purchase the home originally.

Effect of violations: Violation of Regulation Z provisions can lead to both civil and criminal penalties. Civil penalties include a fine of up to $1,000 paid to the borrower, actual damages plus attorney's fees. Criminal penalties include a fine of up to $5,000, up to one year in jail, or both.

TURNAROUND SPECIALIST

A person who specializes in taking over partially completed real estate projects as well as existing structures that are not financially sound and turning them into financially viable projects. Such persons may or may not actually take title to the property.

TURN-KEY PROJECT

A construction undertaking in which the builder/developer completely finishes the building and makes the building(s) available for occupancy. As such, the occupant(s) of the space can "turn the key" and be able to occupy the space.

TURNOVER

The rate at which tenants in a building move in and out. A high turnover may result in added expenses to the owner for refurbishing the space so that it can be rented to someone else. A low turnover may mean that the contract rent is substantially lower than market rents and, thus, tenants have no desire to move.

TWO-FAMILY DWELLING

(See **Duplex***)*

UDAG

(*See* **Urban Development Action Grant**)

ULI

(*See* **Urban Land Institute (ULI)**)

ULLMAN, EDWARD L.

An urban economist who, along with Chauncey D. Harris, is credited with developing the *multiple nuclei growth theory* of urban development. The theory is used to explain how development of different types of land use occurs.

UNDERIMPROVED LAND

A particular land use that, due to the fact the land is not being used to its *highest and best use*, does not generate the maximum level of income that could be generated from the land. Because of possible economic, political, physical, and social changes that affect land use, any parcel of land may have an existing use that becomes an underimproved use. In contrast, a parcel of land that has attempted to combine more factors of production inputs with the land than the land can profitably absorb is referred to as *overimproved land*. (*See* **Highest and Best Use**)

UNDERINSURANCE

Insurance coverage for an amount less than the value of the property being insured. (*See* **Coinsurance, Insurance**)

UNDERWRITER

Someone, such as an employee of a lending institution or mortgage banking company, who reviews an application for a loan and makes a recommendation to a loan committee as to the desirability and risk of the institution making the loan. The *underwriting* process is an integral part of the lending process.

UNDEVELOPED LAND

Land that has not had improvements made either to the land or on the land. The term *raw land* is sometimes used to refer to this type of land.

UNDISCLOSED AGENCY

A situation in which a person is dealing with a third person, but does not notify or inform the third person that an agency relationship exists. (*See* **Agency, Undisclosed Principal**)

UNDISCLOSED PRINCIPAL

A situation in which a third person is not advised of the existence of an agency relationship and, thus, is unaware that a principal-agent relationship exists. The unknown person for whom the agent is acting is referred to as an undisclosed principal. If an undisclosed principal exists, the agent is personally liable under the contract. (*See* **Agency, Disclosed Principal**)

UNDIVIDED INTEREST

The legal interest of co-owners in property in which the individual interest of each individual is indistinguishable. For example, in a tenancy in common each co-owner has an undivided fractional interest in the land and a right to use the whole property. No tenant may exclude a co-owner from any portion of the property. (*See* **Joint Tenancy, Tenancy by the Entirety, Tenancy in Common**)

UNDUE INFLUENCE

Any action or urgency by a person in a fiduciary capacity or in a position of authority that causes someone else to act in a way contrary to what would have been done had the party been free of the influence. The essence of undue influence is mental coercion by one person over another. Contracts induced by undue influence are *voidable* at the option of the injured party. (*See* **Contract, Reality of Consent**)

UNENCUMBERED PROPERTY

Property that is free and clear of any legal claims or liens. (*See* **Encumbrance**)

UNENFORCEABLE CONTRACT

An agreement in which something prevents a court of law from hearing disputes regarding the enforceability of the agreement. (*See* **Contract**)

UNIFORMITY

A term used to denote equal treatment in the assessment of various parcels of real estate for property tax purposes. In some jurisdictions all property is assessed at the same percentage of market value and, thus, "uniformity of assessment" is said to exist. (*See* **Property Tax**)

UNIFORM RESIDENTIAL LANDLORD AND TENANT ACT

An act adopted by numerous states which brings about a certain degree of uniformity in the legal dealings between landlord and tenant. The act modifies the duality of property law and contract law that presently determine the rights and obligations under a lease. The shift is toward more adherence to contract law. Substantive provisions of the act include disposition of security deposits by landlords, ensuring the habitability of the dwelling, and restricting the landlord's remedies. The act establishes the requirement on the landlord's part to mitigate damages in cases of tenant abandonment, abolishes distraint for rent, provides for a grace period for late payment of rent, prohibits exculpatory clauses, and prohibits retaliatory conduct on the part of the landlord after a tenant seeks to assert legal rights by complaining or by joining tenants' rights organizations. As the reader will note, the uniform act is very pro-tenant. It is an attempt to remove the old feudal principles which define the relationships of landlords and tenants. The uniform law has no legal effect until passed by a state's legislature.

UNIFORM SETTLEMENT STATEMENT

A standard settlement or closing statement required to be used for any real estate closing covered under the *Real Estate Settlement Procedures Act (RESPA)*. (*See* **Real Estate Settlement Procedures Act**)

UNIFORM VENDOR AND PURCHASER RISK ACT

A law adopted in many states that addresses the question of who has legal title to property if an event such as damage due to fire occurs prior to the time of delivery and acceptance of the deed. Under common law when a real estate sales contract is signed which is not subject to any unfulfilled contingencies *equitable conversion* occurs and *equitable title* passes to the purchaser. The result of this is that the risk of loss also passes to the purchaser. If the subject matter is destroyed before closing, the purchaser suffers the loss. The Uniform Vendor and Purchaser Risk Act provides for risk of loss to shift only if either legal title or possession has been transferred. However, even with adoption of the act, the purchaser and seller may specify in the contract who has the risk of loss. (*See* **Contract**)

UNILATERAL CONTRACT

An agreement in which one party promises to pay consideration for the performance of an act by another party. The party promising to pay consideration is not legally obligated to act unless the party promising to perform the agreed-to act actually performs. An *open* or *general listing* is a unilateral contract. Under this contract the property owner is only obligated to pay a commission to the broker who is the efficient and procuring cause of the sale. More than one broker may be employed and the owner is not obligated to pay anyone a commission if the owner personally sells the property. (*See* **Contract**)

UNILATERAL MISTAKE

A misunderstanding or mistake of a material fact made by just one of the parties involved in a contractual agreement.

UNIMPROVED LAND

Land in which neither improvements to the land or on the land have been made. Sometimes the term *raw land* is used to denote land in which no improvements have been made. (*See* **Highest and Best Use**)

UNINSURABLE TITLE

Title to real estate that is not marketable and one that a title insurance company refuses to insure due to some existing claim or encumbrance against the property. (*See* **Marketable Title, Title**)

UNIT

That portion of a condominium intended for the exclusive use and possession of the individual unit owner. The individual arranges for separate financing for his or her individual unit and has fee simple title to the unit. (*See* **Condominium**)

UNITED MORTGAGE BANKERS OF AMERICA

An association of minority mortgage bankers. The group is headquartered at 2902 Cadillac Towers, Detroit, Michigan 48226.

UNITED STATES LEAGUE OF SAVINGS ASSOCIATIONS

This league serves as a trade organization for the savings and loan associations in the United States and serves as a spokesman for its members. The mailing address is 111 East Wacker Drive, Chicago, Illinois 60601; (312) 644-3100.

UNIT-IN-PLACE METHOD

A method or technique used in appraising the value of real estate under the cost approach to value where the cost of replacement or reproduction is grouped by stages of construction. For example, the cost of heating and cooling, drywall, carpeting, painting, and other components are costed out on a square foot basis, and when these numbers are multiplied by the number of square feet in the building, a total cost of construction can be estimated. (*See* **Cost Approach**)

UNITY (UNITIES)

The requirement(s) necessary for a joint tenancy form of ownership to exist, specifically the unities of *interest, possession, time*, and *title*. (*See* **Joint Tenancy**)

UNITY OF INTEREST

A requirement necessary to create a joint tenancy which states that each joint tenant must have the same estate and an equal fractional share in the property as every other joint tenant.

Example: Jim conveys Prettyshore to Jack and Pam in joint tenancy. Jim specifies Jack is to have 60% interest in the property and Pam is to have 40% interest. Despite Jim's attempt to create a joint tenancy, all he was able to create would be a tenancy in common. (*See* **Joint Tenancy**)

UNITY OF PERSON

A necessary requirement for the creation of a *tenancy by the entirety* under which property which is held is owned as a whole by the husband and wife and not in undivided shares. There is no individual interest which may be conveyed, and the tenancy cannot be terminated without the consent of both. The public purpose for this form of concurrent ownership is to help preserve the assets of the family unit. Both parties must sign any conveyances in order to make them legally effective. If the husband and wife are divorced, the unity of person is broken, and the tenancy changes into a tenancy in common with each party having an undivided half interest. While the unity of person is intact, there can be no action for *partition* by one party. (*See* **Tenancy by the Entirety**)

UNITY OF POSSESSION

The right of each tenant to the possession and use of the whole property. This unity means that even though one of the joint tenants owns 50 percent of the interest in the property, he or she does not own a legally defined 50 percent of the area. Unity of possession is one of the unity requirements for the creation of a joint tenancy and is the only necessary unity for the creation of a tenancy in common. (*See* **Joint Tenancy, Tenancy in Common**)

UNITY OF TIME

A requirement of a joint tenancy which states that all interests of the joint tenants must have been acquired at the same moment.

Example: Jay owns Blackvalley in severalty. He marries Barbara and wishes to hold Blackvalley as joint tenants with his wife. In order to do this, Jay must convey the property to some third party known as a *straw man* or *nominee* who in turn reconveys the property "to Jay and Barbara as joint tenants with right of survivorship and not as tenants in common." Some states have modified the rule that a person cannot grant property to himself and would allow Jay to directly create the joint tenancy without the process of using a nominee. (*See* **Joint Tenancy**)

UNITY OF TITLE

One of the unity requirements of a joint tenancy which states that the joint tenancy interests must be created in a single conveying instrument. This means that if a joint tenant sells his or her interest to a third party, the joint tenancy is terminated in relation to the third party. If originally two joint tenants owned the property and one of these conveyed his or her interest to a third party, a tenancy in common would be created. If there are more than two joint tenants, the conveyance by one tenant of his or her interest would not terminate the right of survivorship among the remaining tenants as to their interest but would create a tenancy in common only insofar as the purchaser was concerned.

Example: Mary, Kris, and Fred own Hillystreet as joint tenants. Kris sells an undivided one-third in Hillystreet to Sam. Mary and Fred remain joint tenants in two-thirds of Hillystreet while Sam holds one-third interest as a tenant in common. If Sam were to die, his interest would pass on to his heirs or devisees. If he left no heirs or devisees, the interest would pass to the state by escheat. If either Mary or Fred were to die, the survivor would automatically acquire the deceased's interest. (*See* **Joint Tenancy**)

UNIVERSAL AGENT

A type of agent characterized by having the authority to do all acts that can be lawfully delegated to a representative. Ordinarily, a universal agent is created by a *power of attorney*. Anyone of legal capacity may be an attorney in fact, a position created by the power of attorney. Care should be taken not to confuse this status with an attorney at law, a person who must be admitted to an appropriate bar. Power of attorney is useful when a principal wishes to empower a broker to sell a house while the principal must be out of the country and, thus, is unable to personally sign appropriate documents to convey title. It should be noted that power of attorney may be limited in authority so that a universal agency is not necessarily created.

UNLAWFUL DETAINER

The unjustifiable retention or possession of land by someone whose original entry and possession was legal.

UNMARKETABLE TITLE

Title to real estate that is not marketable and one a title insurance company refuses to insure due to some existing claim or encumbrance against the property. (*See* **Marketable Title, Title**)

UNRECORDED INSTRUMENT

Any legal document such as a mortgage or deed of trust that has not been properly placed in the public records. Recordation of the instrument gives the world *constructive notice* as to the legal claims or interests in the property. (*See* **Deed**)

UNSECURED LOAN

A loan made only on the signature and credit of the borrower and, thus, not secured by collateral. By definition, a loan in which property is used to secure the debt is a *secured loan*. (*See* **Mortgage**)

UPLAND

Land bordering a body of water.

UP RENT POTENTIAL

The forecasted amount that rental rates can be reasonably increased over a specified period of time. The ability to forecast future income flows to rental property is contingent on being able to estimate the up rent potential of the property.

UPSET PRICE

The lowest or minimum price as set by a court of law at which property can be sold at public auction. For example, a court may set an upset price at which property being foreclosed and sold cannot sell below. This price is sometimes referred to as the *minimum price*.

URBAN DEVELOPMENT ACTION GRANT (UDAG)

A federal funding program administered through the *Department of Housing and Urban Development (HUD)* for the purpose of making funds available to revitalize commercial areas.

URBAN LAND INSTITUTE (ULI)

A nonprofit research and educational association involved in providing information on intelligent land use. The institute publishes numerous textbooks and research papers on topics related to land use. The mailing address is 1090 Vermont Avenue, N.W., Washington, D.C. 20005; (202) 289-3307.

URBAN RENEWAL

The process by which property is acquired by government action for the purpose of redevelopment and upgrading of the land use. Urban renewal projects include such land uses as public housing, parks and recreational areas, public libraries, and other such uses.

URBAN SPRAWL

The unplanned and often haphazard growth of an urban area throughout a larger geographic area.

USEFUL LIFE

The period of time over which property is expected to have utility.

USE VARIANCE
(See **Variance**)

U-STORE-IT-FACILITY
(See **Miniwarehouse**)

USUFRUCTUARY RIGHT
The personal right to make reasonable use of someone else's property such as the rights received through an easement.

USURY
The charging of more for the use of money than the legal rate of interest. A number of states have laws which limit the interest rate that can be charged to individuals borrowing money in that state. These laws affect all lenders in a state regardless of what federal or state agency issued their charter. It should be noted that if there is a national economic emergency the federal government may temporarily suspend state usury laws. While usury laws are intended to protect the borrower, these laws can, in times of rising interest rates, result in there being less money available than if there were no such laws. If a state sets a certain interest rate ceiling and the effective rate necessary to induce a loan to be made is greater than this ceiling, the result can easily be: (1) no loans made, (2) lenders charging applicants certain fees which in effect raise the effective yield, or (3) funds normally available in that state flowing to other parts of the country where interest rate ceilings are higher. This latter action can result in fewer dollars being available in the state with low usury ceilings. Another reason why there is little or no money available in a certain location is the result of *disintermediation*. Disintermediation refers to the withdrawing of funds from financial institutions by the depositors, generally so as to invest in higher interest-paying instruments, which results in less mortgage money being available for loans.

UTILITY (UTILITIES)
In appraisal theory, the term refers to the usefulness or satisfaction one receives from a good or service. In development, the term refers to the private or public service facilities such as telephone, water, and sewer that are provided as part of the development of the land.

V

VA

(*See* **Veterans Administration (VA) Mortgage**)

VACANCY ALLOWANCE (RATE)

The percent of a building's gross rentable space not currently rented. Vacancy can be a function of numerous factors including over-supply in the marketplace, tenant turnover, poor maintenance and upkeep, as well as locational obsolescence. The vacancy allowance or rate, when subtracted from *potential* or *gross income*, equals *effective gross income*, the amount of income actually collected.

VACANT LAND

(*See* **Unimproved Land**)

VACATE

To give up possession.

VACATION HOME

A residence normally located in a recreational or vacation area used as a second home. Quite often such homes are rented during the periods of time when they are not being occupied by their owner(s). (*See* **Rental Pool**)

441

VALID (CONTRACT)

Legally sufficient or binding, as in a valid contract which contains all of the essential legal elements. (*See* **Contract**)

VALUABLE CONSIDERATION

A right, interest, or benefit accruing to one party, or some loss or forbearance to act by the other party. Valuable consideration is not always money or property. Some examples of consideration include: a promise to do something (I promise to mow the lawn); a promise not to do something (I promise not to smoke for one year); an act (a person painting a house in response to an offer to pay him or her to paint the house); a cancellation of an obligation (a mutual rescission of a contract); and the giving up of a legal right (the cancellation of all rights to an existing easement). (*See* **Consideration**)

VALUE

The ability of a good or service to command other goods or services. Historically, this definition of value has been termed *value in exchange* and denotes how one good exchanges in the marketplace for other goods. For the investor in real estate, another definition of value, namely *value in use*, enters into the analysis. This explanation of value is defined as the present worth of the future rights to income and involves calculating the income generated from a particular use of real estate. The basic concepts of land use are built on certain economic principles. These principles influence the value of the real estate. The more important basic value principles include highest and best use, substitution, conformity, competition, contribution, increasing and decreasing returns, change, anticipation, and supply and demand. (*See* **Market Value**)

VARIABLE EXPENSES

Expenses incurred with the operation of a building and its grounds, such as utilities and maintenance, which are not the same each month.

VARIABLE INTEREST

A financing technique by which the interest rate charged on a mortgage can be legally adjusted by the lender if and when an agreed-upon index changes. Variable interest rate loans have been an important part of construction lending and development loans for many years. Such loans typically require the borrower to pay a specified rate of interest over and above the current *prime rate*. For example, "prime plus two" would mean that if the prime rate is currently eight percent, the construction loan is at ten percent; and if the prime goes to nine percent, the interest rate charged on the construction loan will also increase one percentage point to eleven percent. In recent years variable interest loans have also become an important component of permanent single-family lending. This has been especially true as inflation and uncertainty have made lenders reluctant to make long-term fixed rate mortgages. (*See* **Construction Loan, Variable Rate Mortgage**)

VARIABLE RATE MORTGAGE (VRM)

A mortgage characterized by an interest rate that can move either up or down depending upon the agreed-to index. Under a variable rate mortgage the interest rate charged by the lender can vary according to some reference index not controlled by the lender, such as the interest rate on three- to five-year United States government securities. For the lender this means that as the cost of money increases, the interest rate being charged on the existing mortgage can be increased, thus maintaining the gap between the cost of money and return. Either the monthly payment, the maturity date, or both can be changed to reflect the difference in interest rates. In addition, the mortgage usually stipulates a maximum annual charge and a maximum total increase in the interest rate the lender may charge.

VARIANCE

A type of safety valve provided through local zoning ordinances which allows a property owner who is unfairly burdened by a zoning restriction to find relief. Some properties may be adversely affected by a zoning ordinance and thus a unique hardship may be imposed upon them. For example, a lot may be irregularly shaped and a zoning setback requirement of fifteen feet would result in a planned building not properly fitting on the lot. In order to seek relief from the harshness of the zoning restriction, a property owner may seek a variance from the local zoning board of appeals or zoning board of adjustment. If the proposed variance is approved, the owner of the land is then able to construct the hoped-for structure on the lot. (*See* **Zoning**)

VENDEE

A purchaser or buyer of real estate.

VENDEE'S LIEN

A legal claim held by the purchaser for the purchase price paid for property if the seller defaults on the delivery of the deed. This is an *equitable lien* on the land of a seller after the purchase price has been paid or after expenditures were made to improve the property on the understanding that a deed would be delivered. If the seller defaults on the delivery of the deed, a vendee's lien can be placed on the land. The lien is for the money actually given to the seller and for some additional expenditures made in anticipation of the sale. (*See* **Lien**)

VENDOR

A seller of real estate.

VENDOR'S LIEN

A legal claim held by the seller of real estate which originated in equity and arose when a seller of land financed the purchase price without taking back a mortgage to secure the payment of a promissory note. Thus, the seller has a lien on the unpaid balance. Vendor's liens have been codified as a *statutory lien* in most states. (*See* **Lien**)

VESTED INTEREST

A present right or title to property even though the right of occupancy or possession may be delayed until some time in the future. For example, when Don creates a life estate for Shirley, the estate reverts to Don upon the death of Shirley. The *reversion* is a vested interest held by Don. (*See* **Life Estate**)

VETERANS ADMINISTRATION (VA)

An agency of the federal government created by the *Servicemen's Readjustment Act of 1944*. While the agency is involved in numerous programs dealing with the return of veterans to civilian life, the most important component of its work in real estate is a loan guaranty program which enables qualified veterans to finance real estate purchases with a higher loan-to-value ratio than is normally possible with conventional financing. (*See* **Veterans Administration (VA) Mortgage**)

VETERANS ADMINISTRATION (VA) MORTGAGE

A means of financing real estate by qualified persons who meet certain minimum standards as established by the Veterans Administration. Included in the *Servicemen's Readjustment Act of 1944* were provisions covering the compensation to lenders for losses they might sustain in providing financing to approved veterans. The maximum guaranteed amount, which has periodically been increased, is set by the VA as is the maximum interest rate charged by lenders. There are no provisions on the upper limits of the loan-to-value ratio, which means that it is quite common for an approved veteran to receive 100% VA financing. It should be noted that some lenders set limits on how much they will finance using VA financing. VA guarantees loans up to thirty years. To qualify for VA financing the veteran applies for a *certificate of eligibility*. The property as well as the borrower must qualify. If the property is approved, a *certificate of reasonable value* is issued. As is true with FHA, junior financing is essentially prohibited under a VA mortgage. (Junior financing is rare and its terms keep it rare.) Coverage also extends to the financing of mobile homes, condominiums, and non-real estate purchases such as farm equipment and business loans. A VA loan is assumable; however, unless released by the lender, the veteran who initially borrowed the funds remains liable to the lender. Lenders cannot insert prepayment penalties under VA loans. A mortgage without a prepayment penalty is commonly referred to as an open mortgage while one that cannot be prepaid is a closed mortgage. VA limits the points charged to the buyer to one, commonly referred to as an *origination fee*. Any other points must be paid by the seller.

VIRGIN LAND

Land on which or to which improvements have not been made. Such land is in its natural state and is commonly referred to as *unimproved land* or *raw land*.

VOID CONTRACT

An agreement which is totally absent of legal effect. The law will give neither remedy nor otherwise recognize a duty in a case where a void contract is involved except to prevent a gross injustice. Ordinarily, a void contract is a contract (agreement) which is missing an essential element of a valid contract or involves some kind of illegality. *(See* **Contract***)*

VOIDABLE CONTRACT

An agreement in which one or more of the parties may elect to avoid or ratify the legal obligations created by the contract. Many real estate contracts are voidable on the part of one party and valid on the part of the other party. Contracts may be avoided on the basis of fraud, limited legal capacity of one party, or other such reasons for which the law will give relief to one party, but not to the other. *(See* **Contract***)*

VOLUNTARY ALIENATION

The transfer of title to real property by a deed from one party to another. *(See* **Deed***)*

VOLUNTARY LIEN

An encumbrance placed on the property of an owner through some willful act of the owner. *(See* **Lien***)*

VOLUNTARY WASTE

The impairment of the rights of a person owning a future interest which occurs when a tenant abuses the realty. For example, the cutting down of trees or the demolishing of improvements by a tenant is voluntary waste on the part of the tenant.

W

WAIVER

The voluntary or intentional giving up of a claim or privilege. Most modern real estate sales contracts contain a clause which states that no waiver or modification of the contents of the contract can occur without the written consent of all parties to the contract.

WALK-THROUGH INSPECTION

The physical inspection of property that takes place immediately prior to closing for the purpose of ensuring the new owner that the property is in the same physical condition as when the sales contract was signed.

WALKUP

A building at least two stories in height containing no elevator. Such buildings, quite common in large metropolitan areas, are used for both commercial and residential use.

WAREHOUSE

A building used to receive and store goods and merchandise. In terms of classifying such property, warehouses are normally located in an area zoned for either commercial or industrial property.

447

WAREHOUSING

The process by which a mortgage banker or mortgage broker assembles mortgages that he or she has made and prepares the mortgages to be sold in the *secondary mortgage market*. By selling these mortgages the originator now has additional capital that can be used to make more mortgages which in turn may be sold in the secondary mortgage market. (*See* **Mortgage Banker, Secondary Mortgage Market**)

WARRANTY

A promise or assurance that a set of facts or a statement is true and correct. The warranty can be either oral or written, and in the case of real estate both types of warranties exist. Written warranties are often given by suppliers of equipment, such as appliances or materials, while *implied warranties of fitness and merchantability* are given by contractors and sellers of homes.

WARRANTY DEED

A type of deed used to convey real property in which the grantor makes formal assurance as to the quality of title to the property. Warranty deeds, both *general* and *special*, are commonly used to convey real estate. (*See* **General Warranty Deed, Special Warranty Deed**)

WARRANTY OF TITLE

(*See* **Covenant of Warranty of Title**)

WASTE

The destructive use of property by someone in possession who holds less than full and clear title such as a tenant or mortgagor. For example, in terms of rental property, the tenant is expected to return the property to the tenant in the shape in which the property was received. To do otherwise, with the exception of normal wear and tear, is to commit waste. Owners of property who mortgage their property are required to keep the property taxes paid, maintain adequate insurance coverage, and do anything else necessary to protect the property which is the security for the loan. To do otherwise is to commit waste on the part of the borrower.

WASTELAND

Land which is considered to be economically unfit for production, such as swampland or desert land.

WASTING ASSET

A natural resource such as timber, oil, or gas which has a limited useful life and thus is subject to amortization (depletion) during the life of the asset.

WATER COURSE

A natural stream of running water being fed by a natural source such as a stream or river.

WATER RIGHTS

A legal right to use the water from a natural stream or canal for such purposes as irrigation, power, or private consumption.

WATER TABLE

The distance from ground level to natural groundwater, be it above or below the earth's surface.

WEAR AND TEAR

The lessening in value of an asset such as real estate due to ordinary and normal use. (*See* **Physical Deterioration**)

WENDT, PAUL

A real estate appraiser who throughout the 1960s and 1970s offered numerous ideas on real estate appraising. Wendt drew attention to a number of weaknesses in traditional capitalization theory and attempted to bring into clear focus the relationship between current practice and appraisal theory. He is the author of *Real Estate Appraisal.*

WETLANDS

Lowlying land adjacent to water which may be periodically covered by water or the remains of flooding. Such land is normally restricted as to development that can take place and in many instances is owned by the federal government or a state government to insure the ecological protection of such land and its animal inhabitants.

WILL

A legal declaration in which a person disposes of property to take effect upon his or her death. In order to make a valid formal will a person must be of statutory age, generally eighteen or twenty-one in most states, although some states set the age as low as fourteen. In addition, the person must be of "sound mind" at the time of the execution of the will. A formal will must be in writing, which may be typed, printed, or handwritten. Real estate must be described with sufficient certainty, but it is not required that a complete legal description be included. In addition, a formal will must be signed.

WITHOUT RECOURSE

(*See* **Nonrecourse Loan**)

WOMEN'S COUNCIL OF REALTORS (WCR)

An affiliate of the National Association of Realtors whose members have expressed an interest in furthering the role of women in real estate brokerage activities. The mailing address is 430 North Michigan Avenue, Chicago, Illinois 60611; (312) 440-8083.

WORK LETTER

A letter given by a landlord to a tenant detailing the amount and type of work the landlord and the tenant will each do in preparing the property for occupancy by the tenant.

WORKOUT (LOAN)

A loan which is technically in default but under which the lender (mortgagee) is attempting to assist the borrower (mortgagor) in restructuring the terms of the loan or the time of repayment rather than proceeding with foreclosure.

WRAPAROUND MORTGAGE

A method of acquiring additional financing on real estate by placing the additional funds in a secondary or junior position to the existing debt. As its name implies, a wraparound mortgage "wraps around" an existing first mortgage. This method of obtaining additional capital is often used with commercial property where there is substantial equity in the property and where the existing first mortgage has an attractive low interest rate. By obtaining a wraparound, the borrower receives dollars based on the difference between current market value of the property and the outstanding balance on the first mortgage. The borrower amortizes the wraparound mortgage which now includes the balance of the first mortgage and the wraparound lender forwards the necessary periodic debt service to the holder of the first mortgage. Thus, the borrower reduces the equity and at the same time obtains an interest rate lower than would be possible through a normal second mortgage. The lender receives the leverage resulting from an interest rate on the wraparound greater than the interest paid to the holder of the first mortgage.

WRIT OF EXECUTION

A court order instructing an officer of the court to carry out the decision of the court, such as the selling of foreclosed property or the removal of a tenant at sufferance.

X

A notation made by an individual who has not learned to write or is paralyzed, to show intent to sign an instrument such as a deed or will. In regard to the conveyance of real property, such a handicapped grantor would be required to make such a mark or at least a thumbprint which manifests intent to sign. Both the marking and the statement or declaration of intent by the grantor would need to be witnessed.

YARD

The portion of a lot not occupied by a building. Minimum yard requirements are included in most zoning ordinances. (*See* **Zoning**)

YEAR TO YEAR TENANCY

(*See* **Estate from Year to Year**)

YIELD

The interest earned or return by an investor on an investment, stated as a percentage of the amount invested.

YIELD TO MATURITY

The annual return on an investment equal to the annual interest rate plus or minus the discounted gain or loss realized at time of maturity.

YTM

(*See* **Yield To Maturity**)

ZECKENDORF, WILLIAM

A real estate developer noted for being able to divide real estate legal interest into various legal interests that could be sold to several parties. Zeckendorf referred to his theory as the "Hawaiian technique" or the "pineapple technique," apparently in reference to the place where he first thought of the idea. By dividing the various legal rights and interests into numerous interests, he was able to put developments together that otherwise would not have been financially possible. He is perhaps most noted for the United Nations Plaza building in which three different fee interests, a leasehold interest, and five mortgage interests were created, a total of nine different interests in the property.

ZERO LOT LINE

The location of a structure on a building lot so that one or more of the sides of the building rest directly on the boundary line(s) and, thus, on that particular side of the structure there is no setback. Zoning ordinances normally require *minimum setback requirements* and, thus, prohibit zero lot line construction. However, under certain zoning provisions such as may be the case with *planned unit developments* zero lot line construction is permitted. Such permission allows the developer more flexibility in the design and placement of buildings within the development. (*See* **Planned Unit Development, Zoning**)

ZONING

A police power device which allows for legislative division of space into districts, and imposition or regulations prescribing use and intensity of use to which land within each designated district may be put. Although rudimentary land-use regulations have existed in this country since early Colonial days, zoning is a relatively new technique. It was not until 1916 that the first comprehensive zoning ordinance was passed in the City of New York. In 1926, the U.S. Supreme Court upheld the constitutionality of zoning in the landmark case of *Village of Euclid v. Ambler Realty Co.* on the basis of police power. A local government receives the power of zoning from the state in much the same way it receives its power to plan. Ordinarily, authority is given in a state enabling act. Most zoning enabling legislation is based on the *Standard State Zoning Enabling Act* which was developed by the *U.S. Department of Commerce* in 1922 and revised in 1926.

A zoning ordinance has two major parts: (1) the *text* which contains various regulations and standards, and (2) the *map* which divides an area into different districts. The zoning map is constantly updated and indicates the zoning status of each parcel of land in the community. The Standard Act indicates that zoning shall be made in accordance with a comprehensive plan, and both the text and the map are designed to help carry out the plan. A second overall purpose of zoning is to preserve property values. When zoning helps carry out a plan, it is called *directive zoning*. When it helps preserve value, it is called *protective zoning*. To carry out these two general purposes, zoning provides the following techniques to a local government:

1. Zoning establishes *land-use districts* and provides for different restrictions and standards within each use district. Use districts are divided into four basic categories: (1) residential, (2) commercial, (3) industrial, and (4) agricultural. Each of these basic categories may be further divided. For example, the industrial uses may be divided into light and heavy industrial zones. Further, an ordinance may provide for special-use districts such as a historical district or a downtown shopping district. Each district is composed of uses which are relatively homogeneous or compatible. If two districts adjoin which have incompatible uses, planners normally try to place a *buffer zone* in between the two zoning districts. A buffer zone consists of uses which are compatible with uses in each adjoining district. A zoning ordinance may provide for either *exclusive-use districts* or for *cumulative districts*. If the ordinance specifies exclusive zones, only appropriate uses specified in the text may be permitted in a particular zone. For example, only industrial uses would be permitted in industrial zones. However, if the ordinance permits cumulative zoning, uses which are not specified in the text may be permitted in a particular zone. For example, cumulative zoning places all uses into a hierarchy with residential uses at the top. Uses at the top of the hierarchy may exist in lower zones but not vice versa. Thus, a residential use could be permitted in a commercial zone, but a commercial use could not be permitted in a residential zone.

2. Zoning establishes *height restrictions*. This is done to protect the sunlight and flow of air to adjoining properties.

3. Zoning establishes *area* and *bulk restrictions*. This is a means of regulating the intensity of development to prevent the overloading of public services and the infrastructure. Area and bulk restrictions include setback and side yard requirements, minimum lot sizes, and minimum and maximum *floor area ratios (FAR)*. A setback or side yard requirement specifies how far a building must be from the road and from the property line of adjoining properties. A requirement may be included for a *buffer*. A buffer is created by distance and barriers, such as fences or planting of bushes, and is intended to protect an adjoining property from noise, light and unsightliness of a particular land use or activity. Minimum lot sizes and minimum and maximum floor area ratios are used primarily to protect residential neighborhoods. A minimum lot size requirement might be a two-acre lot for each house. A minimum floor area might be 2,000 square feet of living space. These two types of restrictions have been criticized for raising the cost of housing so that lower socioeconomic groups are unable to afford houses in a particular neighborhood. This is referred to as *exclusionary zoning* since it tends to exclude the poor and minority groups. FAR indicates the relationship between a building area and land. For example, a 2:1 FAR means that two square feet of floor space may be constructed on one square foot of land. In other words, a two-story building covering the entire lot could be built. If only one-half of the lot were covered, a four-story building could be constructed, while if only one-quarter of the lot were covered, an eight-story building could be developed.

4. Zoning establishes *other restrictions* such as off-street parking requirements, open space requirements, prohibitions against unrelated and unmarried persons living in a household (usually used to regulate fraternity houses, boarding houses, and such), prohibitions against building in flood plains, performance standards for noise or pollution, restrictions favoring housing for the elderly, restrictions against socially offensive uses and others. Performance standards are ordinarily used in conjunction with industrial uses to ensure that the quality of the environment will be maintained. When a zoning district is created, some uses may exist which are not consistent with the zoning ordinance. Pre-existing uses which do not conform to the zoning ordinance are called *nonconforming uses*. A nonconforming use may ordinarily remain; however, certain restrictions are usually imposed. For example, the property owner may not expand a nonconforming use. If a building which is nonconforming is destroyed or damaged to a significant degree, the owner may not replace or repair it. If a property owner wishes to change the zoning on his or her property, the procedure is to seek an amendment to the map. Ordinarily, requests for rezonings are heard by a zoning board which is appointed by a local governing board. The zoning board considers recommendations of the planners and listens to citizen groups. The zoning board makes its recommendations to the legislative body of the local government who will make the final decision. If the rezoning will create hazards or adversely affect surrounding properties, it will ordinarily be turned down. When the rezoned use is significantly different and involves only a small piece of property, the rezoning may be called a *spot zone*. Spot zoning is illegal in most states.

Example: Jack wishes to have his lot, which is in the middle of a residential neighborhood, rezoned so that he may build a convenience store upon it. This rezoning would be termed spot zoning.

Some properties may be adversely affected by a zoning ordinance and a unique hardship may be imposed upon them. For example, a lot may be 60 feet deep and a setback requirement may be 30 feet from the road, while a rear yard requirement may be 20 feet from the rear property line. This would leave only 10 feet upon which to place a structure. In order to seek relief from the harshness of the zoning restrictions, a property owner may seek a *variance* from the zoning board of appeals or zoning board of adjustment which may exist in the community. A variance is a type of safety valve to allow property owners who are unfairly burdened by zoning restrictions to find relief. Certain uses such as churches and child day-care centers do not fall within any zone. In order to allow these uses, zoning ordinances provide for conditional or special-use permits or exceptions. These permits are granted if the use meets standards specified in the ordinance. Zoning regulations are enforced by court injunctions (a building which is built in violation to the zoning ordinance can be ordered torn down), by fine (each day a structure violates the zoning ordinance may be treated as a separate violation), or by imprisonment.

APPENDIX A

ABBREVIATIONS

A

AAE   Accredited Assessment Evaluator

ABA   American Bankers Association

AEDC   American Economic Development Council

AFLM   Accredited Farm and Land Member

AGCA   Associated General Contractors of America

AIA   American Institute of Architects

AIP   American Institute of Planners

AIREA   American Institute of Real Estate Appraisers

Aka   Also Known As

ALDA   American Land Development Association

ALTA   American Land Title Association

APR   Annual Percentage Rate

ARA   Accredited Rural Appraiser

AREUEA   American Real Estate and Urban Economics Association

ARWA	American Right of Way Association
ASA	American Society of Appraisers
ASFMRA	American Society of Farm Managers and Rural Appraisers
ASHI	American Society of Home Inspectors
ASREC	American Society of Real Estate Counselors
ASPO	American Society of Planning Officials
ATCF	After-Tax Cash Flow

B

BMIR	Below-Market Interest Rate Mortgage
BOCA	Building Officials and Code Administration International
BOMA	Building Owners and Managers Association International
BPI	Buying Power Index
BTCF	Before-Tax Cash Flow

C

CAE	Certified Assessment Evaluator
CAI	Community Associations Institute
CBD	Central Business District
CCIM	Certified Commercial Investment Member
CCRs	Covenants, Conditions and Restrictions
CD	Certificate of Deposit
CED	Certified Economic Developer

CEQ	Council on Environmental Quality
CID	Certified Industrial Developer
CMB	Certified Mortgage Banker
CMO	Collateralized Mortgage Obligation
CO	Certificate of Occupancy
COL	Cost of Living Clause
CPA	Certified Public Accountant
CPE	Certified Personalty Evaluator
CPI	Consumer Price Index
CPM	Certified Property Manager
CRA	Certified Review Appraiser
CRB	Certified Residential Broker
CRE	Counselor of Real Estate
CREA	Certified Real Estate Appraiser
CRS	Certified Residential Specialist
CRV	Certificate of Reasonable Value
CSHA	Council of State Housing Agencies

D

DBA	Doing Business As
DCF	Discounted Cash Flow
DREI	Designated Real Estate Instructor

E

ECOA	Equal Credit Opportunity Act
EGI	Effective Gross Income
EIS	Environmental Impact Statement
E & O	Errors and Omissions Insurance
EPA	Environmental Protection Agency
Et al	"And Another"
Et ux	"And Wife"

F

FAR	Floor Area Ratio
FASA	Fellow, American Society of Appraisers
FDIC	Federal Deposit Insurance Corporation
FHA	Federal Housing Administration
FHLBB	Federal Home Loan Bank Board
FHLMC	Federal Home Loan Mortgage Corporation
FIABCI	International Real Estate Federation
FLB	Federal Land Bank
FLIP	Flexible Loan Insurance Program
FmHA	Farmers Home Administration
FMRR	Financial Management Rate of Return
FMV	Fair Market Value
FNMA	Federal National Mortgage Association

FRM	Fixed Rate Mortgage
FRS	Federal Reserve System
FSBO	For Sale By Owner
FSLIC	Federal Savings and Loan Insurance Corporation
FTC	Federal Trade Commission

G

GIM	Gross Income Multiplier
GLA	Gross Leasable Area
GNMA	Government National Mortgage Association
GPM	Graduated Payment Mortgage
GRI	Graduate, Realtors Institute
GRM	Gross Rent Multiplier

H

HAC	Housing Assistance Council
HFA	Housing Finance Agency
HOW	Homeowner's Warranty Program
HUD	Department of Housing and Urban Development

I

IAAO	International Association of Assessing Officers
ICBO	International Conference of Building Officials

ICMA	International City Management Association
IFA	Independent Fee Appraiser
IFAC	Appraiser/Counselor, National Association of Independent Fee Appraisers
IFAS	Senior Member, National Association of Independent Fee Appraisers
IREM	Institute of Real Estate Management
IRB	Industrial Revenue Bond
IRR	Internal Rate of Return
IRS	Internal Revenue Service
IR/WA	International Right of Way Association

L

LHA	Landed Homes Association
L.S.	Locus Sigilli ("in place of seal")
LTV	Loan-to-Value Ratio

M

MAGIC	Mortgage Guaranty Insurance Corporation
MAI	Member, Appraisal Institute
MBA	Mortgage Bankers Association of America
MBS	Mortgage-Backed Securities
MGIC	Mortgage Guaranty Insurance Corporation
MIP	Mortgage Insurance Premium
MLS	Multiple Listing Service
MREA	Master Real Estate Appraiser

N

NAA	National Apartment Association
NAAO	National Association of Assessing Officers
NAHB	National Association of Home Builders
NAHM	National Association of Home Manufacturers
NAHRO	National Association of Housing and Redevelopment Officials
NAIFA	National Association of Independent Fee Appraisers
NAMSB	National Association of Mutual Savings Banks
NAR	National Association of Realtors
NARA	National Association of Review Appraisers
NARC	National Association of Regional Councils
NAREB	National Association of Real Estate Brokers
NAREIT	National Association of Real Estate Investment Trusts
NARELLO	National Association of Real Estate License Law Officials
NCHM	National Center for Housing Management
NEPA	National Environmental Policy Act
NIBD	Net Income Before Depreciation
NIFLB	National Institute of Farm and Land Brokers
NLA	Net Leasable Area
NLC	National League of Cities
NOI	Net Operating Income
NSREA	National Society of Real Estate Appraisers

O

OPM	Other People's Money
ORR	Overall Rate of Return

P

PE	Professional Engineer
P & I	Principal and Interest
PITI	Principal, Interest, Taxes, and Insurance
PMI	Private Mortgage Insurance
POB	Point of Beginning
PUD	Planned Unit Development

R

RA	Residential Appraiser
REEA	Real Estate Educators Association
REIT	Real Estate Investment Trust
REMIC	Real Estate Mortgage Investment Conduit
RESPA	Real Estate Settlement Procedures Act
RESSI	Real Estate Securities and Syndication Institute
RLI	Realtors Land Institute
RM	Residential Member
RMU	Registered Mortgage Underwriter
RNMI	Realtors National Marketing Institute

ROA	Return on Assets
ROE	Return on Equity
ROR	Rate of Return
RPAC	Realtors Political Action Committee
R/W	Right of Way

S

SAM	Shared Appreciation Mortgage
SBA	Small Business Administration
SEC	Securities and Exchange Commission
SIOR	Society of Industrial and Office Realtors
SIR	Specialist in Industrial Realty
S & L	Savings and Loan Association
SMMEA	Secondary Mortgage Market Enhancement Act of 1984
SMSA	Standard Metropolitan Statistical Area
SOYD	Sum of the Years' Digits
SRA	Senior Residential Appraiser
SREA	Senior Real Estate Analyst
SREA	Society of Real Estate Appraisers
SRPA	Senior Real Property Appraiser
SRS	Specialist in Real Estate Securities
SR/WA	Senior Right of Way Agent

T

TDR	Transfer of Development Rights
TFTV	Total Financing-To-Value Ratio

U

UCC	Uniform Commercial Code
UDAG	Urban Development Action Grant
ULI	Urban Land Institute
USGS	United States Geological Survey

V

VA	Veterans Administration
VRM	Variable Rate Mortgage

W

WCR	Women's Council of Realtors

Y

YTM	Yield to Maturity

APPENDIX B

REAL ESTATE RELATED ORGANIZATIONS: ADDRESSES AND TELEPHONE NUMBERS

American Bankers Association
1120 Connecticut Avenue, N.W.
Washington, D.C. 20036
(202) 663-5000

American Economic Development Council
Suite 22
4849 North Scott Street
Schiller Park, Illinois 60176
(312) 671-5646

American Institute for Property
and Liability Underwriters
Providence and Sugartown Roads
Malvern, Pennsylvania 19355
(215) 644-2100

American Institute of Architects
1735 New York Avenue, N.W.
Washington, D.C. 20006
(202) 626-7300

American Institute of Planners
1776 Massachusetts Avenue, N.W.
Washington, D.C. 20036
(202) 872-0611

American Institute of
Real Estate Appraisers
430 North Michigan Avenue
Chicago, Illinois 60611
(312) 440-8141

American Land Development Association
1200 L Street, N.W.
Washington, D.C. 20005
(202) 371-6700

American Land Title Association
1828 L Street, N.W.
Washington, D.C. 20036
(202) 296-3671

American Real Estate and
Urban Economics Association
School of Business
Indiana University
Bloomington, Indiana 47405
(812) 335-3297

American Society of Appraisers
P. O. Box 17265
Dulles International Airport
Washington, D.C. 20041
(703) 478-2228

Appraisal Institute of Canada
177 Lombard Avenue
Winnipeg, Manitoba, Canada
(204) 942-0751

American Society of Consulting Planners
Suite 647
210 7th Sreet, S.E.
Washington, D.C. 20003
(202) 544-0035

Associated General
Contractors of America
1957 E. Street, N.W.
Washington, D.C. 20006
(202) 393-2040

American Society of Farm Managers
and Rural Appraisers
Suite 106
950 South Cherry Street
Denver, Colorado 80222
(303) 758-3515

Building Officials and
Code Administration
1313 East 60th Street
Chicago, Illinois 60637
(312) 799-2300

American Society of Home Inspectors
7th Floor
3299 K Street, N.W.
Washington, D.C. 20007
(202) 842-3096

Building Owners and
Managers Association
234 South Michigan Avenue
Chicago, Illinois 60604
(312) 236-5237

American Society of Planning Officials
1313 East 60th Street
Chicago, Illinois 60637
(312) 947-2560

Community Associations Institute
1423 Powhatan Street
Alexandria, Virginia 22314
(202) 548-8600

American Society of
Real Estate Counselors
430 North Michigan Avenue
Chicago, Illinois 60611
(312) 440-8091

Council of State Governments
P. O. Box 11910
Lexington, Kentucky 40511
(606) 252-2291

Appraisal Foundation
1029 Vermont Avenue, N.W.
Washington, D.C. 20005
(202) 347-7722

Council of State Housing Agencies
444 North Capital Street
Washington, D.C. 20002
(202) 624-7710

Housing Assistant Council
1025 Vermont Avenue, N.W.
Washington, D.C. 20005
(202) 842-8600

Institute Of Real Estate Management
430 North Michigan Avenue
Chicago, Illinois 60611
(312) 661-1930

International Association
of Assessing Officers
1313 East 60th Street
Chicago, Illinois 60637
(312) 947-2069

International City
Management Association
1120 G Street, N.W.
Washington, D.C. 20005
(202) 626-4600

International Conference of
Building Officials
5360 South Workman Mill Road
Whittier, California 90601
(213) 659-0541

International Real Estate Federation
777 14th Street, N.W.
Washington, D.C. 20005
(202) 383-1167

International Right of
Way Association
Suite 515
9920 LaCienega Boulevard
Inglewood, California 90301
(213) 649-5323

Manufactured Housing Institute
1745 Jefferson Davis Highway
Arlington, Virginia 22301
(703) 979-6620

Mortgage Bankers Association of America
1125 15th Street, N.W.
Washington, D.C. 20005
(202) 861-6500

Mortgage Insurance Companies of America
1615 L Street, N.W.
Washington, D.C. 20006
(202) 785-0767

National Apartment Association
1111 14th Street, N.W.
Washington, D.C. 20005
(202) 842-4050

National Association for
Community Development
1424 16th Street, N.W.
Washington, D.C. 20036
(202) 293-7587

National Association of Corporate
Real Estate Executives
Suite 8
471 Spencer Drive, South
West Palm Beach, Florida 33409
(407) 683-8111

National Association of Counties
440 1st Street, N.W.
Washington, D.C. 20001
(202) 393-6226

National Association of Home Builders
15th & M Streets, N.W.
Washington, D.C. 20005
(202) 822-0200

National Association of
Home Manufacturers
1619 Massachusetts Avenue, N.W.
Washington, D.C. 20036
(202) 822-0200

National Association of Housing
and Redevelopment Officials
2600 Virginia Avenue, N.W.
Washington, D.C. 20037
(202) 333-2020

National Association of
Housing Cooperatives
2501 M Street, N.W.
Washington, D.C. 20037
(202) 887-0706

National Association of
Independent Fee Appraisers
7501 Murdoch Avenue
St. Louis, Missouri 63119
(314) 781-6688

National Association of
Master Appraisers
P. O. Box 12617
San Antonio, Texas 78212
(512) 271-0781

National Association of
Mutual Savings Banks
200 Park Avenue
New York, NY 10017
(212) 973-5432

National Association of
Pension Funds
Suite 500
1150 Connecticut Avenue, N.W.
Washington, D.C. 20036
(202) 457-1049

National Association of
Real Estate Brokers
4324 Georgia Avenue, N.W.
Washington, D.C. 20011
(202) 289-6655

National Association of
Real Estate Investment Trusts
1101 17th Street, N.W.
Washington, D.C. 20036
(202) 785-8717

National Association of
Real Estate License Law Officials
P. O. Box 129
Centerville, Utah 84014
(801) 298-5572

National Association of Realtors
430 North Michigan Avenue
Chicago, Illinois 60611
(312) 440-8000

National Association of
Regional Councils
1700 K Street, N.W.
Washington, D.C. 20006
(202) 457-0710

National Association of Review
Appraisers and Mortgage Underwriters
8715 Via De Commercio
Scottsdale, Arizona 85258
(602) 998-3000

National Center for
Housing Management
1275 K Street, N.W.
Washington, D.C. 20005
(202) 872-1717

National Committee Against
Discrimination in Housing
1425 H Street, N.W.
Washington, D.C. 20005
(202) 783-8150

National Forest Products Association
1250 Connecticut Avenue, N.W.
Washington, D.C. 20036
(202) 463-2700

National Housing and Economic
Development Law Project
2313 Warren Street
Berkeley, California 94704
(415) 548-9400

National Housing Conference
1126 16th Street, N.W.
Washington, D.C. 20036
(2020 223-4844

National Housing
Rehabilitation Association
1726 18th Street, N.W.
Washington, D.C. 20009
(202) 328-9171

National Institute of
Farm and Land Brokers
430 North Michigan Avenue
Chicago, Illinois 60611
(312) 440-8000

National League of Cities
1301 Pennsylvania Avenue, N.W.
Washington, D.C. 20004
(202) 626-3000

National Leased Housing Association
2300 M Street, N.W.
Washington, D.C. 20037
(202) 785-8888

National Realty Committee
230 Park Avenue
New York, New York 10017
(212) 697-1750

National Rural Housing Coalition
2001 S Street, N.W.
Washington, D.C. 20009
(202) 483-1504

National Savings and Loan League
1101 15th Street, N.W.
Washington, D.C. 20005
(202) 331-0270

National Society of
Real Estate Appraisers
1265 East 105th Street
Cleveland, Ohio 44108
(216) 795-3445

Real Estate Educators Association
Suite 1200
230 North Michigan Avenue
Chicago, Illinois 60601
(312) 372-9800

Realtors Land Institute
430 North Michigan Avenue
Chicago, Illinois 60611
(312) 670-3520

Society of Industrial
and Office Realtors
430 North Michigan Avenue
Chicago, Illinois 60611
(312) 440-8000

Society of Real Estate Appraisers
645 North Michigan Avenue
Chicago, Illinois 60611
(312) 346-7422

Southern Building Congress International
3617 8th Avenue South
Birmingham, Alabama 35222
(205) 591-1853

United Mortgage Bankers of America
111 East Wacker Drive
Chicago, Illinois 60601
(312) 644-3100

Women's Council of Realtors
430 North Michigan Avenue
Chicago, Illinois 60611
(312) 440-8083

APPENDIX C

REAL ESTATE COMMISSIONS

Alabama

Real Estate Commission
State Capitol
Montgomery, Alabama 36130
(202) 261-5544

Alaska

Division of Occupational Licensing
Suite 722
3601 C. Street
Anchorage, Alaska 99503
(903) 563-2169

Alberta

Deputy Superintendent of Real Estate
Department of Consumer
and Corporate Affairs
19th Floor
10025 Jasper Avenue
Edmonton, Alberta, Canada T5J 3ZB
(403) 422-1588

Arizona

Commissioner
Department of Real Estate
202 E. Earll Drive
Phoenix, Arizona 85012
(602) 255-4670

Arkansas

Executive Secretary
Real Estate Commission
Suite 660
One Riverfront Place
North Little Rock, Arkansas 72114
(501) 371-1247

British Columbia

Secretary
Real Estate Council
626 West Pender Street
Vancouver, British Columbia, Canada V6B 1V9
(604) 683-9664

California

Commissioner
Department of Real Estate
2201 Broadway
P.O. Box 187000
Sacramento, California 95818
(916) 739-3600

District of Columbia

Commission Support Officer
Real Estate Commission
P.O. Box 37200
614 H Street, N.W.
Washington, D.C. 20013
(202) 727-7468

Colorado

Director
Real Estate Commission
1776 Logan Street
Denver, Colorado 80203
(303) 894-2166

Florida

Director
Real Estate Commission
P.O. Box 1900
Orlando, Florida 32802
(305) 423-6053

Connecticut

Director
Real Estate Division
165 Capital Avenue
Hartford, Connecticut 06106
(203) 566-5130

Georgia

Commissioner
Real Estate Commission
40 Pryor Street, S.W.
Atlanta, Georgia 30303
(404) 656-3916

Delaware

Administrative Assistant
Real Estate Commission
P.O. Box 1401
Margaret O'Neill Building
Dover, Delaware 19903
(302) 736-4522

Guam

Administrator
Real Estate Agency
Department of Revenue and Taxation
855 West Marine Drive
Agana, Guam 96910
(671) 477-1040

Hawaii

Executive Secretary
Real Estate Commission
Professional & Vocational
Licensing Division
P.O. Box 3469
Honolulu, Hawaii 96801
(808) 548-7464

Idaho

Executive Director
Real Estate Commission
State Capitol Building
Boise, Idaho 83720
(202) 334-3285

Illinois

Commissioner
Department of Professional Regulation
320 West Washington
Springfield, Illinois 62786
(217) 785-0800

Indiana

Deputy Director
Real Estate Commission
1021 State Office Building
100 North Senate Avenue
Indianapolis, Indiana 46204
(317) 232-2980

Iowa

Executive Secretary
Real Estate Commission
Department of Commerce
1918 S.E. Hulsizer
Ankeny, Iowa 50021
(515) 281-3183

Kansas

Director
Real Estate Commission
Room 501
900 Jackson Street
Topeka, Kansas 66612
(913) 296-3411

Kentucky

Executive Director
Real Estate Commission
Suite 300
222 S. First Street
Louisville, Kentucky 40202
(502) 588-4462

Louisiana

Executive Director
Real Estate Commission
P.O. Box 14785
Capital Station
Baton Rouge, Louisiana 70898
(504) 925-4771

Maine

Director
Real Estate Commission
4th Floor, State Office Building
Augusta, Maine 04333
(207) 289-3735

Maryland

Executive Director
Real Estate Commission
Suite 804
501 St. Paul Place
Baltimore, Maryland 21202
(301) 333-6230

Massachusetts

Executive Secretary
Board of Registration of
Real Estate Brokers & Salesmen
Room 1518
100 Cambridge Street
Boston, Massachusetts 02202
(617) 727-7376

Michigan

Administrative Secretary
Department of Licensing & Regulation
Real Estate Division
P.O. Box 30018
Lansing, Michigan 48909
(517) 373-0490

Minnesota

Director of Licensing
Department of Commerce
500 Metro Square Building
St. Paul, Minnesota 55101
(612) 297-4630

Mississippi

Administrator
Real Estate Commission
1920 Dunbarton Street
Jackson, Mississippi 39216
(601) 987-3969

Missouri

Executive Director
Real Estate Commission
P.O. Box 1339
Jefferson City, Missouri 65102
(314) 751-2334

Montana

Administrator
Board of Realty Regulation
1424 Ninth Avenue
Helena, Montana 59620
(406) 444-2961

Nebraska

Director
Real Estate Commission
301 South Centennial Mall
Lincoln, Nebraska 68508
(402) 471-2004

Nevada

Administrator
Real Estate Division
201 South Fall Street
Carson City, Nevada 89710
(702) 885-4280

New Brunswick

Licensing Supervisor
Real Estate Council
P.O. Box 785
Fredericton
New Brunswick, Canada E3B 5B4
(506) 455-9733

New Hampshire

Executive Director
Real Estate Commission
3rd Floor, Johnson Hall
107 Pleasant Sreet
Concord, New Hampshire 03301
(603) 271-2701

New Jersey

Executive Director
Real Estate Commission
20 West State Street
Trenton, New Jersey 08625
(609) 987-2010

New Mexico

Executive Secretary
Real Estate Commission
4125 Carlisle Boulevard
Albuquerque, New Mexico 87107
(505) 841-6524

New York

Director
Department of State
Division of Licensing Services
162 Washington Avenue
Albany, New York 12231
(518) 473-2419

North Carolina

Executive Director
Real Estate Commission
1313 Navaho Drive
Raleigh, North Carolina 27619
(919) 733-9580

North Dakota

Secretary-Treasurer
Real Estate Commission
P.O. Box 727
314 East Thayer Avenue
Bismarck, North Dakota 58502
(701) 224-2749

Nova Scotia

Superintendent
Consumer Services Division
P.O. Box 998
Halifax, Nova Scotia, Canada B3J 2X3
(902) 424-4690

Ohio

Superintendent
Division of Real Estate
Two Nationwide Plaza
Columbus, Ohio 43266
(614) 466-4100

Oklahoma

Executive Director
Real Estate Commission
Suite 100
4040 North Lincoln Boulevard
Oklahoma City, Oklahoma 73105
(405) 521-3387

Ontario

Registrar
Ministry of Consumer
and Commercial Relations
Business Practices Division
555 Yonge Street
Toronto, Canada M7A 2H6
(416) 963-0406

Oregon

Commissioner
Real Estate Agency
158 12th Street, N.E.
Salem, Oregon 97310
(503) 378-4170

Pennsylvania

Administrative Secretary
Department of State
Professional & Occupational Affairs
Real Estate Commission
P.O. Box 2649
Harrisburg, Pennsylvania 17105
(717) 783-3658

Quebec

Superintendent
Service de Courtage Immobilier du Quebec
Ministere de la Justice
220 Grande Allee Est
Quebec, Canada G1R 2J1
(418) 643-4597

Rhode Island

Deputy Administrator
Real Estate Division
100 North Main Street
Providence, Rhode Island 02903
(401) 277-2255

Saskatchewan

Superintendent of Insurance
Consumer and Commercial Affairs
1871 Smith Street
Regina, Saskatchewan, Canada S4P 3V7
(306) 787-2958

South Carolina

Commissioner
Real Estate Commission
Suite 1500
1201 Main Street
Columbia, South Carolina 29201
(803) 737-0700

South Dakota

Executive Secretary
Real Estate Commission
P.O. Box 490
Pierre, South Dakota 57501
(605) 773-3600

Tennessee

Executive Director
Real Estate Commission
1808 West End Building
Nashville, Tennessee 37219
(615) 741-2273

Texas

Administrator
Real Estate Commission
P.O. Box 12188, Capital Station
Austin, Texas 78711
(512) 459-6544

Utah

Director
Real Estate Division
160 East 300 South
Salt Lake City, Utah 84145
(801) 530-6747

Vermont

Executive Director
Real Estate Commission
Pavilion Office Building
Montpelier, Vermont 05602
(802) 828-3228

Virginia

Director
Department of Commerce
Real Estate Commission
3600 W. Broad Sreet
Richmond, Virginia 23230
(804) 367-8552

Virgin Islands

Director
Real Estate Commission
Property and Procurement Building
St. Thomas, Virgin Islands 00802
(809) 774-3130

Washington

Executive Secretary
Real Estate Division
P.O. Box 9012
Olympia, Washington 98504
(206) 753-0775

West Virginia

Executive Secretary
Real Estate Commission
Suite 400
1033 Quarrier Street
Charleston, West Virginia 25301
(304) 348-3555

Wisconsin

Bureau Director
Department of Regulation & Licensing
Real Estate Examining Board
1400 East Washington Avenue
Madison, Wisconsin 53708
(608) 266-5450

Wyoming

Executive Director
Real Estate Commission
4301 Herschler Building
Cheyenne, Wyoming 82002
(307) 777-7141

APPENDIX D

REAL ESTATE FORMS

SETTLEMENT STATEMENT

UNIFORM RESIDENTIAL APPRAISAL REPORT

LAND DEED OF TRUST

TRUTH-IN-LENDING DISCLOSURES

A. Settlement Statement

U.S. Department of Housing
and Urban Development

OMB No. 2502-0265 (Exp. 12-31-86)

B. Type of Loan

1. ☐ FHA 2. ☐ FmHA 3. ☐ Conv. Unins.
4. ☐ VA 5. ☐ Conv. Ins.

6. File Number	7. Loan Number	8. Mortgage Insurance Case Number

C. Note: This form is furnished to give you a statement of actual settlement costs. Amounts paid to and by the settlement agent are shown. Items marked "(p.o.c.)" were paid outside the closing; they are shown here for informational purposes and are not included in the totals.

D. Name and Address of Borrower	E. Name and Address of Seller	F. Name and Address of Lender

G. Property Location	H. Settlement Agent	
	Place of Settlement	I. Settlement Date

J. Summary of Borrower's Transaction		K. Summary of Seller's Transaction	
100. Gross Amount Due From Borrower		**400. Gross Amount Due To Seller**	
101. Contract sales price		401. Contract sales price	
102. Personal property		402. Personal property	
103. Settlement charges to borrower (line 1400)		403.	
104.		404.	
105.		405.	
Adjustments for items paid by seller in advance		**Adjustments for items paid by seller in advance**	
106. City/town taxes to		406. City/town taxes to	
107. County taxes to		407. County taxes to	
108. Assessments to		408. Assessments to	
109.		409.	
110.		410.	
111.		411.	
112.		412.	
120. Gross Amount Due From Borrower		**420. Gross Amount Due To Seller**	
200. Amounts Paid By Or In Behalf Of Borrower		**500. Reductions In Amount Due To Seller**	
201. Deposit or earnest money		501. Excess deposit (see instructions)	
202. Principal amount of new loan(s)		502. Settlement charges to seller (line 1400)	
203. Existing loan(s) taken subject to		503. Existing loan(s) taken subject to	
204.		504. Payoff of first mortgage loan	
205.		505. Payoff of second mortgage loan	
206.		506.	
207.		507.	
208.		508.	
209.		509.	
Adjustments for items unpaid by seller		**Adjustments for items unpaid by seller**	
210. City/town taxes to		510. City/town taxes to	
211. County taxes to		511. County taxes to	
212. Assessments to		512. Assessments to	
213.		513.	
214.		514.	
215.		515.	
216.		516.	
217.		517.	
218.		518.	
219.		519.	
220. Total Paid By/For Borrower		**520. Total Reduction Amount Due Seller**	
300. Cash At Settlement From/To Borrower		**600. Cash At Settlement To/From Seller**	
301. Gross Amount due from borrower (line 120)		601. Gross amount due to seller (line 420)	
302. Less amounts paid by/for borrower (line 220)	( )	602. Less reductions in amt. due seller (line 520)	( )
303. Cash ☐ From ☐ To Borrower		603. Cash ☐ To ☐ From Seller	

L. Settlement Charges

		Paid From Borrower's Funds at Settlement	Paid From Seller's Funds at Settlement
700. Total Sales / Broker's Commission based on price $ @ % =			
Division of Commission (line 700) as follows:			
701. $ to			
702. $ to			
703. Commission paid at Settlement			
704.			
800. Items Payable In Connection With Loan			
801. Loan Origination Fee %			
802. Loan Discount %			
803. Appraisal Fee to			
804. Credit Report to			
805. Lender's Inspection Fee			
806. Mortgage Insurance Application Fee to			
807. Assumption Fee			
808.			
809.			
810.			
811.			
900. Items Required By Lender To Be Paid In Advance			
901. Interest from to @$ /day			
902. Mortgage Insurance Premium for months to			
903. Hazard Insurance Premium for years to			
904. years to			
905.			
1000. Reserves Deposited With Lender			
1001. Hazard insurance months@$ per month			
1002. Mortgage insurance months@$ per month			
1003. City property taxes months@$ per month			
1004. County property taxes months@$ per month			
1005. Annual assessments months@$ per month			
1006. months@$ per month			
1007. months@$ per month			
1008. months@$ per month			
1100. Title Charges			
1101. Settlement or closing fee to			
1102. Abstract or title search to			
1103. Title examination to			
1104. Title insurance binder to			
1105. Document preparation to			
1106. Notary fees to			
1107. Attorney's fees to			
(includes above items numbers:)			
1108. Title insurance to			
(includes above items numbers:)			
1109. Lender's coverage $			
1110. Owner's coverage $			
1111.			
1112.			
1113.			
1200. Government Recording and Transfer Charges			
1201. Recording fees: Deed $; Mortgage $; Releases $			
1202. City/county tax/stamps: Deed $; Mortgage $			
1203. State tax/stamps: Deed $; Mortgage $			
1204.			
1205.			
1300. Additional Settlement Charges			
1301. Survey to			
1302. Pest inspection to			
1303.			
1304.			
1305.			
1400. Total Settlement Charges (enter on lines 103, Section J and 502, Section K)			

I have carefully reviewed the HUD-1 Settlement Statement and to the best of my knowledge and belief, it is a true and accurate statement of all receipts and disbursements made on my account or by me in this transaction. I further certify that I have recieved a copy of HUD-1 Settlement Statement.

_____   _____

Borrowers   Sellers

The HUD-1 Settlement Statement which I have prepared is a true and accurate account of this transaction. I have caused or will cause the funds to be disbursed in accordance with this statement.

_____   _____

Settlement Agent   Date

WARNING: It is a crime to knowingly make false statements to the United States on this or any other similar form. Penalties upon conviction can include a fine or imprisonment. For details see: Title 18 U.S. Code Section 1001 and Section 1010.

UNIFORM RESIDENTIAL APPRAISAL REPORT File No. _____

SUBJECT

Property Address	Census Tract _____	LENDER DISCRETIONARY USE

City _____ County _____	State _____ Zip Code _____	Sale Price $ _____
Legal Description		Date _____
Owner/Occupant	Map Reference _____	Mortgage Amount $ _____
Sale Price $ _____ Date of Sale _____	PROPERTY RIGHTS APPRAISED	Mortgage Type _____
Loan charges/concessions to be paid by seller $ _____	☐ Fee Simple	Discount Points and Other Concessions
R.E. Taxes $ _____ Tax Year _____ HOA $/Mo. _____	☐ Leasehold	Paid by Seller $ _____
Lender/Client	☐ Condominium (HUD/VA)	
	☐ De Minimis PUD	Source _____

NEIGHBORHOOD

	Urban	Suburban	Rural	NEIGHBORHOOD ANALYSIS	Good	Avg.	Fair	Poor
LOCATION	☐ Urban	☐ Suburban	☐ Rural					
BUILT UP	☐ Over 75%	☐ 25-75%	☐ Under 25%	Employment Stability	☐	☐	☐	☐
GROWTH RATE	☐ Rapid	☐ Stable	☐ Slow	Convenience to Employment	☐	☐	☐	☐
PROPERTY VALUES	☐ Increasing	☐ Stable	☐ Declining	Convenience to Shopping	☐	☐	☐	☐
DEMAND/SUPPLY	☐ Shortage	☐ In Balance	☐ Over Supply	Convenience to Schools	☐	☐	☐	☐
MARKETING TIME	☐ Under 3 Mos.	☐ 3-6 Mos.	☐ Over 6 Mos.	Adequacy of Public Transportation	☐	☐	☐	☐

PRESENT LAND USE	%	LAND USE CHANGE	PREDOMINANT	SINGLE FAMILY HOUSING					
				PRICE $ (000)	AGE (yrs)	Recreation Facilities	☐	☐	☐	☐
Single Family	___	Not Likely ☐	OCCUPANCY			Adequacy of Utilities	☐	☐	☐	☐
2-4 Family	___	Likely ☐	Owner ☐			Property Compatibility	☐	☐	☐	☐
Multi-family	___	In process ☐	Tenant ☐	Low		Protection from Detrimental Cond.	☐	☐	☐	☐
Commercial	___	To: _____	Vacant (0-5%) ☐	High		Police & Fire Protection	☐	☐	☐	☐
Industrial	___		Vacant (over 5%) ☐	Predominant		General Appearance of Properties	☐	☐	☐	☐
Vacant	___			—		Appeal to Market	☐	☐	☐	☐

Note: Race or the racial composition of the neighborhood are not considered reliable appraisal factors.
COMMENTS: _____

SITE

Dimensions _____						Topography _____	
Site Area _____			Corner Lot _____			Size _____	
Zoning Classification _____			Zoning Compliance _____			Shape _____	
HIGHEST & BEST USE: Present Use _____			Other Use _____			Drainage _____	
UTILITIES	Public	Other	SITE IMPROVEMENTS	Type	Public	Private	View _____
Electricity	☐	_____	Street	_____	☐	☐	Landscaping _____
Gas	☐	_____	Curb/Gutter	_____	☐	☐	Driveway _____
Water	☐	_____	Sidewalk	_____	☐	☐	Apparent Easements _____
Sanitary Sewer	☐	_____	Street Lights	_____	☐	☐	FEMA Flood Hazard Yes* ___ No ___
Storm Sewer	☐	_____	Alley	_____	☐	☐	FEMA* Map/Zone _____

COMMENTS (Apparent adverse easements, encroachments, special assessments, slide areas, etc.) _____

IMPROVEMENTS

GENERAL DESCRIPTION	EXTERIOR DESCRIPTION	FOUNDATION	BASEMENT	INSULATION
Units _____	Foundation _____	Slab _____	Area Sq. Ft. _____	Roof ☐
Stories _____	Exterior Walls _____	Crawl Space _____	% Finished _____	Ceiling ☐
Type (Det./Att.) _____	Roof Surface _____	Basement _____	Ceiling _____	Walls ☐
Design (Style) _____	Gutters & Dwnspts. _____	Sump Pump _____	Walls _____	Floor ☐
Existing _____	Window Type _____	Dampness _____	Floor _____	None ☐
Proposed _____	Storm Sash _____	Settlement _____	Outside Entry _____	Adequacy ☐
Under Construction _____	Screens _____	Infestation _____		Energy Efficient Items ☐
Age (Yrs.) _____	Manufactured House _____			
Effective Age (Yrs.) _____				

ROOM LIST

ROOMS	Foyer	Living	Dining	Kitchen	Den	Family Rm.	Rec. Rm.	Bedrooms	# Baths	Laundry	Other	Area Sq. Ft.
Basement												
Level 1												
Level 2												

Finished area **above** grade contains: _____ Rooms: _____ Bedroom(s): _____ Bath(s): _____ Square Feet of Gross Living Area _____

INTERIOR

SURFACES	Materials/Condition	HEATING	KITCHEN EQUIP.	ATTIC	IMPROVEMENT ANALYSIS	Good	Avg	Fair	Poor
Floors	_____	Type _____	Refrigerator ☐	None ☐	Quality of Construction	☐	☐	☐	☐
Walls	_____	Fuel _____	Range/Oven ☐	Stairs ☐	Condition of Improvements	☐	☐	☐	☐
Trim/Finish	_____	Condition _____	Disposal ☐	Drop Stair ☐	Room Sizes/Layout	☐	☐	☐	☐
Bath Floor	_____	Adequacy _____	Dishwasher ☐	Scuttle ☐	Closets and Storage	☐	☐	☐	☐
Bath Wainscot	_____	COOLING	Fan/Hood ☐	Floor ☐	Energy Efficiency	☐	☐	☐	☐
Doors	_____	Central _____	Compactor ☐	Heated ☐	Plumbing-Adequacy & Condition	☐	☐	☐	☐
		Other _____	Washer/Dryer ☐	Finished ☐	Electrical-Adequacy & Condition	☐	☐	☐	☐
		Condition _____	Microwave ☐		Kitchen Cabinets-Adequacy & Cond.	☐	☐	☐	☐
Fireplace(s)	# ___	Adequacy _____	Intercom ☐		Compatibility to Neighborhood	☐	☐	☐	☐

AUTOS

CAR STORAGE:	Garage ___	Attached ☐	Adequate ☐	House Entry ☐	Appeal & Marketability	☐	☐	☐	☐
No. Cars ___	Carport ___	Detached ☐	Inadequate ☐	Outside Entry ☐	Estimated Remaining Economic Life				___ Yrs.
Condition ___	None ___	Built-In ☐	Electric Door ☐	Basement Entry ☐	Estimated Remaining Physical Life				___ Yrs.

Additional features: _____

COMMENTS

Depreciation (Physical, functional and external inadequacies, repairs needed, modernization, etc.) _____

General market conditions and prevalence and impact in subject/market area regarding loan discounts, interest buydowns and concessions _____

UNIFORM RESIDENTIAL APPRAISAL REPORT   File No. _____

Purpose of Appraisal is to estimate Market Value as defined in the Certification & Statement of Limiting Conditions.

COST APPROACH

BUILDING SKETCH (SHOW GROSS LIVING AREA ABOVE GRADE)
If for Freddie Mac or Fannie Mae, show only square foot calculations and cost approach comments in this space

ESTIMATED REPRODUCTION COST-NEW-OF IMPROVEMENTS:

Dwelling _____	Sq. Ft. @ $ _____	= $ _____
	Sq. Ft. @ $ _____	= _____
Extras _____		= _____
		= _____
Special Energy Efficient Items _____		= _____
Porches, Patios, etc. _____		= _____
Garage/Carport _____ Sq. Ft. @ $ _____		= _____
Total Estimated Cost New		= $ _____

	Physical	Functional	External
Less Depreciation			

Depreciated Value of Improvements	= $ _____
Site Imp. "as is" (driveway, landscaping, etc.)	= $ _____
ESTIMATED SITE VALUE	= $ _____
(If leasehold, show only leasehold value.)	
INDICATED VALUE BY COST APPROACH	= $ _____

(Not Required by Freddie Mac and Fannie Mae)
Does property conform to applicable HUD/VA property standards? ☐ Yes ☐ No
If No, explain: _____

Construction Warranty ☐ Yes ☐ No
Name of Warranty Program _____
Warranty Coverage Expires _____

The undersigned has recited three recent sales of properties most similar and proximate to subject and has considered these in the market analysis. The description includes a dollar adjustment, reflecting market reaction to those items of significant variation between the subject and comparable properties. If a significant item in the comparable property is superior to, or more favorable than, the subject property, a minus (−) adjustment is made, thus reducing the indicated value of subject; if a significant item in the comparable is inferior to, or less favorable than, the subject property, a plus (+) adjustment is made, thus increasing the indicated value of the subject.

SALES COMPARISON ANALYSIS

ITEM	SUBJECT	COMPARABLE NO. 1		COMPARABLE NO. 2		COMPARABLE NO. 3	
Address							
Proximity to Subject							
Sales Price	$		$		$		$
Price/Gross Liv. Area	$ ☑	$ ☑		$ ☑		$ ☑	
Data Source							
VALUE ADJUSTMENTS	DESCRIPTION	DESCRIPTION	+ (−) $ Adjustment	DESCRIPTION	+ (−) $ Adjustment	DESCRIPTION	+ (−) $ Adjustment
Sales or Financing Concessions							
Date of Sale/Time							
Location							
Site/View							
Design and Appeal							
Quality of Construction							
Age							
Condition							
Above Grade Room Count	Total ¦ Bdrms ¦ Baths	Total ¦ Bdrms ¦ Baths		Total ¦ Bdrms ¦ Baths		Total ¦ Bdrms ¦ Baths	
Gross Living Area	Sq. Ft.	Sq. Ft.		Sq. Ft.		Sq. Ft.	
Basement & Finished Rooms Below Grade							
Functional Utility							
Heating/Cooling							
Garage/Carport							
Porches, Patio, Pools, etc.							
Special Energy Efficient Items							
Fireplace(s)							
Other (e.g. kitchen equip., remodeling)							
Net Adj. (total)		☐ + ☐ − $		☐ + ☐ − $		☐ + ☐ − $	
Indicated Value of Subject		$		$		$	

Comments on Sales Comparison: _____

INDICATED VALUE BY SALES COMPARISON APPROACH .... $ _____

INDICATED VALUE BY INCOME APPROACH (If Applicable) Estimated Market Rent $ _____ /Mo. x Gross Rent Multiplier _____ = $ _____

This appraisal is made ☐ "as is" ☐ subject to the repairs, alterations, inspections or conditions listed below ☐ completion per plans and specifications.

Comments and Conditions of Appraisal: _____

RECONCILIATION

Final Reconciliation: _____

This appraisal is based upon the above requirements, the certification, contingent and limiting conditions, and Market Value definition that are stated in

☐ FmHA, HUD &/or VA instructions.
☐ Freddie Mac Form 439 (Rev. 7/86)/Fannie Mae Form 1004B (Rev. 7/86) filed with client _____ 19 _____ ☐ attached.

I (WE) ESTIMATE THE MARKET VALUE, AS DEFINED, OF THE SUBJECT PROPERTY AS OF _____ 19 _____ to be $ _____

I (We) certify: that to the best of my (our) knowledge and belief the facts and data used herein are true and correct; that I (we) personally inspected the subject property, both inside and out, and have made an exterior inspection of all comparable sales cited in this report; and that I (we) have no undisclosed interest, present or prospective therein.

Appraiser(s) SIGNATURE _____	Review Appraiser SIGNATURE _____	☐ Did ☐ Did Not
NAME _____	(if applicable) NAME _____	Inspect Property

Freddie Mac Form 70 10/86

Fannie Mae Form 1004 10/86

LAND DEED OF TRUST

THIS INDENTURE, made and entered into this day by and between _____

_____

whose address is _____

(Street No. or RFD No. and Box)   (City)

_____ , as Grantor (herein designated as "Debtor"), and

(County)   (State)

_____

as Trustee, and _____

_____ of _____ ,   as Beneficiary

(herein designated as "Secured Party"), WITNESSETH:

WHEREAS, Debtor is indebted to Secured Party in the full sum of _____

_____

Dollars ($ _____) evidenced by _____ promissory note of even date herewith

in favor of Secured Party, bearing interest from _____ at the rate specified in the note _____ ,
providing for payment of attorney's fees for collection if not paid according to the terms thereof and being
due and payable as set forth below:

WHEREAS, Debtor desires to secure prompt payment of (a) the indebtedness described above according
to its terms and any extensions thereof, (b) any additional and future advances with interest thereon which
Secured Party may make to Debtor as provided in Paragraph 1, (c) any other indebtedness which Debtor
may now or hereafter owe to Secured Party as provided in Paragraph 2 and (d) any advances with interest
which Secured Party may make to protect the property herein conveyed as provided in Paragraphs 3, 4, 5
and 6 (all being herein referred to as the "Indebtedness").

NOW THEREFORE, In consideration of the indebtedness herein recited, Debtor hereby conveys and
warrants unto Trustee the land described below situated in the

City of _____ County of _____ State of _____

together with all improvements and appurtenances now or hereafter erected on, and all fixtures of any and every description now or hereafter attached to, said land (all being herein referred to as the "Property").

THIS CONVEYANCE, HOWEVER, IS IN TRUST (subject to the covenants, stipulations and conditions below), to secure prompt payment of all existing and future indebtedness due by Debtor to Secured Party under the provisions of this Deed of Trust. If Debtor shall pay said indebtedness promptly when due and shall perform all covenants made by Debtor, then this conveyance shall be void and of no effect. If Debtor shall be in default as provided in Paragraph 9, then, in that event, the entire indebtedness, together with all interest accrued thereon, shall, at the option of Secured Party, be and become at once due and payable without notice to Debtor, and Trustee shall, at the request of Secured Party, sell the Property conveyed, or a sufficiency thereof, to satisfy the indebtedness at public outcry to the highest bidder for cash. Sale of the property shall be advertised for three consecutive weeks preceding the sale in a newspaper published in the county where the Property is situated, or if none is so published, then in some newspaper having a general circulation therein, and by posting a notice for the same time at the courthouse of the same county. The notice and advertisement shall disclose the names of the original debtors in this Deed of Trust. Debtors waive the provisions of Section 89-1-55 of the Mississippi Code of 1972 as amended, if any, as far as this section restricts the right of Trustee to offer at sale more than 160 acres at a time, and Trustee may offer the property herein conveyed as a whole, regardless of how it is described.

If the Property is situated in two or more counties, or in two judicial districts of the same county, Trustee shall have full power to select in which county, or judicial district, the sale of the property is to be made, newspaper advertisement published and notice of sale posted, and Trustee's selection shall be binding upon Debtor and Secured Party. Should Secured Party be a corporation or an unincorporated association, then any officer thereof may declare Debtor to be in default as provided in Paragraph 9 and request Trustee to sell the Property. Secured Party shall have the same right to purchase the property at the foreclosure sale as would a purchaser who is not a party to this Deed of Trust.

From the proceeds of the sale Trustee shall first pay all costs of the sale including compensation to Trustee of ten percent of the sale proceeds; then the indebtedness due Secured Party by Debtor, including accrued interest and attorney's fees due for collection of the debt; and then, lastly, any balance remaining to Debtor.

IT IS AGREED that this conveyance is made subject to the covenants, stipulations and conditions set forth below which shall be binding upon all parties hereto.

1. This Deed of Trust shall also secure all future and additional advances which Secured Party may make to Debtor from time to time upon the security herein conveyed. Such advances shall be optional with Secured Party and shall be on such terms as to amount, maturity and rate of interest as may be mutually agreeable to both Debtor and Secured Party. Any such advance may be made to any one of the Debtors should there be more than one, and if so made, shall be secured by this Deed of Trust to the same extent as if made to all Debtors. However, on all transactions covered by Truth in Lending, when Debtor's notes, debts, obligations and liabilities to Secured Party (in any form) arising out of existing, concurrent and future credit granted by Secured Party are secured by this Deed of Trust, it will be so indicated on the document that evidences the transaction. Therefore this Deed of Trust will in no way secure any form of credit governed by the Truth in Lending Act unless the document which evidences the Credit Transaction indicates by proper disclosure that the Transaction is secured by this Deed of Trust.

2. This Deed of Trust shall also secure any and all other indebtedness of Debtor due to Secured Party with interest thereon as specified, or of any one of the Debtors should there be more than one, whether direct or contingent, primary or secondary, sole, joint or several, now existing or hereafter arising at any time before cancellation of this Deed of Trust. Such indebtedness may be evidenced by note, open account, overdraft, endorsement, guaranty or otherwise. However, on all transactions covered by Truth in Lending, when Debtor's notes, debts, obligations and liabilities to Secured Party (in any form) arising out of existing, concurrent and future credit granted by Secured Party are secured by this Deed of Trust, it will be so indicated on the document that evidences the transaction. Therefore this Deed of Trust will in no way secure any form of credit governed by the Truth in Lending Act unless the document which evidences the Credit Transaction indicates by proper disclosure that the Transaction is secured by this Deed of Trust.

3. Debtor shall keep all improvements on the land herein conveyed insured against fire, all hazards included within the term "extended coverage", flood in areas designated by the U.S. Department of Housing and Urban Development as being subject to overflow and such other hazards as Secured Party may reasonably require in such amounts as Debtor may determine but for not less than the indebtedness secured by this Deed of Trust. All policies shall be written by reliable insurance companies acceptable to Secured Party, shall include standard loss payable clauses in favor of Secured Party and shall be delivered to Secured Party, Debtor shall promptly pay when due all premiums charged for such insurance, and shall furnish Secured Party the premium receipts for inspection. Upon Debtor's failure to pay the premiums, Secured Party shall have the right, but not the obligation, to pay such premiums. In the event of a loss covered by the insurance in force, Debtor shall promptly notify Secured Party who may make proof of loss if timely proof is not made by Debtor. All loss payments shall be made directly to Secured Party as loss payee who may either apply the proceeds to the repair or restoration of the damaged improvements or to the indebtedness of Debtor, or release such proceeds in whole or in part to Debtor.

4. Debtor shall pay all taxes and assessments, general or special, levied against the Property or upon the interest of Trustee or Secured Party therein, during the term of this Deed of Trust before such taxes or assessments become delinquent, and shall furnish Secured Party the tax receipts for inspection. Should Debtor fail to pay all taxes and assessments when due, Secured Party shall have the right, but not the obligation, to make these payments.

5. Debtor shall keep the Property in good repair and shall not permit or commit waste, impairment or deterioration thereof. Debtor shall use the Property for lawful purposes only. Secured Party may make or arrange to be made entries upon and inspections of the Property after first giving Debtor notice prior to any inspection specifying a just cause related to Secured Party's interest in the Property. Secured Party shall have the right, but not the obligation, to cause needed repairs to be made to the Property after first affording Debtor a reasonable opportunity to make the repairs.

Should the purpose of the primary indebtedness for which this Deed of Trust is given as security be for construction of improvements on the land herein conveyed, Secured Party shall have the right to make or arrange to be made entries upon the Property and inspections of the construction in progress. Should Secured Party determine that Debtor is failing to perform such construction in a timely and satisfactory manner, Secured Party shall have the right, but not the obligation, to take charge of and proceed with the construction at the expense of Debtor after first affording Debtor a reasonable opportunity to continue the construction in a manner agreeable to Secured Party.

6. Any sums advanced by Secured Party for Insurance, taxes, repairs or construction as provided in Paragraphs 3, 4 and 5 shall be secured by this Deed of Trust as advances made to protect the Property and shall be payable by Debtor to Secured Party, with interest at the rate specified in the note representing the primary indebtedness, within thirty days following written demand for payment sent by Secured Party to Debtor by certified mail. Receipts for insurance premiums, taxes and repair or construction costs for which Secured Party has made payment shall serve as conclusive evidence thereof.

7. As additional security Debtor hereby assigns to Secured Party all rents accruing on the Property. Debtor shall have the right to collect and retain the rents as long as Debtor is not in default as provided in Paragraph 9. In the event of default, Secured Party in person, by an agent or by a judicially appointed receiver shall be entitled to enter upon, take possession of and manage the Property and collect the rents. All rents so collected shall be applied first to the costs of managing the Property and collecting the rents, including fees for a receiver and an attorney, commissions to rental agents, repairs and other necessary related expenses and then to payments on the indebtedness.

8. This Deed of Trust (indenture) may not be assumed by any buyer from Debtor. Any attempted transfer of any interest in this property (including, but not limited to possession) will constitute a default and Secured Party may accelerate the entire balance of the indebtedness.

If Secured Party elects to exercise the option to accelerate, Secured Party shall send Debtor notice of acceleration by certified mail. Such notice shall provide a period of thirty days from the date of mailing within which Debtor may pay the indebtedness in full. If Debtor fails to pay such indebtedness prior to the expiration of thirty days, Secured Party may, without further notice to Debtor, invoke any remedies set forth in this Deed of Trust.

9. Debtor shall be in default under the provisions of this Deed of Trust if Debtor (a) shall fail to comply with any of Debtor's covenants or obligations contained herein, (b) shall fail to pay any of the indebtedness secured hereby, or any installment thereof or interest thereon, as such indebtedness, installment or interest shall be due by contractual agreement or by acceleration, (c) shall become bankrupt or insolvent or be placed in receivership, (d) shall, if a corporation, a partnership or an unincorporated association be dissolved voluntarily or involuntarily, or (e) if Secured Party in good faith deems itself insecure and its prospect of repayment seriously impaired.

10. Secured Party may at any time, without giving formal notice to the original or any successor Trustee, or to Debtor, and without regard to the willingness or inability of any such Trustee to execute this trust, appoint another person or succession of persons to act as Trustee, and such appointee in the execution of this trust shall have all the powers vested in and obligations imposed upon Trustee. Should Secured Party be a corporation or an unincorporated association, then any officer thereof may make such appointment.

11. Each privilege, option or remedy provided in this Deed of Trust to Secured Party is distinct from every other privilege, option or remedy contained herein or afforded by law or equity, and may be exercised independently, concurrently, cumulatively or successively by Secured Party or by any other owner or holder of the indebtedness. Forbearance by Secured Party in exercising any privilege, option or remedy after the right to do so has accrued shall not constitute a waiver of Secured Party's right to exercise such privilege, option or remedy in event of any subsequent accrual.

12. The words "Debtor" or "Secured Party" shall each embrace one individual, two or more individuals, a corporation, a partnership or an unincorporated association, depending on the recital herein of the parties to this Deed of Trust. The covenants herein contained shall bind, and the benefits herein provided shall inure to, the respective legal or personal representatives, successors or assigns of the parties hereto subject to the provisions of Paragraph 8. If there be more than one Debtor, then Debtor's obligations shall be joint and several. Whenever in this Deed of Trust the context so requires, the singular shall include the plural and the plural the singular. Notices required herein from Secured Party to Debtor shall be sent to the address of Debtor shown in this Deed of Trust.

IN WITNESS WHERE OF, Debtor has executed this Deed of Trust on the _____ day of _____, 19_____ .

CORPORATE, PARTNERSHIP OR ASSOCIATION SIGNATURE

_____
          Name of Debtor

By _____

_____
                         Title

Attest: _____
                         Title

(Seal)

INDIVIDUAL SIGNATURES

_____

_____

_____

_____

_____

_____

INDIVIDUAL ACKNOWLEDGEMENT

STATE OF

COUNTY OF _____

This day personally appeared before me, the undersigned authority in and for the State and County aforesaid, the within named_____

_____who acknowledged that ___ he ___ signed and delivered the foregoing Deed of Trust on the day and year therein mentioned.

Given under my hand and official seal of office, this the _____ day of _____, 19 _____ .

My Commission Expires _____

_____
                         Notary Public

LAND DEED OF TRUST

from

to

_____ Trustee
══════════════════════════════════════

Filed for Record _____ , 19 _____

_____ o'clock _____ M.

_____ , Clerk
══════════════════════════════════════

STATE OF MISSISSIPPI   Chancery
                                            Court
_____County

    I certify that this Deed of Trust was filed for record

in my office at _____o'clock _____ M., on

the _____ day of_____ , 19 _____

and was duly recorded the _____day of

_____ , 19 _____ , on page_____

Book No. _____ in my office.

    Witness my hand and seal of office, this _____

day of _____ , 19 _____ .

_____Clerk

_____ , D. C.

_____

		Loan Number _____
		Date _____
		Mat. Date _____
		Loan Amount $ _____
BORROWER'S NAME AND ADDRESS	**LENDER'S NAME AND ADDRESS**	

TRUTH-IN-LENDING DISCLOSURES
"I" MEANS THE BORROWER AND "YOU" MEANS THE LENDER

ANNUAL PERCENTAGE RATE The cost of my credit as a yearly rate.	**FINANCE CHARGE** The dollar amount the credit will cost me.	**AMOUNT FINANCED** The amount of credit provided to me or on my behalf.	**TOTAL OF PAYMENTS** The amount I will have paid when I have made all scheduled payments.	I have the right to receive at this time an itemization of the Amount Financed
_____ %	$	$	$	I _____ do _____ do not want an itemization.

My **Payment Schedule** will be:

Number of Payments	Amount of Payments	When Payments Are Due
	$	
	$	
	$	
	$	
	$	
	$	

☐ **Demand:** ☐ This loan has a demand feature. ☐ This loan is payable on demand and all disclosures are based on an assumed maturity of one year.

☐ **Variable Rate:** (check one below)

☐ My loan contains a variable rate feature. Disclosures about the variable rate feature have been provided to me earlier.

☐ The annual percentage rate may increase during the term of this transaction if _____

_____

Any increase will take the form of _____

If the rate increases by _____ % in _____ , the _____

will increase to _____ . The rate may not increase more often than once _____

and may not increase more than _____ % each _____ . The rate will not go above _____ %.

Security: I am giving a security interest in: ☐ (brief description of other property) **Filing/Recording Fees:** $ _____

☐ the goods or property being purchased.

☐ collateral securing other loans with you may also secure this loan.

☐ my deposit accounts and other rights I may have to the payment of money from you.

☐ **Late Charge:** If a payment is late I will be charged _____

Prepayment: If I pay off this loan early, I ☐ may ☐ will not have to pay a penalty.

☐ may ☐ will not be entitled to a refund of part of the finance charge.

☐ **Assumption:** Someone buying my house ☐ may, subject to conditions, be allowed to ☐ cannot assume the remainder of the mortgage on the original terms.

I can see my contract documents for any additional information about nonpayment, default, any required repayment in full before the scheduled date, and prepayment refunds and penalties. "e" means an estimate.

CREDIT INSURANCE - Credit life insurance and credit disability insurance are not required to obtain credit, and will not be provided unless I sign and agree to pay the additional costs.

Type	Premium	Term
Credit Life		
Credit Disability		
Joint Credit Life		

I ☐ do ☐ do not want credit life insurance.

X _____

I ☐ do ☐ do not want credit disability insurance.

X _____

I ☐ do ☐ do not want joint credit life insurance.

X _____

X _____

I ☐ do ☐ do not want _____ insurance.

X _____

PROPERTY INSURANCE - I may obtain property insurance from anyone that is acceptable to you. If I get the insurance from or through you I will pay

$ _____ for _____ of coverage.

FLOOD INSURANCE - Flood insurance ☐ is ☐ is not required. I may obtain flood insurance from anyone that is acceptable to you. If I get the insurance from or through you I will pay

$ _____ for _____ of coverage.

ITEMIZATION OF AMOUNT FINANCED

Amount given to me directly $ _____

Amount paid on my (loan) account $ _____

_____ $ _____

AMOUNTS PAID TO OTHERS ON MY BEHALF:

Insurance Companies $ _____

Public Officials $ _____

_____ $ _____

_____ $ _____

_____ $ _____

_____ $ _____

_____ $ _____

_____ $ _____

_____ $ _____

_____ $ _____

_____ $ _____

_____ $ _____

_____ $ _____

_____ $ _____

_____ $ _____

_____ $ _____

(less) PREPAID FINANCE CHARGE(S) $ _____

Amount Financed $ _____

(Add all items financed and subtract prepaid finance charges.)

BY SIGNING BELOW - I ACKNOWLEDGE RECEIPT OF A COPY OF THIS DISCLOSURE ON THE DATE INDICATED ABOVE.

X _____ X _____ X _____